Recursive Desire

Recursive Desire

Rereading Epic Tradition

Jeremy M. Downes

The University of Alabama Press

Tuscaloosa and London

∞

The paper on which this book is printed meets the minimum requirements of
American National Standard for Information Science–Permanence of Paper for
Printed Library Materials, ANSI Z39.48–1984.

Library of Congress Cataloging-in-Publication Data

Downes, Jeremy M., 1961–
Recursive desire : rereading epic tradition / Jeremy M. Downes.
p.   cm.
Includes bibliographical references and index.
ISBN 0–8173–0841–5 (alk. paper)
1. Epic literature—History and criticism.   2. Desire in literature.   I. Title
PN56.E65D69   1997
809.1'3209353—dc20   96–9789

British Library Cataloguing-in-Publication Data available

You have toiled without cease, and what have you got?
Through toil you wear yourself out,
you fill your body with grief,
your long lifetime you are bringing near to a premature end!
Mankind, whose offshoot is snapped off like a reed in a canebrake

. . . .

For how long do we build a household?
For how long do we seal a document?
For how long do brothers share the inheritance?
For how long is there to be jealousy in the land?
For how long has the river risen and brought the overflowing waters
so that dragonflies drift down the river?
The face that could gaze on the face of the Sun
has never existed ever.
How alike are the sleeping and the dead.

—*Epic of Gilgamesh*

... AOI.
Li quens Rollant, par peine e par ahans,
Par grant dulor sunet sun olifan.
Par mi la buche en salt fors li cler sancs,
De sun cervel le temple en est rumpant.

—*La Chanson de Roland*

Contents

Preface

Through Smoking Pyres

In medias res

LOVE AND WAR, coupled together, command our attention as few other things can: Sex and violence, desire and death, loves and wars form a binary complex with deep roots in the Western tradition, and perhaps in the human psyche more generally. The alternative couplings possible under the general opposition show that there are many ways to encode the basic pair, and it was while I considered the multiple expressions of this complex in epic poetry that this book found its beginnings: war and peace, glory and death, love and duty, fierce warres and faithfull loves, fierce loves and faithless wars, love and art, the smoking pyres of love and death, *l'amour/la mort*. These last two formulations—Hart Crane's and H.D.'s—illustrate the deep interrelation of the terms, an ultimate similitude. Recognizing this interrelation, I try in this book to search *"through the smoking pyres of love and death"* (Crane 1966, 115; my emphasis) that make up our usual understanding of epic toward both a less obscured perspective and a better understanding of this fundamental dyad.

Exordium

From the kiln-fired bricks of Uruk to an underworld lesbian bar, from the ringing plains of Troy to the islands of the Caribbean, this book traces only a few repeating patterns in the endlessly iterative, cyclical, and transformative journey of epic. Like any work asserting the importance of epic poetry, it is fundamentally conservative; like any poststructuralist text (by aim if not execution), potentially inflammatory, even when it embraces moderation and common sense. In short, it is a book like any other, only as liberating and empowering as its readers can construe it.

Since I began this work, many books have been published on subjects it touches, and not a few of them have been written on epic. As a colleague recently remarked, "It's in the air." The best recent scholarship on epic, though it generally fails to quarrel with the death of epic, does provide more rigorous and theoretically astute readings of older epic texts, exploring the constructedness and multiplicity of this semi-mythical genre, examining its ideological and sociocultural embeddedness. I am less indebted to this contemporary renascence in epic studies than I would like, since the erudition and depth of scholarship now available would have been very helpful in formulating the entire study. As it is, works by Elizabeth J. Bellamy, Colin Burrow, D. C. Feeney, David Quint, and Susanne Wofford have all helped to confirm my conviction that even older epic poetry is alive, well, and pertinent, and I would urge the reader to consult them, not only for their differences, but for a larger consonance of thought. My own contribution (somewhat tardy) tries to bring about a broader, more inclusive vision of epics ancient and contemporary. This goal left me with far too many epics to discuss (and even more not to), but happily so, for what I really wanted to talk about was poetry.

Apart from the thousand inevitable shocks that adhere to any text, there are two troubling concerns I should address more fully. One is this book's perilously chronological sweep, which might tempt a developmental, even a meliorist view of the whole. This is hard to eradicate without endangering the book's coherence more than I already have. Suffice it to say here that though there is much change, little changes. A second concern is my eclectic use of scholarship; I am willing to overlook contention in favor of cooperation, and I often prefer not to bother with naming guilty parties or constructing straw persons. Though strong disagreements between scholars (as between countries) are occasionally productive and mutually beneficial, more often they are symptomatic of a breakdown in communication or (much the same thing) mere rhetorical posturing. Thus, rather than constructing an "evil empire" in some other writer, I would prefer to recognize and work against that imperialist claim in my own writing. This is unevenly achieved here; only because of this writing did I begin to realize the hazards of the traditional scholarly clear-cutting of terrain and decide—yet once more—to work *through* the fires of love and death toward a different kind of scholarship. To take a pertinent example, this book reacts strongly against Harold Bloom for reasons laid out in the introduction; but insofar as it reacts, it is also a rewriting of Bloom (as it is even more of Ker, of Tillyard, and so forth). More, it is not even a "strong" rewriting, for he and I have far more in common than I (or he, I expect) would like to admit. Rather, it is a repetition, a recursive structure established about a set of (not inconsequential) differences. It is a common joke in recent studies of tradition and influence to mention Bloom and then pointedly deny being influenced by him. Any text takes and twists its precursors only a little as it repeats them; mine readily admits that recursive structuring, indeed valorizes such recursion as one of the few things we hold in common, again and again, as this text too tries to tell its story, the tale of the tale of the tribe.

Invoking the Muse

There are always too many people to thank, and too little space to do them justice. In particular, however, I would like to express my gratitude to Cyrena N. Pondrom of the University of Wisconsin at Madison, who despite the hubris of the project allowed me to form the necessary theoretical framework, and then encouraged me to persevere. Nick Doane has my thanks for his years of support as well as for his incisive readings of the *Beowulf* chapter. The insightful and generous anonymous reader for the University of Alabama Press encouraged and gave new hope to the whole enterprise, as did editor Nicole Mitchell's persistent interest in the manuscript.

Special acknowledgment goes to Dr. Tom Winnifrith and other scholars of the University of Warwick, whose generous expertise in the field of epic studies has been of great benefit to my work; to Susan Koenig, Dawn Hutchison, and my sister Melissa, for their expertise and wide reading in feminist theory, as well as for the loan of many texts. My colleagues Jim McCormick and Jill Adair McCaughan had the considerable burden of responding to this project from its inception, and their patience and comradeship through many nights at the Plaza Tavern are greatly appreciated.

Wiebke Kuhn's wide reading, linguistic skill, and critical acumen have been of crucial import to the final form of the work, and she has made the many tasks of completing (and re-completing) the project surprisingly happy ones.

The support of my family has been vital. Though they still await the movie version, their patience and good humor in reading and correcting the roughest of drafts, outlines, and vague conceptions have been immeasurable. Most of all, I would like to acknowledge the incalculable resources provided by my parents, without whom none of this would have been possible, and to whom this work is dedicated.

Permissions

Cover illustration: Arnaldo Pomodoro, *Sfera con Sfera* (Sphere with Sphere) 1982–83, bronze. Berkeley Library Podium, Trinity College, Dublin. Photograph by the author. Used by permission of Trinity College. Pomodoro has remarked that he wanted "to find out what is inside a form that seems so perfect and absolute, superficially . . . to investigate the energy inside of a form" (Daniel Wheeler, *Art since Mid-Century*, 113).

Parts of Chapter 2 were originally published in *Oral Tradition in the Middle Ages*, edited by W. F. H. Nicolaisen, Medieval & Renaissance Texts and Studies, vol.

Recursive Desire

1

Fierce Warres and Faithfull Loves

Violence, Sex, and Recursive Desire in Epic Tradition

Genre and Gender: All's Fair in Love and War

All is flux, nothing solid.
—Herakleitos

THE CENTRAL PROBLEM of any genre criticism is the problem of identity through change; the Heraclitean dictum is clear in its judgment that identity, the actuality of sameness, is impossible. In another Heraclitean formulation, one cannot step in the same river twice. The water moves, the context changes, the perceiver changes. The same radical discontinuity inheres in a genre such as epic: That the *Odyssey* is not the same as *Paradise Lost* is hardly a useful observation to make; that the *Odyssey* is not the same as the *Aeneid* is only slightly more informative. However, a significant implication of Herakleitos' statement is that the *Odyssey* is not even the same as the *Odyssey*. As with the river, the context changes, the reader changes, the edition or perhaps the translation changes, the physical book itself changes from reading to reading. In earlier oral contexts the changes from performance to performance are far more drastic: Scenes are lengthened, descriptions and actions elaborated and elided, due to the context of utterance and the vagaries of oral composition. Rather than a single, identifiable *Odyssey*, innumerable *Odysseys* present themselves. Each performer and each member of the audience creates his or her own new and constantly changing version, with each and every "repeated" performance. This radical discontinuity holds true for our experiences (our "performances") of literary as well as oral texts.[1] Clearly, if a reputedly "single" text is

1

thus already subject to such infinite difference or unrepeatability, the implications for a more general term are rather staggering.

Fortunately for our chances of living within the world with an apparent coherence, we have learned ways of coping with this radical discontinuity of experience; by means of conceptual and linguistic tools, in particular, humans establish underlying "samenesses" (Aristotelian *substrata*) that work against the inexorable flux of experience. This means that I can step into the Mississippi River at Itasca, and twenty years later at New Orleans, and still be stepping into the same river. More precisely, at any point and any time I am stepping into the same *name* for a river. Though our experiences of the *Odyssey* as a text are radically different from those of readers in an earlier setting, our name for those experiences is similar.[2] These names, labels, terms (in less abbreviated form, these conventional schemata for organizing experience) function as convenient tools indeed.

The name *epic*, for example, works as a tool or map for organizing our experience of the textual world; it provides us with a set of expectations to be met (or more rarely, not met) by a text.[3] These preconceptions allow us to construct—in more or less useful ways—the textual material with which we interact. Understanding genre as a conceptual tool, as an instrument for dealing with textual portions of our environment, we begin to realize the generic nature of *all* our linguistic interactions with reality, since even our most particular nouns are generic labels: Socrates is not an indivisible unit (a particular human), but rather a humanly constituted label for a set of perceptual and conceptual experiences. What's difficult is that these names are all we have: as Richard Rorty and other philosophers point out, "the universal-particular distinction is the *only* metaphysical distinction we have got."[4]

This "universal-particular distinction," then, clearly has some fundamental importance, not only for genre studies, but for the human condition itself. A *universal*, a generic term such as epic, puts things together (i.e., organizes individual texts into a group). A *particular* term, such as the title of an individual text, takes things apart. More accurately, each term participates in both activities, in that the universal *epic*, while it serves to organize our experience of a combined group of particular texts, at the same time also takes apart larger universals such as poetry, or discourse, breaking up those universals into particular kinds. What surprises, though, is the striking *familiarity* of this distinction, "the only one we have."

Freud's famous twin drives of love and death offer significant parallels, since what he calls the "only two basic instincts, *Eros* and *the destructive instinct*" work the same way as the universal-particular distinction: "The aim of the first ... is to establish ever greater unities and to preserve them thus—in short, to bind together; the aim of the second is, on the contrary, to undo connections and so destroy things" (Freud 1940, 5–6). Moreover, those "only two basic instincts" are paradoxically linked. We must struggle to perceive "*through* smoking pyres of love and death" to a linkage beyond that apparent opposition. Both "instincts" strive toward an ideal *wholeness* or absolute: Eros does so at the cost of the self, the destructive instinct at the cost of everything *but* the self. The destructive instinct, that is, severs connections between things—dissecting, analyzing, labeling the environment—and thus the human incorporates its environment within the autonomous whole of the self: By naming the animals, the mythical Adam makes them contingent on his own consciousness, of a piece with himself. In the case of Eros, on the other hand, by avoiding self-definition in favor of the "oceanic feeling" of connectedness, the human becomes of a piece with its environment: Continuing the illustrative tale of origins, the mythical Lilith, resisting Adam's particularizing and hierarchical impositions, both establishes and disappears into a larger unity of herself with the wilderness and with the region of air.

Seen in this way, the entire spectrum of human behavior lies somewhere between these extreme poles of "putting things together" and "taking things apart." The case for genre outlined above can be similarly polarized, but just as in the human psyche, the practical enactments of such constructions tend to be more complex and more ambiguous, falling between these extreme polar strategies for reaching the desired wholeness. The Heraclitean "all" is one such extreme form of generic description, clearly (but oxymoronically) denoting the loss of self, of order, of "all," in the contiguous flux of experience. The opposite view is that of the solipsist, which in its inexorable self-aggrandizement eliminates difference entirely; rather than the loss of self in the Other (the environment, experience), we are presented with a sublime egotism, the loss of everything Other by its incorporation in the self. In the pertinent example of genre, we can see that "epic," which by its abstraction destroys our experience of the individual performance, at the same time creates a larger unity, allowing us to organize and engage with a wider set of experiences in a useful way.

Like any other part of our approach to reality, then, the construction of epic is an "adaptation in the functional sense," something *useful* to us in our engagement with the world.[5] As Hans Vaihinger notes, "what we generally call truth, namely a conceptual world coinciding with the external world, *is merely the most expedient error*" (Vaihinger 1925, 108). That is, our constructed reality (including the reality of epic, of genre, and so forth) is fundamentally expedient, "a system of ideas which enables us to act and to deal with things most rapidly, neatly, and safely" (108). Such a view of reality, and of literature as part of that reality, opens the way to an improved understanding of both our subject matter and our own discursive practices; recognizing the basic pragmatism of human action, and of discourse *as a performative act,* allows us to begin an examination of such acts *as* acts, that is, as rhetorically and pragmatically directed errors, hypotheses, or fictions that allow action within certain realms of experience.

The Tactics of Mistake

Putting things together and taking things apart thus constitute basic tactics or rhetorical tropes by which we negotiate our interaction with the world. While both are ultimately directed toward the same goal, they often work against each other as well as in combination.[6] In discussing these "two basic instincts" rather more neutrally as "tactics" or "tropes" of existence, Freud's terminology of Eros and Death begins to seem heavy-handed. A more neutral terminology avoids the too-easy Freudian equations of sex with Burke's less objectionable "putting things together" and of destruction with "taking things apart." However, Freud's understanding of destruction and Eros as equivalent to "take apart" and "combine" does suggest the thorough connection between these basic tropes of existence and our cultural milieu—a connection worth exploring.

Certainly, even a cursory glance at Western culture shows the powerful linkage between sex and violence, sex and death. Not only are these often seen as essential ingredients for the popular success of a novel or film in modern culture (as well as a primary focus of censorship), but they also share a traditional and highly valorized coupling as the primary thematic material of epic poetry. This culturally supported coupling of the two themes is also widely proclaimed as innate or "instinctual" by descriptions of the human psyche.

The cultural inscription of sex and violence on more basic tactics of existence is rather troubling, not least because women are traditionally excluded from power in these two realms of action. Rather, women are expected (and trained) to act as the passive recipients, the objects, of both sex and violence.[7] By assigning both Eros and Thanatos to the primary "instinctual" drives, then, Freud suggests that women are *by nature* lesser (if not purely secondary) creatures. Freud's sketch of the "human" instinctual drive both asserts and extends a cultural exclusion of women from sexual and martial power, implying that women are *not even human* within these realms of action. The discourses (epic, film, theory) that replicate this imbalance of sexual and physical power only serve to entrench this exclusion. The idea that men, and only men, are permitted to assert their power in sexual or violent ways is one that has sustained a prolonged—a too well prolonged—empire over intellects. Thus, the encoding of *power* along gender lines becomes crucial, since, naturally enough, we discover that for men the assertion of power through violence is culturally linked to the assertion of sexual power, to the whole definition of what it is to "be a man." In contrast to this, women who assert their power in violent ways tend to be seen as asexual or unfeminine, at the very least. Similarly, women who exert control over their own sexuality are viewed as sorceresses, prostitutes, or both. The difficulty lies not in women's sexuality or violence as such, but in women's assertions of power, or more accurately, in cultural resistance to women's assertions of power.

Returning to the notion of tactics, however, we can propose that a relationship exists between combining and dissecting on a more fundamental level than the cultural, *beyond* "the smoking pyres of love and death." If we assume only the primary importance to the human condition of consciousness and the desire for wholeness, then we can begin to re-envision the connection between sex and violence apart from its investment within the cultural power-structure.

First of all, the desire for union has a paradoxical goal; wholeness or union is achieved at the cost of the dissolution of the Self seeking union. For the Self to exist *as* Self it must be separated from the whole.[8] For us to know ourselves and our desires there must be consciousness, itself dependent upon separation.[9] The human project of desire—to overcome that separation—can be realized in the form of two antithetical descriptions of human behavior.[10] The first—implicit in Love—involves the actual realization of the desire's fulfillment, accomplished by entirely extinguishing or incorporating the Self in the Other, as in the earlier quotation from Herakleitos. The second—implicit in War—would utterly extinguish and incorporate the Other in the Self, the extreme form of solipsism outlined earlier. But the paradox is immediately apparent, and the intrinsic necessity for the reversal of the poles in this bipolar description of human experience is equally clear. For the incorporation of the Self in the Other is in fact the death of the Self—an image of violence. And the overwhelming of the Other by the Self, in what seems clearly an act of violence, in fact leads to union. Thus conceptually the apparently distinct metaphors collapse into one another. In a sense, then, we have a merely apparent duality expressed in phrases that rise easily to the tongue: sex and violence, love and death, fierce wars and faithful loves, fierce loves and faithless wars, *l'amour et la mort,* Eros and Thanatos, etc. The very interchangeability of the terms suggests the linkage; the strategic goal is ultimately the same, but the tactics involved differ, changing even as they repeat: All's fair in love and war.

What I suggest here is a linkage of two distinct tropes through the mechanism of a prior, preoedipal form of desire that is basically narcissistic.[11] As different human tactics for existence, both are vital to the temporary easing of unfulfillable desire. The Oedipal plot (adopted by Freud to explain a typically masculine engagement with desire) shows a gender-linked encoding of basic narcissistic maneuvers (or processes) of union and separation. By separation from the paternal, usually portrayed as the violent destruction of the father, union with the maternal is made possible—a union most frequently portrayed as sexual. In less loaded terminology, the separation from the father is realized as the tactical trope of metaphor: The discrimination between two terms allows a realization of likeness without enforcing identity. This trope fulfills the parental injunction, to be like and yet unlike the parent. In relation to the maternal, the tactical trope of metonymy may be similarly invoked as a realization of unity without the utter loss of identity. Taken to the extreme of preoedipal desire, these tactics would end in the absolute forms of difference and sameness described above, with the same ultimate reversal of poles. In actual practice, however, metaphoric and metonymic strategies (like violence and sex themselves) are not so thorough, but rather can only assuage desire through the attainment of more or less happy substitutes for the absolute fulfillment of desire.

Refiguring desire as formed within narcissistic concerns of connection and separation demonstrates clear advantages over an exclusively Oedipal inscription of desire. Though women's assertions of sexual and violent power are traditionally invalidated by culture, this refiguring recreates desire and its tactical expressions beyond such invalidations. Though preoedipal desire is reinscribed and/or suppressed by later or simultaneous cultural inscriptions, such a theory of desire provides an explanation of the experienced reality of female desire, in contrast to Freudian and Lacanian dismissals. Recognizing that both female and male infants are required to adjust their relations (of separation and connection) with the mother and with other powerful forces in their environment, and considering these adjustments as formative of subjectivity and of a child's later tactics for interaction with the world, enables us to see desire (and epic) as not *necessarily* masculine and patriarchal, and likewise, tradition as not *necessarily* Oedipal. Adjusting Freudian "instincts" to a relatively neutral terminology of tactical metaphor and metonymy simplifies the analysis by losing the freighted "violence" and "sex." While the new terms connect easily to the more sensational labels, they expand even more clearly to poetic concerns with the issues of self and poem, with poetic precursors and tradition.

Thus, while "sex and violence," "love and war," "*l'amour/la mort*," come trippingly to the tongue as cultural pairs and binary opposites, they are not "opposed" at all, but merely *different* tactics for dealing with essentially the same kind of existence, somewhere *through* love and death.[12] The *usual* trope of love/sex/*eros* is metonymic in its relation to the whole, stressing the sense of contiguity, connectedness, interdependence. The *usual* trope of war/violence/*thanatos* is metaphoric, the relation between two distinct objects (as I have said elsewhere, "for every monster, there must be an equal and opposite hero").[13] I stress the "usual" here because these behavioral clusters tend to overlap; we are all aware of sexual relationships where the other is only perceived as "a distinct object"; likewise, we all know of metonymically engaged violence, in civil wars, domestic violence, and so forth.[14]

Much recent criticism has a metonymic focus, in that it seeks to valorize the connections, the embeddedness, of texts in their cultural milieux: the new historicism, cultural studies, much of psychoanalytic criticism. A particularly interesting illustration of this is the contemporary focus on the body, where the individual performances of a physical body become the locus for resistance, and "writing from the body" (or with the body) becomes *de rigeur* for properly "feminine writing." As Teresa Ebert and Judith Butler demonstrate, however, there is never yet a "body" or a performance outside of culture: the body is always already "body," part of a pattern of totalizing concepts.[15] The further we retreat from determinism's force, the clearer it is that we cannot escape. The best possibility for analyzing differing strategies for dealing with this world that we (and our bodies) are embedded in still appears to lie in Julia Kristeva's distinction between the symbolic and the semiotic, between the so-called "law of the father" and "writing from the body" (Kristeva 1980). Now, if this distinction is immediately relegated to traditional cultural dichotomies between male and female, then the entrenchment of female expression within "feminine writing" seems only to replicate and extend the patriarchal hegemony. That is, it perpetuates the exclusion of women from power; it is "ludic feminism" only, in Ebert's words. If we realize, however, that the tactics of representation Kristeva outlines are just that, relatively neutral strategies like the tactics of metaphor and metonymy, then the vital issue becomes the play between the uses of these strategies (regardless of the writer's gender). Kristeva makes the same point rather eloquently:

> On the one hand, there is pain—but it also makes one secure—caused as one recognizes oneself as subject of (others') discourse, hence tributary of a universal Law. On the other, there is pleasure—but it kills—at finding oneself different, irreducible, for one is borne by a simply singular speech, not merging with the others, but then exposed to the black thrusts of a desire that borders on idiolect and aphasia.... Within that vise, our only chance to avoid being neither master nor slave of meaning lies in our ability to insure our mastery of it (through technique and knowledge) as well as our passage through it (through play or practice). In a word, jouissance. (Kristeva 1980, x)

The serious pleasure of "jouissance" as it plays itself out in epic informs the next section, and this book as a whole. Having paid some attention to the critical valuation of metonymy, however, it seems only fair to turn to a primarily meta-phoric criticism, Harold Bloom's violent form of "revisionism."

Bloom's theory of the modern poet's "belatedness" and the Oedipal relation between poet and precursor is a useful one for many reasons. Working hard to earn his inheritance as a son of T. S. Eliot, he develops extensively the long-lived familial metaphors of literary continuity, an organic analogy in contrast to Eliot's chemical and physical analogies. Moreover, in applying Freudian psychoanalysis to a rereading of poetic tradition, he critiques simplistic theories of tradition as a beneficent "happy family," showing instead the darker sides of struggle and flight within the family romance of literature. Finally, he emphasizes the decentering inevitability of repetition, the way that all of us are—as Kristeva points out—trapped in words and language not our own. Each of us is always a "revisionist" in Bloom's view.

There are a number of difficulties and contradictions to his theories as well, of course, which we will glance at throughout this text. The most dangerous of these, and the most appropriate for discussion in this section, is his glorification of the *agon,* the struggle, as central to all poets as they try to compose. In revising his theory to extrapolate backward from his earlier focus on anxiety of influence among the Romantic poets, Bloom laments that "Revisionism prag-matically has become only a trope for Romanticism, just as Romanticism earlier became a trope for the European Enlightenment, the Enlightenment for the Renaissance, and the Renaissance for the Ancients. But there is a telling (and a killing) difference. Revisionism, as Nietzsche said of every spirit, unfolds itself *only in fighting.* The spirit portrays itself as agonistic, as contesting for supremacy, with other spirits, with anteriority, and finally with every earlier version of itself" (1982, vii–viii). To revise is to fight, according to Bloom. But if unrepeat-ability (or *différance*) is inevitable, then so is revisionism. Does one rereading struggle for supremacy with another? Is there warfare between the opening and closing nights of a performance? Strife between one snowflake and the next? Only if the agon loses all meaning, becoming the merest trope of all. Bloom, just as he acoustically tropes "telling" into "killing," also imposes violent sim-plicity on far more delicate and inevitable processes of change.[16]

The "fierce process" of revisionism contrasts with chronological periods or modes in this passage, but Bloom makes the "trope" equation not to break it, but to improve it as a poetic agon—"a loving conflict with previous poetry" (viii). At ease with turning historical discontinuities into assimilable "chunks" (Romanticism, *the* Enlightenment, etc.), Bloom—like an oral poet—implies that the agon of poetry is like the loving rivalry of Roland and Oliver, not the pure hostility of Roland and the Saracens. This complexity at least is worthwhile; what Bloom fails to realize, however, is that both forms of rivalry work as heuristic fictions for far less violent and less easily polarized processes. Just as terms like "the Ancients" are relevant to critical usage rather than to knowable historical realities, so the competition and violent exchange between Roland and Oliver work to delineate their differences concerning the olifaunt (which in turn portrays philosophical differences—in large, the distinction between *fortitudo* and *sapientia*).[17] Similarly, Bloom's heroic Freud, an early fighting spirit of revisionism ("the prophet of agon" [viii]), makes little sense except as a metaphorical exaggeration of the bookish Freud, rereading European tradition in the developing terms of an already established system of inquiry.[18] Continuing the analogy, in applying the *agon* as motivating principle in that particular product of Western European culture known as Freud, Bloom exaggerates his heroism, much as the violence of Pagan and Christian in the *Chanson de Roland.* Not because it happened, but because Roland (or Freud) is the hero, he will slice through warrior and mount together; will destroy ten thousand Saracens; will be lamented by earthquake and storm (and the successive violence of Charlemagne's campaign). Placed above reproach, above all consideration of contradictory evidence, is the *agon* itself, which provides the support for a well-defined character. Bloom, like the poet of the *Roland,* is certainly correct to some degree; Freud *was* somewhat different from many of his contemporaries. The poet of the *Roland* is a bit more accurate; an actual battle did take place: The fact that it was fought against Christian Basques (perhaps Gascons), not Saracens, was not important enough to the poet's audience nor to the poet to be the object of devoted remembrance. This last raises an important question for Bloom's theory: While the inclusion of conflict is vital to an oral epic (making the story more memorable and thereby more permanent), should the same also be said of literary criticism, when more adequate—if less comforting—explanations may be found?

I hope one example will illustrate sufficiently the danger of such a form of criticism. Ronald R. MacDonald's otherwise valuable *Burial-Places of Poetic Memory* (1987) uncritically applies Bloom's theory to a reading of Virgil, Dante, and Milton. Unsurprisingly, MacDonald has significant difficulty in assigning a conflict—a conflict he is sure must exist—to the relations between epic poets. Dante's relation to Virgil is perhaps the most difficult, for in the *Commedia* the poet so very deliberately and literally follows in his master's steps; moreover, Dante's actual difference or "swerve" from the precursor is delineated neither as conflict nor subterfuge, but as the accident of history that left Virgil a pagan. Dante's engagement with Virgil from within the new dispensation of Christianity is far more clearly a recursion to and rescue of Virgil than it is a form of the struggle.[19] And thus, for MacDonald, Dante is "mildly astonishing" due to the lack of conflict, "the apparently serene confidence with which he extends the Vergilian way with regard to Vergil himself. For the *Commedia* is not only full of Vergilian quotation . . . but the figure of Vergil himself is allowed into the poem, and not, as we have already seen, in the guise of the 'Medieval Vergil,' but as a carefully restored approximation of the historical figure" (188–89). Dante's active recursion—the focal desire to remember the precursor—works strongly not against tradition itself, but against an exaggerated *theory* of tradition. A far simpler theory, less sensational than that of the *agon*, but one that makes more sense, is revealed in MacDonald's throwaway image of a Dante who joins Virgil "quite as if he had joined with the master as apprentice or junior partner" (189). A theory of epic based on this model of craft-allegiance would have more to be said for it than the exaggerated agonistic model, but holds, I think, less attraction than the more dynamic, fundamental and heuristically powerful explanations of a balanced psychoanalytic model.

To sum up, the epic dyad of love and war is a culturally and traditionally enshrined usage of a simpler and more neutral set of actions or tactics with regard to the fundamental separation at the core of the human condition—actions of putting things together and taking things apart. This exaggerated usage of metaphor and metonymy, both in epic and in psychological theory (and—as in Bloom—in other realms of discourse), tends to entrench and legitimate the dominant strata of society.

Masterplots and Recursive Desire

Nihil sub sole novum.
—Ecclesiastes

Nothing new under the sun, says Ecclesiastes; as a response to Herakleitos it makes perfect sense, for we experience similitude as much as we experience difference. Often, however, we fail to recognize sameness simply because it is the same. "Difference is the meaning of an allusion," but only *after* the more basic recognition of similitude. The kernel of an allusion lies in its status as repetition. Similarly, the fundamental commonalities of human experience exist in repetition, in the way each of Lacan's "small human animals" is born into a world of fragmented perception and unfulfillable desire, and in our parallel birth into language, into a conceptual system of cultural codes. Though language is largely alien to this organism suddenly "caught up in the word not [its] own" (Bloom 1975, 13), it does allow us to mediate (not heal) the psychological split implicit in consciousness.

Thus it is difficult to overestimate the importance of repetition to our lives.

One illustration of it is David Hume's skeptical argument about the relation of causes and effects, and how that relation demonstrates repetition or "Custom" as "the great guide of human life." Here we can see the fundamental utility of repetition, and our desperate desire, even need, for the recursive structure of experience. Sharply questioning the empirical and rational basis of any "necessary connection" between cause and effect, Hume demonstrates that what gives rise to the reified law of cause and effect is exactly and merely the *apparent repetition* of the "constant conjunction" between two events, rather than any *necessary* connection between the two. And if, as he says, "All reasonings concerning matter of fact seem to be founded on the relation of Cause and Effect," then all "matter of fact" and existence itself are jeopardized when the relation of cause and effect are shown as faulty.[20] Though Hume never impugns the usefulness of or the human desire for the cause and effect relation, he does reduce it from the status of Law to that of an unreasoned *custom*, merely a convenient story that we tell ourselves.[21] By imposing this habitual narrative of "Custom" on the environment, we begin already to tell the same old epic story, the same old plot of connection and separation, of desire and violence.[22]

This thesis, that each and every utterance enacts the psychological drama of human desire, should not seem unfamiliar, nor too great an imaginative leap. If current understandings of human psyches and their interaction with the world are valid, then it only makes sense that human productions bear significant traces of that psyche. While this can be seen as true of any and all products of human effort from the lighting of a cigarette to the building of the pyramids, it is especially so of language, the fundamental tool of the conceiving mind, which mediates all—or almost all—of our engagement with the world around us.

This understanding of language is paralleled, even magnified, in recent theories of narrative. Peter Brooks suggests that the psychological model of narrative, and of "the dynamics of memory and desire" within narrative, may allow us "to reconnect literary criticism to human concern" (1984, xiv). Literary criticism never really abandoned such a concern, I think, but Brooks's exploration "of the motor forces that drive the text forward, of the desires that connect narrative ends and beginnings, and make of the textual middle a highly charged field of force" (xii–xiv) can provide a useful way into the difficulties of epic.[23]

Brooks develops Freud's view of repetition as an attempt at mastery; while this recursive desire is characterized by Freud as a "compulsion to repeat," my comments above suggest that recursion is really *all* there is: *Nihil sub sole novum.* Brooks also summarizes conveniently some literary applications of repetition: "Now, repetition is so basic to our experience of literary texts that one is simul-

taneously tempted to say all and to say nothing on the subject. To state the matter baldly: rhyme, alliteration, assonance, meter, refrain, all the mnemonic elements of literature and indeed most of its tropes are in some manner repetitions
that take us back in the text, that allow the ear, the eye, the mind to make connections, conscious or unconscious, between different textual moments, to see
past and present as related and as establishing a future that will be noticeable as
some variation in the pattern" (Brooks 1984, 99). As demonstrated earlier, there
is no exact repetition; but there is also nothing new, only "variation[s] in the
pattern"; the play between these metaphoric and metonymic poles, between
autonomy and contiguity, is expressed by Freud as a relationship of mastery: It
is "the task of the higher strata of the mental apparatus to bind the instinctual
excitation reaching the primary process" (Freud 1920, 306–7; cited in Brooks
1984, 101). Kristeva makes much the same point, but with less admiration for
the "higher strata": "Language as symbolic function constitutes itself at the cost
of repressing instinctual drive and continuous relation to the mother," breaking
with the earlier (preoedipal) semiotic "wandering or fuzziness" implicit in language (1980, 136).

The "cost" of language as symbolic (as Law) is written as repression. That
this cost is replicated and played out in distasteful ways in a phallologocentric
culture is not in doubt. On the other hand, Brooks points briefly to the value of
mastery, to the extreme utility of the "binding" authority of language, in that
it "allows [textual energies] to be mastered by putting them into serviceable
form, usable 'bundles.' . . . Serviceable form must, I think, mean perceptible
form" (101).

The difficulty with using the claims of Oedipal or preoedipal "masterplots"
lies in their extreme universality—if a claim applies equally to each and every
utterance, then how is such a claim special for epic? Genre criticism must demonstrate a difference as well as similarity, and the theory as laid out thus far
shows only a repetitive sameness: The psychological masterplot is enacted in
the word's relation to the real, and to its own more particular environment of
other words; the same dynamic is enacted within all narrative, and even within
the lyrical; if the masterplot is thus inescapable as scripted, how can one define
the apparent difference? While such redundancy does perhaps militate against
the inexorable flux of existence, it also threatens to collapse any and all difference; rather than the infinite difference available in the Heraclitean dictum, we
seem to be left with an infinitude of repetition, the idea that nothing is new
under the sun.

One answer to these paradoxical truths might be Bloom's, believing Ecclesiastes but ignoring Herakleitos: Repetition is inevitable, and difference is

achieved (if at all) only through conflict. A simpler and more adequate answer notes that both are inevitable, and there is no need for struggle: Things change.

What distinguishes epic as a genre, however, is a somewhat different attitude toward repetition, an apparent propensity for recursion itself. As the proverb says, repetition is the mother of memory: Very clearly in oral cultures, the circumstances of epic composition and preservation require specific technologies of repetition, technologies that can maintain a cultural memory of events, of causes and effects. Thus it is telling that in traditional societies, epic tends to be the domain of male artists and audiences, providing through its dominant recursions a substitute contiguity and continuity between men; in short, epic is men's way of making up for the fact that they are not women. Many scholars have remarked on epic's devotion to recursion, speaking of the seamless "whole world" or "rounded cosmos" of the communal ethos and epos of the "heroic age" (Ker 1896, 39; duBois 1982). More substantively, Bakhtin (1981) and Northrop Frye (1957) analyze the chief marker of epos as its monologic quality, its tendency toward "recurrence." Both scholars base their understanding of this recursion in the rhythmical underpinning of epic, Frye commenting that "The regular pulsating metre that traditionally distinguishes verse from prose tends to become the organizing rhythm in epos or extended oratorical forms. Metre is an aspect of recurrence, and the two words for recurrence, rhythm and pattern, show that recurrence is a structural principle of all art, whether temporal or spatial in its primary impact" (251). Frye recognizes the repetition in all art, but he notes the special quality of epic in this regard, where such recurrence is not simply a structuring principle, but the *primary* organizing principle. Similarly (if more antagonistically) Bakhtin declares that within the "monological world" of the epic, recursion and musical devices are used in an authoritarian manner to "concentrate even further the unity and hermetic quality of the surface of poetic style" (298).[24]

Thus, while numerous critics remark on recursion's important role in the internal workings of epic, few observe that this devotion to recursion extends as well to repeated performances of epic. These observations are limited to students of oral cultures that have various technologies precisely for the accurate preservation and repetition of epic. The device of recurrent formulas and epithets is familiar from Milman Parry's (1971) and Albert Lord's (1960) pioneering work in the field of Homeric and Yugoslavian oral composition: "Wily Odysseus," "fleet Achilles," and so forth. In Anglo-Saxon oral poetry, as well, the stress on recursion is clear: Standard formulas such as "we have heard," or "I heard," create a clear chain of recursions, in spite of the fact that the present performer is not an immediate witness; the formula and the tradition suppose a recursive chain of performers and auditors, leading back to the original event and its witnesses. As Walter J. Ong points out, in an oral culture one must "think memorable thoughts":

> [T]o solve effectively the problem of retaining and retrieving carefully articulated thought, you have to do your thinking in mnemonic patterns, shaped for ready oral recurrence. Your thought must come into being in heavily rhythmic, balanced patterns, in repetitions or antitheses, in alliterations and assonances, in epithetic and other formulary expressions, in standard thematic settings (the assembly, the meal, the duel, the hero's "helper," and so on) in proverbs which are constantly heard by everyone so that they come to mind readily and which themselves are patterned for retention and ready recall, or in other mnemonic form. Serious thought is intertwined with memory systems. Mnemonic needs determine even syntax. (1982, 34)

These conventional patternings attempt to counteract the defects of human memory, and help to explain why recursion constitutes a key feature of epic as a genre: These recursions are the only way to maintain the oral tradition, and thereby to maintain the Humean narrative of "Custom . . . the great guide of human life."

This devotion to recursion is not unique to oral epic poets, but constitutes the attitude of epic poets in general. While recursion as a means of survival is less necessary to literate poets, a great deal of value is still associated with such recursions, for they establish the poet as a member of a discursive elite, as an *epic* poet. The elite concerns of oral epic, where tradition acts as a blueprint of the political system (Vansina 1985, 103), are extended and entrenched in literate culture; the reified text (in the Greek valorization of Homeric texts, for example), is used to determine and justify politics, rather than forming an expression responsible only to a particular sociopolitical context of performance.

While it is generally accepted that poets tend to be more conscious of tradition than other literary artists, that such a statement is truer of epic poets is hardly to be denied. Indeed, the writer of epic is in a position like the oral epic poet's; with each performance, the poet is required to re-create, re-member, as it were, the traditional narrative, the "tale of the tribe." Epic is thus never part of an absolute past, but is always both the remaking of the tradition in light of the contingent present, and the remaking of the present in light of the tradition, exactly as it is in oral cultures.

Brian Wilkie suggests a similar point: "Epic is not and never really has been a genre; it is a tradition" (1965, viii).[25] While Wilkie does not address the issue of oral epic, he provides a cogent analysis of recursion in literary epic, where

"Imitation often seems to be an end in itself" (14). The "seemingly compulsive imitativeness" of the writer of epic is a strong reminder of the thematic and formulaic composition of the oral poet; both use the same

> familiar store of props and scenes: bleeding trees, heavenly tempered
> shields and armor, challenges to single combat, councils, nocturnal scout
> ing expeditions, shipwrecks, games, scale images, hunting images, and a
> whole host of minutely detailed verbal echoes often applied to contexts
> utterly unlike the original settings. To read the great epics in succession
> is like walking through a hall of mirrors. Imitative devices like these, and
> not more general or formal traits, are the most dependable signs that a
> work is a candidate for the epic category, although at least some of the
> larger patterns and traits will almost certainly be present too. (14)

The consistent recursive use of "imitative devices" is itself part of a general, and indeed a formal definition of epic. Epic's "compulsive imitativeness" suggests that the genre possesses interesting psychological ramifications, but Wilkie avoids these to follow out the detailed Wittgensteinian "family resemblances" propagated by the epic tradition (14–15); Michael Bernstein's *Tale of the Tribe* (1980) uses a similar grounding, but his analyses are devoted rather to larger structural concerns and patterns of the epic "family" than to the "minutely detailed verbal echoes" and motifs of Wilkie.

This discussion of the genre of epic as a "family," especially in light of our earlier discussion of the psychological "masterplot," invites the question of the "family romance" as it is worked out in the epic tradition. And here we return to Harold Bloom, whose *Anxiety of Influence* frames the Oedipal relation of poet and precursor in antagonistic terms; as in the Freudian account, the son (Bloom's "ephebe") must murder the father in order to sleep with the mother (or Muse). Bloom's "unified meditation on the melancholy of the creative mind's desperate insistence upon priority" (1973, 13) strikes the reader immediately as somewhat unbalanced, since no female poets exist in the author's schema. Moreover, the "desperate insistence upon priority" is odd, especially if the nature of oral productions is taken under consideration. Bloom suggests that "priority in divination is crucial for every strong poet, lest he dwindle merely into a latecomer. My theory rejects also the qualified Freudian optimism that happy substitution is possible, that a second chance can save us from the repetitive quest for our earliest attachments. Poets as poets cannot accept substitutions, and fight to the end to have their initial chance alone" (8). This passage brings out several difficulties with Bloom's thesis. First of all, while Bloom (correctly) assumes that "the repetitive quest" is inescapable, he uses "happy" and "save" in an absolute sense (as though the "strong poet" might find his absolute), whereas Lacan and Freud recognize that there *is* "something fundamentally impossible about satisfaction itself" (see Mitchell's introduction to Lacan 1985, 6). Poets, even *as* poets, can and do accept substitutions, because they (like everyone else) have no choice in the matter. This last points to another difficulty, Bloom's myth of the "poet as poet," the "aboriginal poetic self" (1973, 11), where "the handful—(since the old, great ones) . . . enter into a counter-sublime, a poetry of earth, but such a handful (Milton, Goethe, Hugo) are sub-gods. The strong poets of our time, in English, who enter greatly into the contest of wrestling with the dead, never go so far as to enter this fourth stage or poetry of earth. Ephebes abound, a double handful manage the Promethean quest, and three or four attain the poetry of discontinuity (Hardy, Yeats, Stevens) in which a poem of the air is constructed" (79–80). Apart from the eclectic and mythic mystification of such figures (one supposes divinity is even better than mere canonical sainthood), there is a significant problem with Bloom's wish to separate the "poet as poet" (as special, semi-divine entity) from the human being who lives or lived in a particular human society.[26]

Most important, however, is Bloom's lack of realization that the urge to *recur* is at least as strong as the urge to attempt absolute "priority" through "swerving" or difference. That this recursive desire is especially powerful among epic poets I have already pointed out, but it is worth remarking that people would not become poets at all if the lack of "priority" were so distasteful. One may have difficulty avoiding the parental and cultural impositions of language, but this hardly means that epic poetry is similarly inevitable. Apart from its lack of attention to the specific dynamics of epic tradition, Bloom's theory is rooted only in the relatively recent poetic valorization of originality, the Romantic and Modernist ideal of "making it new."

To epic in particular the idea of "priority in divination" seems incongruous. The very existence of a thing like tradition, and indeed, of a poet, militates against such priority. The dream of "priority" remains a dream: As William Carlos Williams observes, there is no art of poetry, save by the grace of other poetry. Moreover, if the epic poet aims to tell the "tale of the tribe," to construct "the voice of the community's heritage telling itself" (Bernstein 1980, 14), then divination—especially new, unfamiliar divination—is the opposite of what is required. And if we follow Bernstein up on this idea, we find that the kinds of originality and individuality espoused by Bloom as central to the "aboriginal poetic self" do not suit the epic poet at all: "[The epic] must be narrated by a spokesman for values important to community well-being, and should not bear the trace of a single sensibility. It ought to be the voice of the community's heritage 'telling itself' " (14). In contrast to the Bloomian paradigm, recursion is not necessarily a repressed and inevitable compulsion, but rather a fundamental desire on the part of the epic poet. Divination is designed not to attain an impossible "firstness," but to attain a position within an elite as a responding participant in an ongoing tradition. Moreover, the matter divined in epic is that of the change between the last epic performed and the current performance, the discordance between precursor codes and the contingent present. Divination is the result of disconfirmation, and a response explicitly framed not as priority but as recursive adjustment. Wilkie points out that the repudiation of past epics is in itself a traditional move, a *recursion* to those very epics repudiated, like the adjustive strategy of the prophetic divinations: "It is a tradition, however, that operates in an unusual way, for although, like any tradition, it is rooted in the past, it typically rejects the past as well, sometimes vigorously and with strident contempt. The great paradox of the epic lies in the fact that the partial repudiation of earlier epic tradition is itself traditional" (Wilkie 1965, 10). Walt Whitman's stridently new and relatively democratic assertion that the epic muse has emigrated to the United States, where she is quickly "installed amid the kitchenware," is a maneuver as old as Virgil's, transplanting the epic from one shore to another:

> Arma virumque cano, Troiae qui primus ab oris
> Italiam fato profugus Laviniaque venit
> litora.[27]

Virgil downplays the role of the muse in his poem somewhat differently than does Whitman, merely relegating her to second place as speaker, rather than completely domesticizing her: "Tell, O Muse" appears quickly, but not so quickly that the audience misses the emphatic first-person, the "I" who sings of arms and man. Bloom might refer to this kind of recursion as "poetic misprision" (or *clinamen*)—as "a misreading of the prior poet, an act of creative correction that is actually and necessarily a misinterpretation" (1973, 30): It is a defensive pretense that the original has failed, only to be corrected by the poet-ephebe. At first sight, Bloom's view makes some sense, recalling Vaihinger ("what we generally call truth . . . is merely the most expedient error" [1925, 108]). Unfortunately, it is too general to apply only to poets, as Bloom realizes intermittently: "[M]ost so-called 'accurate' interpretations of poetry are worse than mistakes; perhaps there are only more or less creative or interesting misreadings, for is not every reading necessarily a *clinamen?*" (43). If this is the case (and I would agree that it is), then the pertinent question is who judges this "swerving" from the original, since that person (professionally entrenched critic or not), like the poet, also misreads, also engages in a "creative correction" that can be either more or less agonistic in its relation to the original. What Bloom is casting as anxious and agonistic "misreading" can be seen more productively as *rereading*. The changes that necessarily occur are more closely linked to homeostasis, the tendency (of the individual mind, and of whole societies) to maintain equilibrium by shedding that which is no longer useful. This homeostatic process is more easily observed in oral societies than in literate ones, as Ong (following Goody and Watt)[28] remarks: "[O]ral societies live very much in a present which keeps itself in equilibrium or homeostasis by sloughing off memories which no longer have present relevance" (1982, 46). That such a "sloughing off" occurs among literate peoples is clear to anyone who has worked among library discards, but deserves fuller elucidation for those who have not. The process is more familiar, perhaps, in our continuing need for the countering process of "reclamation" and "discovery" of marginalized discourse (discourse by women, by people of color, etc.). Those things (events, texts, people) not immediately useful for the community to remember, the community quickly forgets. When the homeostatic process is selectively reinforced by powerful institutions (e.g., by a heavy-duty tradition like epic), the process may be hastened or retarded, but it does continue.

Thus "misprision," far from being a willful strategy of the mind available only to poets, is rather the normal state of affairs, a functional adaptation to reality as it is perceived. Each epic poet, consciously imitating and recurring to earlier performances, *necessarily* revises the tale of the tribe as he or she engages in a new performance, struggling to adapt the recursive epic to the changing contexts of life. The epic poet's revision of the tale of the tribe is largely inevitable, and is very specifically a re-vision, a new view of the world as attained by one who lives in different times and places than his or her putative "original" or precursor.[29] The supposed *clinamen* of Whitman from the ancient Virgilian shift of muse and scene of action signifies far more broadly in terms of geographical location and contemporary sex roles than it does in those of "misreading." The interesting thing, rather, is Whitman's devoted recursion to the Virgilian shift in this new context, in spite of his repeated disavowals and repudiations of the European past and American "literary flunkyism." As Anthony Easthope remarks concerning all discourse, "Each additional text both repeats the discourse and differs from it, each is a term which conforms to the discourse but (however slightly) transforms it."[30] One way to further examination of the *reasons* behind this persistent recursive desire in epic can be found by taking a slightly different perspective, looking at the question of tradition and recursion as it acts and is acted upon by women writers.

The patriarchal tradition has been described as a hierarchy, a competitive system wherein male poets strive for glory before the "perfect witness of all-judging Jove, / as he pronounces lastly on each deed" (e.g., in Bloom 1994). Though there are vital differences inherent in the dynamics of epic, Oedipal filiation applies fairly well to strictly literate tradition. But this version of the masterplot, however well it explains the dynamics of male relations within the tradition, offers little with regard to the female experience of epos. A number of scholars try to compensate for this flaw in the patriarchal system by providing models of female poetic development along the lines of women's significant pre-Oedipal attachments.[31] All of them emphasize the "anxiety of authorship" (in Sandra Gilbert and Susan Gubar's phrase) imposed upon women by patriarchal tradition, the struggle women face when they choose to write at all within patriarchal culture. Most provide as well a model of female "tradition," casting the writer's relation to female ancestresses and contemporaries in terms of a continuity of connection. Elizabeth Abel analyzes these two tendencies as characterizing women's "dual response to the past": On one hand, the issues of the female Oedipal conflict are seen to reflect women's conflict with patriarchal tradition; on another, "the relation to female tradition reflects the pre-oedipal" issues at stake (1982, 433–34). Though this work is significant, it problematizes the relation of the female epic poet to the specifically epic tradition. Scholars make a strategic shift to women's texts *in general,* concealing to some degree the fact of the traditional generic hierarchy and its power. It is a necessary shift, for there are far fewer texts by women among the "higher" genres. But the anxiety of authorship women face increases dramatically as they attempt to move from marginalized discursive forms to those genres valorized by a culture. Reinforcing this anxiety is the increased scarcity in these genres of exemplary women writers with whom to establish a connective relationship. In the lyric there is the lineage of Sappho, but in the loftiest of kinds there has been not one widely acknowledged woman writer readily available to women readers until the most recent past.[32]

Thus, while much excellent work has been done in terms of women's reactions to the discourses of patriarchy in general, especially in the decision *not* to write in predominantly masculine genres, a far different dynamic operates when a woman poet's *chosen* genre is the prime example of phallologocentric legislation. The psychological quest for the maternal absolute, which lies at the core of the epic and which suggests that epic traditionally has been men's way of making up for the fact that they are not women, requires a substantial re-examination when the task is undertaken by women, who are said to be always already present to their psychological mothers. Though this is more fully explored in Chapter 6, a brief summary suggests that for women writers of epic, the relationship to "tradition" is indeed rather perilous and antagonistic. Women who choose to write epic, however, generally have a certain stake in and value for that tradition. Thus, their recursions to earlier epic can be remarkably similar to men's in that regard, capable of constituting, to borrow

Kolodny's description, a veritable Echo of tradition, with the poet herself becoming a figure of that shadowy nymph (1987, 116). In this study, however, the poems selected highlight the consistent emphasis in women's epic on the need for "re-visioning" traditionally epic and patriarchal (or "masculine") ways of seeing the world, and especially ways of seeing women within that world. Works such as Elizabeth Barrett Browning's *Aurora Leigh* and H.D.'s *Helen in Egypt* are thus similarly confrontational as they concentrate on recreating and revaluing some of the fundamental conceptions of a phallocentric hegemony, but the strategies chosen are remarkably dissimilar. Barrett Browning's strongly contemporary epic of manners appears at first to be designed as an entire evasion of epic precursors; the philosophy of art expressed within the poem suggests exactly the opposite, however. Moreover, the elision of traditional epic conflict—the matter of war—in favor of a recursion to the epic formula that grounds its conflict in "Art," suggests a different view of tradition on the part of this woman poet at least. Similarly, though H.D.'s deliberately archaizing epic, in its resuscitation of the Homeric Helen, takes the form of a direct confrontation with tradition, her goal in doing so is clearly not to *displace* Homer, but instead to *respond* to Homer while permitting that poet to continue speaking. This is, clearly enough, a strategy far different from that of Milton as he energetically confronts and dismisses classical epic.

Particularly interesting in women's epic is the relationship expressed with regard to the maternal, or to the female in general; the expression of preoedipal concerns implies both a more powerful rejection of and finally assimilation to the maternal than is found in poems by men. A vivid example of this sacrifice of the maternal is the centrality of rape in both Barrett Browning's and H.D.'s epics. The re-assimilation, the recursion to the maternal "masterplot," is realized by Barrett Browning in Aurora's relation with Marian Erle, and by H.D. largely in her own poetic relation to Barrett Browning. This form of recursion involves a substantial "re-membering" or reassembly of the rejected, sacrificed mother, and thus in the case of female poets in particular, a reconstruction of the self.

This last enforces a slightly different view of the reasoning I have already put forth regarding epic's devotion to recursion, reasoning which suggests that men use epic to make up for the fact that they are not women. Rather, recursion in epic attempts to make up for much more than a mere deficiency of gender, actually lending a substantial coherency of *self;* by its extension and valorization, the epic can further lend such a self-coherency to audience, to reader, to polis, to the tribe itself.[33] The recursive desire at the heart of epic thus comes to seem far more thoroughgoing and useful. I have already pointed to the important role such recurrence plays in oral societies, where the technologies of recursive structuring act to retard the process of homeostasis, working more or less effectively against the forces of time and change. I have also argued that such recursions act as a fundamental support for the convenient story of causation, and thereby for custom itself, for the laws of a given society. Recurrence constructs a comforting sameness, a coherent background of continuity against which difference can be measured. Members of the community are able to judge recent actions, to see themselves and their community *as a whole* in relation to their heroes and their cultural heritage. Moreover, that cultural heritage itself provides a sense of continuity, of communal identity through change. In short, epic can work as a synecdoche of the entire community, enacting through its metonymic strategy of cyclic recursion a powerful sense of connection and communal coherence—a "happy substitute"—for its audience. The epic poet in his or her work is attempting to provide that coherence, that substitute wholeness, through careful recursions to this synecdoche of culture; is reaching toward wholeness to take on the voice of the tribe.

Notes toward a Definition

Defining a genre is always difficult, but attending precisely to the problem areas of past definitions may gain us some new insights. If we have in mind a provisional definition, one that works right now, rather than for all time, so much the better for our chances of success. Recent scholarship on both epic poetry and the twentieth-century "long poem" suggests a continuing tradition of epic in the nineteenth and twentieth centuries (Wilkie 1965; Miller 1979; Bernstein 1980; McWilliams 1989). The critical establishment, however, assumes for the most part that the only good epic is a dead epic—that the genre dies with the rise of the novel.[34] Important theorists like Georg Lukács and M. M. Bakhtin (1981) add their influence so weightily that, indeed, the "epic to novel" progression comes to seem a commonplace of literary history.[35] Certainly the fortunes of the novel have been on the rise, but it is (at best) misleading for critics to ignore the continuing production of lengthy poetic forms.

Moreover, this epic to novel theory strangely elides the traditional hierarchical difference between the two genres when it tries to install epic energy or "spirit" in the novel.[36] This hierarchical difference is still conveyed to a surprising degree by the different connotations we attach to such terms as "epic" and "prosaic" (and to a lesser degree by "poetic" and "prosaic"). To put this another way, the difficulty with a phrase like "bourgeois epic," which Lukács applies to the novel, is the fact that it is a contradiction in terms. Epic, in oral and literate forms, has always been the concern of a discursive elite, people whose status is directly related to their ability to produce texts; in short, "the unacknowledged legislators of the world."[37] Epic's elite status as the "highest province of poetic lore" is closely connected to the odd criterion of "greatness" that has tradition-ally been demanded of the genre.[38] Even if we (unwisely) ignore the question of who judges this "greatness," the glaring difficulty is that most attempts at epic will be judged, *at best*, "magnificent failures" (since "most" and "great" are in-compatible terms). Obviously, this applies especially to contemporary judg-ments of "epics," but it is true when we judge past epics as well. Dante and Milton, rather than being *added* to the canon (or "pantheon," as Wilkie calls it) of epic poets, instead *replace* Statius and Lucan. Epic, in short, begins to appear as a mythical creature, like the dragon, the hero, and the miracle, a thing that is necessarily defined as being already dead. This kind of definition helps us little, though no doubt it is convenient when constructing glorious etiologies for the rise of the novel.

Radically questioning these assumptions seems more helpful. For one thing, such questioning immediately shows that declarations of the death of epic are practically as old as epic itself: The recurrent assertion of epic's unsuit-ability to "unheroical age[s]," ranges from at least the time of the Anglo-Saxons (as Alcuin asks, "What has Ingeld to do with Christ?") down to our own; the declaration itself becomes a convention linked to the genre. Indeed, the decla-ration of the "death" of epic is in certain respects integral to and coterminous with the genre; in oral traditions as in literate, the repeated tale of the tribe al-ready has the status of an icon or relic—even if it changes with each perfor-mance.

A new, provisional definition of epic is badly needed, one that accounts ade-quately for its continuing production, its elite status, and a few other difficul-ties. I would like to suggest one, developing further certain lines of inquiry sug-gested by Wilkie, Bernstein, and Bloom. In place of definitions that rely on nebulous entities like the "epic spirit" of an age, or formalist definitions de-pendent upon epic "markers" (e.g., beginning *in medias res*, the presence of cata-logues or *ekphraseis*, etc.), a more accurate definition—like Wilkie's—recognizes the important place of the epic *tradition* within the mind of the epic poet. Bern-stein's looser definition of epic according to Wittgensteinian "family likeness" is effective in the treatment of single works, but Bloom's application of the Freudian "family romance" to English poetic tradition provides in addition a powerful way of explaining the intrinsically dynamic relations between epics within that tradition. Bloom and narrative theorists such as Peter Brooks have argued that the Freudian script—the Oedipal scenario—is inescapable in any kind of sustained discursive structure, but they have focused on lyric poetry and novels rather than epic. Perhaps as a result of their specializations, they em-phasize literary attempts to escape the script, and the ultimate futility of these attempts.[39] But epic is a special case. Epic poets, I believe, are not trying to evade their precursors; epics focus instead on the *recursion* to the traditional script, on the quite deliberate (as well as inevitable) assumption of the forms of epic power, voice, and story.

Understood in this way, the writer of an epic is very like the oral epic poet: With each performance, the poet desires to re-create the traditional narrative, the "tale of the tribe." The oral poet has access only to the ephemera of "winged words," thus the individual performer must continually re-create his or her tradition, and the epic must be repeated as exactly as possible, given the technological exigencies of oral milieux. A suddenly skeptical, critical stance becomes available to the literate poet, but the literary tradition—the weight and power of nearly three thousand years of discourse—still appears inescapable, and leads to the "belatedness" emphasized by Bloom. The sense of belatedness certainly present in some poets[40] is indeed pervasive, but is not so agonistic—not so conflict-centered—as all that; epic poets are not really trying to evade or even stage a conflict with their precursors, but instead deliberately recur to them, aiming primarily to repeat them. (It is rare, even today, that one is compelled to write a poem, especially an epic.) Belatedness, thus, is a chosen burden or reward, not a cause of deliberately violent misprision; not surprisingly, belatedness begins to appear most markedly with the advent of literacy. Increasingly written epics show an increasingly threatening series of textual fathers, despite the apparent success of their heroes. In modern epics, where we might expect it, there is a greater emphasis on "making it new," on breaking free of tradition; this denial of connection, however, is itself an invocation of traditional rejections, serving to establish more firmly the importance of tradition to the poets involved.

With this emphasis on tradition, epic can never be part of an absolute past, nor of the present alone, but is always both the remaking of the tradition in light of the contingent present, and the remaking of the present in light of the tradition. Thus, within a certain historical context the epic poet consciously reacts to earlier epics—a tradition—and aligns him/herself with that tradition or reacts against it. In the poem thus produced, the depiction of sex and violence, though rooted firmly in the cultural psyche and epic tradition, imitates or reflects the poet's attitude toward tradition, while adapting itself to the particular historical context in which he or she composes.

2

Worda ond Worca

Oral Epics and Preoedipal Concerns

> It is finer matter than the tale of Oedipus.
> —W. W. Lawrence[1]

A DISTINGUISHING CHARACTERISTIC of *Beowulf* and the *Iliad* is their primarily oral construction; this difference in technology from later epic changes the psychological grounding of the epics significantly. Rather than presenting a clear-cut Oedipal plot, early epics demonstrate the overriding importance of preoedipal psychological configurations in the epic; specifically, these poems show a working out of narcissistic concerns with the individual's separation from unity. Because of the technology of oral composition, recursion is both more thoroughgoing and harder to detect, because the whole woven interplay of the texts is recursive in structure and aim: to retell the story as told before. In the oral epic, thus, the relative fragility and physical absence of the "tradition" in the form of precursor texts act to strengthen the workings of recursive desire. The heroic focus of the *Iliad* can be seen as narcissistic aggrandizement of Achilles, but the heroism of Beowulf is tempered from the Greek extreme, and mediates more consistently the alternate concerns with personal fame (*lof*) and with the cohesion of society. As Kenneth Rexroth suggests, *Beowulf*, in contrast to the Homeric epics, "fulfills our insistence upon a moral heroism" (1968, 167). That is, *Beowulf*, with an emphasis more pagan than Christian, suggests a code of conduct that mediates between the extreme narcissistic assertion of an Achilles and the extreme narcissistic submission of a Christ. *Beowulf* emphasizes neither the one nor the other, but rather its alliterative verse emphasizes the very process of play, the *jouissance* between grandiose assertion and self-sacrifice.[2] This duality of self is explored even more fully in a poem like *The Epic of Gilgamesh,* where the narcissistic hero-king and his sacrificial partner Enkidu function as aspects of one self.

The Oedipal plot tends to work well for explaining the *Odyssey* and after; but as I have suggested, this plot is only the gender-linked coding of the more basic narcissistic plot (or processes) of union and separation. While we *read* the "death and glory" (*thanatos/kleos*) complex as analogous to that of death and love (*thanatos/eros*), this reading is best seen as our own sexualized imposition on a more fundamental script. The Freudian "masterplot" is already a sublimation— a search for the happy substitute.

This new understanding of the masterplot allows certain advantages over the Oedipal script, implying that men have traditionally used epic not only to make up for the fact of lost connection with the mother, but rather to make up for the fact that they are not even themselves.[3] The adoption of the preoedipal better explains the homosocial focus of much epic, even of later, typically romantic epics; it reduces the potential confusion with regard to the homoerotic divergence from the Freudian masterplot; it also sheers nearer the position of the poet in regard to oral tradition. While "Every poet is a narcissist," this statement applies even more forcefully to the *oral* epic poet, who is engaged in an active self-exhibition in a context where all eyes are literally on him or her.

The question of recursion and repetition is somewhat different in oral forms, though it is recognizably much more vital to the oral than to the literate epic. To take a narrow aspect of this repetition, in *Beowulf* approximately 20 percent of the verses are exactly repeated at least once;[4] the Homeric epics show an even higher proportion of recurrent formulas. But it is not so easy to see why the narcissist, in particular, would wish to recur. One would expect the narcissist to do anything to escape such recursion. The answer to such a question, however, lies in the very fact of narcissism and its dual nature. C. Fred Alford (1988) points out the agreement among contemporary psychoanalysts on the symptoms of pathological narcissism.[5] These symptoms include (1) an uneasy co-existence of dual aspects within the individual of "grandiosity and fragile self-esteem"; (2) detachment and withdrawal from interaction, which allows both grandeur and fragility to be maintained; (3) a surprising lack of the rigid superego of "classical" neurotics; (4) frequent feelings of emptiness and isolation, of not being real, of being an observer of one's own life. Though he or she maintains (5) a relatively high level of social functioning, (6) the cost of such functioning is a rigid self-structure, highly resistant to change (Alford 1988, 44–48). This is not to say that epic poets are pathologically narcissistic; rather the paradigm clearly applies insofar as all humans are narcissistic to some degree. No one ever entirely gives up an object of love, as Freud tells us, and the self is arguably the first and most important of these libidinal cathexes. More to the point, however, is the specific "resistance to change" of the narcissist, a resistance closely linked to recursive desire in the epic. In the full development of the Oedipal complex, the conflict between grandiosity and fragility becomes that of ego and superego, where the demands for self-identity are based and judged according to their recursive closeness to the paternal image of self: " 'You *ought to be* like this (like your father).' It also comprises the prohibition: 'You *may not be* like this (like your father)—that is, you may not do all that he does; some things are his prerogative' " (Freud 1900, 373-74). The dual nature of narcissism foregrounds itself with regard to epic as well, where the loftiest of genres acts as both mirroring foil and insulting challenge to the dichotomized self. For the narcissist, the great epics in succession really do form, in Wilkie's apt phrase, "a hall of mirrors" (1965, 14). But to stand in this mirrored hall without an epic of one's own is the poetic equivalent of nonexistence.

The preeminence of the dual narcissistic struggle for self and recursivity does not preclude manifestations of the Oedipal story. W. Thomas MacCary (1982) has stressed the absolute narcissism of Achilles as the primary motivation for the *Iliad*, but in doing so he underdevelops the clearly Oedipal aspects of the epic. It is, after all, the *Iliad*, not the *Achilleid*. Though we are attracted, even fascinated, by the narcissistic fulfillment of the principal hero, the poet brings enough other material to our attention that the weight of our sympathy is neither always nor necessarily with Achilles. The idea of the Rape of Troy as the central event of the *Iliad* is for the most part the Oedipal imposition of a much later age,[6] but the Homeric epic certainly bears significant Oedipal emplotment. G. E. Lessing's cogent analysis of the difference between the scepter of the fatherly, woman-possessing Agamemnon and that of the young, dispossessed Achilles demonstrates the symbolic (i.e., phallic) difference, "giv[ing] us a vivid picture of the different kinds of power which these staffs symbolized":

> One the work of Hephaestus; the other cut in the mountains by an unknown hand. One the old possession of a noble house; the other merely destined for the first fist that seizes it. The one extended by a monarch over many islands and over all Argos; the other borne by a man from among the Greeks, who, together with others, had been entrusted with the duty of upholding the laws. This, in fact, was the distance which separated Agamemnon and Achilles; a distance which Achilles himself, even in the blindness of his anger, could not but admit.[7]

The contrast between the youthful, violent challenger and the entrenched authority of Agamemnon is striking in Lessing's remarks. Agamemnon's theft of Briseis initiates a familiar working out of the Oedipal drama. Achilles must submit, must undergo the removal of a valued possession that represents some aspect of his power. That is to say, Achilles undergoes a narcissistic wounding that he cannot abide: Rather than facing the unequal challenge of all the outraged Greeks, he withdraws himself from the contest, deferring his libidinal involvement. In Freudian terms, he enters a period of latency—the famous absence of Achilles: "He spoke; and furious hurl'd against the ground / His sceptre starr'd with golden studs" (1.325–26).[8] By denying the gift of himself, Achilles is able effectively to castrate Agamemnon and his army, as in the objective correlative of his scepter,

> Which never more shall leaves or blossoms bear,
> Which sever'd from the trunk (as I from thee)
> On the bare mountains left its parent tree.[9]

This solution to the threat to his narcissism, though, is problematic: If Achilles thus denies (i.e., represses) himself, he ceases to exist. When not in battle, it is as if he were nothing at all. In the world of the *Iliad*, as MacCary puts it, "men exist to fight, exist because they fight" (115).

But this unfolding of the Oedipal in the *Iliad* is not the only—not, I think, even the primary—motivation of the epic. Achilles' mother Thetis is, after all, always present to him in an all-pervading way; the father is notably absent and far less powerful than his son.[10] These conditions are the prime requisites of narcissism.[11] Achilles has no need to undergo an Oedipal quest, as he has already displaced his father in the Oedipal pattern. His death, required by the eventual working out of the plot, is the final fulfillment of his narcissism, for only *through* death can he slay death, avoiding his mortal fate through the metonymic agency of *kleos*, his continuing glory among men. The fact that this ultimate union of *thanatos* and *kleos* is not made explicit in the poem, in favor of the rapprochement between Achilles and Priam, undercuts MacCary's narcissistic reading of the text only slightly: Achilles' death is made unfailingly present to us throughout the *Iliad*.

Similarly, the Oedipal plot to *Beowulf* is not the principal motivation of the epic plot (as it is in the *Odyssey*, the *Aeneid*, and other epics of survival and quest).[12] The clearest expressions of such a plot in *Beowulf*, interestingly, do not suggest the sexual element very strongly: No particular fusion with the mother seems to occur. Indeed, the situation is far different from that of Achilles—no overarching mother seems to be present at all, either as goal or as pervasive spirit. There is no Thetis for Beowulf, and the drama of the hero's death fills the last half of the poem. This suggests, at least, a different kind of narcissism, if it is narcissism at all, and an examination of the poem in terms of language, violence, and sex may help to focus on the difference.

The first half of *Beowulf* presents on one level a search for identity. As an Oedipal quester, the hero enacts the search of the narcissistic child for his or her "true" parents, wish-fulfilling versions of his or her own parents. In Hrothgar and Wealhtheow, Beowulf meets a set of potential adoptive parents who in some ways make up for deficiencies in his own parentage. His outlawed father Ecgtheow had married the daughter of King Hrethel (372–73),[13] possibly creating a perceived imbalance of power within the marriage; this imbalance is redressed in part through the conflicts and condensations of the poem.[14] Hrothgar and Wealhtheow fulfill important wishes, becoming the parents that Beowulf never had, but desired. In them, the political situation of the marriage is apparently reversed: The father is the king, and Wealhtheow, whose name means "foreign slave,"[15] is the submissive social adjunct of his power. The primary enactment of the Oedipal conflict in *Beowulf* is literally submerged in the waters of Grendel's Mere. Here Beowulf kills Grendel's mother and administers the final blow to Grendel's dead body, bearing the head back to Heorot and the waiting Scylding court. Why does Beowulf cut off the head of a corpse (1585–91)? Most readers assume two main reasons: first, it is a token of his victory (though it remains unclear why he brings back no evidence of the mother's death); second, it is paralleled in the law of *talionis*—an eye for an eye, Grendel's head for Æschere's. A third reason may be the fact that Grendel changes in death.[16] Two nights before, Grendel was large, but roughly a fit wrestling opponent for Beowulf. Now he becomes parentally huge, his head alone of such size and weight that four "surpassingly spirited heroes" are needed "with labor to carry Grendel's head on a spearshaft to the hall" (1630, 1632).

The appearance of Oedipal features in these oral, narcissistic epics may be recommended as emblematic of the poet's personal, embedded Oedipal concerns, rather than as features of either tradition, or of the hero's "own" psychology. These are hardly separable, but there are three reasons such a recommendation is useful. First, the Oedipal features do not necessarily fit with what we can discern of the hero's life. Despite the attraction of viewing Grendel and his mother as aggressively invested versions, and Hrothgar and Wealhtheow as inverted, libidinally invested versions of Beowulf's parents, this Oedipal paradigm is tangential to the principal focus of the poem as a whole, Beowulf himself. The case is similar with the *Iliad,* as MacCary shows (1982, 55–65). Our interest in an Achilles, a Roland, or a Beowulf, is substantially different from our interest in Hamlet: We are not faced with the insecure dilettantism of the Oedipal revolutionary, but instead with the narcissistic and existential urge toward self-definition or self-creation carried to its logical extreme, that is, to suicide. Second, the heroes are heroes because they escape the compromises of time. Beowulf and Achilles gain their *lof,* their *kleos;* they live on as the subjects of "a song for men to come." More specifically, by their heroism, they step outside of the Oedipal norm: This in itself fulfills an Oedipal fantasy, but can be explained more usefully through the preoedipal framework. Related to this is the fact that heroes in general die young and heroically (unlike the generality of poets), before their well-defended narcissistic orientation can be fully challenged or dismantled by the impingement of external reality. This is far truer of Roland and Achilles than of Beowulf, where it hardly seems true at all. But in *Beowulf* such challenges disappear as the poet shifts immediately to Beowulf's death, after dwelling in lingering fashion on the youthful inception of the heroic career. Oedipal compromises are excised in favor of narcissistic fulfillment. If Beowulf ever suffered a personal defeat before his final meeting with the dragon, we certainly have not heard about it. A third reason to recommend the Oedipal turn as representative of the poet's concerns is that the Oedipal turn to the narrative is consistently conveyed within the terms of signifying systems.

If narcissism is the primary motive for epic, then, how will we expect our epic heroes, and epic poets, to behave in their dealings with language? The narcissism we face here is that emphasized by Bloom, the Romantic and Modernist concern best expressed by Ezra Pound: "Make it new!" When we look at Pound's epic, however, we find this prime directive balanced by (if not over-balanced by) a second and quite different directive: Make it *old*, as old as possible, and repeat that which has gone before:

> And then went down to the ship,
> Set keel to breakers, forth on the godly sea, and
> We set up mast and sail on that swart ship,
> Bore sheep aboard her, and our bodies also
> Heavy with weeping, and winds from sternward
> Bore us onward with bellying canvas,
> Circe's this craft, the trim-coifed goddess.
>
> (1986, 3)[17]

The language of earlier epic heroes is much the same, as it, too, follows somewhat contradictory demands. Adam Parry (1989) discusses this issue in his well-known paper "The Language of Achilles," arguing that the conflict between Achilles' desire to escape from the tragic world and language of the *Iliad*, and his ultimate inability to do so, is the very core of his personal, Achillean tragedy. But in this desire and its failure, Achilles is both merely and fully human; this is life, a thing of compromise. Parry comes close to this realization in his paper, but does not point out the important psychological resonance of this human tragedy, nor its recursive parallels in later epics. The *Odyssey* is linked more strongly to the escapist desire of the human, but it is linked in a more familiar manner, insofar as it recreates the Oedipal drama, rather than an earlier, more basic frame of reference. The *Odyssey* is a quest, a story of compromise; it constructs survival at any cost as a primary goal. Like ourselves, Odysseus moves through life in a series of compromises—happy or unhappy substitutes for the lost, mourned, and unattainable union. The same thing cannot be said of heroes like Aias and Achilles. They do not achieve a happy substitute because they do not compromise. Because they will not compromise, they die. There is no other choice. MacCary follows Parry but frames the Achillean attitude toward language in psychoanalytic terms:

> By speaking in strongly marked antitheses, by refusing to concede points to his interlocutor, or to anticipate objection, or to consider alternatives; by developing "idiosyncratic" images, and providing details of self-relevant background, and elevating "subliminal ideas to consciousness," Achilles shows himself a master of language. Why, then, do his fellows consider him deficient in speaking? Because, of course, he does not speak to or for them. He is an absolute rule unto himself and though they might use him as a model by which to judge themselves, he uses none but himself to judge himself. This we call narcissism: one seeks not the completion of the self in the other, but the assurance and definition of the self in the mirror image(s) of the self in the other. (1982, 57–58)

Achilles, one of the few poet-figures of the *Iliad*, uses language to create a "verbal mirror." Not only is he thus able to represent himself to himself, but he is able to work against the alienation implicit in language. As MacCary emphasizes, the hero foregrounds his creation of speech, trying to recreate the world in his own terms, rather than those of the society in which he has found himself.

In epic poetry the hero's first speech is expected to be impressive. In Achilles' first speech, he calls the assembly to discuss the plague afflicting the Greek army; this is already a revolutionary suborning of Agamemnon's authority, and as the seer Kalkhas makes clear, the implications of the assembly lead to a direct challenge to Agamemnon's position and prerogatives as king of kings, when he is chastised by Achilles, a warrior from among the Greeks. Achilles attempts to remake the world he is embedded in according to his own standards.

In Beowulf's first speech (258–90) a different approach is followed, but one that serves equally well to highlight certain aspects of the hero's narcissistic character.[18] This speech divides quite clearly into two logical parts, the first directly answering the *landweard*'s request by giving the origin of the seafarers and the lineage of Beowulf; the second part addresses the *micel ærende*—the "weighty business"—of the voyagers, that is, tells why they have come so far, ready for battle and without trade-goods, yet not planning a military expedition or raid as such.

The very first sentence conveys the heart of the matter, moving quickly and directly from the generality "of humankind" to the specificity of *Higelaces heorthgeneatas.* The brief eulogy on Ecgtheow (262–66) enriches both the syntax and the rhetorical flair of the speech; while these lines do establish Beowulf's nobility, his mention of Ecgtheow's age and death seem at first somewhat digressive. But this underestimates Beowulf. These few lines, first of all, emphasize Beowulf's filial loyalty, a loyalty that is underscored by, and by analogy related to, the *holdne hige* in which the Geats have come seeking Hrothgar. However, filial loyalty in Germanic culture is not without its possible drawbacks for the Scyldings. Blood-vengeance is always a potential motive for attack, and this is the concern that prompts the coastguard's demand: *ic eower sceal frumcyn witan, ær ge fyr heonan, leassceaweras, on land Dena furthur feran* [I must know your lineage before you go any further in the land of Danes as dissembling spies] (251–54). In response to this understandable concern, Beowulf takes pains to clarify the fact that Ecgtheow "experienced a great number of winters, ere he turned on his way, ancient from the yards" (264–65). In short, Beowulf's father died old, and not by the hand of another, thus (apparently) at peace with his neighbors. Similarly, if the coastguard has heard of Ecgtheow or of his indebtedness to Hrothgar, he is, by way of Beowulfian compliment, included as *witena welhwylc,* one of the wise. If he has not, little is lost; it is suggested that this is someone he should know, but the fact that Ecgtheow and Hrothgar had an earlier relationship of which he is ignorant is not dangled over his head.

This question of the coastguard's knowledge is intriguing, especially as the first part of the speech ends with an invocation of his "good counsels": *Wes thu us larena god!* Throughout the second part of the speech, Beowulf carefully continues to include the Scylding in a community of greater knowledge, effacing or belittling his own. "Not one thing has to be hidden, *as far as I know. You know, if it is* [true]" (272–73).[19] The hero underscores his own ignorance of the situation, and elevates the knowledge of his audience: *sceathona* ic nat *hwylc* [I know *not* which kind of injurers] (274). This apparent humility on the part of Beowulf can be understood at this point as heroic generosity, or, perhaps, as subtle rhetoric.

We know already that Beowulf intends to engage in combat with Grendel and defeat him (189–209). But in the speech to the *landweard,* the still-nameless warrior does not suggest that he will solve the problem himself; rather, he will only "give counsel" as to "how he [Hrothgar], wise and good" (279), may overcome the fiendish Grendel. The hero is tactfully humble, not attempting to usurp the place of Hrothgar as *leodgebyrgea,* the protector of the people. He offers only *ræd,* in hopes that someday a remedy must come.[20] This consistent self-effacement is worthy of further consideration, for though it becomes clear in the

Unferth episode that Beowulf can boast with the best, his boasts tend to be in response to the instigations of others. Doubtless the hero could have demolished
the poor *landweard* completely, through vaunting (or through demonstration) of
his skills. Beowulf chooses not to do so, however, and this seems to argue a high
degree of humility on his part, at least at this point in the poem. In brief support
of this is his exclusion of his own name from his introductory speech. On the
other hand, this "humility" more plausibly points to a brand of pride peculiar
to Beowulf. He may simply be no more willing to waste his words on this coastguard than he is on Wulfgar, Hrothgar's doorwarden, "a proud and mettlesome
man" (342–47). The very brevity of Beowulf's speeches strengthens the emphasis on pride in his character. This is a key feature of the speech of Beowulf: He
is quite stingy with his *wordhord*. In comparison with the coastguard, the only
previous speaker of the poem, our hero is a model of directness. His syntax is
clear, straightforward; he uses remarkably little variation. All of these characteristics contrast with the sometimes confused garrulity of the coastguard,
whose three speeches are made to Beowulf's one, and whose use of variation
may at some points get out of hand (in, for example, his three references to the
ship within one sentence [293–98]).[21]

The first speech, then, establishes that Beowulf is generous, direct, loyal
to ancestral bonds, and concerned with peace. The alternate readings of his
character as humble or as proud can be explicated most easily in terms of narcissism, with its apparently paradoxical mix of "grandiosity and fragile self-esteem" (Alford 1988, 44). It is difficult to believe that Beowulf's speech is indicative of his true feelings, given that his intentions are clearly other than the aims
stated here. It begins to seem more an act of rhetorical posturing, the product
of someone who may be "using his often not inconsiderable charm for strictly
instrumental purposes" (44). On the other hand, we cannot yet place him in the
same class as Achilles; Beowulf is clearly engaged in a communicative act, one
with relevance to the situation despite its multilayered, somewhat calculated,
rhetorical effect. His language use in another situation allows more insight into
the narcissism of this rather different hero.

The confrontation between Unferth and Beowulf (499–603), in which the
hero and his antagonist recount Beowulf's swimming contest with Breca, is an
excellent example of two contrasting narratives of (ostensibly) the same event.
Jan Vansina remarks in this connection that "the use of messages is perhaps
most dramatic in conflict situations. One fights with tradition . . . debates turn
around clan history and it is the use of decisive formulas that make[s] points"
(1985, 102). The political context of the narratives also shows Beowulf in conflict
with a worthy opponent for the first time. The war of words, of challenge and
response, is a type-scene possessing analogues not only in the later hagiogra-

phies, but in other oral societies as well.[22] The scene in *Beowulf* is an example of what Vansina might call "a fight between masters of knowledge" (1985, 102), a confrontation between an entrenched (if endangered) authority, and a challenger who is still largely an unknown. Unferth, the *thyle* or spokesperson for Hrothgar (1165), sits in a position of authority at Hrothgar's feet, and, by his knowledge of the Breca incident, shows that he is the best informed man in the Danish court (Klaeber 1950, 149). During the course of his narrative, he freely accuses Beowulf, though a guest in the hall, of pride (*wlenco*), of foolhardy boasting (*dolgilp*) and worst of all, of not having the greater strength (*mære mægen*) (508-9, 518).

Beowulf, as the newcomer, is in a more delicate situation. He, too, is a "master of knowledge," as shown in this encounter and in his analysis of the impending marriage of Ingeld and Freawaru (2024-68). But here he must assert his own authority and his own knowledge in a way that will not jeopardize his standing with the rest of the court, and particularly with Hrothgar. He does this in part by combining his very particular attack on Unferth with a continuous strain of generosity or magnanimity. Unferth may be drunk, as Beowulf says, but he is still "my friend Unferth" (530-32) and "clever" Unferth until the end of the speech (589), where he is carefully assimilated once again within the community of those "who may go in high spirits to the mead hall" (603-4). Though Beowulf must bring up the obvious fact that Unferth is afraid to face Grendel himself, still, by emphasizing the particularity of his attack with the reiterated second-person address, and by generalizing those things Unferth should be defending, such as "your nation" and the hall of Heorot, Beowulf is able to sidestep the rather too-obvious implication that *Hrothgar* is ultimately the one responsible for "the protection of the Scyldings."

Moreover, while Beowulf's narrative gains in impact in direct proportion to the amount that he can disparage his opponent, it is aided as well by his ability to parade his own knowledge where Unferth seems ignorant. Unferth, it should be recalled, opens his challenge with a question, not a statement of fact: *Eart thu se Beowulf, se the with Brecan wunne . . . ?* (506).[23] Beowulf may not know of any "skilled combats" fought by Unferth, but he most certainly does know (and say) that Unferth killed his own brother (587-88). This argues a thorough knowledge of the ins and outs of the Danish court, comparable to Hrothgar's antecedent knowledge of Beowulf himself. Further, as Unferth's name (usually etymologized as "Mar-peace") suggests, this bit of knowledge is a crucial condemnation of Beowulf's antagonist as a past, present, and potential agent of strife within an ideally harmonious social group (the family, and by implication, the comitatus).[24] This question of kinstrife has further implications for explaining the poem, but the question can be held off briefly until we consider violence as such in *Beowulf*. For now, the purely linguistic violence of the *argumentum ad hominem* is a kind that allows Beowulf to isolate Unferth from the community, undercutting his authority and his position as resident spokesperson. This is related to what seems Beowulf's personal brand of narcissism, a combination of heroic generosity and canny aggression. Unferth is alienated from the society and then restored. The society itself and its ultimate authority are never questioned; indeed, Beowulf takes pains to avoid any imputation of misconduct by those he terms the "victorious Scyldings," the "spear-wielding Danes" (597, 601). In this, he differs from Achilles, whose narcissistic reaction is played out against the whole of the Greek armies, and against the Homeric heroic code itself.

Lingering for a moment on the *way* that the swimming contest is recounted by the different speakers, Beowulf's relation to the Germanic heroic code can be clarified. Here we must remember the marked difference between oral and literate productions, for conventional oral ways of patterning, used to counteract the defects of human memory, act just as powerfully to render a narrative either comprehensible or incomprehensible. In an oral culture, as Walter Ong comments, one must "think memorable thoughts. Your thought must come into being in heavily rhythmic, balanced patterns, in repetitions or antitheses . . . in standard thematic settings [such as] the assembly, the meal, the duel" (1982, 34). A new narrative, in order to be perceived as true, will have to accord with the form of other, earlier narratives. This is Achilles' difficulty, the result of his intensely lived narcissism: Rather than speak within the heroic discourse that his companions understand and expect, he creates a "verbal mirror" for himself. In a more limited sense, we can see this happening in Beowulf's narrative: It is a self-representation, but it is emphatically a presentation to an audience—specifically, to an audience that has just heard a differing version of the same tale.

Both Beowulf's and Unferth's speeches show a strong sense of the sequence of events—the boast, the voyage, the contest, and the outcome. Beowulf's response is not, naturally, one of those peculiarly literary artifacts, a logical point-by-point rebuttal. It is, to a literate mind, hardly the more believable of the two. But few would dispute that Beowulf tells the far better story: *His* swimming contest includes a storm at sea, and much swordplay in a fierce battle by night against sea-monsters. A brief nod is made to Unferth when Beowulf admits the foolhardy high-spiritedness of his own and Breca's youth, but the greater part of his narrative glorifies combat and the heroic ethos, couched in some of the most familiar and striking of poetic formulas.[25] Another crucial difference between the two versions lies in the actual opposition of contestants. With his initial question Unferth stresses that the contest is between Beowulf and Breca. Beowulf, on the other hand, rejects this opposition in favor of other (and greater) ones: The contest of the two young men against the sea, and then his own heroic contest with the sea-monsters. As Beowulf says, there is no rivalry between himself and Breca: *No ic fram him wolde* [Nor did I wish to swim away from him] (543). It is hardly accidental that the contest, thus recounted, meshes far more neatly with the principal events of the poem as whole, the monster-fights. Moreover, due to its inclusion of conflict, Beowulf's narrative is not only more memorable than Unferth's, but it also follows more correctly the conventions of the oral tradition.

As David Crowne analyzes this particular passage in a key study, Beowulf's use of composition by theme here demonstrates "an excellence akin to that of Homer's" and is "an instance of the extreme flexibility with which the *Beowulf*-poet is able to employ the theme" of the hero on the beach. This *topos* or "theme" is explained by Crowne as "a stereotyped way of describing (1) a hero on the beach (2) with his retainers (3) in the presence of a flashing light (4) as a journey is completed or begun."[26] Beowulf himself puts it better, naturally.

Næs hie thære fylle   gefean hæfdon,
manfordædlan,   thæt hie me thegon,
symbel ymbsæton   sægrunde neah;
ac on mergenne   mecum wunde
be ythlafe   uppe lægon,
sweordum aswefede,   thæt sythan na
ymb brontne ford   brimlithende
lade ne letton.   Leoht eastan com,
beorht beacen Godes.

    (562–70)

[These evil-doers had not the joy of eating their fill, of taking me for their food, or of sitting at their feast on the seabottom; rather, in the morning they lay high on the shore left bare by ebbing waves, wounded by blades and sent to sleep by the sword, so that never again would they hinder travelers from their voyage across the seas. Light came out of the east, the bright beacon of God.]

Here, according to Crowne's analysis, Beowulf has transformed the sea-monsters into the retainers in his "description of the sea-monsters' sitting around the banquet-table like a Germanic comitatus." Likewise, when they lie dead upon the shore they are equated with the more usual reference to a live troop of retainers; voyages (coming or going) will no longer be hindered by the monsters' depredations.[27] Beowulf's elegant use of such a theme should make no less of an impression on his dramatic audience than it has on so many readers, especially when another such performance is within immediate memory. And it is easily noted that Unferth's recent account of Breca's landing is literally pale by comparison:

> Tha hine on morgentid
> on Heatho-Ræmes   holm up ætbær;
> thonon he gesohte   swæsne ethel,
> leof his leodum,   lond brondinga.

(518–21)

[Then one morning the high sea washed him ashore in the land of the Heatho-Ræmas; from there he, dear to his people, reached his cherished homeland, the land of the Brondings.]

No *leoht eastan com,* nor is this a "bright beacon of God." Rather, a pale "morning" seems to be the best that Unferth can manage. The "retainers" of the topos are practical nonentities; not only are they quite abstract, but they are in a country far removed from Breca's landing-place.

It could be argued, of course, that since Breca is not the hero, he cannot receive the full heroic treatment, which is precisely my point. Beowulf, by his brilliant (if rather flashy) conformity with the laws of conventional discourse, has firmly established both the truth of his narrative and himself as a hero eminently fit to challenge Grendel. And as if to underscore the truthfulness of his narrative, Hrothgar, the highest ranking member of his audience, immediately "placed trust in his aid" [*geoce gelyfde*] (608).

Beowulf's narrative coup in Heorot is a self-representation, to an extent a verbal mirror like the language of Achilles, one which both aggrandizes himself and diminishes another. But this is not the "idiosyncratic" language of an Achilles—it is clear that Beowulf has spoken within the constraints of social discourse, and spoken exceedingly well. Although he certainly refuses to concede the issue of the swimming contest to Unferth, he does not "refus[e] to concede points" entirely. His generosity to Unferth throughout the speech, his admission of the brashness of youth, and his magnanimous reintegration of Unferth are parts of an exchange, a balance struck, with the otherwise uncharitable speech-act of *thyle*-bashing.

> Hige sceal the heardra,   heorte the cenre,
> mod sceal the mare,   the ure mægen lytlath.
> —*Battle of Maldon*

Dealing with Achilles as a narcissistic hero, MacCary focuses on Achilles' unwillingness to have his narcissism compromised. Thus in Patroklos and Hektor, the principal foci of Achilles' libidinal and aggressive attentions, MacCary finds again the creation of mirrors for the heroic self. They become "partial objects," highlighting aspects of Achilles that he is unable or unwilling to recognize as self-conscious subjects in their own right. Partial objects take the place of the parent, nurse, or other external satisfier of demand; they provide a mediation between the self and the Other (similar to that performed in the post-oedipal "autonomy" of self by the superego with its relative automaticity of self-regulation).[28] They are metonymically linked conceptual tools that allow interaction with the Other without forcing the self to *recognize* that Other. Thus Patroklos, who functions throughout the *Iliad* as an adaptive, compromising force, mediates between the narcissistic rage of the hero and his Greek compatriots, wearing Achilles' armor as a substitute for Achilles himself: when he dies, Achilles must die in consequence; and thus Hektor, also wearing Achilles' armor, functions as the last link holding the hero within the bounds of a definable reality. The hero is maddened at Patroklos' death because his childhood companion is his mirror, *is* that which defines him to himself as the best. Without Patroklos, Achilles as he thinks of himself can no longer exist. According to MacCary, this is closely related to Homeric modes of combat, the intimate pairing of warrior and charioteer (1982, 127–36). Whether or not this reflects actual Bronze Age tactics matters little, but it does highlight the Homeric emphasis on the close dual relation of companions as a means for negotiating social (and martial) demands. As MacCary states it, "The Homeric hero requires his mirror in another closely related hero (or subordinate) to assure himself of his own 'actual' existence" (1982, 133). Given the rather different modes of combat favored by the Anglo-Saxons, however, the issue of violence within the tradition is, as one might expect, differently resolved. The inclusion of violence within Beowulf's narrative—typical of orality's agonistic patterning—renders the narrated experience more forcefully within the oral and socially charged context. In turn, this allows him to present a self-image that is both heightened beyond the norm and still communicable within the social terms of discourse. But rather than the intimate preoedipal pairing characteristic of the fantasies of an Achilles,[29] the focus and fantasy of the Anglo-Saxons involve the group, and the individual's relation to the group.[30] Thus the emphasis in *Beowulf* falls most heavily on the individual as he or she mediates the social demands of the group and the narcissistic demands of self-fulfillment.

The most promising place to begin an examination of the individual in Anglo-Saxon is with the figure of the exile or outcast, the individual without social or political association.[31] The fascination that this figure exerts in Anglo-Saxon poetry and society is reflected as a dominant theme in *Beowulf* as well, where Grendel is repeatedly characterized as an outcast, an *angenga* or lone-goer

who has only "sufficient presence among men to be named," and who through
envy violently rejects "all those commitments that characterize a human society."[32] He is an outlaw, removed from the dynamic warmth and light of social
exchange in the meadhall. He may terrorize and invade, but he cannot approach
the *gifstola,* the throne of Hrothgar, which is literally the source of gift-exchange
and of power in this social realm (168). In a similar way, Beowulf himself is
threatened by this exilic theme, for though he is entrenched within the social
network, we are repeatedly urged to recognize the precariousness of his position as monster-killer. The threat of this position arises not from the monsters
themselves, but from Beowulf's very separation from the coherence of the social
group. Beowulf and the monsters cross boundaries that other men cannot or
will not. By this dangerous separation of themselves from the system of social
exchange, they become in large part undefinable, unknowable (i.e., monsters),
in the terms of the social system. Beowulf's "praiseworthy deeds" (24) are only
deeds *at all* insofar as they work within the confines of the community's social
and linguistic patterns of exchange. The monsters share Beowulf's "dogged
earnestness," in Rexroth's phrase (1968, 169), but this is not all they share. There
are multiple dimensions to this problem, but the basic point can be seen most
clearly in the fact that, if the monster-fights are the core of the poem, as J. R. R.
Tolkien asserts,[33] then Beowulf can only exist by virtue of the monsters. Without
them, he is a thing nearly uncommunicable within the society, a marker of isolation and separation, an exile. This would extend, of course, to the singing of
his praises in communal epics. From hero, he becomes nothing; his song and
he himself do not exist without the monsters.

   These are only some of the ways in which Beowulf and the monsters can
be seen as equivalent. Indeed, one of the most striking things about reading
Beowulf for the first time is discovering the surprising synonymy between the
hero and the monsters, especially Grendel, the most fully developed of the monsters. The poet's use of *aglæca* for either "champion" or "monster," and occasionally both, stresses this relationship of identity.[34] An awkward "Adversary,"
with connotations of "awesome" or "powerful," would be a truer translation,
suggesting the way in which the violence of the antagonists transcends the normal human limitations but is still an essentially equivalent force, as is clear in
the passages below, the first referring to Grendel, the second to Beowulf:

>   Wiht unhælo,
> grim ond grædig,   gearo sona wæs,
> reoc ond rethe,   ond on ræste genam
> thritig thegna.
>
>   (120–23)

[The unholy man, savage and voracious, instantly was ready, fierce and violent, and in their rest he snatched up thirty thanes.]

>   ... he thritiges
> manna mægen-cræft   on his mund-gripe
> heatho-rof hæbbe.   Hine halig god
> for ar-stafum us onsende.

> (379–82)

[He, a renowned warrior, the strength of thirty men has in his hand-grip. Holy god has sent him to us as a kindness.]

As Beowulf is described almost exclusively in superlative terms, so Grendel, "greater than any other man" (1353). His depredations are characterized as exceeding both human scale and human relations: "This strife was too strong, too hateful, too long-lasting" (133–34). Moreover, Grendel is specifically described as breaking the social conventions of violence—the rules of exchange, both the *wrixlan sweordum* that we might find in, for example, the *Battle of Maldon,* as well as the exchange of wealth, of tribute for the cessation of violence.

>   ... sibbe ne wolde
> with manna hwone   mægenes Deniga,
> feorhbealo feorran,   fea thingian,
> ne thærn ænig witena   wenan thorfte
> beorhtre bote   to banan folmum.

> (154–59)

[He had no wish for a settlement with any man of the pick of the Danes, nor to abandon that deadly work of destruction, to negotiate compensation; and none of the wise ones there expected the bright gold reparation at the slayer's hands.]

The impact of Grendel's incomprehensible attacks is the threatened dissolution of Heorot and all it stands for: The Scylding dynasty, Hrothgar and "the authority of his word" (79). Heorot is "the greatest of hall-buildings," and, like other such buildings, it is the center of exchange for wealth as well as for words: Hrothgar "shared out rings and jewels," "everything but communal property and human lives" (67–85). During the twelve years of Grendel's "humiliations," however, the focal point of Danish unity is "desolate and useless to every warrior" (411–13) after nightfall. The metonymic solidarity of the Scyldings breaks down into separate, isolated lives: "The man was easy to find who sought a place in the outlying chambers, once that hall-thane's hatred was made clear ... he who had escaped the foe afterward kept himself further away and safer" (138–44).

As in criminal fiction, Beowulf must assimilate to his opponent in order to bring Grendel back into the circuit of exchange, to make him "pay." The identity of the two is reinforced by this newly formed circuit of exchange. Because the monster "does not bother with weapons in his recklessness" (433–34), Beowulf adopts a similar recklessness, meeting him in wrestling. As Beowulf says, Grendel "does not understand the good of exchanging swordblow for swordblow" (679). The enforcing of exchange upon an outsider is nowhere more clear than in the dynamics of the struggle itself, the contest that, at its height, threatens the very center (psychological and economic) of the warrior-aristocracy, the great hall of Heorot itself (767–82). Gripping Grendel's arm, Beowulf forces the exile to remain within the hall and (not long, but long enough) within this new and harshly enforced system of trade.

> eoten wæs ut-weard;   eorl furthur stop.
> Mynte se mæra,   thær he meahte swa,
> widre gewindan   ond on weg thanon
> fleon on fen-hopu.
>
>   (761–64)

[The giant was moving outward; the earl kept stepping forward. The great one meant, if he could, to twist away to a greater distance, and flee from there, away to his fens.]

The irresistible centrifugal force that is Grendel, both in his current desires and in all his earlier effects upon the hall, meets an opposite force, not an immovable object, but the centripetally bound and binding Beowulf.

From this brief analysis, several things become clear. First, the Beowulf/Grendel coupling shows Grendel as an aggressively invested image of Beowulf himself, the equal and opposite force demanded. Second, it highlights the importance of exchange for the Anglo-Saxon community, an emphasis that is reinforced by the subsequent trade-war of small "tokens of aggression" between Beowulf and Grendel's mother. And third, it brings up more clearly the liminal quality of Beowulf's heroism; the greatness that makes him equal to Grendel renders him a potential monster himself, destroyer of halls.

The linguistic act of violence against Unferth discussed in the previous section shows Beowulf in the act of self-presentation: Though creating a mirror for himself in this process, he constructs as well a refracted image of self for his audience, a social self as monster-killer and contender with the elements. The polysemy of language encourages, even requires, such multiple layers of meaning, particularly (as in this instance) where the audience is widely varied. In a sense, a different Beowulf is created for Unferth, for Hrothgar, and for each member of the audience. The explicit judgment of Hrothgar at the end of Beowulf's speech bears most weight in determining the judgment of the rest of the audience, in its enthusiastic acceptance of the hero's claims.

This self-presentation is at once a self-aggrandizement and an attack on one who is, as we have said, substantially similar to Beowulf. Both Unferth and Beowulf are knowledgeable men, one an actual, the other a potential advisor to the lord of the Scyldings. Unferth, though he is a powerful warrior, is as clearly eclipsed by Beowulf in this regard as he is in the contest of knowledge. Beowulf usurps the *thyle*'s place in Hrothgar's esteem, and that is a great part of the hero's aim. John D. Niles remarks of Unferth that "he has proven himself to be on the side of the monsters. In him one sees their arrogance, envy, and misdirected violence" (Niles 1983, 21). This statement is of especial significance if taken in the appropriate context. In the folktale analogues of *Beowulf,* as Niles notes, the hero's elder brothers enact the role played by Unferth in the poem (21). This structural detail, together with the fact that Unferth is directly accused of fratricide, suggests a potentially illuminating reading of Beowulf's attack as fratricidal, aimed at eliminating the sibling and usurping his place in the hall. With this in mind, the struggle of the twin *aglæcan* Beowulf and Grendel, which threatens to "bring the house down," also clarifies itself. The recurring references to Cain and his progeny elaborate a dominant mythic background to a poem of narcissistic sibling rivalry over scarce parental resources. The pattern of royal deaths in the poem underscores this view: Older brothers do not fare well in *Beowulf.*[35]

The hall is vitally important, as the focus of Beowulf's contest with Grendel, as well as with Unferth. Heorot is the place of Grendel's twelve-year ascendancy, a place that Beowulf invades and usurps; by doing so, the hero becomes "a son" to Hrothgar, as the old king makes clear:

> Nu ic, Beowulf, thec,
> secga betsta,   me for sunu wylle
> freogan on ferhthe.
>
> (946–47)

[Now I wish to hold you to me kindly, Beowulf, best of retainers, as a son.]

This pattern of fratricides could be traced more thoroughly, looking at the intercession of Wealhtheow on behalf of her own sons as heirs a few lines later (1169–87); in turn, Wealhtheow's intercession leads swiftly into the violently exaggerated intercession of Grendel's mother on behalf of her son. But these fraternal tensions, as such, are instrumental rather than focal to the narcissistic complex pursued here, which is even more deeply invested. Indeed, as with the prevalent modern sexualization of narcissistic conflicts (as Oedipal), *Beowulf* demonstrates a fraternal encoding of those deeper narcissistic concerns. This difference in the choice of relational codes, obviously, is in itself of vital importance. But for now the emphasis ought to fall on the objects of Beowulfian violence insofar as they are mirrors of the Beowulfian self.

The most obvious fact concerning Beowulf's principal opponents is not that they are all reflections of Beowulf, but rather that they are all monsters. This difference in itself is a good clue to their relative identity with the hero, that is, to their original source in a single figure. To elaborate on this, the point of creating opponents so utterly "alien" is that of disguising an ultimate (and feared) sameness. Vansina's comment in regard to oral poetry, that we find inventions and heroic qualities coalescing about the figure of the hero, and all the villainous qualities and actions gathered to his or her opponent (1985, 108), is equally applicable to the narcissistic psyche. Like the jagged particle of dirt that an oyster transforms into a pearl, the initial, perhaps uncomfortable reality of the limited self is transformed through repeated performance into the far more comfortably omnipotent center of narcissistic concern. The narcissist, trying to maintain a view of the self as complete, necessarily realizes a view of anything threatening that completion as Other, as alien. This extreme form of metaphoric distancing, however, though it aids immeasurably in the perception of the self as a complete, integrated unit, has a powerful drawback in the fact that it cannot construct the other, the unknowable, except in terms of the known, the self. Thus, while it creates an Other through metaphoric negation and opposition, that other is also created along the lines of metonymic identity, a partial object. This is true of twentieth-century science as well, of course; we reason in a dialectical process of metaphor and metonymy from accepted information (sometimes known as "facts") to an accommodation of new information. The reading of the Other is always a reading of the Self. Moreover, this metaphorical distancing of the Other from the "here and now" grounding of an act of epic discourse is in part an enactment at this macrostructural level of the metonymic ideology basic to epic. By positing or constructing an "outside," an "Other," a *feond*, or "enemy," the poet constructs in the here and now a more coherent and unified "inside," "self," or *freond*, "friend." The similarity of the Anglo-Saxon terms, like the opposed application of *aglæca* to two ostensibly different opponents, resonates with a way of seeing the world that is in some ways peculiar to Anglo-Saxon. In terms of textual violence, however, this process of constructing what is basically the same thing as different is nicely evoked by the image of bright Heorot with its lights and golden-gabled roof ablaze against the dark moors. The relative brightness of the one (e.g., the self) and darkness of the other are *created* only by the juxtaposition of the two terms; when it is not, in Conrad's phrase, so beastly, beastly dark outside, the meadhall loses much of its power as a unifying force. The very binary opposition that reinforces the communal integrity of the opposing "units" is in fact that which constitutes them *as* units by the opposition. To put this another way, the increasing impingement of the outside world should, up to a certain point, enforce a still stronger *self* definition for Heorot as a community. The difficulty with a monster such as Grendel is that his violence is "too strong, too loathsome, and too enduring" (133–34) for the communal self to either accommodate or deny.[36] This agonistic and binary framework of violence supports a system where increased adversity results in a parallel increase in solidity and community. In a sense this is merely a truism. But it illustrates an important point, that in order to attain such solidity and community, the Other is essential. In short, violence for the Anglo-Saxons is a way of making a coherent, unified whole of the community. Similarly, violence and violent separation act as a way of enforcing the integrity of the self. Joan Blomfeld hints at this in the following passage:

> The setting out of the material is not in *Beowulf* an evolution, following one main line or connecting thread. Instead, the subject is disposed as a circumscribed field in which the themes are drawn out by a centre of attraction—in this case, the character of the good warrior. Far-flung tales and allusions, apparently scattered material and disconnected events are grouped in a wide sweep around the hero's character. In fact, these are his character, and their significance in the poem consists in this particular relation; by comparison we are shown Beowulf's nature, by searchlights into the past and future we are to sense the magnitude and true import of his achievements. From this periphery he draws his substance and reality. By these means he lives and his destiny impregnates the whole poem.[37]

I have suggested before that the self is merely an apparently repeated constellation of sensual and conceptual experiences. Blomfeld notes the same thing concerning our experience of Beowulf as a character. He is a "centre of attraction" in a "circumscribed field." Like the Lacanian self, formed through the interaction of the self with its mirror images, Beowulf's enactment of the mirroring processes in the poem shows us the formation of the heroic self.

This parallels Joseph Russo and Bennett Simon's depiction of the sense of self in Homeric culture. Following Hermann Fränkel, they suggest that the "I" or "self" is more akin to an "open force field," having no structured boundaries to separate it or insulate it from forces all around.[38] It is easy to see how this suits Achilles' grandiose self-conception. The removal of anything (e.g., Briseis, Patroklos) from him is interpreted as an assault upon the self, a threat to the sense of narcissistic completion. Achilles isolates himself to such an extent through his idiosyncrasy and fundamental self-involvement that he calls into question the validity of the entire heroic code. In *Beowulf*, it is the dragon who adopts this extreme position, but with much the same result: The dragon, though he has lost only a single gold-ornamented cup from his vast hoard, believes and behaves as if the entire hoard has been ransacked. As a creature exceeding the normal pattern of limits in the epic (Calder 1972), the dragon is so far beyond the range of human heroism that his very Otherness threatens the entire conception of heroic conduct with meaninglessness. This threatened futility of heroic effort shows most clearly in the way critics often interpret Beowulf's final victory as a defeat (Niles 1983, 235–47 and notes).

With Beowulf the self is not so "poorly differentiated"; the limiting effects of social and temporal boundaries, and Beowulf's self-restraint in submitting to them, set up a less extreme narcissistic project. The physical architecture, the landscape of the monster-fights, illustrates this well. The linguistic and physical violence of the metonymically engaged episodes of Unferth and Grendel takes place in Heorot itself. Similarly, though the cavern below the mere is a grim parody of Heorot, it too is consistently denoted as an Anglo-Saxon hall.[39] With the dragon the struggle is entirely alien to the human context and the human community. Unlike the earlier monster-fights, this last conflict takes place in the open, out on the barren windy heights above the sea, and is portrayed as inevitable. Beowulf, as *leodgebyrgea,* the shield of the people, must face his opposite, the *leodsceatha,* the scourge of the people. The human architecture of the hall, so vital to the earlier conflicts, has already been destroyed, and along with it the Geatish *gifstol,* literally the seat of power, significant order, and exchange within the community (2324–26). Beowulf confronts a form of signification that arises outside of the normal systems of exchange, one that reaches out of the depths of time. Three hundred years the dragon has lain upon the hoard, a hoard that becomes—so briefly—Beowulf's in due exchange for the dragon's destruction. The lives and fortunes of both creatures meet their end in this last exchange. The hero takes sensible, realistically human precautions against the monster, but these measures must ultimately prove futile.

Calder's excellent article focuses on the "immeasurability and open-endedness" of the dragon: "[T]he entire universe becomes unfathomable, impervious to man's attempts to measure and explain" (1972, 30). In this, Calder directly complements the work of Edward B. Irving, whose earlier reading focuses on the contrast of the society and companionship of the poem's first part with the stark loneliness of the second.[40] Combining these two readings reinforces the notion that the earlier combats are struggles of same with same, a conflict (like that of the Finnsburh episode) that attempts to resolve the dangers of too-close connection. The very similitude between Beowulf and figures such as Grendel and Unferth necessitates the hero's violent reaction against them; in order to construct a coherent identity for Beowulf as hero, the figures that jeopardize his singularity must be eliminated. In the second part of the poem, however, the poet shows the opposite danger, the consequence of such complete narcissistic individuation. In this connection we should recall the apt terms used by Alford in his discussion of narcissism:

> Separation, loss, and loneliness are heightened for most individuals dur-
> ing the second half of life; but for the narcissist, they are specially intense,
> for such experiences make it more and more difficult for the grandiose
> self to deny the frail, limited, and transitory character of human existence.
> (1988, 47–48)

The second part of *Beowulf* replicates this passage nicely, concentrating its ele-
giac elements and evoking the typical Anglo-Saxon concern that *lif is læne* [life is transitory]. Moreover, in his combat with the dragon, Beowulf undergoes a real crisis of separation in the defection of his picked men from the scene. This dangerous separation very nearly leads to an inglorious defeat for Beowulf, and it is only through the metonymic connection with Wiglaf (through kinship and comitatus bonds) that Beowulf is able to attain victory on any terms. Irving has noted that "Wiglaf is really a part of the character of Beowulf rather than a fully developed individual,"[41] and this observation fits well the conception of Beowulf as narcissist. The young warrior functions as a partial object for the aging king, an image of himself when young, and one through whom the hero is able to live on. He is both Beowulf's heir as lord of the Geats and the immediate recipient of his arms and armor. It would be very difficult to read the dragon in terms of an Oedipal conflict, but in those of narcissistic conflict it makes a good deal of sense. The dragon is not the father, but rather a kind of sheer inevitability. Often enough it is called a figure of time and death, and there is little reason to quarrel with these as universals that concur with the dragon's sig-
nificance in the poem.

The conflict of Beowulf with Grendel's dam partakes of both the earlier metonymic conflict and of this last and purely oppositional conflict. The most complex and easily the eeriest of the combats (for twentieth-century audiences, at least), it is the struggle of the masculine self with that which is the same but different—with the figure of woman. It is closely linked to the Grendel combat not only because of the kinship connection between him and his mother, but also because of the topography involved, once again the same but different.

Many readers try to unravel the landscape of Grendel's Mere into a kind of coherent but naive realism. The balance of criticism aims instead in the direction of myth, attempting to recreate the Mere as a Christian or Scandinavian Hell in opposition to a heavenly Heorot.[42] Without condemning either of these approaches, a reading that emphasizes the functional value of action within the *nithsele* will provide a further understanding of the dynamics of the conflict, and a useful explanation with regard to the dynamics of the epic as a whole.

Whitelock has shown that in presenting the home of Grendel's mother, the poet of *Beowulf* "describes a hall at the bottom of a lake":

> Writers on *Beowulf* may refer to a cave as the scene of Beowulf's second encounter, but the poet never does. He calls it a *hof,* a *nithsele,* a *hrofsele,* a *reced,* a *hus,* all terms that apply to a building rather than a natural cave.[43]

Apart from these descriptive terms, however, the Mere is in every way antithetical to Heorot; Niles even calls it "a kind of anti-Heorot" (1983, 231). Though it is conventionally labeled as "Grendel's Mere," the contrasting descriptions of the setting show that the mere of the second combat is clearly the Mere of the mother, not that of Grendel (841ff. versus 1345–79, 1403ff.). That is, while it is the same location at each juncture in the text, it is clearly a "different place" because of the primary denizen envisioned in the separate descriptions. Similarly, where Heorot is a *heah-stede* with a *geapne hrof* (836), the *nithsele* of the mother is *under gynne grund* (1551), at the very bottom of a *grundleas* pool. Home to sea-serpents as well as the Grendelkin, it is set low among high crags, wolf-infested hills, and an unpleasant wood. But three or four details stand out especially: *fyr on flod,* the fire that burns on the water (1366); the ice-covered trees that overhang the pool (1363–64); the repeated references to "the watery expanse . . . welling with blood, with warm gore" (847–48, 1422–23, 1593–94). All of these have been seen as clear manifestations within the narrative of the female genitalia.[44] The rime-encrusted trees, like the *niceras* that attempt to bind Beowulf during his descent through the mere, threaten him with immobility, impotence on the verge of a powerful Other.

Perhaps most interesting is Hrothgar's statement that

> Theah the hæth-stapa   hundum geswenced,
> heorot hornum trum,   holtwudu sece,
> feorran geflymed,   ær he feorh seleth,
> aldor on ofre,   ær he in wille,
> hafelan hydan.
>
>   (1368–72)

[Though the heath-stepper pressed by hounds, the strong-antlered hart, may be seeking the forest, having been chased a long way, he will first yield up his life and being on the bank, before he will go in there to protect his head.]

This statement is particularly significant in its use of *heorot*. Though the exact significance of the "strong-antlered hart" in this connection has been debated, the animal at least indicates the failure of Hrothgar and his thegns to extend the imposition of phallic order to the mere. The *heorot* simply lies down and dies rather than penetrate this place that is both *heimlich* (for Grendel and his mother) and *unheimlich* (for anyone else).

The vaginal imagery of the mere into which Beowulf must make his descent is strongly marked—indeed, strong parallels are found in Karen Horney's (rather dated) description of some of the dreams of male homosexuals: of falling into a pit, of moving through narrow channels of water, of being sucked down by a whirlpool, of being trapped in a cellar full of "uncanny, blood-stained plants and animals" (in Slater 1968, 19). Throughout the episode, the feeling of closeness, of concealment and uncertainty are emphasized. Though they watch and wait, the Danes and the Geats have no understanding of Beowulf's combat in the mere. Indeed, what clues they do receive (the renewed welling of blood on the water) they misinterpret as emblematic of the hero's death.

While the landscape of the Mere and its surroundings are significant, evoking a traditional masculine fear of woman, the actions that take place within this context signify even more sharply.[45] As we have seen, the specific movements of Grendel and Beowulf in their conflict act as a repetition in physical form of the problem and solution of Grendel as an outlaw, a violent destroyer of the system of exchange. The danger to the social order implicit in Beowulf's contest with his double is made manifest by the shaking of the hall and the tearing loose of meadbenches. In his conquest of the mother, the hero finds himself in an *unheimlich* parody of Heorot, which by its inversion (the same as, yet different from) is strongly evocative of Beowulf's puzzling relationships with women. Niles has suggested ways in which Beowulf assimilates to, or becomes like, the mere-woman, but far more striking is the way that Beowulf (yet once more) becomes Grendel. By the deliberate omission of Grendel's father, Grendel and his mother form "an incestuous primal couple," as Niles has remarked, and thus Grendel has in a sense lived out Beowulf's own incestuous desires. (Indeed, one supposes that it is in part for this crime of invasion that he is punished.) Here Beowulf both visits his punishment on the mother and reenacts Grendel's crime.

After Hrunting fails him, he grabs Grendel's mother "by the shoulder." "Ruthless in the struggle, now swollen with rage" he throws her to the floor (1537–40). She in turn trips him and pins him "so that he was prostrated."

> wolde hire bearn wrecan,
> angan eaferan.   Him on eaxle læg
> breostnet broden;   thæt gebeag feore,
> with ord ond with ecge   ingang forstod.
> Hæfde tha forsithod   sunu Ecgtheowes
> under gynne grund,   Geata cempa,
> nemne him heathobyrne   helpe gefremede,
> herenet hearde.

> (1546–53)

[She meant to avenge her child, her only son. Across his shoulder lay the meshed mail shirt; it saved his life and resisted penetration by point or edge. Ecgtheow's son, the Geatish campaigner, would have perished then down in the vast deep, had not his battle-corselet, his sturdy soldier's mail-coat, afforded him help.]

As in the earlier combat, an invading "hallguest" is met by a stronger defense than expected. In spite of himself and his efforts to maintain a sword's length between them, he is pulled into very close physical combat, "swollen with rage." Both combatants collapse on the floor, where the defender attempts, as in the last combat, to deliver a telling wound to the "shoulder." The *earm ond eaxl* manifest the power of Grendel, and the same object has great signifying power as a *tacen* of the earlier victory. Here, a similar wound is attempted on Beowulf, and it would be disingenuous to ignore the implied threat of castration. The shoulder in Anglo-Saxon plays a role like that of the knees in the Homeric epics, which play (as at least one scholar has suggested) the role of a displaced phallus; comrades in war fight "shoulder to shoulder," Æschere was Hrothgar's *eaxl-gestealla* [shoulder-comrade] (1326), and so forth.[46] But Beowulf, unlike the earlier hallguest, is saved from such a fate, largely because he is not acting independently, as an outlaw or exile, but as an agent of the father, of Heorot and the impotent Hrothgar. Though the scene is not without a strong pattern of images and body positions that can be understood as sexual in content, the primary goal of the hero in this context is defeat of the mother, and this, it appears, can only be accomplished through distancing, separation of himself from her. As in the Grendel combat, there is a danger that the hero will be literally swallowed up by the monster. In that combat, however, the fear is that he will be merged with the group, becoming just one more of the *thritig thegnas* whom Grendel habitually consumes. Here the situation is different. Though the threat of being consumed remains the same, the point of that threat is different, and lies in the possibility that he will never have existed at all. The episode of the Mere has often been seen in a Christian framework as a scene of death and rebirth for Beowulf, but this phrase perhaps runs too easily from our pens. The statement is true, but due to the terms of violence in which this process is described, the possibility of utter extinction is very near. At least in the struggle with Grendel, the valuable mail corselet, token of Beowulf's identity, would have been saved; in this struggle, however, conducted far beneath the surface of the Mere with a being who seems in every way alien to his own conception of self, nothing will be left. (At best, he can hope for blood on the water, quickly dispersing, as a sign of his passing.) When the threat of being devoured in difference is most hazardous—when the *Mere-wif* is above him, like a mother about to give birth[47]—Beowulf is saved only by his identification with other males, a metonymic connection through constructed and exchanged products of masculine labor: the corselet given him by Hygelac, the grace of the *Alwealda*, and the old heirloom, the *ealdsweord eacen*, provide him with an insulating armor, a technology, for separating himself from the fact that he is born not of himself, nor of the same, but of woman. This sense of masculine connection as something that must be constructed or bridged is interesting, and stands in this combat in direct contrast to the dangerous physical closeness of the mother. Only by his self-identification through the masculine accoutrements of warfare, the weapons of men, is the hero's sense of self made coherent enough to repel the *mere-wif*'s assaults and eventually subdue her. This male bonding in the face of the unknown other is the forging of a link that connects almost exclusively with the paternal—the loan from a same-sex fraternal competitor, Unferth's sword Hrunting, has failed early in the combat.

Despite the obviously sexual dynamic here—ostensibly, the Oedipal resolution of the poem—there are some puzzling uncertainties. While there is strong evidence for an interpretation such as that above (along the lines pointed out by Philip Slater in his study of classical Greek mythology), in many ways such an interpretation seems limited. This is less a criticism of Slater or later psychoanalytic classicists than an attempt to outline some of the differences such Mediterranean theories face when they reach an epic of a far different culture.

Philip Slater (1968) and Page duBois both emphasize that the female in Greek texts is always the inscribed, not the scriptor.[48] Woman is *unheimlich*, unknown and yet inscribed by men. Moreover, she is inscribed as passively or statically malevolent, or else (rarely) encoded as masculine, active, and benevolent (e.g., the mother-goddess reduced to the young, masculine virgin in Athena). But neither of these two categories really applies to the Mother in Beowulf. She is a woman with her own interests, though devoted to her family (such as it is), and capable of considerable exercise of power within the realm of significant violence. There is as well some uncertainty as to whether she gives the victory to Beowulf: Both antagonists are on the floor "until he got up again"—the poet does not say how, except through a vague reference to God. Moreover, she keeps in her hall (though not for her own use) the very instrument of her death, an *ealdsweord* suitable not only for cutting her own head off, but for administering the postmortem *coup de grace* to Grendel, despite his earlier imperviousness. Perhaps in Grendel's mother we begin to see the shadow of Kalypso in the *Odyssey*—a woman who is vehemently rejected, but who tenders of her own volition the very tools by which the hero may accomplish that rejection.

In the figure of Beowulf, then, we see a recurrent self-exile, a separation that is made in order to do battle with those forces that impinge upon or threaten the self. The first two battles, those of the Grendelkin, are a struggle for differentiation from those forces that threaten to overwhelm, or swallow the hero: the threat of losing one's self among the same (in Grendel, or in Unferth's narrative of Breca), and the threat of losing one's self to the mother. The third, final, and deadly contest is that of the dragon, in which the dangers of such self-exile, such narcissistic self-exposure, are themselves exposed. The only way that Beowulf is able to achieve victory is through his metonymic ties of kinship and comitatus to another man (albeit an image of himself). This issue of exile is vital not so much as a way of exploring the self (or more accurately, the "field of self" that we find in *Beowulf*), but rather with an eye to exploring that from which the exile is exiled; what sense of fusion or union is there, if the figure of the mother can be treated with such violence?

The Myth of Narcissism and the Matrix of Exchange

The question of exile leads us to the way the absolute is portrayed in Anglo-Saxon society. What constitutes the ideal of narcissistic fulfillment for the Anglo-Saxons? Twentieth-century theories generally assume that the mother, as vaguely fantasized by the child, is the source of narcissistic pleasure, a narcissistic pleasure that develops into Oedipal desires and thence, with the impingement of reality, into the resultant complex.

Inroads have been made against this assumption in recent years. In later periods of socialization, and indeed, through much of the history of Western culture, it appears to allow a good understanding of human motivations, but in earlier chronological periods this assumption seems less clearly to apply. According to Daniel Stern, the same might even be said for the period of infancy. He concludes that the infant *never* "experiences itself as fused with the mother and the world."[49] Stern's argument needs some answer in this book, for my opening chapter relies heavily on the concept of fusion as the fantasized realm of absolute control and/or absolute negation. An answer of a kind is given by Alford in *Narcissism,* where he suggests that the actual "experiences" of the child do not really matter; what matters is only "the intensity of the ideal" (1988, 9).

In this suggestion, Alford extends some conclusions from my introductory chapter, where I stress the importance of the expedient error, the convenient fiction. That is, it is particularly *useful* to imagine that total fusion is possible, whether or not such existence ever did or will occur. The opposite poles of the absolute (death and union) work as a useful shorthand for an existence we do not comprehend. The virus culture constituting the physical body that we associate with "humanness" continues to survive long after what we consider "death." Similarly, we construct a state of complete being that we believe or hope to have been possible before separation (birth, consciousness, it matters little). But the world of lack and the exigencies of reality already impinge upon the fetus by means of genetic codes, nutritional imbalances, the effects of the mother's external environment, and so forth. The story of an absolute primal narcissism, like the story of the Garden of Eden, may be only another, similarly useful myth.

The Christian myth is particularly persuasive, placing the absolute at the end as well as the beginning of time. James Earl points out the relative rarity of this formation, especially of the imagined revelatory fusion of the Apocalypse, which is "by no means a universal myth. It is in fact unique to Judaism and Christianity" (1982, 364). Earl asserts that it is the insistent Judaeo-Christian historicization of myth in human lives that distinguishes it from other eschatological myths, pointing out the incidental relation of human to divine in other mythic structures, which include but hardly dwell upon humanity or its place in the grand scheme of things. The creation of humans in the *Voluspá* is particularly poignant, where the gods merely happen upon lifeless driftwood on the newly created beach, and, in fewer lines than are devoted to their game of drafts, construct the race.[50]

This hints at two important things. First, our current psychoanalytic theories of narcissism, with their emphasis of Wordsworthian "clouds of glory," may be more deeply (and hence insecurely) rooted in the Judaeo-Christian cosmology than we think. That is, our very understanding of narcissism may be a construction, a myth of "an idealized past from which we are alienated by some act of separation" (Earl 1982, 363). Second, outside that tradition, these theories may require substantial revising; such revision seems necessary in reading a text like *Beowulf.* Although it is a heavily Christianized poem, and although as an end-product it is undoubtedly the work of a Christianized society, the poem is, as many have noted, essentially pagan. Earl is aware of this, of course. As he says, the Germanic mythic structure "tends to blunt the apocalyptic theme with its starker eschatological analogue, stressing transience, death, doom—that is, judgment—and punishment, rather than redemption, salvation, and revelation. The result is part of a peculiar contribution of the Anglo-Saxons to Christianity, that dark Christian realism which is not only so attractive to us in retrospect, but was so influential in the development of English and other medieval Christian literature" (364). Briefly to illustrate this conception, it might be noted (following Tolkien) that there are two kinds of *lof* (praise, glory) in the Anglo-Saxon worldview.[51] To extend the traditional analogy of illumination that Earl invokes, there is the dark pagan *lof* that is seen as glory among men, the way the tale of a man's *worca* spreads out around him while he walks upon the earth, and more emphatically, the way remarkable deeds live beyond the individual in the mouths of the children of men. The other kind of *lof*, bright and Christian, is the praise among the angels that is due to the heaven-bound man after his death. In both of these, the emphasis is laid on death or distance: *Lof* is that which lives on, allowing a kind of continuity, even immortality. As with the Greek *kleos*, within the etymology of the word there is already a distinction to be made between this metonymic linkage of the self and the modern conception of the narcissistic self as autonomous, complete and fulfilled. The imagined metonymic goal here is entirely social, an acoustic reflection of the self through the voices of others.

In *Beowulf*, moreover, the kind of *lof* available is "dark," restricted to the earthly and the social. When Beowulf is characterized as *lofgeornost* at the end of the poem, the adjective comes among a variety of others that have specific references to his life on earth:

> cwædon thæt he wære   wyruld-cyning,
> manna mildust   ond mon-thwærust,
> leodum lithost,   ond lofgeornost.
>
> (3179–82)

[They said that among the kings of this world he had been the most compassionate of men, and the most humane, the most kindly to his people and the most eager for fame.]

The radically social, pre-Christian view of human life is thus outlined in *Beowulf*, but it finds more concise expression elsewhere. As Bede records the famous rationale given to King Edwin for the Anglo-Saxon conversion to Christianity:

> This is how the present life of man on earth, King, appears to me in comparison with that time which is unknown to us. You are sitting feasting

with your ealdormen and thegns in winter time; the fire is burning on the hearth in the middle of the hall and all inside is warm, while outside the wintry storms of rain and snow are raging; and a sparrow flies swiftly through the hall. It enters in at one door and quickly flies out through the other. For the few moments it is inside, the storm and wintry tempest cannot touch it, but after the briefest moment of calm, it flits from your sight, out of the wintry storm and into it again. So this life of man appears but for a moment; what follows or indeed went before, we know not at all.[52]

Charles Dahlberg has rightly pointed out that "the question of the lighted hall and the surrounding darkness is just as pressing" to the *Beowulf*-poet. However, he goes on to say, in opposition to most readings of the poem, that "the hall has become more problematic and the stormy darkness filled with light."[53] While one can easily agree that the hall is "problematic," there is little evidence for the last half of Dahlberg's statement. The point where the Christian god can be imagined as bright lord amid his Anglo-Saxon comitatus of saints and angels has not been reached in *Beowulf.*

What appears to happen here to the concept of transcendent fusion is parallel to the "force field" earlier linked to the Anglo-Saxon self-concept. Rather than a *point* of transcendent union or fusion, we have a "field" wherein desire finds satisfaction, a web or matrix of happy exchange that is imagined socially and architecturally in familiar terms.[54] Perhaps it is less accurate to say there is no happy substitute, than to say that there appears to be no absolute point of thoroughly transcendent fusion, no time, for the Anglo-Saxon, of absolute control. The closest approximation we have of such a thing is found in the Anglo-Saxon equivalent of the *locus amoenus,* the life of lord and thanes in the meadhall.[55] In the passage from Bede above, this topos is invoked to describe the brief pleasure of the sparrow in the ordered circle of warmth and light.

Thus, if human life is implicitly akin to the sparrow's fragmented experience of the meadhall, then there is no narcissistic core of self, nor a sense of absolute control to which one's fantasies can return. That there is no core *is* an answer of sorts. This understanding of the ideal fusion as a nebulous "field" of exchange and social life seems counterintuitive to us, trained as we are in the myths of our own cultures to view the mother as both source and most basic goal of all human effort. In a similar projection, we feel that Beowulf ought to have more to do with women. But he does not. He does not marry; he produces no heir as we understand the term. His closest female associate is Hygd, the young queen of Hygelac, who offers him the throne of the Geats after Hygelac's death (2370–71); but only when all of Hygelac's sons have been killed in battle does Beowulf finally take the throne and rule the Geats.

The Mirroring Threshold

Counterintuitive or not, the evidence of oral epic suggests that this narcissistic masterplot precedes and later coexists with the Oedipal plot; indeed, that the Oedipal plot is inscribed upon a receptive set of conflicts and repressions in the process of formation and reformation. Comparing a recursive pattern from three different oral traditions may show the broad importance of the preoedipal plot in forming an epic, as these different cultures develop a structurally similar story within very different contexts. The conflict of Beowulf and Grendel within Heorot provides a convenient and familiar illustration, showing the symmetrical and antagonistic relation of a rivalrous twinning. In the Anglo-Saxon context, as the reading of figural and postural relations shows, Beowulf works to restore the system of exchange, exerting a centripetal force toward coherence against Grendel's centrifugal aims of isolation and miserly solipsism; he represses chaos in favor of order and community. The adversaries are (only just) contained within the boundaries of culture as the meadhall shakes around them. The other Geats look on, helpless, while the Danes hear the struggle and worry.

In the *Epic of Gilgamesh,* a parallel scene of conflict takes place as Enkidu confronts the haughty Gilgamesh at the sacred marriage-house in Uruk. In the *Iliad,* the climactic conflict of Hektor and Achilles takes place before the walls of Troy. A much longer episode, it uses the pursuit of Hektor by Achilles to provide a veritable catalog of culturally liminal sites, from the Skaian to the Dardan gates, from the lookout point to the wild fig tree, to the hot and cold running springs of the Skamandros, where the women of Troy would bring their laundry in days of peace.

Where Beowulf and Grendel threatened to bring down Heorot, the struggle of Gilgamesh and Enkidu "broke the doorposts and the walls shook" (69).[56] In the *Iliad* the struggle has little immediate effect. Even though Hektor is the bulwark of Troy, the resultant sack of the city is deferred—the Homeric heroes seem to have less impact on the larger cultural matrix.

The dramatic audiences serve to magnify the conflict of Beowulf and Grendel; in *Gilgamesh,* the audience serves only to set up the conflict and applaud its results, explaining Gilgamesh's abuses of privilege to Enkidu and celebrating their union after the fact. The *Iliad* shows a different register of pathos and of distance between heroes and audience. Hektor's mother and father urge their son inside, back within the community. But Hektor, heroically adult, resists the potential shame of his father's mutilation as well as his mother's bared breast and remains outside with his fixed resolve like a snake's "evil poisons" seething inside him (22.93–96). Achilles, in turn, heroically narcissistic, resists the help of the Akhaians, never letting them throw their spears at Hektor "for fear the thrower might win the glory, and himself come second" (22.205–7). Moreover, the wall of Troy and the repeated similes of isolated figures in sky or wilderness reinforce this insulating distance.

The similarities among the epics are striking, considering the thousands of years and the distances that lie between them. An invader arrives to "change the old order" (68) through combat; the combat takes place at the center of the civilization, shaking it to its foundations; it occurs in the presence of a dramatic audience, and signals a significant change in the structure of the society. Most important is the relative identity between the two contestants, fraternal figures who are almost equal—"second selves," as Thomas Van Nortwick (1992) points out regarding *Gilgamesh* and the *Iliad.*

Beowulf's destruction of Grendel is, I have argued, a wounding of himself; he severely represses an insatiable narcissism in favor of coherence, community, and order. He freely compromises himself in the interests of the social contract of the meadhall. This repression can never be complete, however, as demonstrated by Grendel's mother, the dragon, and the eventual destruction of Heorot (regardless of all heroic action). In *Beowulf* the source of disorder is projected outside of culture, language, and law, into the archaic, bestial, and isolated Grendel, who is explicitly depicted as unassimilable within the social web of exchange.

In contrast, *Gilgamesh* presents the source of disorder *within* culture, indeed, as Gilgamesh himself in the arrogance of his power (more like Heremod than like Grendel).[57] Order is achieved by a partial return to the natural virtues and natural order of the bestial, half-civilized Enkidu. (Enkidu apparently promotes improved relations between Gilgamesh and the folk of Uruk by redirecting Gilgamesh's energies.) Perhaps even more important is the fact that order is not based on the complete repression of the second self, but upon a harmonious linking of the two. For Gilgamesh to kill Enkidu would be to kill himself, as the later parts of the epic show more clearly. But to join with him by shifting his stance, by a slight compromise, allows something else entirely, as their struggle shows: "Mighty Gilgamesh came on and Enkidu met him at the gate. He put out his foot and prevented Gilgamesh from entering the house, so they grappled, holding each other like bulls. They broke the doorposts and the walls shook, they snorted like bulls locked together. They shattered the doorposts and the walls shook. Gilgamesh bent his knee with his foot planted on the ground and with a turn Enkidu was thrown. Then immediately his fury died. . . . So Enkidu and Gilgamesh embraced and their friendship was sealed" (69). The centripetal and centrifugal forces of *Beowulf* become in *Gilgamesh* the power of two forces striving directly against each other—"like bulls locked together"—

emphasizing the social context somewhat less and the adversaries more. In my
reading of this fragmented passage, Gilgamesh then backs off, shifting his
weight so as to channel his and Enkidu's strength in the same direction: Enkidu
goes flying, carried onward by his own force coupled with that of Gilgamesh.
This physical struggle is repeated in the larger structures of the narrative. Their
married strengths enable them to defeat Humbaba, spurn Ishtar, and slay the
Bull of Heaven. When death comes, as it must, Enkidu is thrown forward again
as a surrogate, encouraging Gilgamesh again to a natural balance, an eventual
tactics of compromise in the face of his own death.

In the *Iliad*, where he is neither violently repressed nor comfortably affi-
anced, the insatiable beast is victorious. Though Achilles knows full well that
his own death follows hard on the heels—so to speak—of Hektor's, he kills him
and wishes for even more:

> "I wish only that my spirit and fury would drive me
> to hack your meat away and eat it raw for the things that
> you have done to me. So there is no one who can hold the dogs off
> from your head, not if they bring here and set before me ten times
> and twenty times the ransom, and promise more in addition,
> not if Priam son of Dardanos should offer to weigh out
> your bulk in gold; not even so shall the lady your mother
> who herself bore you lay you on the death-bed and mourn you:
> no, but the dogs and the birds will have you all for their feasting."
>
> (22.346–54)

The bestiality of Achilles is emphasized throughout his lengthy aristeia, but especially in his encounter with Hektor. The long race and the final struggle are
suspended again and again by similes, retarded by the plangent details of the
surroundings and by the machinations of the gods. Rather than a few simple
actions with serious implications for the culture and for the larger narrative, we
face a multitude of actions that seem to have relatively little impact. Most simply, the retardations work to build suspense—in contrast with the scenes in the
other epics, this is the key fight of the poem. More broadly, however, the heroic
activity within this agonizingly slow and systematic narrative shows itself
as futile, having little lasting impact. Both men—both aspects of the self—are
locked in a perpetually self-defeating competition. Racing three times around
the walls of Troy (to no practical purpose), they reverse the Beowulfian paradigm of repression. Achilles, Grendelishly invulnerable, pursues himself in the
figure of Hektor, but ends up taking Hektor's place. He now guards the gates
of Troy from Hektor's return. Hektor, in Achilles' armor, now tries to reach the
gates, now turns and advances, the hunted becoming the hunter. Achilles casts

his spear—and misses. Hektor casts his, striking the center of that wonderful shield—uselessly. It is not merely that these multiple actions defer the inevitable; that is the case in *Beowulf,* certainly, but Homer is demonstrating more than that. Not only are chaos and narcissism more powerful, more likely to be in the ascendant provisionally as well as inevitably (as is shown in both poems), but the interpenetrating struggle is perpetual, taking place on the battlefield as it is on the shield of Achilles, taking place within the mind as between combatants,

> As in a dream a man is not able to follow one who runs
> from him, nor can the runner escape, nor the other overtake him,
> so he could not run him down in his speed, nor the other get clear.
>
> (22.199–201)

Achilles' killing of Hektor is constructed as a kind of perpetual moment that seems to respond directly to the ordered cosmos of the shield; where the artist Hephaistos balanced war and peace delicately, interlinking them, that vision remains a vision only. Neither Hektor nor Achilles can achieve or affect that balance: Hektor, trying to balance the demands of homelife and warfare, makes a "dead-center hit" but it never touches that remote vision, glancing away uselessly. Achilles has already made his famous choice, but he cannot erase the eventual compromise the shield intimates, any more than he can stop Hektor's (or the poet's) final words—"the ash spear heavy with bronze did not sever the windpipe, so that Hector could still make exchange of words" (22.328–29). And indeed, Achilles lives only long enough to fulfill Hektor's words and give his own the lie. No dog or bird feeds on Hektor's body, Achilles does ransom the body to Priam, and then dies in the dust himself before the Skaian Gates.

> Its rhythms have the tone of pre-emptory challenge
> and the clang of iron.
> —Rexroth

In *Beowulf,* as in all oral epic and perhaps all poetry, time (and its representative in the human, death) can be seen as an ultimate enemy. The major goal of the epic is to provide a sense of coherence, of recursion, of continuity despite time, change, and death. Poetry has been described as "eternity's hostage in the hands of time."[58] But "Words move . . . only in time," and the words of the *Beowulf*-poet are no exception. They cannot avoid time or eliminate death, though through their form as *lof,* they come the closest of any human endeavor. In oral epic this attempt at continuity is allowed, as we have said, by the technologies of oral-formulaic verse. In *Beowulf* in particular, the primary organizing device is alliteration, the recursion of similar initial sounds, usually within a given line (that is, within the acoustic frame of four repeated stresses, which are split over a medial pause). The alliterative formula is in general more flexible than Homeric dactylic verse, and this accounts to some extent for the difference in the percentage of repeated formulae in the respective epics.[59] This microstructural dynamic plays itself out in especially interesting ways in the larger structures of the poem. Much has been written on this subject, highlighting the thoroughgoing bipartite structure of the verse style as it extends outward into Anglo-Saxon culture.[60] Rexroth (1968, 168) has remarked on the "clang of iron" implicit in the very rhythm of the work; he refers to the clash of the harsh alliterating consonants, the kind we find, for example, when the dragon wakes to find his hoard robbed:

> Tha se wyrm onwoc,   wroht wæs geniwad;
> stonc æfter stane,   stearc-heort onfand
> feondes fot-last;   he to forth gestop
> dyrnan cræfte   dracan heafde neah.
>
>   (2287–90)

[When the worm awoke, wrath was renewed; stark of heart, he smelt about the rock, found the track of the foe; he had stepped forth with crafty stealth very near the dragon's head.]

We should briefly note the poet's skillful modulation in acoustic values as the focus shifts from the *stearc-heort* to the *dyrnan cræfte* of the thief. But more conventional formulas may demonstrate better the way the Anglo-Saxon mind patterns. In a common phrase like "words and deeds" (*worda ond worca*), for instance, an interesting set of contrasts and similarities appears (698, 1273). According to the Scylding coastguard, the "shrewd warrior" must be able to distinguish between the two as he makes judgments concerning these, the only effects that men can produce (289). The implicit judgment is that there should be a synonymy between them, that one should reflect the other, in much the same way as the terms alliterate. The examples in the poem, however, of Unferth and other speakers unfaithful to their vows, suggest that the potential difference between the similar terms is immense. In the Finnsburh episode as well, an attempt is made to guarantee peace, a harmony between Danes and Frisians to be broken neither by *wordum ne worcum* (1100). And indeed, we find that an integrity is maintained between words and deeds, but that the third term, the treaty itself (*wære*), is broken entirely.

Saussurean linguistics suggests that *worda* only means what it does because it is not *worca*. But more important, just as a great part of Beowulf's meaning as hero and character comes from the fact that he *is* Grendel, so in linguistic terms *worda* means what it does because it is the *same* as *worca.* The vital thing is not in the binary *opposition* as such, but in the relation of similarity between the two terms. John Leyerle's conception of the way the "interlace structure" of Anglo-Saxon and Celtic art is reflected in *Beowulf* is apropos here, and Niles has drawn on this conception to focus on the way that the similar always evokes the dissimilar in *Beowulf,* particularly in the Anglo-Saxon preference for the "play of light and shadow," as in the image of Heorot and the surrounding darkness of the moors: "This tendency to antithesis, frequently verging on paradox, and the constant play of irony are but stylistic manifestations of those movements of the poet's thought which shape the very stuff of the poem" (1982, 58). John Miles Foley, attempting to define the Anglo-Saxon oral formula, points out that it is "better to conceive of a lexical core or kernel at a stressed position and of a looser (and therefore more variable) aggregation of material forming a shell."[61] This nicely parallels my discussion of the difficulty of defining the self against the group for the Anglo-Saxon. Like Beowulf, the "core or kernel" of the narrative, the core of the alliterative formula requires at least two basically equivalent terms, which can be opposed or parallel. Tolkien remarks that opposition is the more prevalent kind of relation. But we should recall that the alliterative elements are not the only ones within the verse. There is a variable number of syllables, as Foley points out, which are not bound in this manner. In Foley's metaphor, these elements form a looser "shell," what we might in the terms of this essay call a "field" of relatively indeterminate energies. It has been pointed out above how the "fields" of self and society in Anglo-Saxon times are defined and rendered coherent largely through a violent opposition, that is, through the erection of aggressively invested "mirrors" of that self or society. The extension of this understanding to the mechanics of alliteration seems intuitive, as it appears above. But this mirroring effect of the verse form is apparently not achieved without violence. Energies are bound, mastered, within a sameness of initiation, a sameness of beginnings.[62]

This suggestion allows a simple answer to Alcuin's famous reprimand of the Bishop of Lindisfarne: *Quid Hinieldus cum Christo?* [What has Ingeld to do with Christ?]. In a cultural context that emphasizes the interchanges of sameness and differences, Ingeld and Christ have *everything* to do with one another. As heroic characters representative of two cultural myths that are in the process of being forged (with a "clang of iron") into unity, these two figures (like those of Heremod and Sigemund in *Beowulf*) become like the waves on a pattern-welded blade. Simply put, the concept of Christ and the concept of Ingeld alliterate with one another in the Anglo-Saxon mind. This is particularly suggestive if we consider the role of the monastic houses in Anglo-Saxon England as "alliterating" with the earlier men's hall, as Earl's essay invites us to do.[63] Tolkien, too, emphasizes the importance of this collision in *Beowulf* between the old Germanic heroic ideals and the new dispensation of Christian-Stoic ideals. In this collision, this complex process of cultural *wrixlan*, lies the source of *Beowulf*'s energy.

The other suggestion this argument pushes forward is the uncomfortable sense that epic as a genre may require a kind of violence. We could say this is true of any poetry, since poetry as a discursive product allows the liberation (and likewise enforces the realization) of the word as a thing, as a tool for the construction of reality. In a purely oral culture this is especially true, since poetry establishes for itself a margin of silence, a boundary that controls energies and maintains the narrative of important events. By means of this (clearly necessary) violence, the poet is able to create a unity, weld the community. A separative violence appears to be a condition of the genre, so long as the epic purports to be the tale of the tribe, or is constructed in order to solidify some community. It is not clear that this violence need be intentional.[64]

The oral poet's antagonism toward the tradition, such as it is, is a narcissistic orientation in favor of his or her own coherent individual performance, implying that the *here and now* is a unified whole, a sparrow in the meadhall, as opposed to the outside, where it is so beastly, beastly dark. With the oral epics, we can understand this as a grim necessity. The violence implicit in this separation is externally imposed. It is an aspect of time and the human, and perhaps not so necessary to literate productions.

To conclude, the oral battle epics argue strongly a search that is neither for mother nor father but for death—or, if we must have the Oedipal reading, to find both of them through death. Death is seen as a perfect union, for death, as Wallace Stevens suggested, is the mother of beauty. The hero's goal is to find glory, and thus slay death. Death is, to use inadequate terms, a win-win situation for the hero. It allows him or her a changeless beauty, a metonymic contiguity through glory; it allows the conquest of death—that is, of time, of change, of narcissistic injury; at the same time, it allows the most thorough form of self-punishment for the narcissistic assertion, through the hero's submission to death. Agamemnon, Odysseus, even Aeneas—each mourns the fact he did not fall at Troy. Only Achilles (and hundreds of others, of course) need not mourn.

This suggests that there are at least two kinds of epic: Those characterized above, of death; and others we may characterize as epics of survival, of heroically enduring the narcissistic injury and attempting to come to terms with it through more or less happy substitutes. Oral epic is the child of glory and death, *kleos* and *thanatos;* later epic especially tends to highlight culturally acceptable forms of accommodation to the forces of the external world: happy substitutes.

3

Twice Faithless Troy

The Happy Substitute

All men's thoughts have been shaped by Homer from the beginning.
—Xenophanes

EXPLORING SAMENESSES—the way time is always out of joint—requires a close look at differences; and exploring differences between oral and literate epic discovers a complex of change. Though the preoedipal story of separations and connections remains, it is encoded differently; an ephemeral, cyclical world of song rewrites itself within "history" as a progressive journey, as a surviving of past history for the continuing challenge and compromise of futurity. It rewrites itself as Oedipal, and in terms of a long string of substitutions. If the oral poets see and hear a world full of voices, literate poets begin to see a written world; the visual field creates a fiction of progress and/or loss wherein one writes or—increasingly—is written. From preoedipal adjustment and narcissistic insistence one moves to the Oedipal complex and survivalist compromise. From orality to visuality, from ear to eye and tongue to pen: With these shifts come others. Narrative turns predominantly Oedipal: The *Odyssey*'s attenuated paternal figures modulate to the threatening Aietes and Pelias in the *Argonautica,* and then to their heavily intertextual equivalents in Chaucer's *Troilus and Criseyde.* A parallel but distinctly different change affects the female characters of the epics: they gain greater prominence and power, but are also more suspect and more self-divided.

Is it progress or is it loss, this illusory sense of change? Most often it is both, to judge from these poems. Focusing on the mourning process the hero undergoes in the Homeric *Odyssey* emphasizes loss; but his reconstruction as survivor elicits the happiest of substitutes to be found in this chapter. His extended, ambivalent struggle ends (provisionally) with a legal, socially acceptable substitute—Penelope—for the maternal but necessarily foregone object of desire. The too happy ending of Jason and Medea's epic voyage deliberately invites our contemplation of their approaching loss, and the frailty of all substitutes. Similarly, Troilus discovers his happy substitute in Criseyde, but this happiness cannot last, as "the storie telleth," enforcing their mutual betrayals. It is progress, it is loss, it is change without change: It is the same story.

"My Life is Pain": The Homeric *Odyssey*

> What you have gotten off your fathers—
> Earn it, to make it your own.
>
> —Goethe

An Oedipal reading of the *Odyssey* is simple. The poet speaks of a man with bad feet, consistently comparing him to the "great Gamelegs," Hephaistos.[1] Its hero wanders blindly for years—having blinded an image of himself in the Cyclops[2]—after his mother has arguably killed herself for love and lack of him.[3] Though this kind of reading highlights important aspects of the text, usefully suggesting that the *Odyssey* records the results of (real or fantasied) Oedipal success, it does tend to reduce the greater scope of epic to a structural simplicity more characteristic of other genres. Examining the recursive structures of the epic, on the other hand, demonstrates more substantially the organizing dynamic of sex and violence at play in the epic.

The *Odyssey* is probably the most-read classical text of the twentieth century, and its appeal is familiar. It bears significant traces of oral composition,[4] but the poem develops a somewhat skeptical response—an incipient literacy— in reaction to the oral and narcissistic ethos of the *Iliad*.[5] Its hero is literally "the man of many tropes" or tactics for dealing with the world (*polytropos Odysseus*). While he is "much-turned" by forces outside himself, he is also—literally— "troping against death," executing his own "turns" upon his environment. Not only do his "many turnings" help him evade physical death, but they also keep him from narrative death, from the final end of the story. The hero's numerous accounts of his adventures since the Fall of Troy show the *Odyssey* more than any other early epic as a story about stories and their making. These infratextual fictions shed valuable light on the way oral texts are formed and guided by the psychological, political, and generic constraints of the specific context of utterance.

But the epic is "oral" in more ways than one. Henry Fielding describes the *Odyssey* as "that eating poem,"[6] and his assessment is accurate: The subjects of food, drink, or eating appear just about every thirty lines.[7] Since the tendency in the poem is—through hospitality and feasts—to link the action of speaking with the action of eating, this recursive pattern becomes so insistent as to seem obsessive. How do these actions of eating and speaking signify, especially in their repetition?

Eating is violence, bearing within it a desire that is sexual in its metonymic aim. As Freud suggests, "the act of eating is a destruction of the object with the final aim of incorporating it" (1940, 6). Seemingly divergent aims coalesce in this act: The desire for the maternal breast, for a metonymic sense of union, combines with the aggressive urge to destroy (and thus incorporate) the powerful agent that can remove the source of pleasure. In the Oedipal script, this aggression is usually seen as directed against the father. Some of Freud's notes, however, and the *Odyssey* itself suggest that the *mother's* assertions of power are equally the target of such violence (e.g., Freud 1923a, 370n1): In order to gain a sense of wholeness in the absence of the mother, the child tries to gain control over that power which can give and take away the feeling of wholeness. At first glance, this kind of orality seems far removed from that of story-telling, but the connection is actually rather strong. Indeed, we find that there is an inverse relation between the two actions—eating and speaking—within the framework of the *Odyssey*. Paraphrasing Freud's description of eating, the act of speaking is the creation of an object contiguous with the self, with the final aim of separation (violence), of *excorporating* that object. Freud remarks, "The creative writer does the same as the child at play. He creates a world of fantasy which he takes very seriously—that is, which he invests with large amounts of emotion—while separating it sharply from reality" (1908b, 144). According to Freud's vision of the creative process, "a happy person never fantasies, only an unsatisfied one. The motive forces of fantasies are unsatisfied wishes, and every single fantasy is the fulfillment of a wish, a correction of unsatisfying reality" (1908b, 146). Many of Odysseus' stories seem particularly designed as fantasies of convenience, "objects" that serve a primarily practical purpose by their operation apart from their speaker; the stories of himself that he tells for the benefit of Eumaios and the Suitors are the obvious examples. Though they issue from the mouth of Odysseus, they are "separat[ed] sharply from reality" for both Odysseus and the audience of the epic. They are clearly presented as *other* than the "real" story of Odysseus.[8] Like all the gifts he gives, in their deceptively connective presentation his stories conceal a metaphoric (and sometimes aggressive) distancing.[9] Yet if Freud is correct, and Odysseus by lying corrects "unsatisfying reality," then a question arises: What is the nature of Odysseus' dissatisfaction?

Two important events frame the "wanderings" of Odysseus (as he describes them in books 9–12): The poem's exordium, however, wrongly suggests that the story begins "after he plundered the stronghold on the proud height of

Troy," and carries through to the crime of his men on Thrinakia, where "they killed and feasted on the cattle of Lord Hêlios, the Sun" (1.4–13). The long-discussed discrepancies of this opening suggest that the violation of divine cattle causes the long wanderings of the hero, but this leaves unsettled both case and cause (Heubeck 1988, 68). Long before the Thrinakian episode, Odysseus blinds Polyphemos, and his father Poseidon still bears a grudge. But Odysseus says that his "wanderings" begin even earlier: Before his meeting with the Cyclops, Odysseus encounters both the Kikonês and the Lotos Eaters (and in these episodes, he is already losing companions). Likewise, Zeus has already set him to wandering, "rous[ing] in the north a storm against the ships" (9.71–72); similarly, the sea-current (9.84) and then "dangerous high winds" leave Odysseus and his fleet to "drift" for nine days (9.87–88).[10] Apparently the punishment of exilic wandering predates the cattle-feasting "crime" of the exordium by a good bit. But perhaps the crime has already occurred. George deForest Lord proposes that the attack on the enigmatic Kikonês at Ismaros can be key to our understanding of the *Odyssey*. The unprovoked raid is, he says, "an act of violence that becomes . . . the typical crime of the *Odyssey*."[11] And as far as it goes, Lord's observation is certainly accurate. But the too-briefly recounted incident, an extreme act of violence, actually conflates the two crimes of the exordium, crimes of killing and consuming:

> "I stormed that place and killed the men who fought.
> Plunder we took, and we enslaved the women,
> to make division, equal shares to all—
> but on the spot I told them: 'Back, and quickly!
> Out to sea again!' My men were mutinous,
> fools, on stores of wine. Sheep after sheep
> they butchered by the surf, and shambling cattle,
> feasting . . . [The Kikonês] came
> with dawn over that terrain like the leaves
> and blades of spring. So doom appeared to us,
> dark word of Zeus for us, our evil days."
>
>   (9.44–57)

This episode, the most "realistic" of Odysseus' recounted adventures, vividly evokes the crime (or indiscretion, at least) of "feasting," paralleling the Cattle of the Sun episode. Second, as Lord points out, this segment of Odysseus' tale to the Phaiakians becomes the formulaic prototype of his later "pseudo-auto-biographies" (e.g., 14.285ff., 17.494ff.). If these "fantasies" of Odysseus constitute the "fulfillment of a wish," it is an odd wish, and worth a closer look. Third, the rape of Ismaros (on a smaller scale, with a vital difference) replicates the destruction of Troy. The war at Troy is the other primary act of the exordium, and the song of Troy on Skheria has just evoked a cathartic release of grief in Odysseus (8.544ff.). The raid on Ismaros is, as George Dimock notes, "the Sack of Troy in its predatory essentials, with the glamor stripped off" (1962, 108). The primary acts related in the exordium begin to appear as recursive analogues, as differently worded versions of the same story, a story of conquest, violation, and retribution that can be seen as the narrative structure of the entire poem.

Of many repetitive stories in the *Odyssey* perhaps the clearest "versions" or fictional recursions are those told latest in the poem. The story Odysseus relates to Eumaios in book 14 displaces the violent, unexpected raid onto the magical land of Egypt: "[H]ow I wish that I had died in Egypt, on that field" (300–301), he says. Instead, he begs asylum from the Egyptian king, "embracing and kissing his knees" (306), while his companions are slaughtered. The later version for the Suitors is nearly identical. After his crewmen plunder the Egyptian farms, killing the men and carrying off the women, the defenders come upon them: "Their scything weapons left our dead in piles, but some they took alive, into forced labor, myself among them" (17.511–13). All three stories are basically equivalent; in the Ismarian raid, the harsh punishment of the native army is merely the first stage of a long exile; in the two recursions, the violation is followed again by punishment and by labor in exile.[12]

The Rape of Troy, with added detail, is nearly the same story: "We killed the men who fought and carried off the women." The striking difference lies in the lack of parallel punishment. The Rape of Troy is a renowned success, "a song for men to come." This suggests that the wish Odysseus attempts to fulfill with the later fantasies is a wish for punishment. And Alkinoös intimates a psychological resonance to Odysseus' "terrible" grief, suggesting that a relative, someone "next your own blood most dear" died at Troy, and that Odysseus' tears are compensatory for that loss (8.601–10).[13] In Freudian terms it is easy enough to trace this story, this "song for men to come" to the son's primal conflict with the father for the mother's affections. In the Fall of Troy, however, as in Sophocles' *Oedipus*, the father *is* killed (along with a number of competitive siblings), and the mother *is* carried off.

The Fall of Troy plays a traumatic role in Odysseus' psychomachia: All traces in the text seem to lead back to this cataclysmic event. From the opening references (in the exordium and the council of the gods) until the memory-jarring speech of Eupeithes (24.440–52), the Trojan War and the many "Bitter Homecomings of the Akhaians" are insistently present.[14] Especially important is the Trojan Horse, the vehicle of Odysseus' fame as the most prominent conqueror of Troy. This is a little surprising since Odysseus himself speaks of it rarely; when he does it is rather significant. He asks Demodokos to "sing that wooden horse Epeios built, inspired by Athena—the ambuscade Odysseus filled with fighters and sent to take the inner town of Troy" (8.511–14). Requesting the very song that will make him weep is puzzling, as Alfred Heubeck notes (1988, 381).[15] Moreover, Odysseus' request is deeply rooted in the dynamics of recursion that continue throughout the poem; as with his fictions, Odysseus is reiterating his punishment, recalling yet once more that which appears to him as a great crime, the Fall of Troy. Snider's conception of it as "the grand estrangement" (in Steiner 1962) captures nicely the archetypal role the Trojan war and its outcome play in the poem, both for poet and for hero.[16] The Fall of Troy is the murder of the father, the rape of the mother.[17] Gendered parental figures are synthesized in the image of Troy, suggesting a need to assert control over maternal as well as paternal power.[18] We shall return to this point, but at least the purely Oedipal struggle of father and son outlined by Freud and modified by Bloom does not fully explain the *Odyssey*. Rather, the struggle of Odysseus (and the poet) is a narcissistic struggle of individuation; but unlike the dynamics of narcissism at work in the *Iliad* and *Beowulf*, the *Odyssey* does develop an ambivalent struggle against *parental* proscriptions. Troy is not the scene of Odysseus' biographical Oedipal struggle; Troy explains itself more effectively as the scene of the *Odyssey*-poet's somewhat anxious separation from the poet (or the tradition) of the *Iliad*; Troy is, however, imbricated with Odysseus' Oedipal situation. Sounding surprisingly like an oral theorist, Freud remarks that "[Fantasy] hovers, as it were, between three times. . . . What it thus creates . . . carries about it traces of its origin from the occasion which provoked it and from the memory. Thus past, present, and future are strung together, as it were, on the thread of the wish that runs through them" (1908b, 147–48).[19] A "provoking occasion" like the struggle over Helen and the city of Troy is clearly a suitable vehicle for the expression of powerful repressed wishes, those of the *Odyssey*-poet as well as our own.[20]

The vital contrast between the story of Troy and other episodes, as we have seen, lies in the absence of punishment immediately following the act. The rape of Troy is successful. Unfortunately for the Akhaians, the punishment for living out their incestuous desires is eventually enacted upon them in the *Odyssey*'s depiction of their many "Bitter Homecomings." Odysseus' own homecoming is in some ways the bitterest of all, for the *Odyssey* insists on his unceasing recursions to the rape of Troy, each time including his own punishment. Just as the rape of Troy becomes the paradigm lived out in the bitter homecomings, so the whole of the *Odyssey* becomes the story of Odysseus coming home to Ithaka *as to a version of Troy*, and hence a recursion to the Iliadic precursor. Odysseus throughout the *Odyssey* is engaged in the process of mourning over both the victory and loss at the Fall of Troy, a process so drawn-out and repetitive that it has attributes of melancholia.

In "Mourning and Melancholia" Freud points out that the two processes are similar, often having the same initial causes (1917, 251). He characterizes mourning as "the reaction to the loss of a loved person, or to the loss of some abstraction which has taken the place of one, such as one's country, liberty, an ideal, and so on" (252). Hans Loewald generalizes this reaction, seeing it as subsuming all the loss and renunciation that takes place with regard to the psyche (in Earl 1982, 363). Symptoms of mourning and melancholia are also quite similar: "profoundly painful dejection, cessation of interest in the outside world, loss of the capacity to love, inhibition of all activity"; in melancholia, moreover, where the loss is typically unconscious and the original love deeply ambivalent (as in the case of Odysseus), there is found "a lowering of the self-regarding feelings to a degree that finds utterance in self-reproaches and self-revilings, and culminates in a delusional expectation of punishment" (Freud 1917, 252). That is, the aggression once focused on the lost person or object now turns against the ego, since the ego has come to identify with the lost object. This in turn leads to the melancholic's repetitive self-exposure or exhibition, more exaggerated than, but parallel to, the self-mortification and self-abasement characteristic of Homeric mourners.

This tendency toward self-exposure has often been remarked in Odysseus—indeed, George Dimock argues that self-exposure is the typical Odyssean strategy (1962, 109). In the *Odyssey* and in Freud, exhibition of this type is paired with its opposites, the loves of the gaze and of research (scopophilia and epistemophilia). Exploring the development of these tendencies in increasingly literate epic is one aim of this chapter, but for the *Odyssey* one example will have to suffice.[21] Though the hero's love of exploration and discovery runs all through the poem, perhaps the most neatly condensed illustration is Odysseus' encounter with the Sirens. Verging on disobedience to Teiresias' explicit warnings, the solitary Odysseus deliberately exposes himself to new and dangerous knowledge, telling his crew (falsely) that Kirke urged him to it:

> Therefore
> you are to tie me up, tight as a splint,
> erect along the mast, lashed to the mast,
> and if I shout and beg to be untied,
> take more turns of the rope to muffle me.
>
> (12.160–64)

Not only does the episode bring together the love of knowledge and self-exposure, but they are tied up with one of the more famous images of self-punishment, a bondage necessary to this kind of knowledge. Especially striking (and fitting to an oral context) is that the knowledge gained is not the Freudian scopophilic *vision*, but rather the "honey-sweet" *song* of the primal fields of Troy:

All feats on that great field
  In the long warfare,
Dark days the bright gods willed,
  Wounds you bore there . . .
    (12.189–90)[22]

But how is melancholia linked with the two significant threads of recursive orality—eating and speaking—which run throughout the *Odyssey?* Freud mentions both of them in connection with mourning and melancholia, both closely associated with the eventual healing process. Generally, people strongly oppose abandoning an object of love, "even, indeed, when a substitute is already beckoning to them. This opposition can be so intense that a turning away from reality takes place and a clinging to the object through the medium of a hallucinatory wishful psychosis" (1917, 253). Like the "fantasies" explored earlier, the much-remarked romance of *Odyssey* in books 9–12 ("a turning away from reality") constitutes a wish-fulfillment[23] that—literally—allows Odysseus to get on with his life. Reality must be obeyed, but not all at once; its injunctions can only be carried out "bit by bit, at great expense of time and cathectic energy, and in the meantime the existence of the lost object is psychically prolonged. Each single one of the memories and expectations in which the libido is bound to the object is brought up and hypercathected, and detachment of the libido is accomplished in respect of it" (1917, 253). By means of his tale of adventures Odysseus wishfully recreates his activities at Troy, including his own punishment (either as his own, or through the punishment of his companions). Hypercathexis (over-indulgence) allows him to cherish, temporarily, each recursion, and then separate himself from it. Through the medium of his story on Skheria, Odysseus finally begins to put his past behind him. Whether he is able to do so entirely is unclear.

So much for speech. But what of eating? This other orality is specifically linked to the melancholic "regression from object-cathexis to the still narcissistic oral phase of the libido" (1917, 259), a phase more generally connected with establishing the superego. The process of "introjection" or identification with the desired but lost object (e.g., the parents) lets one recreate that object inside one's own ego, thus gaining some measure of control over the object. The formation of the super-ego is accomplished by identifications, particularly by those primary identifications with the parents, which form a kind of "precipitate" in the ego; the precipitate then "confronts the other contents of the ego as an ego ideal or superego" (1923a, 373). "The super-ego is, however, not simply a residue of the earliest object-choices of the id; it also represents an energetic reaction-formation against those choices. Its relation to the ego is not exhausted by the precept: 'You *ought to be* like this (like your father).' It also comprises the prohibition: 'You *may not be* like this (like your father)—that is, you may not do all that he does; some things are his prerogative' " (1923a, 373–74). Elsewhere, Freud draws a parallel between this process of identification and the beliefs of "primitive peoples . . . that the attributes of animals which are incorporated as nourishment persist as part of the character of those who eat them" (1923a, 378n; see also *Totem and Taboo*, 1913a). Though such an incorporation of the object (through introjection or ingestion) reestablishes the individual's sense of wholeness in the absence of the loved object, it also extends the control that the object has over the person. In order to become like the parents, the child must consume them, and Odysseus has done essentially this in the Fall of Troy. However, in doing so (even in fantasy), the child realizes a crime, a separation; in order to atone for this destruction of his or her object-cathexes, the child must be punished, that is, eaten. The difficulty suggested by the passage above for Odysseus will be readily apparent: He has already usurped his father's role, both figuratively, in his conquest of Troy, and actually, in that Laertes, though alive, is no longer king of Ithaka. His ambivalent love and hatred for the lost parental object "takes refuge in narcissistic identification" where sadistic impulses and hatred especially come to the fore in his treatment of "the substitutive object [himself and his crew], abusing it, debasing it, making it suffer and deriving sadistic satisfaction from its suffering" (1917, 260). While all of Odysseus' "debasing[s]" of himself are in some sense his own tropes or stratagems, they also suggest the uncertainty of his own identity in the face of the constantly expected punishment. "My life is pain," as Odysseus says (7.150).

There appear to be two contradictory imperatives at work in the poem to make Odysseus' life "painful": From the narcissistic life-instincts there arise the many repetitions of desire, most prominently represented by hunger, the recurrent evocations of Odysseus' (and his men's) desire and need for nourishment.

> Belly must be filled.
>
> (7.230)

> There's no part
> of a man more like a dog than brazen Belly,
> crying to be remembered . . .
>
> (7.225)

> how many bitter seas men cross for hunger!
>
> (17.475)

On the other hand, a powerful directive is issued by the superego: Thou shalt not eat, a command which carries with it the implicit threat of being eaten. This threat is made explicit in the eventual destruction of Odysseus' entire fleet and his own ship's crew. The ego, caught in the conflict between desire and the parental figures of the superego, will suffer a narcissistic wound, a castration. Dimock has seen the dangers of the *Odyssey* in terms of a threatened loss of identity, primarily to those forces (the sea, Kalypso, the Lotos) which threaten to swallow or overwhelm the ego. In the case of the man-eating monsters, the Laistrygonês, Polyphemos, Skylla, and perhaps the Sirens, the threat is even clearer. The most obvious lesson occurs in book 11, the descent to the under-world.[24] Here Odysseus is faced with Tityos, whose punishment for the rape of Leto is to have his belly torn out repeatedly by vultures. For a crime analogous to Odysseus', he is condemned to being eaten (11.588–99).[25] The punishment of Tantalos is also to the point: Surrounded by water, he is not permitted to drink. With food in easy reach, he is not permitted to eat (11.600–610). Some of the confusion about the purpose of the poet in placing these figures here, however, arises from the seemingly explicit moral guidance provided by Teiresias.

According to Teiresias, if Odysseus wants to negotiate the continued anger of Poseidon, there is only one way: "One narrow strait may take you through his blows: denial of yourself, restraint of shipmates" (11.110). "Recklessness" has long been recognized as one of Odysseus' major flaws in the *Odyssey*, an aspect of his character that is reputed to improve throughout the poem. If we consider this difficulty too long, however, the hero's reputation for "cunning" is rather suspect. Dimock, trying to reconcile these two attitudes, has suggested that "to be Odysseus, then, is to adopt the attitude of the hunter of dangerous game: to deliberately expose one's self, but thereafter to take every advantage that the exposed position admits; the immediate purpose is injury [of the quarry], but the ultimate purpose is recognition and the sense of a great exploit" (57). Odysseus' "self-exposure" is one of the characteristics of melan-cholia; Dimock's explanation, at first glance, is sound. But what, in most cases, can we consider Odysseus to be "hunting"? Ithaka? "Men and manners"? The episode of the boar was long ago, and far away from the Cyclops' cave. More-over, especially among hunters, to "expose one's self," to beard the lion in his den, so to speak, is sheer foolhardiness, not "cunning." He appears to be hunt-ing both self-aggrandizement—"recognition"—and simultaneous punishment, *self*-injury.

Questions of "restraint" and of Odyssean "strategy" are both important. But Odysseus clearly shows restraint *before* his meeting with Teiresias. Upon his arrival at the land of the Lotos Eaters, perhaps having learned from his encoun-ter with the Kikonês, his decisions as a leader are characterized by commend-able caution: He carefully sends "two picked men and a runner" (9.87) to in-vestigate. On their surrender to the charms of the plant, Odysseus, in a very physical, almost sadistic image of "restraint," "drove them, all three wailing, to the ships, tied them down under their rowing benches" (9.109) and departed, without tasting of the Lotos himself. His division of the crew into two platoons for the exploration of Kirke's isle (10.200) shows some caution, if not exactly restraint. Similarly, his self-denial (even self-punishment) on the first trip out from the island of Aiolos is rather amazing: "I had worked the sheet nine days alone" (10.40). It seems the condemnation of Odysseus' rashness is a little off-target; or, perhaps, his rashness and his caution are mistimed, misapplied. Moreover, can we say that Odysseus improves in self-denial, and restraint of his crew, after his warning from Teiresias? While the episode of the Sirens certainly shows cunning, his self-exposure seems a dismissal of Teiresias: He is physically restrained by his crew from joining the Sirens, but does not deny himself their song (12.150). Not even restraint and self-denial, apparently, can do any good against Skylla and Kharybdis; giving battle to Skylla will only give her time to eat more men (12.110). But as Odysseus admits, "Kirke's bidding against arms had slipped [his] mind" (12.212), and, unrestrained, he takes up spears against the monster. His arming appears to do him neither good nor ill, but it certainly does not follow the advice of Teiresias.[26] On Thrinakia, once he has given in to his crew's understandable demands for rest, he fails, as well, to restrain them from feasting on the Cattle of the Sun. As with Skylla and Kharybdis, of course, there is absolutely nothing that can be done about the matter: Both the storm that keeps them on the island and the sleep of Odysseus are caused by the gods (12.315, 338). There are important lessons here for Odysseus, but they have little to do with rashness and restraint. Rather, the lessons have to do with certain inescapable realities. First of all, the *cost* of survival is always (paradoxically enough) a kind of death, either a surrogate death or a loss to self; there is, necessarily, a narcissistic injury if one wishes to live. The narcissistic heroism of an Achilles or an Aias can lead only to death. Just as clearly, humans are not made of iron; they break: "Belly must be filled." The punishment exacted by the gods (or the superego) can be too harsh, expecting more of humans than such creatures can possibly accomplish. Even the dead cattle can teach Odysseus something:

> The silken beeves of Hêlios were dead.
> The gods, moreover, made queer signs appear:
> cowhides began to crawl, and beef, both raw
> and roasted, lowed like kine upon the spits.
>
> (12.390)

The "queer signs" encode an important lesson for Odysseus, but one that he perhaps never learns entirely. In Freud's account of "primitive peoples," some part of the things that one eats lives on afterward, incorporated in the body; so also on Thrinakia we see the continuing influence of the slaughtered cattle suggested by the queer signs. For Odysseus, the lesson is: Atone or make sacrifices as you will, those lost "loved objects" (here, the parental figures of Troy) that you identified with and incorporated can never be done away with entirely, no matter how many times the Oedipal struggle and self-punishment recur.

What are Odysseus' tactics for mediating these many obstacles? If not through "self-exposure" nor mere "restraint," how does he survive? The simplest illustration lies in the episode of Kharybdis (12.426–46). Odysseus leaps from the remnants of his ship, letting the whirlpool take them, while he hangs all day in the fig tree above. "And Ah! how long, with what desire, I waited!" His raft is regurgitated, he rejoins it, and continues on his way. His raft is the recursive equivalent of the Trojan Horse, a "gift" to Kharybdis. If we look at it in this way, the difficult simile of the "one who hears and judges pleas in the marketplace all day" becomes transparent: The simile refers to Kharybdis, not to Odysseus. The hero, who is literally depending upon the whirlpool's decision, has attempted to sway the judgment in his favor by means of a gift, a bribe. Odysseus' strategy, here and elsewhere, is like that of Rhea, whose substitution of a stone for the infant Zeus allowed him to escape his brothers' and sisters' fate in the belly of Kronos. A substitute is given, a representative of the self. Odysseus' response to the problem of eating or being eaten is straightforward: Eat *and* be eaten (that is, allow a surrogate to be eaten).

A more complex version of this strategy occurs in the cave of Polyphemos, where Odysseus is admittedly rash. More important, however, are the recursions in this bucolic setting to the destruction of Troy, and the strategy by which the hero gains the victory despite his narcissistic loss. His desire to move from the island of wild goats to the land of the Cyclops is already a violation, showing a greed that goes beyond the bounds of need. It is the kind of exposure that Odysseus forces upon himself, asking for punishment. Odysseus himself thinks of this trip as a violation, long before he has any idea what manner of folk inhabit the land. As he says, he brings the Ismarian wine along because "in my bones I knew some towering brute would be upon us soon—all outward power, a wild man, ignorant of civility" (9.220). But it is soon far from clear exactly who is "ignorant of all civility" in this exchange. Odysseus' opening speech is that of the hero of the Trojan War, not that of the supplicant guest.

> We served under Agamemnon, son of Atreus—
> the whole world knows what city
> he laid waste, what armies he destroyed.
> It was our luck to come here; here we stand,

beholden for your help, or any gifts
you give—as custom is to honor strangers.
We would entreat you, great Sir, have a care
for the gods' courtesy; Zeus will avenge
the unoffending guest.

(9.250–60)

Insulting his host's intelligence with what "the whole world knows" but this "shaggy mountain of a man" surely does not, is not exactly endearing. Even if Odysseus were among people bound by the laws of hospitality, his immediate recourse to the idea of gifts and unsubtle reminders of the required "courtesies" could not be considered polite. Of course it is doubtful whether tact would make a difference at this stage, as Odysseus and his men are trapped at the back of the cave where they have been eating cheese (uninvited). The punishment Odysseus expects is not long in coming, and after six of his men (substitutes for himself) have been eaten, Odysseus enters into an exchange of gifts with the giant. The two separate gifts, the Ismarian wine and the name *Outis,* or Nobody,[27] conceal their aggression under the guise of closeness, and Odysseus earns a gift in exchange as well: He is to be eaten last.

Like the city of Troy, the figure of Polyphemos is a condensation of both maternal and paternal qualities; he is male, and a veritable "mountain"; yet he is also the cave within the mountain, the provider of the omnipresent milk and whey of the episode. Despite his men's advice and his own foreboding, Odysseus has returned to the scene of the crime to reenact it, this time including the punishment he deserves (though it is largely visited upon his men). Because Polyphemos' invocation of Poseidon will cause Odysseus to wander aimlessly, his blinding of the Cyclops is a blinding of himself (a self-mutilation like that of Oedipus).[28] His blinding of Polyphemos is also a reaction against the implicit threat of punishment for such crimes; the phallic imagery of the olive stake and the "single eye" of the Cyclops is obvious, and the poet dwells on the "sizzling" of the eye with some relish. It is a remarkable scene, coalescing the different concerns of the Oedipal struggle in a single central image; not without reason is this one of the most popular parts of the *Odyssey* and a common folktale motif. In the very act of punishing himself with blindness, Odysseus strikes out against the towering (but now passive and feminized) father-figure, and simultaneously commits the act of incest he desires; but in striking out thus, he also carries out his own punishment. His blinding of Polyphemos is a psychological self-castration.[29] Though he gains the benefits of identity—the ability to assert himself ("Odysseus, raider of cities, took your eye!")—he simultaneously blinds himself. The shadowy father-figure of Poseidon, the dark brother (or double) of Zeus, ensures that he will indeed wander long before he reaches Ithaka. Odysseus can no longer guide himself.

A few additional features of this encounter are worth mentioning. Apart from the sadistic acts of eating and blinding, bondage appears in the tying of the crewmen beneath the sheep. One commentator calls this a Trojan horse in reverse; but also, as they have been food for the Cyclops, now Odysseus disguises them as food to make good their escape. The olive stake as phallus is emphatically Polyphemos' own extension of phallic power, a club that lies seasoning [i.e., maturing] for use (9.320). This is not, of course, the only time that the olive especially, and trees in general, function as representative of Odysseus' sexual identity: As on Skheria, where the "single branch of olive" is "broken off" and used to "make up for" Odysseus' nakedness, it sets forth the castration of the father (6.130). On Ogygia, the olive appears as the gift of the axehandle, a gift wholly in keeping with Kalypso's role as substitute mother, but one that Odysseus greets with some suspicion (5.236); Samuel Butler remarks on the "minuteness of description" devoted to it.[30] Confirming the olive's involvement with phallic identity is the still-rooted olive tree that holds up the famous marriage bed and serves as the only "sign" by which Penelope will finally recognize the hero (23.160–80). The sexually resonant fig tree over Kharybdis to which Odysseus so desperately clings is similarly significant. Odysseus has undergone a kind of death and loss of his own identity at this point, a loss from which only the seven years of mothering by Kalypso can restore him.[31] His rapprochement with Laertes, confusing though it is, is based upon the organic symbolism of the orchard, the rootedness of the trees and their status as gift. Odysseus, having lost his natural mother, having been reborn, can finally come to terms with his natural father, recognizing their intimate connection in spite of the Oedipal conflict that has separated them. He is not able to do this, however, without aggressive assertion of his own status in the "testing" of Laertes, which has so much puzzled students of the poem.[32]

The poet of the *Odyssey* also undergoes the repetitive mourning process of Odysseus, and this is most clearly marked in the second *nekuia*. Though even the first *nekuia* is redundant (since Kirke knows what Teiresias relates), it can be explained in terms of lessons to be learned, and Odysseus' need to put the past to rest. Stranger still is the second descent. Unwitnessed, apparently inexplicable in its origin, it appears to mark a necessary return (once again) to the scene of the poet's contest with the precursor, and to the prominent victims of this retelling, the Iliadic heroes. Apart from the dead suitors, only the three Trojan heroes are present in Hades, their behavior contrasting with their earlier appearance to Odysseus. The text constructs a poet who desires both to lay the precursor tradition to rest, and to be punished for that poetic transgression; this results in the evocation of these ghosts, and in their frustration of that desire. The heroic ghosts do not die easily.

On the first occasion, Agamemnon recounts his inglorious death, how Klytaimnestra "killed me, after feeding me, like an ox felled at the trough. That was my miserable end" (11.414). Again we see the punishment associated with eating, though in Agamemnon's case it is specifically linked to women, both in the mention of his concubine Kassandra and in Odysseus' stress of "women" in his otherwise formulaic opening question, γυναικων falling heavily at the end of the sentence (Heubeck 1988, 101): "Were you cattle-raiding on the mainland / or in a fight for some strongpoint, or women?" (11.302–3). Even meeting the dead, Odysseus is politic. With Agamemnon he speaks of women, with Achilles of glory. Moreover, while they appear in book 11 to validate his present struggle, he does not do so much for them. Most of Agamemnon's advice goes unheeded by Odysseus, despite his confirmation of Penelope's virtues. Achilles, apart from the single famous speech asserting the infinite value of life over death, is similarly locked into his world of glory and death. In spite of his confirmation of merely surviving (and hence of Odysseus) the great Achilles is primarily concerned with the "rank and honor" of Peleus, and whether his son Neoptolemos was able, like his father, "to make a name in battle" (11.494–500). Once satisfied, he strides off, leaving Odysseus to show his own contrast with Aias, whose silence is a condemnation. Odysseus has learned the value of survival, and has suffered enough to care little about the arms (and aims) of Achilles, but Aias never compromises. The narcissistic wound of losing precedence to Odysseus could not be borne. But here his silence is effective; Odysseus both looks and feels stained by comparison (as he does in Ovid's rendition of the debate in the *Metamorphoses*). The damning contrast of the glorious heroism of Homer's Troy with the survivor's guilty torment is reinforced by juxtaposing the Iliadic heroes with Minos, judge of the underworld, and the figures of punishment. Apart from the oral punishments exhibited, the labor of Sisyphus is offered as an antiphonal prologue to the appearance of Herakles. Odysseus' fate rests somewhere in between the two, but he does not recognize this. His labors are not as infinitely repetitive as those of Sisyphus, but neither are they as varied as Herakles'. In the contrast with the Iliadic epic of death and glory, an epic of survival like the *Odyssey* is most clearly characterized by C. S. Lewis's phrase: "the mere endless up and down, the constant aimless alternations of glory and misery, which make up the terrible phenomenon called a Heroic Age" (1942, 28).

The poet's attempt in the first *nekuia* to bid farewell to arms, to the narcissistic complex of glory and death is not fully successful; while the heroes, except for Aias, are seen for their limitations, the equivocal presentation of Elpenor undercuts the *Odyssey* itself. "No mainstay in a fight or very clever" (9.560), his heroic language and request for a monument seem designed as an ironic comment on the heroism of the *Iliad*. The *Odyssey* concerns itself with living rather than dying. What is strange, however, is that Elpenor should want such a monument. Even stranger, perhaps, is that Odysseus grants the request, building a cairn with the "arms" (i.e., the oar) of Elpenor upon it. The poet's ironic comment goes far enough that it begins to seem self-parodic; though the world of heroes is no more, has it gone so far that monuments are built to those brought low by clumsiness and drink?

In the second *nekuia*, the poet's, we meet only the Iliadic warriors. Achilles greets Agamemnon, and speaks in his old voice, remarking that it would have been better for Agamemnon to have died at Troy. Agamemnon agrees, and his response serves to undermine the *Odyssey*: "You perished, but your name will never die. It lives to keep all men in mind of honor forever, Akhilleus" (24.95). They talk of funerals again, describing the glories that attended Achilles' death. Possibly this is a genre-linked substitution of a funeral in an epic where no "real" funeral takes place. It also emphasizes the unheroic end of Penelope's suitors, who lie "untended still" (24.200). But there is also a sensed inadequacy in the *Odyssey*'s lack of a decent heroic funeral.

Similarly, there is a real question about the heroism of Odysseus in his slaughter of the suitors. While Agamemnon devotes a single phrase to him ("O fortunate Odysseus!"), the bulk of his praise goes to Penelope. Even if one kills 108 strong young men and remains alive, apparently there is little glory in it if one must dress as a beggar to do so. Perhaps Agamemnon is still stuck in his world of women and death, but then his reversal in praise of Penelope is little short of astonishing. The very presence of the second *nekuia* suggests the need for poetic and heroic validation of the victory. What is surprising, I think, is that such a validation cannot be forced from the precursor or the ghosts of the past heroic ethos: The epic of survival cannot fully rewrite the heroic narcissistic narrative of glory and death.

After his discovery in Hades that his mother, the woman who brought him into the world, is dead, and after undergoing a series of punishments that render his very identity questionable, Odysseus is "received" by Kalypso as a gift, much the way that Nausikaa will receive him seven years later, when Kalypso herself "brings him into the world." Thus, Kalypso mothers Odysseus during his time of recovery on Ogygia. It is no accident perhaps that the seven years of exile on Kalypso's isle correspond neatly to the typical stay of the child in the Greek nursery; Odysseus' world, like that of the child, is "an almost entirely feminine one" (Slater 1968, 10). The intervening seven years are unrecorded, but the nymph "ceased to please" at some point. He cannot discontinue his mel-

ancholic position, because (though tired of it) he is still required to sleep with
his mother. Consequently, each day sees the renewal of his self-punishment.

> The sweet days of his life time
> were running out in anguish over his exile,
> for long ago the nymph had ceased to please.
> Though he fought shy of her and her desire,
> each night he lay with her, for she compelled him.
> But when day came he sat on the rocky shore
> and broke his own heart groaning, with eyes wet
> scanning the bare horizon of the sea.
>
> (5.150–58)

The ornate description of Kalypso's isle (5.40–80) is one of the poet's most sen-
suously compelling: "Even a god who found this place would gaze, / and feel
his heart beat with delight" (5.80–81). However, Ogygia no longer has charms
for Odysseus. His desire to escape the overwhelming bounty of Kalypso is apparently so strong that "he longs to die," as Athena remarks in the opening
council of the gods. Yet his desire, though usually seen as a straightforward
longing for home and family, is really more complex, as he himself reveals in
answer to Kalypso's last plea:

> "My lady goddess, here is no cause for anger.
> My quiet Penelope—how well I know—
> would seem a shade before your majesty,
> death and old age being unknown to you,
> while she must die. Yet it is true, each day
> I long for home, long for the sight of home.
> If any god has marked me out again
> for shipwreck, my tough heart can undergo it.
> What hardship have I not long since endured
> at sea, in battle! Let the trial come."
>
> (5.220)

Though he longs for home, Odysseus desires at least as strongly the "trial" of
hardship. George Dimock has pointed out the danger of "nonentity" implicit in
lingering in the immortal absorbing world of Kalypso (1962, 111). Some separation from this otherwise consummate union is necessary, and Odysseus
struggles to maintain as much separateness as he can on this island full of intimations of immortality. Unless Odysseus reacts with a kind of metaphoric distancing, even a kind of violence, to his lush surroundings, he is in jeopardy of
losing himself, of dissolving into that environment. And for at least part of his

seven years, this is exactly the trope he used: He "sat apart," staring out at "that tract of desolation, the bitter sea," carefully cultivating his own sense of difference from the island and the nymph behind him, the deathless fulfillment that threatens to "consume [his] life" (5.94, 161). Similarly, he reacts with suspicion and anger to the goddess' eventual offer of help, seeing in any new proposal a hidden danger ("I take no raft you grudge me out to sea" [5.190]).

To a certain extent, we understand Odysseus' reaction. The human world of lack and the immortal world of fulfillment are difficult to reconcile. But considering the passage of seven years, his opposition and his suspicion seem to overreact. The resonances of melancholia in Odysseus' behavior on Ogygia should be clear; he has so little interest in the island or in any activity apart from mourning his loss, that he seems unaware for seven years of the tools and materials available for an attempt at escape. In a sense, he would rather stay and suffer, feeling that he deserves the punishment. Again, melancholia is connected to an unconscious loss of the object, unlike the consciously realized loss that is healed through mourning. Odysseus' purported loss of Ithaka is a cover for the deeper loss he has suffered, one that takes much longer to work through; this accounts, I think, for the surprising diffidence with which he always approaches the idea of returning home (e.g., the year's delay on Aiaia, or the odd departure from and sudden return to Troy "to please the Lord Agamemnon," which Nestor relates [3.162], and the apparent willingness to remain a year on Skheria [11.360]). Even in his reaction to Kalypso's offer he shows a willingness to back away from the dangerous project of separation and departure that reminds us of the further associations of her name: The verb *kaluptein*—to conceal, or cover—also conveys "protection," to cover (as in the *Iliad*) with a protective veil, or with leaves, as at the end of book 5 (φυλλοισι καλυψατο, 5.491). As with his mother Antikleia's attempt to keep him from going to war, so with Kalypso there is a danger of being too well shielded from the world. Her gift of the axeblade and handle, which he must prepare and wield himself, frees his erotic impulses to his own agency. Her son/lover goes out to seek his fortune.

Hence when he arrives in Ithaka, he approaches the island as a newcomer; he has been reborn with Kalypso, and faces this island as he would almost any other. Indeed his strategy has not changed. He approaches Penelope and the suitors not only, as so many have said, as Agamemnon coming home, but even more as Orestes, back from his long exile to avenge his father at the hands of "handsome" suitors. Incidentally, the approaching death of Laertes, the long-displaced father of Odysseus, is *made* far more imminent than the story line, or Laertes' actions, would suggest. His shroud has been in the making for several years, and thus his death is brought up whenever the story of the loom is told. Antikleia has certainly given the impression of oncoming death, telling Odysseus that Laertes makes his bed in the windrows of leaves. However, Odysseus is also, for the first time, allowed to play the part of his father. Like the city of Troy, his own home is under attack by Akhaians, suitors for the woman of the house. Thus Odysseus, in the final, climactic struggle of the poem, identifies with the outraged father punishing the sons for their sexual crime of eating, *and* identifies with the son, killing yet once more the displaced and multiplied father (the suitors who "possess" the house) to attain the mother's sole affection. In short, he administers the extreme self-punishment, killing his substitute in the usurping son. He can eat and be eaten. Once again Odysseus enters the household as a "gift from Zeus," a beggar. As beggar, as not-himself, he enters Home/Troy/Kharybdis. This is difficult for him, a very real injury to his narcissistic heroic ego. Interestingly, it is here as well that the puzzling similes of Odysseus as food cluster: The remarkable image of the hero as a heated "sausage, big with blood and fat" (20.24–28) combines in a telling manner the themes of bondage and eating, the tightly bound sausage paralleling in many ways the bag of winds obtained from Aiolos so long ago; the explosive storm is not long delayed. Similarly, the likening of his clothes to an onion in the disguised interview with Penelope (19.230), while it heightens the layers of disguise that Odysseus has put on, also reminds us of his possible fate at the hands of the suitors who have swallowed up so much else of his estate. The images of sadism and bondage that fill the following bloodbath need, I hope, no recounting. To close this discussion of the *nostos* of Odysseus, let us return to Freud.

Mania occurs in melancholics when

> as a result of some influence, a large expenditure of psychical energy, long maintained or habitually occurring, has at last become unnecessary, so that it is available for numerous applications and possibilities of discharge . . . when a long and arduous struggle is finally crowned by success, or when a man finds himself in a position to throw off at a single blow some oppressive compulsion, some false position which he has long had to keep up. (1917, 263)

> In mania, the ego must have got over the loss of the object . . . and thereupon the whole quota of anticathexis which the painful suffering of melancholia had drawn to itself from the ego and "bound" will have become available. (1917, 264)

It may not be over entirely, of course. The parental figures in the superego are notoriously persistent, and the sadism of the heroes as executioners may show an overcompensation. But that is the implication of the *Odyssey* as a whole, as well; there is always another journey, another sacrifice to be made in order to survive.

Though not the focus in this reading of the *Odyssey,* women's positions in the poem help to explain some of the changes to an increasingly literate epic tradition. In the *Iliad,* the mother Thetis is always already present, responding to her son's needs. She is mysterious, in that she contains all knowledge but does not divulge it. Other women in the text, however, function principally as emblems of masculine desire and status, as items of exchange. In the *Odyssey,* for whatever reason (incipient literacy? awareness of the *Iliad* as precursor-text?), women's position appears to have changed. Though it never approaches the misogyny of classical Greece, the poem shows a leaning in that direction which could easily be overemphasized. The familiar double standard of the gods, like that of humans, is gently criticized but never really challenged. The landscape through which Odysseus moves, though it combines characteristics of both genders, is figured predominantly as feminine, as a space or Other to be inscribed by masculine desire. Odysseus' strategy of the "Greek gift," despite its neat dialectical complement in Penelope's "circumspect" strategy of receipt without acceptance, is not without flaws. The concealment of metaphoric separation within a metonymic "gift" of love, while it recreates the Other within the Self, and so allows sympathy, at the same time must maintain and prolong the view of the Other as similarly divided: If there is an Athena, there is Skylla; if there is a Penelope, there is also Klytaimnestra. In the mind of Odysseus, women are alternately fascination and peril: Kalypso is "a lovely goddess and a dangerous one" (7.254). The later parts of Odysseus' adventures *may* show a moderation of his strategy, a drawing away from the extremes of violence and love that are synthesized within his gifts; but this is uncertain, and the courtyard littered with dead suggests otherwise.

The framework of the narcissistic plot and the family romance provides a useful way of reading a text, rather than a "truth" about the text's supposed "meaning." Instead, it confirms several deeply held impressions of a text (e.g., that Odysseus' quest is a search for identity, is an epic of survival and accommodation, is antiheroic); but at the same time, the theory allows an explanation of some of the more tightly bound knots of a text, those places within it (e.g., the second *nekuia,* the extremity of violence against suitors and servants, the puzzling similes of hero as food) that, though they exist for some reason, have baffled more conventional ways of reading epic.

The *Argonautica:* Traffic in Women

As a society grows increasingly literate, the coercive power of any single text as the only privileged repository of historical and other truths begins to wane. (Though as letters to the editor and the debate over the canon attest, the *claims* for a single text's authority may grow more vociferous and desperate.) Thus, as the power and direct relevance of Homeric epic decreased, the way opened for new forms of epic. Apollonius of Rhodes was an early literary practitioner of epic recursion, and his epic of Jason and Medea heavily emphasizes the role of the powerful male precursor. This aggrandizement of the paternal role is coupled with an increasingly suspect role for the feminine. In the *Argonautica*, as in *Troilus and Criseyde*, the power of women is paradoxically both lessened and increased. The combined loveliness and danger of the Homeric Kalypso—an extreme form of Penelope's own circumspection—becomes in these later epics the too-familiar dichotomization of women. Medea represents this clearly, not only in the ambivalently figured power she uses in books 3 and 4, but in her later Euripidean role as well.[33] For Criseyde, the traditional story carefully scripts her behavior as a misogynistic lesson in the inconstancy of women: Her courtly rule of love over Troilus shifts directly into her betrayal of him.[34] Hastily condemning this division of women by epic tradition probably misses the point; a strong feminist argument based on the sheer importance of women to these texts would be more useful. Whereas in the *Odyssey* the circumspect Penelope's duplicity, though complementary to that of Odysseus, does not change the fact that she waits quietly on Ithaka, in the *Argonautica*, despite Medea's ambivalent representation, her adoption (or "usurpation") of heroic stature expands both her presentation and her influence within and outside of the text. (Similarly, Chaucer's epic, given the still greater influence of the female character, and the critical energy devoted to her explication, might better be called the *Criseyde* than the *Troilus*.) Barbara Pavlock, noting this ambivalence in Apollonius, remarks that "while adding a new dimension to epic by reflecting the female from within and exploring her passion with great insight and sensitivity, the poet carefully controls this new subjectivity" (1990, 65–66). (It should be added that book 3, the story of Medea's growing passion for Jason, has long been recognized as the most successful part of the epic.) The "new dimension" of love that Apollonius is credited with introducing to epic is an emphasis consonant with the changed psychological dynamic of a written tradition. Moreover, love is a matter of emphasis rather than invention—the Oedipal codes embedded within oral texts are reinforced, becoming the dominant codes of written epic. This shift is framed insistently around an increasing ambivalence toward women, and a parallel ambivalence toward language. As oral theorists have observed, there is a substantial change implicit in writing and its deceptive capacity to make untrue things look true: Jack Goody's comments expand on this: "[W]ords assume a different relationship to action and to object when they are on paper than when they are spoken. They are no longer bound up directly with 'reality'; the written word becomes a separate 'thing,' abstracted to some extent from the flow of speech, shedding its close entailment with action, with power over matter" (1977, 46). This deceptive quality is built in to written language (though it is always potential in oral contexts where it can be reified and decontextualized). It is also, and analogously, "built in" to women by a patriarchal society, which depends on "traffic in women," on their potential for decontextualization and reinsertion or "slydynge."[35] Thus it is not surprising that the *Argonautica* and *Troilus and Criseyde* emphasize women's status as "portable property," as tokens to be exchanged between men. In my reading, the dynamics of this exchange connect closely with the exchange of women's attentions between father and son, and the Oedipal son's interpretation of maternal absence as "slydynge." The surprising aspect of this formulation is that, if written words (and women) are thus subject to multiple interpretation (i.e., exposed as "deceptive"), then writing also opens a way toward increased power and potential freedom. That is, when words (or women) are seen to dominate the system of exchange, their value and hence their power increases—especially when they are able to maintain a sense of personal or group agency in spite of patriarchal strictures. Freedom—such as it ever is—comes about with the proliferation of texts that agree and disagree, and the consequent creation of gaps and spaces of free play.

Apollonius' Jason is a rather hapless epic hero. His most frequent epithet is *amechanos* (without resource), and it applies aptly enough from the very first verses of the *Argonautica,* where King Pelias heeds the oracular warning of a man with one bare foot, and sends Jason (who lost a sandal crossing the Anauros) to find the Golden Fleece; through the epic's penultimate battle with Talos, the brazen giant of Crete, who is defeated by Medea. Borne from episode to episode by the whims and stern directives of more commanding figures, by the elements, and by the magical ship *Argo* itself, Jason emphasizes that aspect of Odyssean heroism which involves being buffeted about, and moves toward the position of Aeneas, "exiled by fate" (*fato profugium*). Chaucer's Troilus exacerbates this heroic lack of agency; in the words of one critic, Troilus is an "anaemic, passive hero," whose passivity "almost makes Pandarus the hero of the poem."[36] The splitting of heroic agency in these epics is a kind of fragmentation to examine more closely in Chapter 5; the increasing passivity of the hero as survivor shows a growing concern with deterministic influence, the way the hero is written rather than writing. Briefly, Odysseus willfully invades and explores each landfall: Every island yields a new story that is an active rewriting of the old. In Apollonius, Jason's repeated transgressions are cast as involuntary actions, often with the additional seductiveness of the environment or inhabitants. This "accidental" and unwitting transgression by the hero plays into the plot of more powerful figures. Jason's opening transgression is a good example, where unknowingly he arrives as the fulfillment of an oracle. The fact that Jason is—in a sense—seduced into this involvement with King Pelias by the goddess Hera is not revealed until later in the epic.[37] In Chaucer's *Troilus and Criseyde*, often seen as an epic of thoroughgoing determinism,[38] such determinism is conveyed primarily through what "the storie telleth"; despite the poet's valiant attempts to mitigate and liberate by reading the gaps in that script, in the end he is coerced into repeating the old story.

The lack of traditional narcissistic heroism in the *Argonautica* is perhaps most apparent in its closing lines, where the poet arrives at the "glorious finish" of the heroic labors after celebrating the mundane task—turned into a game—of stocking the ship's water supply:

> Farewell, heroic, happy breed of men! Your blessing on this lay of mine. And as the years go by, may people find it a sweeter and yet sweeter song to sing. Farewell; for I have come to the glorious finish of your labours. After Aegina you suffered no mishap, no gale opposed your voyage home. The coast of Attica slipped quietly by; you sailed at ease inside Euboea, past Aulis, past the cities of Opuntian Locris; and with joyful hearts you stepped ashore at Pagasae. (195)

Exactly why this should be understood as a "glorious finish" is unclear unless interpreted as irony, for it appears distinctly inglorious—nothing happens. The conclusion seems oddly muted in light of the wide variety of incidents that do occur in Apollonius' epic (and even more so in light of events to follow). Indeed, the charge often leveled against the "episodic" nature of the *Argonautica* has its origins in the confusing array of encounters.[39] The relative calm in which the *Argo* sails to its end is indicative of both the relative calm attained in the happy substitute, and an intimation of the storm that arises after such calm, when the substitute is deemed insufficient to reiterated human desire. The very insistence Apollonius displays concerning the tranquillity of the scenes raises our suspicions, particularly when the well-known—perhaps better known[40]—outcome of the story is so violent.[41]

In the *Odyssey*, the paternal figure splits into opposing roles—played by Zeus and Poseidon—both of them significant to the Odyssean sense of self and development. In the *Argonautica* a similar splitting of the powerful male precursor takes place, but almost all of these figures appear in a negative light, usually quite hostile to the young quester. Pelias of Iolkos and Aietes of Kolkhis are the most important of these, governing the initiation of the quest, the goal (and its consequences), and hanging like a repressed shadow over the ending of the epic.[42] Repeatedly, despite the heroic fortitude boasted of the crew, they find themselves at a standstill in any conflict with paternal figures, as if such a con-

flict were indeed forbidden. It is only through highly specific *feminine* agency
that such conflicts are brought to an end in favor of Jason and his followers.
This is true not only of Medea's victory over Aietes through her use of Jason,
but of the approaching victory over Pelias. Similarly, only Medea and her magic
can bring down the monsters who substitute for these powerful paternal figures, the towering bronze Talos who "terrified the Argonauts" (191), and the ser-
pent-guardian of the Fleece. The encounter of Jason and Medea with the ser-
pent-guardian of the Golden Fleece provides a useful example. With a hiss loud
enough to alarm not only the waiting crew, but also children in their mothers'
arms, the serpent advances:

> The monster in his sheath of horny scales rolled forward his interminable
> coils, like the eddies of black smoke that spring from smouldering logs
> and chase each other from below in endless convolutions. But as he
> writhed he saw the maiden take her stand, and heard her in her sweet
> voice invoking Sleep, the conqueror of the gods, to charm him. She also
> called on the night-wandering Queen of the world below to countenance
> her efforts. Jason from behind looked on in terror. (150–51)

The phallic significance of the serpent as a representation of the power of Aietes
is clear enough. The ambiguity as to the source of Jason's terror is noteworthy,
for it is an ambiguity that Apollonius plays upon and develops in Medea's assertions of power throughout the epic. When she is only the innocent maiden
carried off—the mere token of desire and victory—all is well; when she asserts
a desire for self-determination, she is met with placation;[43] when she actually
uses the power she has, even on behalf of the Argonauts, she is met with this
ambiguous "terror." The poet himself asserts still more in depicting (and condemning) her destruction of Talos: "[Medea] bewitched the eyes of Talos with
the evil in her own. She flung at him the full force of her malevolence, and in
an ecstasy of rage she plied him with images of death" (192). The poet adds,
with distaste for this death at a distance, "The thought appals me." Similar
but more striking for the poet is "the sorry tale" of Medea's betrayal of her
brother Apsyrtos to the sword of Jason. This tale, though it has bearing on
Medea's future behavior, is even more significant as a variant recursion to the
epic's principal plot, that of "traffic in women." Apsyrtos, "tempted by Medea's
treacherous offer" to steal the Fleece and return with him to their father, seeks
her out in the temple of Artemis.[44] The attempt to establish communication
proves fatal, despite the fact that he and his sister *seem* to agree on every detail
of the plan. However, in a resonant simile that clearly identifies him with Jason,
Apsyrtos is likened to "a little boy trying to ford a winter torrent that a strong
man could not cross" (159). Immediately Jason "butchers" him, an act that the

poet dwells on in some detail despite his distaste, including Jason's lopping off of the corpse's extremities and the ritual use of the dead man's blood.

The simile demonstrates an inverse conclusion to the plot that opened the epic—Jason crossing the River Anauros in winter flood. In the betrayal of Apsyrtos, however, the attainment of the feminine object (Medea, the Fleece) is prevented by the object's current male possessor: Jason himself plays the role of the father, killing himself in Apsyrtos. Both of these identities, however, subscribe to the myth of feminine seduction as a basic principle. This is clearest in the case of Apsyrtos, "tempted" by Medea's pretended treachery. In Jason's crossing it seems at first glance that the contrary is true, as though feminine seduction plays but little part in the opening episode. Though there are Oedipal intimations in the scene—the sandalless Jason confronting King Pelias, who attempts to defer his own deposition and death by substituting the quest for the Golden Fleece—no women appear to be involved. Later in the epic, however, Hera—Jason's patroness, and the primary maternal goddess of the Greeks—reveals her own important role in this episode, and her twofold reasons for helping the hero:

> For I will not have King Pelias boasting that he has escaped his evil doom, insolent Pelias, who left me out when he made offerings to the gods. Besides which I have been very fond of Jason ever since the time when I was putting human charity on trial and as he came home from the chase he met me at the mouth of the Anaurus. The river was in spate, for all the mountains and their high spurs were under snow and cataracts were roaring down. I was disguised as an old woman and he took pity on me, lifted me up, and carried me across the flood on his shoulders. For that, I will never cease to honour him. (111)

The aggression directed against the dominant male, and the "honour" reserved for the young—and largely passive—male, easily matches the pattern of maternal relations with male children in fifth-century Greece, as discussed by Marilyn B. Arthur (1973) and Slater (1974). "Imprisoned and isolated by her indifferent and largely absented husband, some of the mother's sexual longing was turned upon her son. Along with, and in direct contradiction to, her need to belittle and discourage his masculine striving, she attempted to build [him] up into an idealized replacement of her husband, fantasying that 'her little man' would grow up to be the perfect hero and take care of his mother all of her days" (Slater 1974, 22–23). In the expanding social and economic world of the Hellenistic age, however, opportunities for women to assert power in the public realm were increasing; perhaps in consequence, an epic like the *Argonautica* allows the (quite temporary) establishment of a happy couple as a form of the happy substitute, a balancing point for gender relations.[45] In contrast, though we know the happy substitute in the *Odyssey* is tenuous, this homecoming satisfies us because of its steadiness as a goal and the vagueness of the destiny implied beyond the epic. (Chaucer's placement of the happy substitute in the medial position seems to emphasize the brevity of human forms of fulfillment.) Though the terminal position of the happy substitute in Apollonius is similar to that of the *Odyssey*, the overly calm conclusion to the poem only highlights the grimness of subsequent events. The persistent thread of allusions to the Euripidean tragedy lends significant irony to the lightness of the ending (Pavlock 1990, 52, 61). Moreover, the substantial confusion of the goal of the quest bodes ill for the relationship of Jason and Medea. The Fleece is the goal at first, yes, but in Medea's dream she herself is the object Jason seeks; in the last third of the epic, her analysis seems most correct: The Fleece is mentioned only as an adjunct to the marriage ceremony.

The Fleece itself, due to its importance in the first half of the epic, deserves fuller explication. It is most easily explained as a condensation of Oedipal desires, containing on the one hand symbols of the maternal and the absolute—the gold, the fleece as representative of pubic hair, its status as a token of power, its power to "bear" children (i.e., Phrixos and Helle). On the other hand, it is the fleece of a slaughtered male sheep, the Ram slaughtered, moreover, as a sacrifice in a fantasy of paternal approval.[46] The Golden Fleece thus acts as a concretely realized crystallization of slaying the father and sleeping with the mother. As such, its "dismantling" or displacement into the paternal and maternal figures of Aietes and Medea is much clearer. The fact that the ram originally carried two children (one who lived, one who died) is primarily significant as an echo of the act—repeated throughout the epic—of *carrying* the maternal figure (carrying *Argo* through the Libyan desert, carrying Hera across the Anauros, or carrying Medea off from Kolkhis), and of being carried or borne by that maternal figure.[47] In particular, this image of bearing the maternal freight is significant as a repetition of the plot discovered in the simile of Apsyrtos, the seduction over the winter flood.

The epic revolves around this recursive complex, particularly insofar as the maternal *Argo* itself carries the entire epic.[48] The ship also functions as a fundamental indicator of the poet's role in the poem. Explicating this recursion in terms of psychoanalytic theory would be useful, for its dynamics seem to contrast significantly with the "Greek gift" characteristic of the *Odyssey*.

I have argued that the Oedipal inscription of the narcissistic masterplot is the principal story repeated in these three epics, and have remarked that the roles of scopophilia and epistemophilia—loves of the gaze and of knowledge—are heightened. In part, it is simply that the increasingly visual world of literacy—its "visuality"—strengthens this "desire for research," but further discussion of the Freudian concepts and its intersection with the Oedipal narrative may illuminate other aspects of the text and of literacy itself.

Scopophilia and epistemophilia are a set of early instincts that are only later subsumed under the primacy of genital sexuality. As such, they form the principal component in the sexual researches of children.[49] This research is conducted on two fronts, the question of sexual difference and the question of origins—of where babies come from. Most important for this discussion is the second question, for it concerns very closely the issues of fidelity, centrality, and replaceability that *Troilus and Criseyde* addresses; it also suggests the connection with the *Argonautica* and the *Odyssey* in terms of "bearing" and rebirth.[50] As is usual with the Freudian instincts, there are active and passive forms: The active form of scopophilia, looking, is paired with the passive form, exhibitionism, which plays a significant part in the *Odyssey*. The question of origins is not without its narcissistic basis: "It is not by theoretical interests but by practical ones that activities of research are set going by children. The threat to the bases of a child's existence offered by the discovery or the suspicion of the arrival of a new baby and the fear that he may as a result of it, cease to be cared for and loved, make him thoughtful and clear-sighted" (1905b, 112). Freud notes that while "under the influence of seduction the scopophilic perversion can attain great importance in the sexual life of a child," but remarks that children's interest in exposing and viewing genitalia is also general, a "spontaneous manifestation" (1905b, 110). Other forms of research besides the strictly scopophilic include the asking of questions, testing the value of competing theories (e.g., the theories heard from other children, the "theories" provided by parents), additional observation. Especially important (traumatic) observations for the child are those of the primal scene (of parental intercourse) and of the genitals of the opposite sex. In Freud's schema, these tend to result, respectively, in a sadistic view of intercourse, and in the much-criticized "castration-complex" for males and "penis envy" for females (1905b, 113–15). I am less interested in Freud's questionable and certainly limited conclusions than in the import of these observations so far as they have impact upon the poems under consideration. Thus, though not necessarily interpretable in the Freudian manner, the following (not untypical) touristic "observations" of Apollonius are of particular interest as they address questions of origin and sexuality:

> [The Argonauts] sailed in safety past the country of the Tibareni. Here, when a woman is in childbirth, it is the husband who takes to his bed. He lies there groaning with his head wrapped up and his wife feeds him with loving care. She even prepares the bath for the event.

> Next they passed [the land of] the Mossynoeci. . . . What we as a rule
> do openly in town or marketplace they do at home; and what we do in
> the privacy of our houses they do out of doors in the open street, and no-
> body thinks the worse of them. Even the sexual act puts no one to blush
> in this community. On the contrary, like swine in the fields they lie down
> on the ground in promiscuous intercourse and are not at all disconcerted
> by the presence of others. (101)

Typically, the sexual researches of the child end in a failure that can have divergent results, either in "a renunciation" (1905b, 115) of research and inquiry, or
in the sublimation of sexual researches in other forms of research, depending
upon the experiences associated with the initial curiosity.[51] Either way, however,
due to the "mystery-making" habits of adults (i.e., the highly suspect "customary answers given to the child in the nursery," of the stork, etc. [1907, 174, 177]),
the child is alienated from the parents, and "begins to mistrust grown-up
people, and to keep his most intimate secrets from them" (1907, 178). Freud
spells out the psychological dynamics somewhat more clearly in "The Sexual
Theories of Children": "The set of views which are bound up with being 'good',
but also with a cessation of reflection, become the dominant and conscious
views; while the other set, for which the child's work of research has meanwhile
gained fresh evidence, but which are not supposed to count, become the suppressed and 'unconscious' ones" (1908c, 192). In the next sentence, Freud describes this first "psychical conflict" as establishing the "nuclear complex of a
neurosis"—as the establishment, that is, of the Oedipus complex (191–92 and
notes). Importantly, Freud here bases the Oedipal complex on a collision of texts,
a text received from the parents, and a text that is to be suppressed (detectable
largely through its questioning stance). As with the quite similar collision of
precursor and poets' texts in the epic tradition, the "truth" of the earlier narrative is opened to question by the later; the child explores the gaps in the parental tale of origins through further research and reflection—conducted, as Freud
notes, in secrecy—until questions cannot be answered, can be answered with
a suitable theory, or are met with a forbidding agent intimidating enough to
squelch further inquiry.[52] The persistent questions of the unconscious are not
eradicated by intimidation, of course, but can remain as unanswered questions,
or emerge in temporarily satisfactory truths—the infantile theories of generation. Unanswered questions, on the other hand, when subject to repression, may
lead to their own neurosis of "obsessional brooding" and doubt (1925, 162ff.;
1907, 178, etc.).

In explaining the *Odyssey* as a work that mourns the Oedipal victory,
though I drew attention to the scopophilic aspects of the text, I developed only
partially the poem's focus on exploration and discovery. Whether produced by

contingency or the hero's own narcissistic exhibitions, the explorations of Odysseus appear as experiments in happy substitution. Due in part to Odysseus' rashness, however, these substitutions lead most frequently to self-punishment, emanating usually from the paternal figure. In the *Argonautica*, though the voyage is more clearly plotted by paternal figures, there is a similar investment in the exploration of unknown lands, and an increased reliance on the gaze (particularly in developing the relationship between Jason and Medea). The resolution of the Oedipal conflict is deferred, in order to maintain the illusion of the happy substitute attained through "traffic in women." In the story of Troilus and Criseyde, which revolves precisely around the traffic in women allowed by Criseyde's "slydynge," survival appears to lose credibility as an epic goal. Similarly, since apart from the limited exchange between Greek and Trojan camps the poem shows no concern with voyaging, it may be difficult to understand the applicability of exploration or discovery. Whatever "voyaging" takes place in *Troilus and Criseyde*, one would think, would have to take place in bed (where Troilus spends most of his time). Given the nature of research and exploration involved, that is exactly the point; Troilus' investigations into the nature of sexual difference and into his own replaceability (that is, into the question of origins) *are* conducted in bed. His radically disconfirming discoveries suggest a new meaning for the "double sorwe of Troilus." Chaucer's poem also emphasizes the narrator's involvement (and through him that of the audience) with research into the matter of the story. Moreover, the recurrent imagery of the ship tossed about on this "tempestuous matere" (2.5) (applied to both Troilus and the narrator) not only provides a fortunate image of physical voyage, but also suggests that parallel interpretations may be fruitful when applied to ships in the *Odyssey* and the *Argonautica*. A ship, in common parlance and in the interpretation of dreams, is feminine, by its association with other forms of vessel (e.g., in Freud 1933, 156). The various "ships" of Odysseus are routinely gained from women—Kirke, Kalypso, even Kharybdis. The *Argo*, of course, is specifically linked with the maternal. But beds in these epics should not be underestimated, since they are the primary locus of the happy substitute itself. The famous bed of Odysseus is indeed the key to his ultimate recognition and thereby the happy substitute. In the *Argonautica*, the honeymoon bed, spread with the Golden Fleece ("to grace the wedding and make it famous in story" [178]) underscores the temporary quality of the happy substitute achieved; Jason and Medea, "though they loved and delighted in each other, were haunted by fear" (178-79).

However, the act of "bearing the mother" or "traffic in women" has not been fully explicated, and the good ship *Argo* provides a fairly clear example. The nymphs in the Libyan desert (where the *Argo* is grounded) suggest this as they "reprove" the *amechanos* Jason and his crew for their self-abandonment: "You must repay your mother for what she suffered all the long time she bore you in her womb" (183). As Peleus interprets this vision, "As for our mother, I take her to be none but the ship herself. *Argo* carried us in her womb; we have often heard her groaning in her pain. Now, we will carry her. We will hoist her on our shoulders, and never resting, never tiring, carry her across the sandy waste" (184). The mother, abandoning or being abandoned by her usual partner (the sea), provides the opportunity for Oedipal involvement. A similar incident, showing more precisely that "belatedness" itself allows intercourse or posses-sion of the feminine, immediately follows the nine-day portage. Searching for water in the desert, the Argonauts come upon the garden of the Hesperides, where Herakles, just the day before, has slain the serpent and stolen the golden apples.[53] One of the Hesperides describes his rape of the garden and his break-ing open of the rock to find water:

> "You have indeed been fortunate," she said. "There was a man here yes-terday, an evil man, who killed the watching snake, stole our golden apples, and is gone. To us he brought unspeakable sorrow; to you release from suffering.
> . . . he rushed about the place in search of water; but with no success, till he found the rock. . . . He struck [the base of the rock] with his foot, water gushed out, and he fell on his hands and chest and drank greedily from the cleft." (185–86)

The simile that follows, in which the crew "milled round the cranny in the rock, like a swarm of burrowing ants busy round a little hole" (186), almost enforces a sexual reading of the scene. The precursor has invaded and spurned; the po-lite followers are invited to take advantage of that despoiling. Disturbingly enough, once their thirst is sated, the crew speak only of Herakles, and attempt to follow him further. That this transgresses farther is apparent from the deaths of Kanthos and (notably) Mopsos, the seer (187–88).

This reading of *Argonautica* as a sequence of seductions or invitations by maternal figures, and following the paternal traces of involvement and aban-donment, suggests an analogous involvement on the part of the poet. That is, the epic is achieved because of the initial expression of powerful epic precur-sors, and their later abandonment of such projects. Apollonius, the first poet to attempt the genre for some three centuries, begins his epic with a disclaimer of surprising relevance: "The ship was built by Argus, under Athene's eye. But as poets before me have told that tale, I will content myself by recounting the names and lineage of her noble crew, their long sea voyages, and all they achieved in their wanderings" (35). Though he recognizes the "poets before,"

Apollonius distances himself from their matter not at all; rather, he explicitly takes up where they left off. He "contents himself" with an already-completed object, rather than with the making of that object.

Jason's cloak (55–57), described in an ekphrasis that reflects the poet's view of his own work, is similarly completed, a "gift" from Athena.[54] Two of its scenes comment quite clearly on the issues under discussion: that of the young Apollo slaying Tityos "who was boldly dragging off his mother Leto" (56), and that of Zethos and the singer Amphion laying the foundations of Thebes, "as yet un-fortified." While Zethos, laboring hard, goes before, the poet "Amphion walked behind" (56).

Exactly why writing an epic should seem so easy to Apollonius is unclear; perhaps the way he "walks behind" Homer, by singing the foundations of epic a generation earlier—the epic "as yet unfortified" by the Trojan War—helps significantly. For Chaucer, who places his story in the midst of things Trojan, matters seem more complex.

Troilus and Criseyde: "Lechery, lechery, still, wars and lechery"

Certain features of Chaucer's *Troilus and Criseyde* make it a useful text to consider at this point. As the recursion to a precursor narrative—the matter of Troy—its status is relatively clear; moreover, Chaucer takes pains to show the debt owed to at least one precursor: "For as myn auctour seyde, so sey I" (2.18). Because "myn auctour" Lollius is a fiction deliberately adopted by Chaucer, his authority as a precursor is extremely malleable. Apart from this important paternal figure fantasized as supporting the poet's narrative, the script to be followed is rather restrictive: It requires both involvement with and abandonment of (or abandonment by) the feminine form of the happy substitute. The traditional story of Troilus and Criseyde is readily seen as a recursion to the action of the *Argonautica,* but Chaucer presents the audience with a highly limited narrative exchange of the woman between men.[55] Rather than a maternally approved script of feminine seduction and consequent Oedipal theft, Chaucer and his literate precursors develop a narrative of faithless abandonment: The traitorous father Calkas abandons Criseyde in a show of indifference; Troilus and Criseyde enjoy their union in a love seemingly approved by the father's absence; however, Calkas reasserts his authority to summon Criseyde, and Troilus must convey the woman to the forbidding father; the woman, in turn, is "untrewe," establishing a new connection with Diomede. Chaucer adds a number of complexities to this basic narrative frame, but even in this structural repetition of the Oedipal quest, the increased dominion of the father is apparent, particularly in the resurgent expression of his power despite his apparent abandonment.

A striking aspect of this epic as recursion, especially important to this chapter, is that the Troilus-Criseyde story, cloaked though it is in the matter of Troy, is entirely a product of literate societies in the medieval period.[56] The earliest version of the story is contained in *Le Roman de Troie* of Benoît de Sainte-Maure (c. 1155 CE), out of which arise numerous retellings, including that of Chaucer.[57] The written quality of the tale is pointedly revealed in the fears of scriptedness attributed to Benoît's Briseida: "Henceforth no good will be written of me, nor any good song sung. No such fortune or happiness will be mine henceforth."[58] In Chaucer's poem the written quality is highlighted; for example, Criseyde's first appearance marks her as a primarily—and primary—textual creature:

> Among thise othere folk was Criseyda,
> In widewes habit blak; but natheles,
> Right as oure firste lettre is now an A,
> In beaute firste so stood she, makeles.
>
> (1.169–72)

This short comparison—a significant departure from Boccaccio's rose among the violets—is usually seen, following J. L. Lowes, as a compliment to Queen Anne.[59] While a plausible reading, it limits the passage and hence Criseyde to little more than a consequential historical pun. Just as in the letters exchanged by the lovers, identity is here reduced to a cipher, and a thoroughly ambivalent cipher at that.[60] Criseyde, "In widewes habit blak," implies death and the end of things, in addition to her status as "makeles" point of origin. This is already significant in the context of her relations with Troilus, but the familiar line from Revelation ("I am the Alpha and the Omega" [1.8]) adds considerably. The comparable lines from Isaiah are also pertinent: "I am the first and the last; besides me there is no god. Who is like me?" (44.6). "Who is like me?" forms a suitable comment considering the critical history of Criseyde, and her role as an unknowable signifier.[61] Interpreting Criseyde as a textual token of the beginning and end of all things in Chaucer's poem is not too surprising: She quite clearly works this way for Troilus in the initiation and conclusion of his "double sorwe." The paradoxical double status of Criseyde is reinforced by what Donald Howard has called the "cinematic" effect of her introduction, in black, among the knights and ladies who are "Ful wel arayed . . . both for the seson and the feste" (1.167–68). Similarly, though she stands meekly "ful lowe and stille allone, Byhynden other folk," last in the temple, she is "first" as well, "With ful assured lokyng and manere" (1.178–82).[62] Though textually and visually more emphatic, this doubleness of Criseyde is directly akin to that of Medea, and continues throughout the epic. Criseyde's doubleness *appears* to present the traditionally dichotomous feminine, madonna and whore, a dichotomy that applies comfortably enough to other inscriptions of Criseyde, but that remains unsatisfying for explaining her role in Chaucer's epic.

Arthur Mizener and, more recently, Carolyn Dinshaw, have summed up earlier positions on the status or "character" of Criseyde. Mizener glances at the attitude of Root, calling his version of the heroine "calculating, emotionally shallow, and a drifter from the first."[63] Kittredge contrasts sharply, seeing Criseyde as "amorous, gentle, affectionate, and charming altogether, but fatally impressionable and yielding."[64] Dinshaw updates this with her feminist critique of E. Talbot Donaldson and D. W. Robertson, two similarly influential, diametrically opposed critics. She points out that although they are "theoretically antagonistic, in practice they make very similar critical moves: a vigorous limitation of the disturbing, a rigorous structure controlling the unstable and threateningly destabilizing, are the foundations of both approaches . . . the delimitation of the text's meaning is achieved through a rejection or containment of what is constituted as feminine" (1989, 37–38). According to Dinshaw, in short, both Donaldson and Robertson "read like men" in their desire to "totalize" the poem. Where Robertson's exegetical reading allies Criseyde strictly with Fortune and the mutable world, and hence rejects her, Donaldson's argument is based in part upon the notion outlined above of her character as duplicitous and paradoxical. He argues, in fact, that this is the whole point, that her complexity is "the unpredictability, the instability, of even the most lovely of mortal women" (in Dinshaw 1989, 37). As Dinshaw points out in this connection by paraphrasing Donaldson, " 'You can never understand a woman' is a way of understanding her. Criseyde becomes a sign of instability, compared to and subsumed by Heavenly stability, and the poem's totality is asserted and assured" (1989, 37). That is, while the traditional dichotomy applied to the feminine may indeed provide the kind of "complexity" labeled as "psychological" in the portraits of Medea and Criseyde, it also provides an excuse for closing down the feminine as limited to one, the other, or (as in the case of Donaldson) both. Thus Criseyde appears to be not only the marker or mirror of desire for Troilus, but a mirror of critical desire as well.

In recent criticism Criseyde has been read as embedded quite thoroughly in the scripts of others. Dinshaw, for example, analyzes Criseyde's "slydynge" as integral to patriarchal structures of control, as part of the "traffic in women." This is intimately connected, I think, with the notion of Criseyde as fundamentally a literary token, one that mediates Chaucer's interaction with tradition.

As Mieszkowski notes, Criseyde's self-reproachful speech in Chaucer ap-

pears largely unmotivated when compared to the corresponding passage in
Benoît (cited above). Briseida has had good evidence of her name being ill-used;
Troilus' vociferous insults are being repeated "a hundred times a day" in both
of the warring camps. In Chaucer, however, Criseyde's speech is based on the
intertextual reputation of Criseyde—"her fourteenth-century position as an antifeminist type of the fickle woman":[65]

> Allas! of me, unto the worldes ende,
> Shal neyther ben ywriten or ysonge
> No good word, for thise bokes wol me shende.
> O rolled shal I ben on many a tonge!
> Thorughout the world my belle shal be ronge!
> And wommen moost wol haten me of alle.
> Allas, that swich a cas me sholde falle!
>
> Thei wol seyn, in as much as in me is,
> I have hem don dishonour, weylaway!
> Al be I nat the first that dide amys,
> What helpeth that to don my blame awey?
>
>   (5.1058–68)

This lament over her literary fate manages to suggest the possible unfairness of
her condemnation, as well as its status as a violation, a "shending" that reiterates the (sexual as well as linguistic) promiscuity of Criseyde: "O rolled shal I
ben on many a tonge!"

Moreover, her status as sexual and textual token is strongly emphasized by
the narrator's attempts to excuse her despite what "the storie telleth us" (5.1037,
1051). Phrases like this (applied to the already scripted narrative) surround
Criseyde's speech. In addition, her lament is followed by the narrator's quibble
over the time required for Criseyde's second seduction (couched again in terms
of "auctour" and "bokes"), and his celebrated desire, even so, to excuse her:

> But trewely, how longe it was bytwene
> That she forsok hym for this Diomede,
> Ther is non auctour telleth it, I wene.
> Take every man now to his bokes heede;
> He shal no terme fynden, out of drede.
> For though that he bigan to wowe hire soone,
> Er he hire wan, yet was ther more to doone.
>
> Ne me ne liste this sely womman chyde
> Forther than the storye wol devyse.
> Hire name, allas! is punysshed so wide,

That for hire gilte it oughte ynough suffise.
And if I myghte excuse hire any wise,
For she so sory was for hire untrouthe,
Iwis, I wolde excuse hire yet for routhe.

(5.1086–99)

This desire to excuse, one of the pillars of Donaldson's argument that the narrator himself falls in love with Criseyde, displays the ambivalent stance of the
narrator toward that which "the storie tells." That is, Criseyde herself serves as
the ground of the poet's ambivalent relationship with tradition: Just as the attempt is made to provide an "excuse" for her, so she provides an "excuse" for
him to detach himself from exact repetition. On the one hand, the poet needs
to repeat that old story faithfully—must be like the father; on the other hand,
the poet perceives that story as both constrictive and insufficient (locking
Criseyde into actions but failing to account for such actions), and this allows
the poet to distance himself from the precursor narratives. "The storie telleth
us," but it never tells enough to satisfy. In the passage above, for example, the
lack of a specific duration for the betrayal provides a gap for the curious—a gap
that is carefully exposed, and then as carefully *not filled* by the infinitude of acts
required of Diomede ("Er he hire wan, yet was ther more to doone").[66] This strategy is repeated any number of times in *Troilus and Criseyde* (Donaldson 1983, 65–
83). There are two points especially worth emphasizing in Chaucer's strategy
of questioning the precursor, however: First, the heightened (and often visual)
awareness of the written letter as a powerful determinative force (unsurprisingly, a force inscribed almost exclusively by male "auctours"); second, the
specific techniques Chaucer uses to deal with such paternal, originative inscriptions.

Most simply, this strategy involves the reification and consequent dismantling of the earlier narrative. That is, the mere act of saying that "the storie
telleth," rather than simply telling the story, is an act of metaphoric distancing
that gains power for the naming agent; similarly, as Lord and Goody point out,
such forms of artful, skeptical distancing, unlike the examples from oral cultures given earlier, are inextricable from literacy (Goody 1977, 43; Lord 1960,
129–31). Thus the narrator, choosing from his stock of "bokes olde," establishes
his greatest difference from the epic tradition in choosing the matter for recursion. This act of differentiation is not as easy as it may appear, despite the opening lines of the poem:

The double sorwe of Troilus to tellen,
That was kynge Priamus sone of Troye,

In lovynge, how his aventures fellen
Fro wo to wele, and after out of joie,
My purpos is, er that I parte fro ye.

    (1.1–5)

"My purpos is," he says, but fifty lines later the poet is still attempting to find
a way "streght to [his] matere,"

In which ye may the double sorwes here
Of Troilus in lovynge of Criseyde,
And how that she forsook hym er she deyde.

    (1.53–56)

"*Streght* to my matere," however, hardly does justice to the process involved;
there follows a stanza to summarize the setting—already well known from
other poets. Following this is the extended discussion of the poem's primary
paternal figure, the "lord of gret auctorite," Calkas. The linguistically powerful Calkas himself, through his "forknowynge" and through the god of poetry,
Apollo, knows that Troy will be destroyed, and his actions parallel those of
the poet:

For which to departen softely
Took purpos ful this forknowynge wise
And to the Grekes oost ful pryvely
He stal anon; and they, in curteys wise,
Hym diden bothe worship and sevyse,
In trust that he hath konnynge hem to rede
In every peril which that is to drede.

    (1.78–84)

Calkas and his "purpos"—to depart (and hence survive by telling)—echo, in
inverted form, the poet's described purpose of telling "er that I parte fro ye."
In some sense, the poet cannot go straight to his "matere" until Calkas has departed. Even Calkas' paternal abandonment, however, allows only a few stanzas
dealing with Criseyde before the poet must return to, even name, certain precursors. Venturing to say that the poet's "matere" is also his *mater*, and that this
maternal figure is specifically Criseyde, may seem to border on the playful, since
he clearly indicates his argument as "the double sorwe of Troilus." The doubleness of Criseyde as origin and end, however, and hence her status as the "double
sorwe" itself, put in question the precise centrality of Troilus. More telling,
though, is the particular question of "the matere" that drives the poet back to-

ward his precursors in the traditional story—toward, as it were, the patter of Troy.[67]

> But wheither that she children hadde or noon,
> I rede it naught, therfore I late it goon.
>
> The thynges fellen, as they don of werre,
> Bitwixen hem of Troie and Grekes ofte . . .
>
> . . . .
>
> But how this town com to destruccion
> Ne falleth naught to purpos me to telle;
> For it were here a long digression
> Fro my matere, and yow to long to dwelle.
> But the Troian gestes, as they felle,
> In Omer, or in Dares, or in Dite,
> Whoso that kan may rede hem as they write.
>
> (1.132–47)

The first question above, that of Criseyde's offspring, is deliberately exposed and left as question. In Benoît, the character is *la pucele,* a virgin; in Boccaccio, the question is answered in the negative;[68] in Chaucer, a gap is created in the precursor narratives, highlighting their insufficiency ("I rede it naught"), but at the same time emphasizing the narrator's fidelity to those inscribed narratives ("therfore I late it goon"). The juxtaposition of his concern with maternity and his retreat into paternal narratives is not puzzling, simply Oedipal. The puzzling thing is that the narrator's fidelity is explicitly phrased as an abandonment: "[T]herfore I late it goon." This is puzzling only for the moment. The following stanzas remind us that to inscribe the paternal narrative (actions "as they felle, In Omer, or in Dares, or in Dite") is precisely to abandon the question of maternity and of "matere" in favor of masculine metonymic bonding (through inscription and through combat). As in the psychoanalytic formulation of male identity (as contingent upon separation from the mother), so the identity of the faithful male inheritor of Homer, Dares Phrygius, and Dictys Cretensis would depend on "a long digression / Fro my matere." Moreover, this would be an identity based on aggression—"The thynges [which] fellen, as they don of werre, / Bitwixen hem of Troie and Grekes ofte"—and on other kinds of exchange, as the balance of the stanza makes clear, and as we have seen before in discussing *Beowulf.*

What requires more explanation, however, is the poet's adoption of a clearly different identity. Rather than aligning himself fully with the patriarchal tradition, he shifts back and forth, almost himself "Bitwixen hem of Troie and Grekes ofte." In one sentence he as much as calls the *Iliad* "a long digression," but in the next refers his audience to Homer and the pseudo-historians as the ultimate "auctorite." This ambivalence—repeating but refusing to repeat—is well conveyed in the ambiguity of the phrase I have read as "abandonment" above; "therfore I late it goon" leaves the question of who abandons whom distinctly undecided, just as it does the question of Criseyde's maternity.[69] The narrator's ghostly precursor, his pretended "source" in Lollius, creates additional complexity for the narrator's identity. Before adding this complexity to the present discussion, however, the narrator deserves some attention within a psychoanalytic frame: His careful attention to the omissions of his precursors, as well as to their commissions, strikes responsive chords throughout the epic and, not surprisingly, in twentieth-century psychoanalytic theory.

The scopophilic instinct discussed earlier can be seen as having special applicability to *Troilus and Criseyde;* the ethos of courtly love in which the poem is framed makes the human gaze essential to the poem. Freud discusses the gaze in more detail in the following passage: "It is usual for most normal people to linger to some extent over the intermediate sexual aim of a looking that has a sexual tinge to it; indeed, this offers them a possibility of directing some proportion of their libido on to higher artistic aims. On the other hand, this pleasure in looking [scopophilia] becomes a perversion (a) if it is restricted exclusively to the genitals, or (b) if it is connected with the overriding of disgust (as in the case of *voyeurs* . . .), or (c) if, instead of being *preparatory* to the normal sexual aim, it supplants it" (1905b, 69–70). The active form of scopophilia, looking, is paired with the passive form, exhibitionism. This in itself is suggestive enough to a reading of Chaucer, but becomes particularly so in Freud's application of the scopophilic instincts to "the development of beauty in the sexual object": "The progressive concealment of the body which goes along with civilization keeps sexual curiosity awake. This curiosity seeks to complete the sexual object by revealing its hidden parts" (1905b, 69). In light of this passage, what has been labeled as "courtly love" explains itself readily as a forerunner of Freud's scopophilic instinct and more recent theories of the gaze. An ingenious medieval amalgam of Platonism and heterosexuality, courtly love tries to theorize the erotogenic power of the gaze in terms of the nearly unattainable object (deliberately chosen as above the lover's station), and the necessarily furtive means by which the love affair is conducted. "Love" is defined sensually, according to Andreas Capellanus, as "a certain passion, born within one and proceeding from sight of, and from immoderate reflection upon, the physical appearance of a person of the opposite sex; because of it one desires above all things to become possessed of the other's embraces and to fulfill all the promptings of love, by common consent, in the other's arms."[70] A courtly love, necessarily "illicit and, for the most part, adulterous," is one that must needs be kept secret, and involves the "furtive" conduct of the lovers as they exhibit and conceal their desires—*Qui non celat, amare non potest.*[71] A necessary aspect of the system is that the love thus created must not be too easily obtained,[72] but rather depends for much of its power on the higher position of the woman, who should be embedded within a marriage. The issue that creates barriers to the culmination of (as Freud would put it) "the normal sexual aim" is not that of chastity or physical fidelity, but the social force of shame or scandal, most frequently expressed by means of the forbidding figure of the powerful lord who was the lady's husband. As Dodd remarks, "Chastity might be dispensed with without scruple, but a sullied reputation was unbearable."[73] Freud formulates his own version: "The force which opposes scopophilia, but which may be overridden by it . . . is *shame*" (1905b, 70).

The scopophilic instinct, then, provides an Oedipal focus to much of the interaction between Troilus and Criseyde, as well as appropriately emphasizing the role of the gaze in the initiation and maintenance of their relationship. It also explicates the "vicarious" involvement of Pandarus and of the narrator in the love-relationship—their voyeuristic and "abnormal" satisfaction in abetting, orchestrating, and observing others' behavior in love. Similarly, the extreme intertextuality of the poem, the narrator's insistent presentations of text and of the gaps within texts, make sense in light of the textual collision that generates the Oedipus complex. The parental text, associated with "cessation of reflection," becomes dominant, while the child's ongoing research creates a new text that (until its suppression) questions the precursor (1908c, 192).

In the parallel collision of texts observed in Chaucer's epic, the "truth" of the earlier narrative is opened to question by the later; the child, through further research and reflection—conducted, as Freud notes, in secrecy—explores the gaps in the parental tale of origins until questions cannot be answered. Quite significantly, then, the first gap the narrator opens in the precursor's story is "wheither that she children hadde or noon." Similarly, the first speech of Troilus suggests that his own researches are sexual in nature:

> "I have herd told, pardieux, of youre lyvynge,
> Ye loveres, and youre lewed observaunces."
>
> (1.197–98)[74]

Since his research thus far appears to be through hearsay, in the opening scene he goes about "On this ladye, and now on that, lokynge," until his sudden access to new knowledge conveyed in the vision of Criseyde:

> ... thorugh a route
> His eye percede, and so depe it wente,
> Til on Criseyde it smot, and ther it stent.
>
>   (1.269–73)

The nature of Troilus' discovery is not yet clear to him, but it leaves him at an impasse, brooding throughout most of book 1. Not only is he deliberately speechless in his encounter with Pandarus, but immediately upon the exchange of glances with Criseyde, an awareness of danger seems to affect his sight, conveyed with the analogous phallic "drawing in of horns" and abstention from further research:

> And though he erst hadde poured up and down,
> He was tho glad his hornes in to shrinke;
> Unnethes wiste he how to loke or wynke.
>
>   (1.299–301)

The reasons for such a withdrawal from further research may be best explicated in the similar unwillingness to speak Criseyde's name, and the uncertainty of Troilus as to the results of his new knowledge.[75] The fact that Pandarus suggests as much in the following passage—that Troilus has perceived something he cannot fully comprehend—hints at the importance of sexual difference to childhood sexual research.

> "What! slombrestow as in a litargie?
> Or artow lik an asse to the harpe,
> That hereth sown whan men the strynges plye,
> But in his mynde of that no melodie
> May sinken hym to gladen, for that he
> So dul ys of his bestialite?"

> And with that, Pandare of his wordes stente;
> And Troilus yet hym nothyng answerde,
> For-why to tellen nas nat his entente
> To nevere no man, for whom that he so ferde,
> For it is seyd, "man maketh ofte a yerde
> With which the makere is hymself ybeten
> In sondry manere," as thise wyse treten.
>
>   (1.730–42)

The radical disconfirmation of his former system of knowledge develops a set of unanswered questions that are repressed in favor of "cessation of reflection," as in the "bestialite" of the ass. In Freudian terms, for the male child to admit to the fact of female sexuality—what Freud sees as the appearance of castration—is to admit to the possibility of being castrated himself (1908c, 195; 1924, 321). Hence arises the fear of realizing such a possibility in speech, as well as the telling aphorism—being punished through the rod of one's own making.[76]

An explanation of this first vision of Criseyde as a discovery of sexual difference is reinforced by Criseyde's initial presentation as "so bright a sterre" placed "under cloude blak" (1.175).[77] In the passage above, the threat of castration is conveyed by means of proverbial wisdom, a form of precursor text expressly associated with Pandarus. Troilus attempts to deny the further applicability of such narratives (1.752-60), but the flexible Pandarus is not the forbidding agent that Troilus initially fears. Rather, his proverbial wisdom is, exactly like the fabricated precursor narrative of Lollius, flexible, and susceptible of multiple interpretations. To extend this, just as Calkas is allied with the discursively powerful paternal "auctorite" that counsels the abandonment of the maternal "matere," so Pandarus is allied with Lollius, making vision, speech, seduction (and epic) possible. These possibilities are only allowed, however, through various and ample refractions: the many fabrications;[78] the gaps and lacunae afforded by patriarchal codes as well as texts;[79] the vicarious satisfactions of voyeurism and instrumentality.[80]

Troilus' conversion to love, aided by the agency of Pandarus as an approving father, is a conversion to a fantasy of Oedipal fulfillment—to Criseyde as a happy substitute. In this Troilus is parallel to the narrator, who converts to the "matere" of love by means of the fantasized Lollius. The reiterated image of the "sterelees" boat (1.415-18, 2.1-5) seeking safe harbor in this "tempestous matere" provides the clearest example of their parallel situations.[81] The narrator, of course, has an additional distance that makes him more like Pandarus than Troilus, gaining satisfaction like Pandarus through his attention to others' acts of love: As Pandarus puts it, they both "hoppe alwey byhynde" in the dance of love (2.1106-7). The ghostly presence of Lollius functions, then, as a textual father who authorizes the narrator's investigation of his "matere," and further authorizes the stance of skepticism, questioning, and difference toward other versions of the story.[82] In the close of Chaucer's epic, however, as the abandonment and consequent displacement of Troilus become crucial, the narrator turns more steadily against this "auctorite" as well. While Lollius authorizes much, he cannot condone an utter disregard for the story so well known. Arthur Mizener justifiably emphasizes the determining power of "the story," in reaction to the many "character studies" of Criseyde: "It may appear gratuitous to say that Criseyde is unfaithful because the story makes her so, but it is just the insufficient attention to this possibility which has made it seem necessary to prove that there was from the start some tragic flaw in her character which motivated her betrayal of Troilus."[83] Mizener's emphasis on the scriptedness of the abandonment is related to many studies concerned with determinism in *Troilus and Criseyde*.[84] The traditional story, the constraining patriarchal culture, the machinations of fortune and destiny, the internal inconsistencies of the characters' views, even the actions of Calkas himself—all are circumstances that militate against the continuance of union, and, as suggested at the opening of this chapter, militate in the form of patriarchal supervention of the relationship. As this submission to "necessitee" (as he sees it) is forced upon Troilus, so the pattern of the story is forced upon the narrator.[85] Both Pandarus and Lollius, unwilling to shrink from the hard lessons of book 5, retreat from their positions as beneficent authorities as they acquiesce in the forces of closure—the abandonment of the "matere," and as well the abandonment of Criseyde to her textually mandated abandonment of Troilus. Pandarus' silence is often quoted: "I kan namore seye" (5.1743); Lollius, on the other hand, is last mentioned by name a little earlier (5.1653), where he describes the coat "rent from Diomede" that Troilus reads and weeps, for he

> on the coler fond withinne
> A broche, that he Criseyde yaf that morwe
> That she from Troie moste nedes twynne,
> In remembraunce of hym and of his sorwe.
> And she hym leyde ayeyn hire feith to borwe
> To kepe it ay! But now ful wel he wiste,
> His lady nas no lenger on to triste.
>
> (5.1660–66)

The problem with this otherwise affecting scene is that this brooch that was Troilus' (as "the storie telleth us" [5.1037–41]) appears to be a creation of book 5. Possibly this is a newly invented brooch, but there appears to be a rather sharp inconsistency with the actual exchange of gifts in book 3, where the lovers "entrechaungeden hire rynges"; these the narrator cannot describe, as there is no authority for it. However, when he comes to the book 3 brooch, he is most emphatic, as though his authority were certain as well:

> [They] entrechaungeden hire rynges,
> Of which I kan nought tellen no scripture;
> But wel I woot, a broche, gold and asure,
> In which a ruby set was lik an herte,
> Criseyde hym yaf, and stak it on his sherte.
>
> (3.1368–72)[86]

Criseyde here gives Troilus the brooch. While this is a minor point, it seems worthy of remark that the fabricated precursor is specifically implicated in the textual error that fabricates the clinching proof of Criseyde's transfer of affections. It may be merely that Chaucer, like Homer, nods. But it may be more satisfying to attribute such nodding to Lollius. To suppose that this carefully described gift and its giving are intended to have *no* consequence is disingenuous. To suppose them mistakes, given the redundancy of specification, the important last, end-stopped line in the stanza that the act of giving occupies, as well as the manner that the ruby "set lik an herte" reiterates the imagery of Criseyde's earlier dream, would be, I think, rather odd. The puzzle that remains for such an argument, one that must be left, unfortunately, for a later study, is the following: If the invention of the book 5 brooch is intended as a significant gap in the narrative of Lollius, why does the narrator not bring it more clearly forth, make something of it? One might revert to the parallel example of Pandarus, whose condemnation of Criseyde is allowed to stand, despite Troilus' disagreement, his inability, as he says "To unloven [Criseyde] a quarter of a day" (5.1698).

The conclusion of *Troilus and Criseyde* has with good reason been likened to "a literary and linguistic apocalypse."[87] The contradiction and collision of texts is unnerving, and we are indeed at the end of things, for as Troilus has been forced to a recursion—to the abandonment of the happy substitute—so too the narrator must abandon his "matere." Again, as in the poem's opening, at least one collision is phrased in terms of the difference between the "matere" of the poem and that other, *Aeneid*-like poem which would more directly recur to the precursor: "The armes of this ilke worthi man" (5.1766). The battles of Troilus, it should be noted, involve the continuing rivalry with Diomede, which is both an extension of the Oedipal conflict and a narcissistic attempt at reestablishing the autonomy and centrality of the self. That is, like Achilles, but with the additional burden of the Oedipal struggle, Troilus attempts to eradicate that mirroring other—the aggressively invested fraternal version of self in "this sodeyn Diomede." The narrator's brief gestures toward writing (so Homerically) "[t]he wrath, as I bigan yow for to seye, / Of Troilus" (5.1800), are interrupted by a fragmented digression and next by Troilus' death. The digression *appears* to involve the abandonment or sacrifice of the "matere" to the patriarchal tradition, the precursors (5.1770, 5.1786–92), thus establishing the poet's metonymic continuity with the tradition of epic.[88] Sandwiched between Dares and Virgil, however, between these forms of atonement and masculine solidarity, is the critical puzzle of the address to women in his audience: The speaker distances himself from those "other bokes" that record the guilt of Criseyde, and suggests that his own book, by its speaking *between* these "other bokes," may be read, indeed,

should be understood as not only for men, "But moost for wommen that bitraised be / Thorugh false folk" (5.1776–81). How this advice works within the
poem needs to be more fully explored in terms of the figure of Criseyde, but in
this context it clearly reinforces the substantial critique of the precursor texts;
indeed, it seems to be allowed only because of the otherwise devout recursions
that cluster round.[89]

> "What aileth yow to be thus wery soone,
> And namelich of wommen?"
> *Troilus and Criseyde* 2.211–12

With the ending of *Troilus and Criseyde* we can also bring together other aspects of this chapter. The *Odyssey* requires the continuing sacrifice of the hero—
the continuing cost of survival with the happy substitute—as a series of narcissistic compromises, scripted beyond the epic in Odysseus' future pilgrimage to
a loss of identity, to the place where the defining oar is no more than a winnow-
ing fan. Similarly, Jason's union with Medea, which appears as an ongoing
struggle with the paternal, is a union ultimately doomed (in the traditional
story) to death and fragmentation. In Chaucer's recursion to the matter of Troy,
however, the focus developed is that of the "double sorwe": Troilus desires but
fears the cost of his desire, and Troilus desires but is displaced. Each of these
sorrows, however, is consequently ameliorated by different forms of the happy
substitute: first in the maternal, metonymic union of the love affair with
Criseyde; second in the metaphorically distanced, vicarious form of metonymy
found in Troilus' postmortem vision. As many a reader of the epic has remarked, this final vision with its accompanying "disembodied laughter" is profoundly unsatisfying. It echoes with familiar kinds of patriarchal closure used
(before and after Chaucer) to isolate the traditional Criseyde as an emblem of
the threatening female; moreover, concluding the poem this way appears to contradict strongly much of the earthly love the poem itself has celebrated.

   This contradiction lies between, on the one hand, a form of fulfillment that
is consonant with a patriarchal understanding, and, on the other hand, a form
of fulfillment that is more directly understood as Oedipal in focus, in direct disregard of the paternal role. That is, it lies between recursion to the precursor
and involvement with the "matere." A more familiar view of the same contradiction is that of C. S. Lewis, who remarks on the conflict in the poem between
Augustinean *contemptus mundi* and the opposed *joie de vivre,* which seems, at
times, so characteristic of Chaucer.[90] After his death, Troilus moves on to a state
of vast indifference, a contempt of the world. Frequently this is equated with an

increasing likeness to God as Troilus grows indifferent to the things of earth, but the poet's view of God seems far different from his view of Troilus. Such an "indifference" as the dead Troilus assumes, dependent as it is upon those very things of earth that he looks back upon, is hardly an attitude one feels comfortable *calling* indifference. Rather, in this final vision, Troilus regresses to the point at which he began the epic, in mockery of, but seemingly obsessed by, the "lewed observaunces" of lovers. From this pretended state of indifference (cloaking, as will be recalled, a penetrating curiosity) that seemed to arise from ignorance, Troilus has moved to a form of indifference that is plainly hostile, and moreover, is now aggressive in its voyeuristic observance of the same acts, the primal scene writ large:

> And down from thennes faste he gan avyse
> This litel spot of erthe, that with the se
> Embraced is, and fully gan despise
> This wrecched world. . . .
>
> . . . .
> . . . he lough right at the wo
> Of hem that wepten for his deth so faste;
> And dampned al oure werk that foloweth so
> The blynde lust, the which that may nat laste.
>
> (5.1814–24)

The difference lies in his willingness to "despise" and condemn the "embrace" and "al oure werk" devoted to "blynde lust" (including, of course, the poet's "matere of lovynge"). In this carefully distanced act of violent indifference Troilus repeats the patriarchal narrative of Calkas—the abandonment of women.[91]

In spite of Chaucer's interesting assertion that *this* is the end of Troilus and "Swych fyn hath al his grete worthynesse" (5.1829), which reads in divergent ways, he does not avoid the patriarchal abandonment of women as effectively as we might wish. The repetition of the precursor may appear to dominate, even though he addresses the "yonge, fresshe folkes" ("he *or* she") (5.1835) in the image of God, and even in spite of his too-formulaic reiteration, in the final line, of the "matere" of his epic: "For love of mayde and moder thyn benigne" (5.1869).

The pivotal point of the story is the transfer of Criseyde from Troy to the Greeks, and this act of traffic in women clearly raises concerns with fidelity, centrality, and most important, replaceability. Clearly enough it is the instigation of Calkas—the returning authority of the father—that abridges the happy substitute of union with the maternal so recently achieved. The paternal authority, however, is not that which seals the second of Troilus' sorrows; rather, the metonymic union is abridged directly and symmetrically by Troilus' mirroring opposite, the "sodeyn Diomede" who appears as if from nowhere to displace the hero. The "traffic in women" is not in this poem merely Oedipal but fraternal. Indeed, when compared with Apollonius, the Oedipal concern in Chaucer seems—not exactly weakened—but rather diffused into the patriarchal social structure. That is, while the paternal assertion is conveyed as more efficacious in Chaucer, its intimidating quality appears to have diminished.[92] The exchange of Criseyde results not merely in the birth of Diomede as the usurper of Troilus' place, but in the similarly symmetrical appearance of two other figures, Antenor and Toas (or Thoas): the Greeks, that is, trade the (later traitorous) Antenor for Criseyde and Toas (4.137–38). The appearance of Toas is especially brief (this line alone), and therefore rather puzzling. While the splitting of Troilus into two distinct fraternal (but opposed) images is simple enough to explicate, the splitting into three significant and one insignificant brothers-in-arms is distinctly less so. What appears to be happening, given the psychoanalytic frame thus far found useful, is a doubled splitting reflective of the new sibling relationship. On the one hand, Criseyde's departure creates a new, usurping other (Diomede); on the other, it adds to the "Troian" fold a (suspect) brother-in-arms (Antenor). Similarly, though in the main Troilus is forced to follow the traditional masculine path of separation, he too is split. Some aspect of himself—the wishful "kyng" among the Greeks, Toas—remains closely connected with Criseyde:[93] Calkas bids the messengers that "for Antenor [that they] bryngen hom kyng Toas and Criseyde" (4.137–38).

A more complete reading of the poem would also examine the important dream of Troilus (with its primal scene); the hero's increasing disenchantment with the "matere" of love; and Troilus' abandonment of feminine narratives in his aggressive scorn for Cassandre (5.1520–26); but Criseyde awaits us.

Janet Adelman, in her analysis of Shakespeare's *Troilus and Cressida*, explains clearly a stance similar to the one I have sketched thus far with regard to the way Criseyde is viewed by Troilus, by patriarchal society, and by the literary tradition that Chaucer struggles with but also repeats: "Her sexual betrayal is of course the ultimate sign of her status as opaque other: when she gives herself to Diomed, she demonstrates to Troilus that she is both unknowable and unpossessable. . . . At issue here, I suspect, is a primitive fantasy in which separation is infidelity: for the infant, the mother's separateness constitutes the first betrayal; insofar as she is not merely his, she is promiscuously other. . . . [S]eparation, opaque otherness, and sexual betrayal are one."[94] Dinshaw, by her adaptation of Lévi-Strauss, suggests a similar conclusion for Criseyde, arguing that the famous "slydynge of corage" attributed to Criseyde is exactly what is *required* for the maintenance of the patriarchal status quo

(1989, 57–62). Women in Chaucer's Troy, as in Homer's, are tokens, "crystallizations of patriarchal exchange."[95] That is, they are read rather than readers, bodies or texts passed between groups of men at war (56). In Dinshaw's perceptive argument on the scenes of reading in *Troilus and Criseyde*, she suggests Chaucer's awareness that the totalizing exclusion of the feminine—the act of "reading like a man"—*is* only an act, not a "natural" way of reading. Criseyde's acts of reading thus contain "hints" toward a different kind of reading, one that "keeps the whole in view—every word of it" (1989, 55). Dinshaw deals in similar fashion with Pandarus' adoption of the "masculine" pose—"I hate, ywys, Crysede" (5.1732). By its status *as pose* his act of reading undermines the "natural" assumptions of the patriarchal system.

The difficulty with Dinshaw's reading is that, having deconstructed the bases of patriarchal reading which appear to govern the text, she does not deconstruct that reading itself, and thus sees the deliberate confusion of the conclusion (which Donaldson calls "a kind of nervous breakdown in poetry" [1983, 91]) as "markedly gendered," a typically masculine response conveying "movement toward unity, solidity and closure as an intense, emotional urgency. . . . Chaucer's critique reasons not the need but a misogynistic formulation and fulfillment of it" (1989, 47). This reading accepts too easily a monolithic understanding of the ending as a desperate drive toward closure, and tends to seal off even the "internal warfare" of the narrator suggested by Donaldson (1983, 91). In other words, Dinshaw is, in her own terms, "reading like a man." Clearly this position, like that of Pandarus, is expedient, and well within the tradition of twentieth-century criticism. But Chaucer's pyrotechnics in the ending of *Troilus and Criseyde* exaggerate (rather than close down) the distinction between a narrative of closure and an open-ended text, and leave the audience with the turmoil that lies between them. Moreover, insofar as the narrator has suggested a reading "moost for wommen that bitraised be," it seems unfortunate indeed not to approach that reading instead.

The poem does end, admittedly, but it is an ending that explicitly extends the doubled movement and sympathies of the poem. Donaldson's analysis, for example, in general pays close attention to this doubled pattern to the poem (where "every resolute thrust forward ends with a glance backward" [1983, 100]), and leaves the ending less monological than Dinshaw's: "The world he knows and the heaven he believes in grow ever farther and farther apart as the woeful contrast between them is developed, and ever closer and closer together as the narrator blindly unites them in the common bond of his love" (Donaldson 1983, 100). As the narrator, here quite Christ-like, attempts to unite heaven and earth through the "common bond of his love," so he attempts to resolve through love's mystery—the third term of the Trinity—the bipolar extremes that rule the narrative. His resolution of these extremes is most clear in terms of sexual difference, in his invocation of Christ's mercy for the sake of the "love of mayde and moder." Christ, like the narrator trying to bridge two contrasting narratives by (or as) love, is that which binds heaven and earth. The explicit contrast of the "sothefaste Crist" and Criseyde three stanzas earlier is here reiterated through the important term of "mercy" (5.1860, 1867, 1868), and sets up interesting reverberations in the text. For in the person of Criseyde such mercy is difficult to read, as Troilus acknowledges, seeing what he wants to see: "Though ther be mercy writen in youre cheere, God woot, the text ful hard is, soth, to fynde!" (3.1356–57). That is, though Christ appears legible, Criseyde does not. This is emphasized in the contrast that discusses Christ at the poem's end:

> For he nyl falsen no wight, dar I seye,
> That wol his herte al holly on hym leye
> And syn he best to love is, and most meke,
> What nedeth feynede loves for to seke?
>
>   (5.1845–48)

Though not without some trepidation ("dar I seye"), the text of Christ is more easily read than that of Criseyde. Christ's meekness leads to an ultimate victory. In the "muwet, milde, and mansuete" Criseyde (5.194), on the other hand, her meekness leads to her ultimate condemnation, or at least to her condemnation by what "the storie telleth." What "Men seyn" and what "the storie telleth" are throughout the poem exposed to question as possible lies, and occasionally to outright disagreement: "Men seyn—I not,—that she yaf hym hire herte" (5.1050). The question is actually left open: Does one believe what "Men seyn" about a woman? Does one believe what the narrator says? Moreover, what the narrator says is interesting, because he does not say that Criseyde did not give Diomede her heart, but rather, depending upon the manuscript or edition used ("nat," or "not") says either that he does not know, or that he does not say. My point is not, of course, that Criseyde is actually "true" to Troilus. My point, rather, is that, aware that his own perspective—like those of the *auctorites* he cites—is faulty, the narrator resists the urge to condemn her. This deliberately inscribed unknowability to Criseyde, the mystery of her which likens her to Christ (in her temporary appearance incarnate to Troilus) is not elided by the conclusion of the epic. Whereas Christian revelation allows a vision that is unbounded and inclusive of all—"Uncircumscript, and al maist circumscrive" (5.1865)—the Chaucerian revelation attempts to "uncircumscribe" the woman most subject to the limited human circumscription of "wikked speche" and what "Men seyn." Like the "mayde and moder" of the last line, who escapes traditional misogynistic condemnation by means of her connection with the "Uncircumscript," so Criseyde escapes such condemnation (in Chaucer) by means of the carefully unwritten.

To reiterate an earlier caution: This is not to say that Chaucer has faith or trust in Criseyde at all, only that he is aware that she need not be condemned by men for her guilt. Like the world itself, Criseyde is at once "a faire . . . that passeth soone as floures faire" (5.1840–41), and full of "this false worldes brotelnesse" (5.1832), and she goes beyond the human attempt to inscribe, just as she goes beyond the ending of the text itself.

Chaucer illustrates this difficulty of perspective better than I, through the process of Troilus' misguided and finally regressive attempts to deal with the absence of Criseyde. Once he knows Criseyde must leave, Troilus is unable to see her except as a positive or negative reflection of himself—that is, as a presence or an absence *to him.* This attitude is only emphasized by the violent indifference of his gaze from the eighth sphere, his abandonment of sympathy or mercy for those below. The merciless denial of worth to the world and the denial of sympathy to those "that wepten for his deth so faste" (5.1822), marks his denial of connection, and a creation (*contra* Robertson) of extreme solipsism. The poet's sympathetic view, on the other hand, is paralleled by that of Christ in its intimate connection and infinite mercy to the world. Moreover, this view allows us to suppose that existence on "this litel spot of erthe, that with the se Embraced is"—for all, but especially for the survivors "that wepten for his deth"— has unknown significance in a sympathetic and "Uncircumscript" heaven beyond the cynical laughter of Troilus.

Thus, it is precisely by means of her unknowability that Criseyde in Chaucer's poem escapes the traditional scripts of her behavior.[96] She cannot be entirely read or possessed by any of the men—characters or critics—who make the attempt. The poet's relative victory over the precursor may come about as a result of this awareness of—indeed, his construction of—Criseyde as an unknown. This is not to say that Criseyde becomes *merely* the "opaque other"; she is that, transparently enough. But Chaucer consistently attempts to develop her as a subject, and moreover, a subject who forms herself—in all her ambiguity— through language. Always, from the first letter she ever writes to the last, her words appear (to Troilus) to be "covered . . . under sheld" (2.1327), much as they appear in her dialogue. Though she is always more formed by what "Men seyn" than she is able to form herself through language, still, through the discrepancy between these systems of language, and through the fact that none of them can fully account for her, she escapes the poem with her subjectivity and her life intact. This description of Criseyde, however, sounds very like the description I have applied to Chaucer's recursion to his epic precursors: He reaches his "matere" by a carefully displayed pretense of being "like the father"; all the while he is writing something else, something "covered ... under sheld." Chaucer criticizes a too-simple view of the conventional *contemptus mundi,* but also acknowledges the value of that vision, if corresponding value and sympathy are maintained for "al oure werk," and "this litel spot of erthe." As Criseyde notes in her last letter,

> Ek gret effect men write in place lite;
> Th'entente is al, and nat the lettres space.
>
> (5.1630)

4

Fierce Loves and Faithless Wars

Milton, Macpherson, and the Inverted Epic

T HE EPIC POETS of the last chapter turn on their traditions as they confront an increasingly present, disturbingly parental written tradition, rather than an ephemeral oral tradition. The epics themselves thus turn from immediate narcissistic fulfillment toward the necessary (and occasionally happy) substitute. The earlier narcissistic narrative—achieving glory through death—is repeated, but it repeats by encoding the parental figures more powerfully as both source and object of the quest. The metonymic fulfillment through glory (*kleos*) best attained in oral epics through the ultimate separation of death (*thanatos*) undergoes its first and most important shift of emphasis, moving in the written epic (in part because it is written) toward a poetry of survival rather than of death. This new poetry necessarily focuses on strategies for negotiating a world in which fulfillment cannot be finally discovered. Such negotiations must be made from the perspective of the fallen, the "scattered remnant" that is left of a real or imagined (narcissistic) unity. The turning away from absolute narcissistic fulfillment in glorious death is a turning toward the "happy substitute," the near-perfect union figured in the Oedipal script as fusion with the maternal. As we move through the epic "hall of mirrors," however, we seem to find an increasing distortion, an increased inability to achieve the happy substitute. The "Fierce warres and faithfull loves" that can be seen as characteristic of the "successfully" negotiated Oedipal project (in the at least occasional displacement of the paternal for the poet's own recursion, and the happily substituted maternal), as seen briefly in the adventures of Spenser's Redcrosse Knight, are left behind. Instead of these, the Byronic formulation that heads this chapter suggests that the poet can be seen as inverting the tradition:

> "Fierce loves and faithless wars"—I am not sure
>   If this be the right reading—'tis no matter;
> The fact's about the same, I am secure;
>   I sing them both.[1]

The metonymic engagement becomes "fierce," intense but fraught with conflict, and violence becomes not "faithful" but radically unstable, an acting out of inconstancy and uncertainty. The explicit uncertainty—"I am not sure"—highlights the ambivalence clearly marked in the inverted epic. The "heroic self" within such poems is divided at its core and in all its expressions; the figure of narcissistic fulfillment balances against a background that appears as the very expression of the patriarchal script: As Pope phrased it, "To copy Homer is to copy Nature." Odysseus is able to return home; Jason and Medea return to Iolkos and the troubled continuation of Oedipal success.[2] The inverted epic, however, displays the interaction of conflicting forces or strategies, neither of which can clearly and finally be decided upon as effective, but which through the very process of their interaction allow a free space for poetic agency.

This inversive or ironic strategy reaches its most influential and perhaps simplest expression in John Milton's *Paradise Lost;* a more complex inversion takes place in the Ossianic epics of James Macpherson, and much of the chapter concerns his *Fingal* (first published in 1762). Though these strategies certainly appear in earlier epic, the "long century" of English literature (1660–1800) shows a marked predilection for the ironic doubling characteristic of inverted epic (what Margaret Anne Doody [1985] calls its "double-tonguedness"). This doubleness of voice manifests itself in an apparently strange division of epic discourse. On the one hand there is evidence of the power of the precursor texts: The famous translations of Homer and Virgil, combined with a significant number of "slavishly imitative" epics, suggest the dominance of the ancient models.[3] On the other hand, the marked reaction against those models is conveyed by the prevalence of satiric and parodic forms of the epic.[4] The wealth of criticism produced in these centuries, as well, bears witness to a powerful ambivalence with regard to the precursors. As Howard D. Weinbrot reminds me, Homer was "attacked throughout Europe as a poet unfit for a civilized world," yet remained "at the center of the battle between the ancients and the moderns."[5] Few epic works mediate effectively between the poles of devotion and antagonism, but many projected epics remained unwritten, imagined at least as neither imitative nor parodic. Milton's early desire to "break the Saxon phalanxes with British war" is well known,[6] but many of the poets who followed had similar desires. Dryden wanted to write an epic on the Black Prince, or else, following Spenser's voice (and Milton's desire), an Arthurian epic; Pope's youthful attempt to "collect all the beauties of the great epic writers" into his early, admittedly imitative *Alcander* gave way in later years to his dreams of an epic on Brutus, the mythical founder of Britain.[7]

These different manifestations of epic reflect a doubled (and in the case of

writers such as Thomas Chatterton and Macpherson, duplicitous) attitude toward tradition. The consistently realized separation of warfare from love (despite the intermingling of such concerns in classical sources) constitutes a strategic—and Oedipal—shift from an epic concern explicitly linked with warfare,
to a parodic concern with sexuality and, more generally, society. Dryden's prefatory "Account" of *Annus Mirabilis*, for example, asserts that war is the only great
subject for poetry: "All other greatness in subjects is only counterfeit . . . the
greatness of arms is only real."[8] On the other hand, writers like William Cowper
choose to "sing the Sofa" rather than arms and the man.[9] Pope provides a more
concentrated form of this division, his translation of the *Iliad* contrasting pointedly with *The Rape of the Lock* and the *Dunciad*.[10] In an Oedipal framework, the
aggressive attitude of the parodist appears to allow poets access to the feminine
or the maternal. By remaining passive before the law of the father, by abdicating the Oedipal conflict, poets can identify with the maternal and the feminine.
This passivity and feminine identification, however, lead the poets to a view
of themselves as threateningly feminine, and hence, to the misogyny and militant overcompensation common to an age of imperialist expansion.[11] While this
reading is useful as far as it goes, the dynamic is potentially more complex
than the gender-inflected hierarchy suggests. Macpherson's scornful reaction to
Gray's *Elegy* comments on the conflict over subject matter, but he draws the
boundaries of genre in terms of occupational status rather than gender status:
" 'Hoot!' cried Fingal [Macpherson], 'to write panegyrics upon a parcel of
damned rascals that did nething but plough the land and saw corn.' He considered that fighters only should be celebrated" (Boswell 1950, 186). This senti-
ment, like Dryden's, expresses the old and powerful notion that "serious" poetry is the domain of a discursive elite, concerning itself with ruling elites in
their proper realms of action.[12] It also hints that the basis of the conflict lies in
the apportionment of power, rather than, strictly speaking, either gender or oc-
cupation. Persistent metaphors of feminization, of degeneracy, of the unheroic
"age too late" (indeed, of Bloom's "belatedness" itself) *are* only metaphors for
a sense of passivity and powerlessness before the determinative force of the
past. Peter Laslett remarks on the lack of substantial critique of "placement" or
status within English society, but his remarks clearly apply to the important
place and dominant status of epic tradition as well: "In this society, subordina-
tion and politics were founded upon tradition. Therefore critical examination
of the reasons why some men were better placed than others was unlikely to
come about. This submissive cast of mind is almost universal in the statements
made by the men about themselves" (Laslett 1971, 183). As this chapter moves
from the age of Milton to that of Macpherson, we detect increasing effects of

social change in the strategies of the two poets, the first emphasizing the "more heroic virtue" of patience and submission over a Satanic narcissism, and the second depicting an inversion of that balance.[13]

> But first he grasps within his awful hand
> The mark of sov'reign pow'r, his magic wand.
> —Dryden, *Virgil's Aeneid* 4.354–55[14]

I have suggested a common bifurcation of the impulse toward epic among seventeenth- and eighteenth-century poets, conveying through translations and imitations the powerful urge toward recursion, and conversely a parodic, often aggressive reaction against the precursor.[15] Most often we encounter these in texts where one or the other goal appears to exercise the dominant influence, and we hesitate to apply the name of epic to Pope's Homer, or to his *Dunciad*, without insisting on the disclaimers of "translated" or "mock" (especially given the poet's own feeling that his *real* epic had yet to be written). Some works, however, orchestrate their struggles with precursor-epics so that their "double-tonguedness" appears—without qualifications—as epic. Rather than emphasizing one goal or the other, epics such as Milton's *Paradise Lost* and Macpherson's *Fingal* deliberately highlight *both* their metaphoric opposition to tradition *and* their metonymic contiguity with tradition; therein they find, at least temporarily, workable forms of agency, of narcissistic wholeness.

A closer look at the psychological ramifications of this divided impulse yields, not surprisingly, an analogue in Freud's formulation of the joke (*Witz*) and the uncanny (*unheimlich*): Both, as Elizabeth Wright points out, "participate in the double movement of the return of the repressed and the return of the repression."[16] Simultaneous metaphoric and metonymic goals are played against one another, resulting in a permitted form of rebellion against authority. As Freud puts it, "They make possible the satisfaction of an instinct (whether lustful or hostile) in the face of an obstacle that stands in its way. They circumvent this obstacle and in this way draw pleasure from a source which the obstacle had made inaccessible" (1905a, 105). As with the Oedipal narrative of exhibitionism explored in discussion of the *Odyssey*, jokes have the maternal as their aim, and the paternal as the primary obstacle. ("Smut" in particular is seen as "originally directed towards women" and "equated with attempts at seduction" [1905a, 97]). The joker, "hold[ing] fast to the original sources of verbal pleasure" in the preoedipal and prelinguistic, subverts the linguistic law of the father ("Reason, critical judgment, suppression") (1905a, 137). Inevitably, however, this return of the repressed must conclude with the return of the repression; as linguistic play, the joke is framed within patriarchal language, set aside as "joke."

Jokes, like analogous but more extensive forms in literature, enact this doubled movement most often by holding up for comparison contrasting systems of discourse.[17] Parody involves a careful, highly wrought "mis-translation" of one (usually elevated) discursive structure into another structure or set of structures. The latter is usually that of an assumed social context and language, one that the parodist and his or her audience share. This is related to our more usual understanding of translation, in that both involve a movement between the language of the originary text and the new poet's "mother tongue." The difference arises in the different strategies by which a new text is created. While both strategies affirm the influence of the original, parodic translation is most frequently an aggressive strategy, a joke on the tradition shared among contemporaries.[18] The metaphoric distance thus established between the original and the poet's own work highlights the earlier poem's weaknesses and pretensions, to the detriment of the original and to the narcissistic aggrandizement of the parodist.[19] Conventional translation, on the other hand (though still a "mis-translation"), is dedicated to the preservation and extension of the domain of the earlier poem. Rather than the "subversive mimicry" or "distorting mirror" of parody, we are presented with a loving mimesis of the precursor placed within the words of the mother tongue.[20]

These typically destructive and creative strategies show us, in simple form, two ways of reacting to the epic tradition. The simplest *combination* of these two is readily seen in the young Alexander Pope. "When I was twelve I wrote a kind of play. . . . It was a number of speeches from the *Iliad,* tacked together with verses of my own."[21] Taking apart and putting back together a precursor—the construction of a pastiche—did nothing new. The practice of centonism (the creation of "new" works from the dismembered corpus of an authority) was a common aspect of the medieval use of Virgil and other canonical authors; like the commonplace book, the cento is a useful tool. The important point, however, is that while the cento or pastiche (like translation) can have a destructive or a creative goal, in either case the text of the "father" must be (temporarily, at least) dismembered, in order to be re-membered.[22] As Ben Jonson put it in his *Discoveries,* a good writer learns from his or her poetic father by consuming his textual body, "not as a creature that swallows what it takes in, crude, raw, or undigested, but that feeds with an appetite, and hath a stomach to concoct, divide, and turn all into nourishment."[23] The point, of course, is not merely the consumption of the text, but the "turn[ing]" or troping of text into nourishment—into a usable, empowering past. This passage suggests the chief difficulty with recursive strategies such as translation, parody, and pastiche; they tend to emphasize the dominance of the precursor text without allowing the narcissistic fulfillment of the new poet—they remain, in Jonson's terms, "crude, raw, or undigested." They present the poet with an unacceptable lack of differentiation, a metonymic crisis. While *a* product is created, that new product is still overshadowed by its source, the poem of the precursor. As in oral cultures, the poetic precursor has a separate identity which allows him or her to operate as representative of the culture as a whole. But in an oral culture the mere passage of time and the young poet's simple repetition of stories will allow the same identity with separation: In time, that is, he or she will replace the elder poet. With the advent of the written word, and much more forcefully with the printed word—where the elder poets do not die—the process of becoming a poet is increasingly uncertain, even anxious.

Both Walter Jackson Bate and, more recently, Harold Bloom, discuss a "crisis of creativity" taking place in the Enlightenment, but hesitate to specify causal connections, leaving the crisis to some unspecified social factors that rise (teleologically) toward Romanticism.[24] Weinbrot, in a paper on William Collins, focuses astringently on such ahistorical critics as maintaining a "well-marinated fantasy," and his reaction is not without justification.[25] Indeed, it is perilous to ignore the immediate contexts of literary production. Equally perilous, however, is denial of larger contexts—generic, psychological, etc.—and denial of our own entrapment within particular historical contexts. Though there will still be readers who see my own work as "ahistorical" in a negative sense, I feel obliged to clarify that human repetitions of the past—through their epics—are recursions conditioned by change. With the two (widely separated) epics considered here, however, the historical context can be defined loosely enough as an increasingly literate print society, where epic poetry is still considered, in Hayley's phrase (written in 1782), the "highest province of poetic lore."[26] Laslett tellingly hints at the effect that their fathers' possible *illiteracy* had on writers such as Shakespeare and Isaac Newton: "It would seem that a man born into a bookless household could die as the writer of momentous books" (1971, 209). Most other writers, their contemporaries and those who followed them, were not so fortunate.

Reacting slowly to changing contexts of production, poetry remained more closely tied to the lettered elite's habitual circulation of manuscripts until Ben Jonson's time, responding more conservatively to the changes in their reading audience.[27] With the development of a much-expanded (though still far from widespread) reading audience,[28] the social status of readers necessarily fell rather sharply, though the size of that audience was greatly increased. The elite audience for whom *epics* were produced continued to exist, but their elite status was being undermined by new genres and a market that catered increasingly to a somewhat different taste. As Jonson put it, "it is not that the better have left to [i.e., ceased to] write or speak better, but that they that hear them judge worse."[29] Moreover, elite discursive structures faced new competition in what was fast becoming a literary marketplace; this forced (and forces) epic poets—engaged in an act of recursion—to try as well to "make it new" in a way they had not before. Formal innovations indicate this most clearly, especially where they conceal these innovations as returns, as rememberings of an earlier (and in the case of Milton, an earlier and *higher*) set of principles. In an oral culture, "What oft was *Thought*" is an excuse for repeating the saying: *hwæt, we gardena . . . oft geheardon*. Only in later chirographic and in print societies does this become a problem, reaching the point where the old story is so well-known, so eternally present, as only to bear repeating if it has remained "ne'er so well *Exprest*."[30] Earlier in *An Essay on Criticism*, Pope expresses the same idea in slightly different terms:

> When first young *Maro* in his boundless Mind
> A Work t' outlast Immortal *Rome* design'd,
> Perhaps he seem'd *above* the Critick's Law,
> And but from *Nature's Fountains* scorn'd to draw:
> But when t' examine ev'ry Part he came,
> *Nature* and *Homer* were, he found, the *same*.
>
> (130–35)

Pope's simple equation of the environment with the textual precursor is an index to a prevailing sense among poets that the precursor was nearly inescapable. (Virgil can be considered the primary commentator.) Simple forms of recursion—what we can see as the active "translation" of the father from one context (time or language) into another—are no longer enough, because the printed, textual father, like Milton's God, is ominously and eternally present. The texts of Homer and Virgil are insistently present for comparison.[31] No matter how one "translates" the inscribed precursor as a way of gaining access to both the linguistic mother and thus to metonymic glory one arrives only, *at best*, at the "spi't'n' image" of the father.[32] The translator functions mainly as an intermediary—not to say Pandarus-figure—between the poetic father and the translator's mother tongue.

At first the case of close parody seems different, since it is clearly based in differentiation, in viewing the earlier text as explicitly Other. But though this distinction by negation is indeed made, it allows no identity for the new poet within the epic tradition. By the aggressive metaphoric distancing of parody, one achieves at best a temporary victory over the precursor. The victor becomes only a diminished reflection of that precursor and the tradition (as with Satan's parodic—and temporary—victory over God). Like the joke, parody involves the return of the repressed, but also the return of the paternal repression, and remains a hermetic, limited form of identity. And thus, insofar as the parodist has by deconstruction of the origins deconstructed him or herself as well, any sense of poetic identity is undermined. The simultaneous prevalence of translations and parodies of the epic forms a doubly focused index to the classic (and classical) "double-bind" inflicted upon an age, the conflicting demands to be "like your father" and "not like your father."[33]

Though the texts mentioned all bear traces of this continuing conflict, epics that synthesize the metaphoric and metonymic relations to tradition are most interesting. By allowing the dialectical play between the two extremes, they enact what we have characterized as a typically Odyssean strategy. Disguising their aggression as a metonymic gift of repetition, they allow themselves to be consumed by the tradition, in order to emerge triumphant, deconstructing the tradition by their very reconstruction of it. Milton's *Paradise Lost* and Macpherson's *Fingal* exemplify such a strategy, but differ radically in their means of enacting that strategy.

> When we behold their battles, methinks the two poets resemble
> the heroes they celebrate. Homer, boundless and resistless as
> Achilles . . . Virgil, calmly daring like Æneas. . . .
> —Pope[34]

Milton's *Paradise Lost* has been called an epic without a hero; the poet "begins his poem of things, and not of men," as Charles Gildon observed.[35] This itself shows Milton's decentering irony, an irony he applies not merely to himself, but to humans in general, and which draws attention to the fact that precursors had (wrongly) emphasized the heroic aspect of the human, a conception that Milton wished to expose as an empty fiction. However, this very act of inversion or decentering leads to a foregrounding of the poet, and hence to another recurrent strain in Milton studies that promotes Milton himself as the hero created by his own epic.[36]

James Macpherson's *Fingal,* on the contrary, constructs a vital myth of the ancient poet as the "all-pervading, omnipresent personality" so common to eighteenth-century epic (Hägin 1964, 126).[37] Ossian is not only the aged bard and "original" but he is also one of his own preeminent heroes, the son of Fingal himself and a warrior of great power (particularly emphasized in book 4 of *Fingal*). Unfortunately, he is almost wholly a fiction, a fraudulent cover for Macpherson himself. The dynamics of such an illusion need to be more fully explored, but we can see immediately how these two epics end at much the same point, despite their different pathways: Milton creates a text emptied of heroes, which must ultimately construct him as the heroic poet; Macpherson constructs a heroic poet who creates an ultimately empty—that is, fraudulent—text.

The contrast between Milton and Macpherson is similar to that noted by Pope between Virgil and Homer: "We oftener think of the author himself when we read Virgil, than when we are engaged in Homer; all which are the effects of a colder invention, that interests us less in the action described."[38] The "Heroic Poet" to whom Gildon accorded a place beside Homer and Virgil is clearly paralleled in Pope's description of Virgil.[39] The Ossianic poems, on the contrary, are full of action: Intimate violence and the figure of woman form the basis of all, or nearly all, of the original *Fragments;* the same story is repeated in Macpherson's longer poems, where the principal additions are political and military context and the aggrandizement of the single bardic figure of Ossian; the episodes of love and death (many of them directly transposed from their places in the *Fragments*) still form the bulk of the matter in the epics of *Fingal* and *Temora,* as well as *casus belli* of the former.[40] The fact that "the same story" is present in all of these, however, reminds us that the masterplot of epic—the Oedipal plot inscribed upon the narcissistic narrative—may be the basis of Milton's poem as well, at least if we are to read Milton as repeating the epic tradition in his own poem.

> For never since created man,
> Met such imbodied force, as nam'd with these
> Could merit more than that small infantry
> Warr'd on by Cranes. . . .
> *Paradise Lost* 1.573–76

William Kerrigan highlights the Oedipal concerns of Milton and his poetry rather neatly:

> One cannot begin to think psychoanalytically about Milton without realizing that the oedipus complex is the generative center of his character and his art. . . . Concerns prominent in his epic—the justification of the ways of the Father, the freedom found in serving the father, the failed heroism of Satan's rebellion, the tragedy of human disobedience, the reworking of the Trinity into an uncreated Father and an indebted Son—impress the situation of an oedipal child on a religion that already derived our salvation from an identification with a divine and ideally obedient Son whose love was manifested to us through a sacrificial death demanded by

paternal justice. In this sense Milton all but delivers up his religion to the secular verdict of oedipal interpretation.[41]

Seeing this set of Oedipal concerns as working within the context of the epic tradition (as well as within the religious context) requires another step, outlining the jokelike double movement of Milton's epic. In simplest form, the physical return of the repressed in the figure of Satan is followed by the "justif[ied]" return of the repression—the enactment of the Law of the Father. But the two movements secure, on earth, a limited space of free play, where the liberating return of the repressed in the many guises of temptation and sin (within history and within the individual), works together with the restrictive return of the repression to create the oscillation of human life, the error or "wandering" that is human history.

Yet another reading of Satan as the quintessential narcissistic hero of earlier epic, in whom Tillyard (and the Romantic poets) saw "the strenuous Western temper at its height,"[42] seems unnecessary. Modeled strongly on the characters of Achilles and Odysseus, Satan is, as commentators remark, the extreme form of the Homeric hero.[43] The epigraph to this section provides a slightly different passage into the complexities of the epic's interaction with tradition.

The full context of the lines concerning the "small infantry" is that of Satan's review of his troops, one of two significant Miltonic glosses on epic tradition:

> He through the armed Files
> Darts his experienc't eye, and soon traverse
> The whole battalion views, thir order due,
> Thir visages and stature as of Gods;
> Thir number last he sums. And now his heart
> Distends with pride, and hard'ning in his strength
> Glories: For never since created man,
> Met such imbodied force, as nam'd with these
> Could merit more than that small infantry
> Warr'd on by Cranes: though all the Giant brood
> Of *Phlegra* with th'Heroic Race were join'd
> That fought at *Thebes* and *Ilium*, on each side
> Mixt with Auxiliar Gods; and what resounds
> In Fable or *Romance* of *Uther's* Son
> Begirt with *British* and *Armoric* Knights;
> And all who since, Baptiz'd or Infidel
> Jousted in *Aspramont* or *Montalban*,
> *Damasco*, or *Morocco*, or *Trebisond*,
> Or whom *Biserta* sent from *Afric* shore

> When *Charlemain* with all his peerage fell
> By *Fontarabbia*. Thus far these beyond
> Compare of mortal prowess, yet observ'd
> Thir dread commander. . . .
>
> (PL 1.567–89)

The simplest reading suggests that, in comparison to the present array, and to Milton's recent catalogue of the fallen angels and their consequences, all other epic heroes are mere pygmies. Focusing on the dynamics of this encounter with tradition, it is easily seen that Satan's review of his troops is equated with Milton's review of epic heroism. The specular gaze of Satan, which "Darts" through the "armed Files" and "sums" them, is also that of the poet, flipping through the files of epic. Like Satan, Milton "names" the epic past "with these," summing up their "merit" as that of "small infantry." Though all the heroes from all epics were actually added up—"sum[med]"—as the lines imply, they would not only be small, but "unspeaking ones"—infants. Thus Milton, the speaking heroic poet, at the opening of his "high argument," is identified with Satan. However, it remains a question whether or not we should associate Milton so closely (or so exclusively) with Satan. There is a repeated shift of the reader's focal point, emphasized by the simile and the allusions to past epics: Preceding the passage above, the reader has been engaged with the "perfect Phalanx" of the fallen angels en masse, "Awaiting what command thir mighty Chief / Had to impose" (PL 1.535–67). Satan's survey of his troops follows, concentrating almost immediately to the phallic image of his heart, which "Distends with pride, and hard'ning in his strength / Glories" (PL 1.571–73). The simile, as no doubt has been remarked, results in a momentary confusion, due the postponement of the "nam'd" versions of "such imbodied force"; the puzzlement of the simile is deeper, with its negative, its comparative, and its odd linkage as causal of Satan's exultation. His heart "Glories: *For never* since created man, / Met such [as] . . . / Could merit *more* than that small infantry / Warr'd on by Cranes." As though these were not enough, the reader's sense of time, space, and scale is set in suspension, until it is determined that the Homeric pygmies—"that pygmaean race beyond the Indian mount" (PL 1.780)—are meant, and that they are equated not with the still-glorious devils, but with classical and medieval heroes. The fact that the list begins with "the Giant brood" who battle the Olympian gods does not help the reader's sense of perspective. But above all, if the pygmies have been identified, who are the cranes? In the opening of book 3 of the *Iliad*, they are presented in the following simile:

> Now when the men of both sides were set in order by their leaders,
> the Trojans came on with clamour and shouting, like wildfowl,

as when the clamour of cranes goes high to the heavens,
when the cranes escape the winter time and the rains unceasing
and clamorously wing their way to the streaming Ocean,
bringing to the Pygmaian men bloodshed and destruction:
at daybreak they bring on the baleful battle against them.
But the Achaian men went silently, breathing valour,
stubbornly minded each in his heart to stand by the others.

    (3.1–9)

In both Milton and Homer, the epic catalogue has just been completed; in the *Iliad*, the initial combat of Paris and Menelaos is about to occur. The Akhaians, thus, loosely enough, are identified with the pygmy warriors. In *Paradise Lost*, an odd synthesis has taken place. The silence of the Akhaians is reflected in the host of fallen angels, "awaiting" Satan's command, despite the supposition that, like the cranes, they have recently undergone the "storm" of the war in heaven, and are—potentially—preparing to do battle against the pygmaean epic heroes—humanity. It is an odd combination of passive and aggressive stances, which is only stranger given the fact that the "small infantry" are "nam'd with these," not in an antagonistic fashion, but "*with*" in the additive sense that is carried throughout the list of epic hosts. Milton's rapid shifts of perspective, here and throughout book 1, destabilize any sense of certainty, but a focus on the act of "awaiting" is illuminating. This action parallels the strategy in Milton's earlier sonnet on his blindness, where the last line allows the abdication of the struggle for fame: "They also serve who only stand and wait" (168). The division between Satan and the angelic host, then, heightened as it is by their respective activity and passivity, replicates what has been seen as a deep division in Milton himself. The overarching contiguity among them lends a certain irony—all are fallen, "erring," warred on by Christ. Moreover, the extension of that sense of contiguity through the simile only serves to emphasize Milton's involvement with both aspects of this tableau. Milton's complicity is especially clear in Satan's backward reasoning, from anachronistic and unlike things to like, rather than the reverse. He (or at least his heart) "glories" on the basis of the "puny" (from *puis-né*, "later born" [*PL* 2.367]) inhabitants of a world not yet come into being. Satan becomes the current epic poet, delighting in his imagined preeminence, both preceding and following traditional epic narratives by his choice of insurmountable priority—since narrative itself begins with Satan's fall, and ends with his ultimate defeat. The ambiguity, especially, of "Thir number last he sums," suggests with its potential for inversion that while Satan is literally the only one who counts, he is also *the* sum, the topmost (*summus*, top or peak) of them all. He counts their number to the last one, but he is also the "last." The first shall be last, and the last shall be first. It is easy to apply this to Milton, who is often read as writing the last epic and thereby exhausting epic as a genre, but also the summary, the synecdochic "sum" or total of all epics (as Satan is the paradigmatic adversary).

The difficulty with such a reading remains with the cranes, who must in this larger view operate as emblematic of heaven and its inevitable power to shut down narrative entirely. A Freudian reading would emphasize the cranes' castrative power (as in Fitzgerald's translation of the *Iliad*, where the cranes are "beaked for cruel attack"). The attack on the silent host—the "infantry"—is a primal one, taking place in the *Iliad* at dawn, in Hell at the dawn of history (and in the fashion mentioned above, predating it). The understanding of the pygmies as a plural, passive, and unfocused energy—existing only to be "impose[d]" upon by the phallic pride of Satan—leads to the question of their symbolic status as "infants." According to Freud, a child operates for women as a "substitute phallus," a phallic "gift." In Milton, this multiple "infantry" does appear in a similar light. The passive pygmy, which derives from *pugme*, a measure of about thirteen inches in length ("but a cubite in height"),[44] functions as a gift from the passive and metonymic aspect of this dyad to the active "imposer," and the orderly, silent gift serves precisely to heighten that figure's narcissistic pride: "he above the rest / In shape and gesture proudly eminent / Stood like a Tow'r" (*PL* 1.589–91). The cranes remain a puzzle, for their place in terms of epic tradition is difficult to see at this point: In what way can they operate as castrating precursor, if the precursors are included among the pygmies? But in terms of the immediate dynamic, a complex exchange takes place between the poet as one of many lesser epic poets, and the poet as "sum" of all. The dyadic formation of the self—watching narcissistic pride, as it in turn watches the passive (primarily, perhaps, to see itself therein), allows a free play—*jouissance*—that seems interminable, suspended until the reader makes a decision and moves on.

> Sufficient to have stood, though free to fall.
>
> (*Paradise Lost* 3.99)

The dyadic formation of the self explored in the microstructure of this early passage can also be examined in the larger structures of the poem. Not only the major narrative movements of the poem, but also the Miltonic version of the Freudian double-bind—the struggle between fate and free will expressed above—illustrate this dyadic expression of heroism.

The traditional epic hero appears in Satan, and he serves to fulfill a narcissistic fantasy as the rebel twin (to the passive, dutiful son) who lives out the dream, but then is crushed to justify submission to the Father. His close iden-

tification with specifically epic heroism and tradition, however, lets Satan function additionally as a paternal figure to be crushed by the Son in a new type of
heroism. Moreover, *this* precursor—the epic tradition in Satan—is the one that
allows (or seduces) the fall from the Platonically idealized precursor, the
infinite, on the part of both humans and Christ. According to Milton, pagan
epic has in the same way executed a vast and influential—seductive—"misreading" of the father ("thus they relate, / Erring" [*PL* 1.746–47]); John Milton,
like Christ, must swerve enough to redeem such errors (Christ's errancy out of
God's bosom and his eventual return are related at 3.238–65).

Satan, like all repressed material, occasionally returns, and his returns do
secure an Oedipal victory of a kind, even if only within time. Like his colorful,
idiosyncratic language, the tortuous path through chaos leads him out of his
encrypted existence into his successful "attempt at seduction," appearing first
(where else but?) in a dream. Driven off by Gabriel and the Cherubim, he goes
(quite literally) underground again:

> There was a place,
> Now not, though Sin, not Time, first wrought the change,
> Where *Tigris* at the foot of Paradise
> Into a Gulf shot under ground, till part
> Rose up a Fountain by the Tree of Life;
> In with the River sunk, and with it rose
> *Satan* involv' d in rising Mist.
>
>   (*PL* 9.69–75)[45]

Milton's treatment of the epic tradition in the figure of Satan inverts the established epic norms, as he tries to close off this resurgent narcissistic narrative. Satan, a grim parody of God the Father, is also a metonymic recursion to Achilles
(in his wrath and jealous pride) and to Odysseus (in his wanderings and labors,
his disguises and his guile), and Milton aims to repress that narcissistic tradition based in human action: He inverts the poles along which we have judged
Oedipal relations, turning the epic tradition into the narcissistic, wayward
child, associating himself instead with another precursor—the Author waiting
at the end of time and the epic tradition.[46]

The real virtue lies in "the better fortitude / Of Patience and Heroic Martyrdom" (*PL* 9.31–32). Milton's enshrining of an unapproachable patriarchal
authority, and his appropriation of the passive metonymic stance often associated with femininity, are more fully explored by Christopher Kendrick's influential essay on *Comus*. Kendrick summarizes Milton's renegotiation of the Oedipal
pattern through the young poet's "chastity cult": "[H]e gives up the object-tie
with the mother (and with women) only to make himself one with her; in other

words, he identifies, not with the father, but with the mother, that wonder of modest deportment, whose character then overdetermines the ego-ideal. Paradoxically by this same act of abdication, the power behind the father's demand, the law of his desire, is attracted and taken possession of."[47] By abdicating the Oedipal struggle as futile, Milton is enabled to receive the continued love, the "gifts" of the father, and to possess, if only potentially and temporarily, his power. As Kendrick points out, this strategy is in essence a retreat into the world of self-contained narcissism, the potentially static "den[ial] of the law of desire itself." In order to circumvent this problem, the self is split into the passive, undesiring respondent—the good child, Christ, one of those "also" servants "who only stand and wait"—and the active, desiring agent, repressed and ultimately doomed, but necessary as a "conjurer" (in Kendrick's phrase) to display the dangers (over and over again) of narcissistic desire's fulfillment. The conjurer—in the person of Satan, Comus, even Lycidas—is an evil twin to the good, similar in aim and function to the fraternal oppositions of *Beowulf,* and, in some regards, those of *Fingal.* Only through the interplay between these forces is poetry, including *Paradise Lost,* produced. Milton's division of his world into these necessarily linked "twins" of good and evil is thoroughgoing, seen throughout his insistently "double-tongued" work, as in the often-quoted passage from *Areopagitica:* "Good and evill we know in the field of this World grow up together almost inseparably. . . . It was from out the rinde of one apple tasted, that the knowledge of good and evill as two twins cleaving together leapt forth into the World. . . . what wisdome can there be to choose, what continence to forbeare without the knowledge of evill? He that can apprehend and consider vice with all her baits and seeming pleasures, and yet abstain, and yet distinguish, and yet prefer that which is truly better, he is the true wayfaring Christian" (4.310–11). The apple provides an opportunity to engage in a dialectical play of aggression and defense in the service of the Father, and it is worth noting the emphasis on observation of vice, stressing the power of "waiting" or abstention: One must "apprehend and consider vice with all her baits and seeming pleasures, and yet abstain." Only then (and only at the end of Time) will come the ultimate reward, the actual assimilation to the Father, when the Son his "regal Sceptre shalt lay by, / For regal Sceptre then no more shall need, God shall be All in All" (*PL* 3.339–41).

Thus, it is easy enough to see this enactment of the Oedipal drama as key to the overarching structure of the epic, and to recall the parallel view suggested of the "small infantry." It is still difficult to evaluate the relationship of the precursors, as they are doubled, like the loci of "heroism." As in the *Odyssey's* division between Zeus and Poseidon, the paternal in *Paradise Lost* is split into the idealized form of God and the deconstructed or parodic image of God—the "Father of Lies." Though God is the first Author, inscriber of the "poem containing history" par excellence, it seems a trifle ingenuous to read him purely within the epic tradition. Every explanation has its limits. But the understanding of that divine original as a textual "Maker" or poet clarifies the increasing power of the printed text, its status as essentially coterminous with reality itself.

To return to the question of free will with which this section opened, it should be clear that the swerves enacted by Satan and Christ operate as the initiation and the conclusion of narrative. Similarly, these swerves allow the assignment (and comprehension) of vice and virtue: The "free" swerve from perfection is evil; the necessary, sympathetic swerve to restore perfection is good. Perfection can only thus be understood *as* perfection.

Only if humans are created with free will—"Sufficient to have stood, though free to fall"—does God appear in any other than an unjust light; Milton makes this point in the *Areopagitica* discussion of the "mere mechanical Adam," and elsewhere.[48] Milton's "justification" of the "ways of God to Man" rests on this equivocal argument for free will. But as Northrop Frye notes, it is a poor argument: "God knew that Adam would fall, but did not compel him to do so, and on this basis he disclaims legal responsibility. This argument is so bad that Milton, if he was trying to escape refutation, did well to ascribe it to God. Thought and act cannot be so separated: if God had foreknowledge he must have known in the instant of creating Adam that he was creating a being who would fall" (1957, 211).[49] The point in asserting free will as a reality is that of clarifying that responsibility exists, and that it lies within the individual *will*, rather than in the system as a whole (or God). Free will thereby allows punishment, and allows the creation of a scapegoat, an evil twin, who is made representative of evil for the initial deviation. However, free will can also elevate the individual, providing the option of abstaining from vice, as in the *Areopagitica* passage above. It should be clear from this that the question of free will, or agency, also determines the possibility of making judgments of value at all. Frye continues, pointing out that one is only "free to *fall*" in a "use of freedom to lose freedom" (1957, 212), as Milton clarifies later in the same book (*PL* 3.176–77). In the limited sense that being "sufficient" is a "free" condition, however, is encountered the same lack of differentiation faced by Odysseus on Ogygia. One is free only in the sense that one has no identity.

"Sufficient to have stood, though free to fall" thus manifests itself as an expression of the classic double-bind of Oedipal conflict. It is necessary for survival to "stand" for the Father, to "be like me" or come to an equivalence; given the immortality of the Father in the Miltonic schema, however, the strategy of "those who stand and wait," while attractive for the resulting approval and attainment of union, allows no possibility of self; one is an undifferentiated piece of the Father, the merest chip off the old block. Therefore it is likewise necessary that *someone* "fall," enacting a Bloomian "swerve" that allows the establishment of a self, an identity. Since the Father is that which is perfection itself, any swerve thus enacted will appear imperfect—regardless of its necessity. The masochistic "better fortitude / Of Patience and Heroic Martyrdom" (*PL* 9.31–32), however, is a vicarious fall, one that is committed as the agent of the Father, only justified by the "vice" of another. Thus throughout *Paradise Lost* Milton is able to justify his own epic as an inverted, antithetical swerve, through the sympathetic identification with the fraternal deviation from an idealized precursor. In *Fingal,* conversely, we find the poet acting, not only as agent of the father, but also as the precursor himself, in the persona of the third-century bard Ossian.

> We read *Imitation* with somewhat of his languor, who listens to a twice-told tale: Our spirits rouze at an *Original;* that is a perfect stranger, and all throng to learn what news from a foreign land. . . . All eminence, and distraction, lies out of the beaten road.
> —Edward Young[50]

Discussing the Ossianic epics of James Macpherson as representative of epic tradition may seem a questionable enterprise; the aura of fraudulence and forgery that surrounds them has led to their near-total disregard in this century. To consider *Fingal* as member of a genre whose distinguishing characteristic has been said to be "greatness" begs some contradiction. But in opening the question, I am at least in the company of Hazlitt, who as late as 1818, long after the matter appeared to have been settled, could include Ossian with Homer, the Bible, and Dante as one of the "principal works of poetry in the world."[51] According to Thomas Sheridan, one among many contemporary readers, "he excelled Homer in the Sublime and Virgil in the Pathetic" (Boswell 1950, 182).[52] During the century that followed their initial appearance, the work of Ossian was translated into twenty-six different languages (as well as into English *verse,* a fact to which we shall return) and exerted a force in the Romantic movement akin to that of *Childe Harold's Pilgrimage.*[53]

Moreover, given the problem under exploration, the question of fakes and frauds needs an explanation, insofar as it constitutes an extreme (so extreme as to be the inverse) form of the strategy we have found most applicable in Milton. Whereas in Milton the repressed and heroic narcissism of Satan returns only to be brought down (though never eradicated) by the return of the repression, in Macpherson's Ossianic poems we encounter a different kind of joke. This second kind is the Freudian *Aufsitzer,* what we might call a "take-in" joke or a shaggy-dog story, where the only joke is that there is no joke. Hence, it is not merely a joke on the tradition in the manner of parody, or a joke in common with contemporaries, in the manner of satire. Rather, the joke is on everyone and everything but the joker, and involves a great deal of aggression directed, not only at tradition and authority, but, more pointedly, at the joker's very contemporaries. It is not without reason that Samuel Weber characterizes the shaggy-dog story as "the most narcissistic" kind of joke.[54] Indeed, we (who share in being butts of the joke) begin to understand Freud's condemnation of this type as illegitimate, as "idiocy masquerading as a joke" (1905a, 138–39n).[55] However, the idiosyncratically "double-tongued" nature of the escape (and the aggression) offered by such "idiocy" renders the shaggy-dog story (and its literary equivalents) a highly plausible solution to a complex problem. First, as an inside joke, it gratifies narcissistic desire. Second, as a joke *upon* the audience, it satisfies as an aggressive move. Third, by its appearance in disguise as a conventional joke, it lures the audience into a supposed intimacy that is violently disrupted—a literary version of the Trojan horse. The relationship of the fraudulent joke in its manifestation as epic to its different audience—the tradition—is somewhat simpler. It is plainly designed as a recursion, a metonymic extension of the precursor's power. The desire to "be like" the precursor is achieved; but the narcissistic aim is also achieved, in the secret knowledge that one *is* (or has displaced) one's own precursor. This strategy seems particularly effective for dealing with an antagonistic world of competitors and of immortal, unapproachable precursors.[56] In addition to the interesting psychological complexity of the fraudulent epic, Macpherson's work is historically (if not aesthetically) rather more significant than brief comments in literature survey courses tend to admit.

Anthony Grafton suggests a number of possible motives for forgery and imposture: social or professional ambition; amusement, in particular "the sadistic pleasure derived from seeing others fooled"; love, surprisingly, in cases where impostors have "attributed greater deeds, more magnanimous sentiments, and more eloquent words"; and hatred.[57] All of these have been suggested above in the discussion of the Ossianic poems as a kind of inside joke, though we may see that ambition is dependent to a greater extent on the maintenance of the joke's disguise—hence a joke inside a joke.

In spite (and in part because) of the question of authenticity (raised immediately), the poetry of Ossian had a profound impact on English and European thought. The substantial disregard with which it has been treated in the twentieth century is itself a legacy of the nineteenth-century rebellion against "neoclassical" traditions, and of that rebellion's "new" traditions of "originality" and "sincerity."[58] Macpherson's attitude toward epic is not difficult to discern in *Fingal* and in his later, much-encouraged (and much-criticized) translation of Homer's *Iliad* in cadenced prose "after the manner of Ossian." "A Poet, like Caesar, ought to own no superior. The moment he acts a secondary part, he sinks into a slave" (1773, v–vi). For Macpherson, it was not the "original genius" of Homer that had allowed that poet his "despotism" over the field of poetry (ii–iii). Rather, Homer, being dead, had earned a magnified and idealized reputation in the minds of his eighteenth-century readers, since he had escaped the persistence of "Envy, which is almost inseparable from the nature of mankind" and which "throws a cloud on the merit of their contemporaries" (i). The lack of authorial intrusion in Homer was seen as a response to this force of "Envy, the never-absent attendant of merit": "His silence concerning himself is a sort of proof, that he foresaw the benefit, which an uncertainty of this kind, might bring to his fame" (iii). Macpherson's view of Homer is not without its own "Envy," of course. But there is a note of satisfaction that such "uncertainty" also surrounds his own work. Macpherson's "silence" concerning the accusations of imposture was, he believed, "a sort of proof" of his honesty, and he knew full well that the notoriety of such "uncertainty" had not been without benefits. His lack of response was seen by commentators as a symptom of his "Highland pride,"[59] and may also be seen as one of the frequently repeated "withdrawals" characteristic of narcissism. He wrote in the preface to the first edition of *Fingal* (1762a) when the question of authenticity had already been raised: Since "Poetry, like virtue, receives its reward after death," "he that was no extraordinary man in his own time, becomes the wonder of succeeding ages." Therefore, according to Macpherson,

> This consideration might induce a man diffident of his abilities to ascribe his own compositions to a person whose remote antiquity, and whose situation, when alive, might well answer for faults which would be inexcusable in a writer of this age. An ingenious gentleman made the observation before he knew anything but the name of the epic poem. . . . When he had read it his sentiments were changed. He found it abounded too much with those ideas which only belong to the most early state of society, to be the work of a modern poet. . . . notwithstanding the disadvantages with which the works ascribed to Ossian appear, it would be a very uncommon instance of self-denial in me to disown them, were they really my own composition. (1762a, vi)

In this chapter I want to deal as succinctly as possible with the question of authenticity. Relatively little new evidence bearing directly on the case has come to light since the publication of Mackenzie's exhaustive *Report* in 1805, though naturally enough the constructions that critics have placed on existing evidence vary remarkably.[60]

In brief, then, some of the original *Fragments* do have an attested source in Gaelic. The overall plot of *Fingal,* and the plots of some few of the episodes, are, loosely, derived from Gaelic ballads.[61] As Derick Thomson puts it, "Macpherson's refining and bowdlerising pen has often changed the atmosphere of the ballads beyond recognition . . . the same may be said of the content as Hector Maclean said of the diction of the Gaelic 'Ossian'—it may be Greek or English, but it is not Gaelic."[62] In all, there appear to be twelve passages of *Fingal* that are in some manner specifically "translated" from the Gaelic. But for the most part, it appears that Macpherson was doing something else entirely, and certainly Hugh Blair's assertion in the prefatory note to the 1760 *Fragments* is fantasy: "The translation is extremely literal. Even the arrangement of the words in the original has been imitated; to which must be imputed some inversions in the style, that otherwise would not have been chosen" (1760b, vi–vii).[63] As Saunders rightly points out, what Macpherson was doing—bringing together scraps of Gaelic song within a loosely traditional plot to form a larger "epic" whole—was not at all new.[64] Saunders concludes his work with a discussion of the parallel constructions of other "ancient" texts, the *Kalevala,* the *Nibelungenlied,* the *Eddas,* even the poems of Homer; the *Nibelungenlied* analogy strikes him as most exact: "The matter of both is a mixture of myth and history, and both are based on songs and ballads of uncertain date and origin. In the one and in the other a fresh and alien element is superinduced; in the *Nibelungenlied* the ideas of the age of chivalry refine the gods and heroes of an earlier mythology: in the Ossianic poems, a literary elegance obscures what was rough and harsh in the old Celtic legends" (1894, 323). Indeed, though the eminent spokespersons for *Liedertheorie* were as yet a century away, Macpherson was in fact a very late practitioner of the arts which they thought Homer and other early poets to have used: a stitching together of smaller, discrete tales to form an epic cycle.

According to Stafford, Macpherson felt that he *was* restoring the work of Ossian to an original unity and purity (1988, 125). Under the influence of such thinkers as Thomas Blackwell at Aberdeen, propelled by the enthusiasm for an early Gaelic epic on the part of his acquaintances in Edinburgh, and no doubt encouraged by the success of his *Fragments,* Macpherson attempted to recreate the original greater poem of Ossian, which had been "broken" by the intervening eras of oral tradition.

The form the poem then took, of course, reflects little, if any, of the Gaelic oral traditions or even what we have come to see as marks of the oral formulaic style.[65] Rather, it reflects far more clearly the state of contemporary epic scholarship—the classical "rules" of epic as seen and imagined. This crafted conformity was powerfully emphasized by the scholarly apparatus that accompanied the epic. Not only Blair's lengthy "Critical Dissertation on the Poems of Ossian," which prefaced the 1763 edition, but the wide range of etymological, historical, and explanatory footnotes served to heighten the classical parallels.[66] Careful to avoid overstating the obvious conclusions, the apparatus led readers of the handsome edition to make an explicit comparison with other culturally valorized texts, as does Sheridan (quoted above) in his comparisons of emotional response. The footnote to the conclusion of *Fingal* is perhaps the best example of this method, where Macpherson draws attention to the fact that "an epic poem ought to end happily. This rule, in its most material circumstances, is observed by . . . Homer, Virgil, and Milton; yet, I know not how it happens, the conclusions of their poems throw a melancholy damp on the mind. One leaves his reader at a funeral; another at the untimely death of a hero; and a third at the solitary scenes of an unpeopled world" (1805, 206). This "curious amphibology," as Malcolm Laing calls it in his own notes, is clearly designed to show the precursors as insufficient, as "less fortunate in their conclusions." *Fingal,* in short, in its opening *in medias res,* its ekphrastic description of the chariot of Cuthullin, its epic machinery of ghosts, is filled with evocations and imitations of, and responses to, earlier models of epic poetry. The aspect of Macpherson's work that stands out most clearly in contrast to prevailing epic practice, however, is the poetic medium involved.

> To break the pentameter—that was the first heave.
> —Ezra Pound

Ramsay of Ochertyre, like many others, focuses on Macpherson's use of "measured prose" in a way that exposes the continuing elite status accorded to poetry rather than prose: "Nothing could be more happy or judicious than his translating in measured prose; for had he attempted it in verse, much of the spirit of the original would have evaporated, supposing him to have had talents and industry to perform that very arduous task upon a great scale. This small publication drew the attention of the literary world to a new species of poetry."[67] The "new species of poetry" that Macpherson initiated with his *Fragments* and carried through in his epics and translations was, perhaps, his singular stroke of luck or genius. The measured prose of Ossian is probably Macpherson's most significant formal innovation in, or deviation from, seventeenth- and eighteenth-century poetic norms.[68]

The dominant poetic form of the period has been seen as the heroic couplet, a strict, but, in competent poets, a balanced and extraordinarily flexible form.[69] Considered on its own, it constitutes a fundamental (and fundamentally divided) building block, as Doody has argued, for the "double-tongued" quality of seventeenth- and eighteenth-century style, where "every line speaks in, as it were, two languages" (1985, 211). Like the oxymoron, or its extension in the favored trope of the zeugma, the couplet persistently "yokes together" meanings (which may stand in various relation to one another), forming an equation of the terms by means of a metonymic contiguity of sound (in the case of rhyme), or of grammar and syntax (in the case of zeugma). The most remarkable of these, naturally enough, are those that convey, in Doody's delicious phrase, "the shock of inappropriate relation" (1985, 218).

This "shock" can be understood as parallel to the Oedipal victory of the joke, where the forbidding law of the father is temporarily circumvented, and the object of incestuous desire attained. But to Macpherson, the strict duality and metrical demands of the heroic couplet have themselves become the arbitrary laws and "fetters" of language into which he was born (or perhaps into which, as a Scot, he was "seduced"). Hence his return to "the original sources of verbal play" primarily involves a Whitmanic "breaking of the pentameter." A binary pattern of recursion and completion continues, but the overall effect is that of overflowing boundaries, an excessive flood of language that allows an openness, a democratic (but dangerously anarchic) freedom not permitted by the highly constricted, limited victories of the couplet. Similarly, the Ossianic diction, with its repetitive use of concrete monosyllables, levels and rejects the reified abstractions of elite seventeenth- and eighteenth-century poetry.[70]

In his rejection of rhyme, Macpherson was not exactly innovative: Milton famously castigated it as "the Invention of a barbarous Age," and saw himself as returning to origins in the unrhymed heroic verse of Homer and Virgil. Thus, Milton's rejection of rhyme with *Paradise Lost* frames itself as a return to the virtues of an elite tradition, that is, to the correct (and dutiful) reading of the law of the father: "This neglect then of Rime so little is to be taken for a defect, though it may seem so perhaps to vulgar readers, that it rather is to be esteem'd an example set, the first in *English,* of ancient liberty recover'd to Heroic Poem from the troublesome and modern bondage of Riming" (1957, 210). Macpherson, on the other hand, though enacting a similar return, attempts to reinvent a (sentimentalized) "barbarous Age" that predates and therefore *ought* to be inadequate to comparison with "modern, connected and polished poetry." Moreover, his decision to use a (rather feebly) "measured prose" is a movement from the opposite direction. Through the use of prose he aligns himself with the writers and readers of sentimental novels, rather than with the elite audience of Homer and Virgil.

This generic boundary between prose and poetry is only one of the markers of status with which Macpherson had to deal seriously. In the preface to the fourth edition, he discusses with some acidity the impact of political boundaries on the reception of his poems:

> When rivers define the limits of abilities, as well as the boundaries of countries, a writer may measure his success by the latitude under which he was born.
> If this [i.e., the imposture] was the case, he was but young in the art of deception. When he placed the poet in antiquity, the translator should have been born on this side of the Tweed. (1805, lxvi)[71]

Macpherson, writing as a Scot, was vigorously marginalized by the English literary establishment from the very beginning of his career. Samuel Johnson indicates the nationalistic flavor of reactions against Macpherson in his aspersions of "a national conspiracy of falsehood." As Saunders reminds us, little since the Act of Union had served to make the Scots popular in English eyes. The rising of 1745 had set opinion firmly against them. Indeed, the savage attacks of the London critical establishment on the first volume of his *History* led David Hume to vow he would never again venture among "the barbarians who inhabit the banks of the Thames" (Saunders 1894, 184).[72]

Moreover, even in Scotland among Scots, as a Highlander representing a "rude and barbaric people," Macpherson was looked on with some misgivings. Boswell, for example, both delighted in and scorned the roughness of his "sublime savage." He noted with some glee Lord Eglinton's remark that Macpherson was "really a Highland claymore. If you was to scour him, you would spoil him" (1950, 110). Though the Edinburgh literati tended to support him publicly, his pride and reticence led them to express graver doubts in their correspondence. David Hume's letters to Blair, and later to William Strahan (the publisher), provide a record of the philosopher's growing disenchantment with the poet's typically Highland attitudes: "Macpherson has style and spirit, but is hotheaded, and without judgement" (Saunders 1894, 225).

As Stafford points out, the poems of Ossian celebrate a "democratized," even revolutionary world, at least in comparison to the refined, carefully stratified world of mid-eighteenth-century England: "In Ossian's age of heroes, men were free from the burden of property and unrepressed by Church or State. There were no class barriers: Fingal was a leader through merit rather than privilege, while his army was tied by bonds of affection rather than by self interest or obligation" (Stafford 1988, 178). Like the vernacular Bibles from which the structure of its cadenced prose sprang, Ossianic poetry created and gave voice to its own revolution. The famous line of Ezra Pound cited above, of course, clearly applies to Walt Whitman; but in many respects it applies more truly to (of all people) James Macpherson. Romanticism and the poetic freedoms of that mode of discourse (and hence, in part, the freedoms of Whitman himself) owe a certain amount to Macpherson's earlier experimentation. Though E. H. W. Meyerstein may overstate his case slightly, his opinion of the revolutionary force of Macpherson's poetry should be given more credence: "Macpherson can, without extravagance, be regarded as the main originator (after the translators of the Authorized Version) of what is known as 'free verse.' "[73] Macpherson himself realized quite early, I think, the difficulties implicit in his chosen form. As he remarked to Blair, he felt himself in some ways unfaithful to "the spirit and force" of the originals, and, moreover, that "they would be very ill relished by the public as so very different from the strain of modern ideas, and of modern, connected, and polished poetry." Though Sheridan asserted that "Mr. Macpherson in his translation of *Fingal* has shown us what dignity the English language is capable of in prose" (Boswell 1950, 83), the fact that he needed to specify "prose" shows the widely felt lack of "dignity" in the medium. That Macpherson's perception of the elitist preference for verse was fully accurate is attested by the many, many "re-translations" of the Ossianic texts into "English verse" (cast in either heroic couplets or, more rarely, blank verse).[74] But Laing, commenting on the "secret . . . irresistible charm" exerted by the poems, exposes still more clearly the dangerous border of class that Macpherson was treading. In Laing's view, Macpherson's imitations of the most beautiful passages from the classics were "a pleasing substitute to the unclassical reader: perpetual efforts at bathos and sublimity . . . adapted to the untutored taste of the multitude" (1805, 208). There were also a significant number of imitations of the Ossianic style. A generation later, nearly all the major poets would at least attempt it; in Macpherson's own age, the Ossianic imitators were many. (Ironically enough, even the other most famously fraudulent writer of the age, Thomas Chatterton, wrote Ossianic imitations.)[75] But Macpherson himself remained somewhat insecure with his position as revolutionary and with his divergence from what he apparently thought of as "real poetry," as his preface to Homer's *Iliad*, translated in the same style, demonstrates.[76] Here he asserts again that his work is not "mere prose," but that "with a minute attention to the very arrangement of words" (1773, xix) he has aimed to translate "Homer as he really is" (xx). We see the Miltonic aspiration to the elite (not "*mere* prose") simultaneously with the aggressive desire to reduce Homer from his "despotism" to the merely mortal. In doing so, like Milton, he casts off the "fetters" of rhyme and meter, the taste that has "seduce[d]" modern translators to present Homer as "too much of a modern beau" (1773, xv–xvi).[77]

To summarize, the form of the Ossianic poems, and especially of the pseudoscholarly *Fingal,* demonstrates a deeply rooted ambivalence, a "double-tonguedness," toward the epic tradition and toward the translator himself. Though Macpherson asserts that a translator ought to be the equal of his original (1760, preface), he cannot recognize translation as a fully fledged poetic enterprise. Thus *Fingal* appears both as a radical insult to epic tradition and as a profound paean to that tradition. Macpherson himself appears, alternately, as epic poet, as mere translator, as utter fraud. The symptoms of pathological narcissism we glanced at in Chapter 2 provide some explanatory parallels in Macpherson's remarkable combination of "grandiosity and fragile self-esteem," and in his feelings of emptiness and isolation, of being an observer of his own life. Recursion, sex, and violence in Macpherson's epic detail this narcissism more thoroughly.

> The plaintive strain, the moving lay,
> Like those they mourn, at last decay.
> —Macpherson

The remarkable thing about recursion in the Ossianic poems is their obsessive return to a particular dynamic of sexuality and violence. Over and over again we are presented with the same tableau: two warriors in conflict, ostensibly over a woman. And over and over again we are brought to the same conclusion: All of the figures die.

> Duchômar came to Tura's cave; he spoke to the lovely Morna.
> Morna, fairest among women, lovely daughter of the strong-armed
> Cormac! Why in the circle of stones? in the cave of the rock alone?
> The stream murmurs along. The old tree groans in the wind. The
> lake is troubled before thee; dark are the clouds of the sky!
> . . . .
> "Long shall Morna wait," Duchômar said, "long shall Morna wait for
> Câthba!"
> Behold this sword unsheathed! Here wanders the blood of Câthba.
> Long shall Morna wait. He fell by the stream of Branno! On
> Croma I will raise his tomb, daughter of blue-shielded Cormac!
> Turn on Duchômar thine eyes; his arm is strong as a storm." "Is the
> son of Torman fallen?" said the wildly-bursting voice of the maid.
> "Is he fallen on the echoing hills, the youth with the breast of snow?
> The first in the chase of hinds? The foe of the strangers of ocean?
> Thou art dark to me, Duchômar, cruel is thine arm to Morna! Give
> me that sword, my foe! I love the wandering blood of Câthba!"
> He gave the sword to her tears. She pierced his manly breast! He

fell, like the bank of a mountain-stream, and stretching forth his
hand, he spoke: "Daughter of blue-shielded Cormac ! Thou hast
slain me in youth! The sword is cold in my breast: Morna, I feel it
cold. Give me to Moina the maid. Duchàmar was the dream of her
night! She will raise my tomb; the hunter shall raise my fame. But
draw the sword from my breast. Morna, the steel is cold!" She
came, in all her tears she came; she drew the sword from his breast.
He pierced her white side! He spread her fair locks on the ground!
Her bursting blood sounds from her side: her white arm is stained
with red. Rolling in death she lay. The cave re-echoed to her sighs.
(1924, 40–41)

When it appeared in the *Fragments*, the episode included the following lines,
emphasizing the erotic component of the death-scene: "As she fell, she plucked
a stone from the side of the cave, and placed it betwixt them, that his blood
might not be mingled with hers."

Macpherson's characters (and by extension, the poet himself) are clearly
engaged in a powerful process of rivalry that can largely be understood as the
rivalry of siblings. It appears as a competition, at any rate, between figures who
are almost invariably portrayed as "brothers" of a kind. The brother marks a
twinning, a doubling akin to that in Beowulf and Grendel, and more recently
in Satan and Christ. Interesting in Macpherson, however, is the occasional addition of a third figure, an actual *enemy*, but one who is *not* the actual antagonist. Through "mistake" or "accident," and in one instance through the actions
of an evil servant, the brother-figures are brought into conflict with each other,
not with the putative antagonist. This conflict is inevitably *over* something, and
on a first reading the object of strife appears to be the freedom of access to the
feminine (i.e., over a woman). However, the feminine is never really attained,
even through victory. As Stafford has observed, "Love seems unable to flourish
in Macpherson's Caledonia. Instead of normal sexual activity, the lovers are
united only in violent death, sleeping together not in bed, but in the grave"
(1988, 105). The female object of an alleged desire always remains unreached,
and indeed seems unreachable: She is almost invariably destroyed in rather
macabre fashion, as in the episode of Morna above. A different formulation for
the goal of narcissistic competition in *Fingal* seems required, as we found, similarly, in the *Iliad* and *Beowulf.*

In two of the repeated episodes, which begin to seem utterly interchange-
able, the object of desire is a bull, once spotted, once white. This traditional
symbol of virility and domination suggests—as expected—that strife in *Fingal*
arises as a result, not of the desire *for* the feminine, but instead as a desire for

separation, for masculine identity. Possession of woman, were it actually to occur, would function only as a symbol, a token of male identity and power.

Unfortunately for the parties concerned, the struggle to differentiate in this
fashion ends not in identity or the assumption of power, but rather in the utter
lack of differentiation implicit in death. Similarly, while the "names" of the
dead lovers and/or combatants are recalled by the aged bards, the names begin to matter not at all; when faced with the same story for the third time, the
reader realizes that the names are merely renaming a set of identical tokens that
struggle and die without any differentiation. This feeling is heightened by the
name-changes that accompany the episodes transferred from the *Fragments* directly into *Fingal*. The struggle itself is futile, and the futility of the interchange
is exacerbated by the outcome of all the struggles: Everyone dies.

This futility in action is underscored by the attitude toward language, especially toward poetry, in *Fingal*. I have argued that violence, in its ultimate aim,
is directed toward the extinction of self and the paradoxical narcissistic fulfillment or aggrandizement in *kleos*. In Macpherson's Ossianic texts, however, this
glory itself is subjected to a substantial critique—similar to Macpherson's critique of the "despotism" of Homer. Ossian himself consistently questions the
power of language even as he composes; words do not bring back the dead, and
even the song itself is in danger of extinction: "Our names may be heard in song.
What avails it when our strength has ceased?" (1924, 195). More telling in terms
of Macpherson's own obsession with the futility of language and ultimately the
futility of any action is his early poem, *The Monument:*

> In vain we toil for lasting fame,
> Or give to other times our name;
> The bust itself shall soon be gone,
> The figure moulder from the stone;
> The plaintive strain, the moving lay,
> Like those they mourn, at last decay.
>
> (1805, 196)

In the actual oral texts we have discussed, *kleos* and *lof* serve as the only means
of maintaining continuity, of attaining (a human and limited) immortality. *Fingal*, however, which pretends to a kind of orality, suggests that even such a limited form of immortality is illusory. Ossian's disillusioned view of the power of
language to preserve directly reflects Macpherson's doubled and ironic relation
to tradition. Though he is eager to attain the poetic power and adulation that
accretes to the established epic poet, his own interest lies as well in asserting
the ultimate futility of epic, since it cannot conserve either the culture or the

heroism of which he is enamored.[78] Through Ossian, Macpherson both laments and celebrates the fact that song cannot preserve the past—that the song itself is subject to time, something that must be (especially in the case of *Fingal* and *Temora*) re-membered, put back together. Perhaps more precisely, Macpherson is interested both in glorifying and belittling Ossian. Glorification is required as part of Macpherson's continuing conflict with his formidable epic precursors— Homer, Virgil, Milton, even Pope. But the belittling is necessary as well, insofar as Ossian is representative of that epic past; the past must be destroyed as well, "fragmented" and shown to be irrelevant to current concerns if it is to be transcended.

This attitude toward the past is perhaps best seen in the epic itself. Cuthullin's response to a song from "the aged Carril" may even suggest the situation of the contemporary reader; in a sense, it functions as a directive for reading an ancient work in the proper spirit: "Pleasant are the words of other times! they are like the calm shower of spring; when the sun looks on the field, and the light cloud flies over the hills" (1924, 49). This in itself need not strike us as odd. Cuthullin's statement shows a sense of the relief given by song, of its ephemeral yet life-giving quality. In context, however, it strikes a discordant note indeed, for it immediately follows a rather horrifying tale of mayhem and violent death.[79] Moreover, the episode is nearly identical to one in which Cuthullin himself has recently taken part, which involved the killing of his closest friend over the "snow-white bull" of Cairbar and Deugala, and which he recounts scant pages further on. "Unhappy is the hand of Cuthullin, since he slew his friend! Ferda, son of Damann, I loved thee as myself! . . . Ferda, from Albion came, the chief of a hundred hills. In Muri's hall he learned the sword, and won the friendship of Cuthullin. We moved in the chase together: one was our bed in the heath!" (1924, 57–58).

Ideally, perhaps, a poet would follow up these similar episodes, enabling us to suppose that Cuthullin's lack of self-recognition is what leads him to such repetitions; that his complacent, superficial attitude toward the bards is his tragic flaw, and his apparent scoffing parallel in some degree to that of Virgil's Mezentius. Unfortunately this is entirely inadequate as a way of reading Cuthullin's behavior (though it might be sufficient for reading Macpherson's). Fingal and Ossian himself use similar phrases in their own reactions to (equally grim) tales. This suggests that Macpherson's reaction to the past displays an apparent openness and receptivity, but actually and actively denies that past. Like Dryden's translations, speaking "that kind of English, which [the poet] would have spoken had he lived in England, and had written to this age,"[80] Macpherson's characters turn their pasts into that which they would have them be. It is a rewriting of the father by the son that "writes out" the power of the father. Unfortunately for the poetic son, however, this writing out of the power of the father is one that is also visited upon the son. Writing the past as we would have it (in order to allow ourselves freedom and control), we find that we have lost power ourselves. Macpherson's epics actually become little more than "the calm shower of spring" moving over the late eighteenth and nineteenth centuries.

> Learn hence for Ancient *Rules* a just Esteem
> To copy *Nature* is to copy *Them*.
> —Pope

The growth of the underworld from early to late epic reflects in part the increasing concern with poetic debts (MacDonald 1987). As I have suggested, the first and second *nekuia* of the *Odyssey* attempt to lay to rest the ghosts of heroic tradition and epos. The *katabasis* in the *Aeneid* fills an entire book, and is the structural center of Virgil's epic. Dante and Milton initiate their poems with "panoramic views of hell," and the *Dunciad* can be seen as depicting the ultimate infernal victory.[81] With Macpherson's *Fingal*, however, there is no explicitly realized descent, and we tarry momentarily over the appropriate "burial place of poetic memory." Pope's epigraph to this section provides an important clue, I think, for *Fingal*'s dead are ubiquitous and never dispelled; in *Fingal*, "Nature" and the threatening precursors form (almost) a single entity. "The ghosts of the lately dead were near, and swam on the gloomy clouds: And far distant in the dark silence of Lena, the feeble voices of death were faintly heard" (1924, 49). The dead in the poems of Ossian far outnumber the living, and they fill and suffuse the landscapes of the poem; in the passage above, "the lately dead" control the battlefield, the heath of Lena.[82] But throughout the epic their presence is repeatedly invoked, as in Ossian's address to the ghost of Carril: "Be thy soul blest, O Carril! in the midst of thy eddying winds. O that thou wouldst come to my hall, when I am alone by night! And thou dost come, my friend. I often hear thy light hand on my harp; when it hangs, on the distant wall, and the feeble sound touches my ear. Why dost thou not speak to me in my grief, and tell when I shall behold my friends? But thou passest away in thy murmuring blast; the wind whistles through the grey hair of Ossian!" (1924, 95).

Here Ossian summons his own precursor, who touches the harp and murmurs; the living bard is left to fill in the balance of the song. The dead, and especially their voices, textualize the landscape, and the bards in the Ossianic poems are the readers and writers of these earthly signs. The earth becomes eerily fraught with voices, and the reader encounters the precursors, like the Romantic versions of God, half-dissolved into the landscape. The more striking ghostly encounters in *Fingal* show this best, the appearance of the ghost of Crugal in book 2, and the tale of Cormar, grandfather of Calmar, in book 3. The first instance, involving the apparition of a former comrade in arms to "the hero" Connal, is modeled on similar epic apparitions in Homer, Virgil, and Milton:

> The hero beheld, in his rest, a dark red stream of fire rushing down from the hill. Crugal sat upon the beam, a chief who fell in the fight. He fell by the hand of Swaran, striving in the battle of heroes. His face is like the beam of the setting moon. His robes are of the clouds of the hill. His eyes are two decaying flames. Dark is the wound of his breast! "Crugal ... Why so pale and sad, thou breaker of the shields? Thou hast never been pale for fear! What disturbs the departed Crugal?" Dim, and in tears, he stood and stretched his pale hand over the hero. Faintly he raised his feeble voice, like the gale of the reedy Lego! (1924, 48–49)

Crugal advises Connal to leave the field, since the Irish are destined to lose in the next day's battle. He then departs "like the darkened moon," despite Connal's plea: "Lay by that beam of heaven. ... What cave is thy lonely house? What green-headed hill the place of thy repose? Shall we not hear thee in the storm? In the noise of the mountain-stream? When the feeble sons of the wind come forth, and, scarcely seen, pass over the desert?" (1924, 49–50). In addition, we learn from Connal's account of the visitation of Crugal that "the stars dim-twinkled through his form. His voice was like the sound of a distant stream. He is a messenger of death! He speaks of the dark and narrow house!" (1924, 50–51). It surprises us, of course, that Connal can recognize this ghost at all, who rides on a meteor, clothes himself in naturalistic phenomena, and remains translucent.[83] Malcolm Laing, in his rather eagerly debunking 1805 edition of the poems, expresses surprise that the ghost is so unlike the form that Crugal bore in life, as compared with the apparition of Patroklos to Achilles in book 22 of the *Iliad* (1805, 59).[84] This is not such a reversal of tradition as Laing suggests, however; more relevant to the passage in question is the appearance of Hector to Aeneas (*Aeneid* 2.375ff.) or even Beelzebub's parallel appearance to Lucifer after the angels' fall from heaven. In these, the emphasis of the interlocutors is on the ghostly change from former glories: "If thou beest he; but O how fall'n! how changed From him" (*PL* 1.84–85). Recalling the *nekuia* of the *Odyssey*, it is worth noting (though it should not surprise) that only the post-Homeric ghosts suffer such a dramatic change in appearance after death, despite the Homeric appellation of "the strengthless dead." More to the point here, though, is the reaction of the hero to the risen spirit. Aeneas, after following up briefly on his "first impulse" to do battle, quickly accedes to his fate and the wishes of Hector's ghost. Satan's response to Beelzebub, who counsels suffering acquiescence ("Too well I see and rue the dire event. . . . What can it then avail . . . ?" [*PL* 1.134–55]), is a model of narcissistic perversion of the law of the father:

Fall'n Cherub, to be weak is miserable
Doing or suffering: but of this be sure,
To do aught good will never be our task,
But ever to do ill our sole delight,
As being the contrary to his high will
Whom we resist.

(*PL* 1.157–62)

In *Fingal,* Cuthullin (like Satan) immediately turns to mustering his forces for battle, in direct and mocking despite of the ghostly advice carried to him by Connal: "He spoke to Connal . . . though stars dim-twinkled through his form! Son of Colgar, it was the wind that murmured across thy ear. Or if it was the form of Crugal, why didst thou not force him to my sight? Hast thou inquired where is his cave? The house of that son of wind? My sword might find that voice, and force his knowledge from Crugal. But small is his knowledge" (1924, 52). The threat made on the world of spirits is not here carried out, but in book 3 it reappears, ascribed to Cormar, a grandsire of the race, whose

black skiff bounded on ocean; he travelled on the wings of the wind. A spirit once embroiled the night. Seas swell, and rocks resound. Winds drive along the clouds. The lightning flies on wings of fire. He feared, and came to land: then blushed that he feared at all. He rushed again among the waves, to find the son of the wind. Three youths guide the bounding bark; he stood with sword unsheathed. When the low-hung vapor passed, he took it by the curling head. He searched its dark womb with his steel. The son of the wind forsook the air. The moon and stars returned! Such was the boldness of my race. . . . They best succeed who dare! (1924, 65)

"They best succeed who dare!" is a fitting motto for Macpherson's epic. In its audacity and surprising success, the work of Ossian bid fair to eclipse the light of the ancient Greeks and Romans. The poem itself, like the character in the passage above, strikes out against the dead. The past, which fills and qualifies the landscape of the poem, is riddled with the sublime and the terrible. The precursor texts—"the angry ghosts of men" (1924, 39)—that inform the Ossianic scenery are temporarily subjected, subsumed, by the living voice, in spite of the persistent frailty of that voice. Though the bardic voice is an ultimately futile gesture, it is the only thing available at all to provide some temporary form of order.

Readers will note that the landscape which I characterize as textually fraught with figures of anxiety—the ghosts of precursors and legible texts—is displayed in the passage above as explicitly female: "He searched its dark womb with his steel."[85] But then the passage presents the seemingly anomalous death of the "son of the wind."

Two readings of this action are possible. First, noting that women in *Fingal* and the other poems are without power except insofar as they are the putative foci of men's desire, it is likewise possible that the feminine agency described in the passage—with its power, akin to Medusa's, of instilling fear in the hero ("He feared, and came to land")—is coded in accordance with eighteenth-century gender roles *as a* male, a "son." That is, rather than suggesting that the spiritual mother behind the fear can act, can have a phallus of her own, her power is encoded as another opponent, a male one. Macpherson attempts (as Freud does later) to elide the power of the mother in favor of that of the father, creating a male spirit who is attacked *through* searching the dark womb. The feminine is not only *not* the actual object of desire, but, stranger still, functions largely as *a means through which* conflict is conducted (as in Starno's pretended marriage offer of his daughter Agandecca to Fingal as a means of luring the young king to Scandinavia [book 3]). More simply put, the attack on the maternal functions primarily as a means of attacking the "ghost in the machine," the male progenitor or precursor. Perhaps this is supported when we learn that Macpherson "hates John Bull but loves his daughters" (Boswell 1950, 258–59), or that he has "no relish for anything in life except women, and even these he cared but little for" (Boswell 1950, 255).

However, a second examination elicits a slightly different view, allowing us to see the "return of the repression" as well as the "return of the repressed" in the killing of the father-figure outlined above. For Cormar is identified in the poem almost exclusively as the primal precursor himself, "the father of my race" as Calmar calls him, and his actions here involve a killing of the "son of the wind." In many ways this is parallel to the Odyssean slaughter of suitors, where, as shown in Chapter 3, the hero returns as both incestuous son and outraged primal father. In addition, the Oedipal conflict with the precursor is assuaged by other aspects of Macpherson's textual strategy. On the one hand, nearly all the young men in the episodes are killed (if not in the actual epic battles, which are—in both senses—relatively bloodless); on the other, far more energy is focused on the fraternal conflict than on parent-child relationships of any kind (apart from the lament for dead sons, as in Fingal's lament for Ryno).

What suggests itself is that Macpherson's relationship with the father is less fraught with anxiety than his relationships with his contemporaries.

This view is borne out upon consideration of the most important "ghost" in the poem, the textual shade of Ossian himself. The blind Bard, blind as Milton and Homer, is always on the verge of fading into the landscape himself when "the wind whistles through the grey hair of Ossian!" (1924, 95). His own frailty, coupled with his deathlessness, is a recurring theme:

> Many were the deaths of my arm! dismal the gleam of my sword! My locks were not then so grey; nor trembled my hands with age. My eyes were not closed in darkness; my feet failed not in the race! (1924, 69)

> When shall I cease to mourn, by the streams of resounding Cona? My years have passed away in battle. My age is darkened with grief! (1924, 74)

These are typical of Ossian's brief digressions. But within the story of the poem, he is associated with the forces of nature not only as reader, but also as creator (even though this passage begins with his voice dying away): "On Lena's gloomy heath, the voice of music died away. The unconstant blast blew hard. The high oak shook its leaves around. . . . [Ossian receives a warning that his son, Oscar, is in danger.] My spear supported my steps; my rattling armour rung. I hummed, as I was wont in danger, the songs of heroes of old. Like distant thunder [the forces of] Lochlin heard. They fled; my son pursued" (1924, 75–76). The mere humming of Ossian emerges "like distant thunder" to frighten the foes. This passage, which is Macpherson's version of the conventional epic night sortie, might be pursued further. The deceitful qualities of Odysseus and Diomedes are transferred to the enemy ("dark advance the sons of Lochlin, over Lena's rustling heath" [76]); the lack of caution in Virgil's Nisus and Euryalus, which seems so noble but which is actually fruitless and fatal, is in *Fingal* rewarded with hardly credible success. Especially interesting is Macpherson's coupling of father and son. The traditional overtones of deceit and same-sex identification (tinged with the homoerotic in Virgil) that the night sortie carries with it irresistibly suggest the connection with Macpherson's own deceptive identification with Ossian. The conflict between father and son before the next day's battle is compelling, hinging as it does on the important question of whose *name* shall be praised. Oscar speaks first, then Ossian replies.

> "O ruler of the fight of steel! my father, hear thy son! Retire with Morven's mighty chief [Fingal]. Give me the fame of Ossian." (1924, 78)

> "Raise Oscar, rather raise my tomb. I will not yield the war to thee. The first and bloodiest in the strife, my arm shall teach thee how to fight. But

remember, my son, to place this sword, this bow, the horn of my deer, within that dark and narrow house, whose mark is one grey stone." (1924, 78–79)

The all-or-nothing mentality of "They best succeed who dare!" that per-vades the poem is not surprisingly embodied to a high degree in Macpherson himself. Nor is it surprising that his vision of the world is to a high degree nar-cissistic, in the terms discussed in Chapter 2.[86] We may suppose Macpherson to have made his eventual compromises with life (though he was buried, at his own request, in Westminster Abbey). But his "very outrageous" attitudes at the height of his fame are consistently characterized by Boswell's valuable commen-tary on the "Sublime Savage" (1950, 265–66). The lack of a strong superego needs little comment in the case of Macpherson. His feelings of grandiosity mixed with insecurity seem nowhere clearer than in *Fingal* itself, where he had the grand ambition to create an epic for Scotland, but the insecurity to name himself only as translator, "sink[ing]," as he said, "into a slave." In par-ticular, Boswell records a number of statements that support the reading of *Fin-gal* thus far:

> Macpherson said he had strong and nice feelings, and therefore was easily made happy or miserable. "But then," said he, "nothing will make me either happy or the reverse above a day. It is hard," said he, "that we tire of everything." (1950, 73–74)

> [H]e said that to retain our high ideas of anything, we should not see it. He said too that few, if any, people were happy. (1950, 249)

While such sentiments are in many ways commonplaces, taken together as a cluster they demonstrate the kind of narcissistic absolutism associated with Milton's Satan. The powerful desire for the absolute ("something in perfec-tion" in another comment), couched in absolute terms, is of a piece with both the supreme rewards for audacity and the ultimate necessity of death in the Os-sianic epic.

The attitudes expressed in *Fingal* toward women, discussed above, are par-alleled by Macpherson's own attitudes, which bring together a multiply-recur-sive approach to union with a marked aggressiveness; in the quotations above from Macpherson, too, it is clear that some other (e.g., John Bull) is being at-tacked *through* women, and that the women themselves are involved secon-darily.

There is greater concord between Macpherson and his precursors than one might initially expect, given the circumstances; Milton's overarching attempt at repression of the recursion—of the Satanic and epic quest for narcissistic fulfillment—is much clearer in comparison. But in a larger sense, the consistent structural patterns of the Ossianic poems strike a similar, and in Macpherson, a discordant note. Not only are the young men effectively silenced by death, but all the words, the songs themselves, are sung by the old.[87] Stafford remarks on the prevalence of aging speakers in the Ossianic poems with a phrase that has surprising resonance: "Ossian is not the only father to outlive his son" (1988, 107). We have discussed Macpherson's ambivalence toward language above; his attitude to the speakers of that language, that is, to Ossian and the other "ancient Bards," is similar, accentuating their age, their frailty, their isolation in the face of approaching death. Since Ossian, like almost all of the narrators in the *Fragments,* is an old man, we have an interesting view of those to whom poetry is possible. *Fortia facta patrum,* Macpherson's family motto as well as the epigraph to *Fingal,* implies in the world of Macpherson a powerful corollary: *infantia facta infantum.* The brave deeds of the fathers allow no space for the still unspoken deeds of the young, except when dead, and then only as textualized, memorialized by the old.[88] As Stafford has pointed out, in this poem "marked by the absence of children and the preponderance of old men," "The obsession with the superiority of the past thus becomes a destructive force, denying the young any opportunity to develop their own potential" (1988, 147). We are forced once again to the sheer immortality of Milton's God, of the deathless and poetically stifling omnipresence of the Father as First Author.[89] In *Fingal,* in consonance with the valorization of the narcissistic heroes, that paternal authority is itself rendered as decayed, tenuous and fleeting. In all cases, however, the father still outlives the son. The return of repressed narcissistic desires is inevitably punished with death, but the paternal authority remains, if "broken" and slightly irrelevant. The very applicability and survival of Ossian's song is in great part undercut by its lack of viability—there are no inheritors in view for "the broken poems of Ossian" (as there are, deferred and metaphysical though they might be, in Milton's world), only fast-fading memories of the lost world. Where the language of Milton's God creates (and largely *is*) the "inform'd" cosmos ("an unpeopled world," as Macpherson noted), the world of Ossian is like the speaker himself, broken, uncontrolled, anarchic. As with the disorder of the measured prose, a freedom is attained for the fulfillment of narcissistic desire; but that desire ceases to have meaning.

Reading Macpherson's doubly inverted epic through Milton's shows an interesting and similar inversion of their social and poetic consequences. Though both poets develop, as we have seen, duplicitous strategies for dealing with tradition—ways of both being and not being the tradition—the worlds they thereby create differ radically, as do the worlds they bequeath to their poetic successors.[90] On the one hand, in Macpherson's epic, godless and disintegrative, existence itself appears futile, and the poet tidily closes down the fantasized world to a nasty, brutish, and very short Hobbesian holiday. On the other hand, Milton, by positing existence and time itself as dependent upon an eternal father, has created a poetry of survival within proscriptive limits; paradoxically, these limits are seen to open outward to include the sum total of human experience: "The world was all before them" (*PL* 12.646).

The results for poetry, however, indicate a different outcome. A plausible reading of *Paradise Lost* is as a work that recreates its author in the image of and as successor to its Author, a work that leaves a deceptively "open" world, but one that actually extends and entrenches the elite script. The only approved heroism is one of masochistic passivity, thus eliminating any agency but *errant* heroism. Any supposed form of agency, likewise, results in one's entrapment in the preordained script of the paternal, for action is possible only within time, and hence within the script of the father, where any swerve is interpreted as fall, and hence "unheroic" in the terms established by Milton. The irony of the poem, the second and Satanic tongue it speaks, though it appears to some critics as only "a heroically embroidered warning" (e.g., Hägin 1964, 159) is equally the only potential source of energy, of escape at all, for the poets who follow in Milton's tradition. Indeed, for Milton, the only potential points for beginning again lie in the reemergence of the narcissistic (in the temptations of Christ and Samson) and in thus putting the question of predetermination aside for the sake of the appearance of temporal agency. It is not surprising that later poets had to do likewise. In the case of Macpherson's *Fingal* we see this narcissistic impulse taken to such an extreme that it threatens to extinguish the tradition it portrays in such decrepitude; and yet the narcissistic impulse toward identity of the poet is to a large degree extinguished in the fiction of "Ossian," just as the heroes themselves are extinguished in the *fictions* of Ossian.

That the Ossianic texts had such a vogue and such an energizing effect on the century that followed, then, is not surprising. *Fingal,* through its fraudulence and its related treatment of the past as irrelevant, eliminates the authority of the tradition it pretends to represent; rendering all customary veneration meaningless, it frees primarily Macpherson himself, but it can also be seen as freeing the poets who follow to erect their own systems, rather than be enslaved by those of others. For the same vital agency (gained precisely to be eliminated in Milton's epic) increases in importance even as the world of the artist is increasingly alienated and fragmented in the nineteenth and twentieth centuries. If value judgments themselves are dependent on the fiction of free will, then virtue, or the good, particularly as it applies to judgment of the self as virtuous (a judgment important to narcissism), becomes dependent on the very concept of the fragment itself.

5

With Half Unravel'd Web

The Fragmented Epic

All that is unknown passes for magnificent.
—Tacitus

THE FRAGMENTED EPIC demonstrates the self-divisiveness urged by the nightmare of history. Keats's *Hyperion*-poems and Hart Crane's American epic, *The Bridge,* exhibit what we might call Oedipal and Oresteian strands in the modern epic; the first of these strands recurs to the father through relations with the maternal; the second recurs to a father already dead. The fragmented epic is a highly productive form, however, not restricted to the so-called Romantic or Modernist periods.[1] The strategy of fragmentation is one, literally enough, of breaking with tradition. In the case of epic, this strategy is fundamentally a breaking *with* tradition, a breakage that is in itself a recursion. While all epics, all human endeavors, are *necessarily* fragmentary products of the human condition,[2] this study uses the term *fragmented* in a more restricted sense, applying it to textual performances that consistently, flagrantly, and often pointedly do not attain to the (conventional and arbitrary) standards of textual coherence and integrity that we are trained to expect.

Lie to us,—dance us back the tribal morn!

Thomas Jefferson, speaking of epics, tells us that in the process of living "things fall off one by one" until we are left with the legendary coherence and completeness of Homer, pointing to an origin that cannot be supplemented or improved: All endeavor since that ideal is marginal, fragmented. Though the fragment as a fallen part of some undivided whole is arguably the most important to epic,[3] we should not neglect other aspects of this relationship. Perhaps I do Jefferson an injustice, since he portrays Homer as a goal toward which "we advance," toward which life tends, and not only as an origin from which life has fallen off. As we grow older, that is, we shed parts of ourselves, growing into or toward an absolute that here is figured as Homer—in my beginning is my end, one might say. The comic figurations of history—Christianity, Marxism—do likewise. Like the *Aeneid*, they project a utopian absolution to the alienation of living within history, an "endlessly receding Italy" that will ideally, like the vanishing mother of Aeneas, make everything whole.[4]

I have just outlined two potentially divergent trends of the fragmented epic—sentimental and utopian visions of an absolute.[5] The particular allegiance of such epics either forward or backward, however, is not so remarkable as the fact that both positions imply a hypotactic relation to the absolute: in one way or another, the fragment is understood as subordinated to some larger whole.[6] Hart Crane, viewed as "the last of the Romantics" by his Modernist contemporaries, illustrates well this hypotactic relation. His epic work on *The Bridge* and poetry itself constitute the attempt at "connective experience," the "bridge" between the fragment and the absolute:

> Poetry, in so far as the metaphysics of any absolute knowledge extends, is simply the concrete *evidence* of the *experience* of a recognition (*knowledge* if you like). . . . When you attempt to ask more of poetry,—the fact of man's relationship to a hypothetical god, be it Osiris, Zeus, or Indra, you will get as variant terms even from the abstract terminology of philosophy as you will from poetry [*sic*]; whereas poetry, without attempting to logically enunciate such a problem or its solution, may well give you the real connective experience, the very "sign manifest" on which rests the assumption of godhead. (225)[7]

The Bridge presents its audience with clear evocations of transcendence as telos: Cathay, Atlantis, the "Answerer of all," the "Everpresence, beyond time" (116–17). What is puzzling about the absolute in *The Bridge* is not so much its consistent presentation as absolute goal, but its status as a goal that remains immediately and practically *irrelevant* to the poetic emphasis. This is demonstrated especially well by the epic's mythic center, "The Dance," and appears most clearly in the speaker's often-quoted invocation of the native American "medicine-man" Maquokeeta:

> Dance, Maquokeeta: Pocahontas grieves . . .
> .   .   .   .
> Dance, Maquokeeta! snake that lives before,
> That casts his pelt, and lives beyond! Sprout, horn!
> Spark, tooth! Medicine-man, relent, restore—
> Lie to us,—Dance us back the tribal morn!

Spears and assemblies: black drums thrusting on—
O yelling battlements,—I, too, was liege
To rainbows currying each pulsant bone:
Surpassed the circumstance, danced out the siege!

  (73)

Through the dance of Maquokeeta, the epic poet's recursive Homeric focus displays a carefully wrought *fiction* of origins, "the tribal morn." The archaic diction (hardly native American) of "siege," "liege," and "yelling battlements" suggests the recursion, and the initial "Spears and assemblies" recur rather precisely to the opening scenes of the *Iliad*.

At first, it seems strange that this fiction of origins is portrayed as a "Lie," and stranger still that this part of the poem is most often read as an ecstatic heterosexual union.[8] Fundamentally, the "Lie" equates with the "snake that lives before, / That casts his pelt, and lives beyond!": Both elide the forces of sexual generation in favor of a myth of self-generation (clearly in consonance with the epic recursion). The heterosexual point of origin, the union of male and female, is largely derealized by its mythic evanescence and the short shrift the poem gives it, especially when compared to the lengthy homosocial interchange. The "dance" is one between men, a metonymic device that enhances— like epic—the homosocial and homoerotic bonds. The principal union takes place between men; the female participates only as incidental ground for masculine connection:[9] "We danced, O Brave, we danced beyond their farms" (75). That is, while there may be a heterosexual union, it is fragmented by the white invasion: "There was a bed of leaves, and broken play" (70).[10] This violent fragmenting of the scene—"a primal scene in both a Freudian and anthropological sense," as Yingling observes (1990, 219)—allows the union between men over the female, the "common basis of our meeting" (Crane 251). This always already fragmenting incursion, then, first allows male conflict and finally male merging. The "conflict between the two races" that Crane describes is one which modulates into full "identifi[cation]"—indeed, into the homoerotic dance of "the serpent with the eagle" (251, 75).[11] This masculine union, as Crane suggests, is "beyond their farms," beyond, that is, the heterosexual cultivation of the virgin soil. Thus, while *a* point of origin arguably resides in the mythic heterosexual coupling, the point of *interest* in "The Dance" is not *that* origin at all, but the "Lie" of Maquokeeta, establishing through its epic recursion a dynamic, recursive, and antitelic narrative. That is, while origin and telos remain fixed and in some way desired, the desire for the maternal goal is more than balanced by antitelic and recursive desire for the paternal.

In a later section, "National Winter Garden," we see a debased inversion of

"The Dance." The female dancer manifests the same earthy feminine principle as Pocahontas: she is the source and ground of *male* acrobatics, she whose "spasm" engenders horror in the male spectators ("we" who "flee through a fleshless door") and, too, she is the ultimate cause of bonding between men ("Always you wait for someone else") (100). Thus, the female in Crane's poem is ambivalently represented as a simultaneously terrifying and enticing telos, the goal to which "each comes back to die alone. / Then you, the burlesque of our lust—and faith, / Lug us back lifeward, bone by infant bone" (101). She is inevitable, but not the immediate object of desire.

Hypotactic fragments often emphasize origin and telos, versions of the absolute. Crane emphasizes instead the bridge, the dance, the lie, the self that lies between them.

With half unravel'd web

We can imagine other relations among fragments themselves, however, as well as with the absolute. *The Waste Land,* for example, offers no redemptive fusion—there *are* only fragments, to shore against ruin as best one can.[12] As Anne M. Janowitz sees this question, such a juxtapositive, paratactic method is typical of the Modernist fragment, contrasting with the hypotactic method of Romanticism. The paratactic fragment denies a traditional unity: "Rather than exemplifying a fracturing of the Romantic organic model of unity, the Modernist fragment collage poem is an anti-Romantic text, and is constructed by arranging discrete fragment elements into wholes which constantly alter as the assemblages generate and proliferate meanings."[13] This view certainly supports Modernism and Romanticism as traditionally conceived, but it is no surprise to find many Romantics among the Modernists, and many Modernists among the Romantics. Rajan usefully qualifies this broad distinction, pointing to the Romantic *valorization* of the fragment as opposed to the "deeply conservative" work of Modernist poets such as Pound, who, like the later Eliot, "returns to the classic unfinished, writing a poem of contestation . . . between the holistic objective and the fragmentary method" (1985, 17).[14] Underscoring this inversion, Rajan sees Byron's *Don Juan* as an epic which is "based on sheer succession, which is not approximative, transformational, or developmental, which is not propelled by its nature to the magnetic north of a final cause, and which is not driven forward by the prospect of emergent understandings or even the hunger for those understandings" (16–17).

In somewhat similar fashion, Keats's fragmentary *Fall of Hyperion* develops a processual theory "decoupled" (in Rajan's phrase) from absolute forms of transcendence. The poem records a surprisingly hopeful interaction with tradition as Keats creates, in his most significant revision of the earlier *Hyperion*, a fiction of agency—a hero, if you will—whose heroism appears to consist precisely in his willingness to sympathize.[15] The difficulty for such an agent is his lack of self, though this is also where his ultimate victory lies. The distinction between the fragmenting strategies of *The Fall of Hyperion* and Byron's *Don Juan* is analogous to the familiar contrast between agnosticism and atheism. In Keats, there is always that unknowing "hunger" for "emergent understandings," but these understandings (epistemes) remain poised, provisional. The emergent understandings are temporary modes of action—acting *as if* such understandings held a kind of truth. The "half unravel'd web" that is *The Fall of Hyperion* captures the poem's fragmentary, atelic and paratactic relation to tradition quite precisely. In addition, its context outlines the swift metamorphosis of understandings possible through the fragmented, processual epic:

> Onward I look'd beneath the gloomy boughs,
> And saw, what first I thought an Image huge.
> Like to the Image pedestal'd so high
> In Saturn's Temple. Then Moneta's voice
> Came brief upon my ear,—"So Saturn sat
> When he had lost his realms"—Whereon there grew
> A power within me of enormous ken,
> To see as a God sees, and take the depth
> Of things as nimbly as the outward eye
> Can size and shape pervade. The lofty theme
> At those few words hung vast before my mind
> With half unravel'd web. I set myself
> Upon an Eagle's watch, that I might see,
> And seeing ne'er forget.
>
>   (1.297–310)[16]

Moneta's whisper, the content of her message, and the speaker's consequent assumption of power imply an Oedipal seduction fantasy. More important, though, is the paratactic relation between "those few words" and the provisional meaning, the "lofty theme" elicited from them: The "discrete fragmentary elements" are read in their relation, not to a unifying completion or telos, but in relation to the "vast," "lofty," but still "half unravel'd" fragment. As reader and visionary dreamer watch, the web ravels and unravels, never reaching nor attempting to reach completion, but only newer thresholds of understanding. To adapt Janowitz here, the weaving reweaves, "constantly alter[ing] as assemblages . . . proliferate meaning."

To "unravel," of course, is to undo, or ravel, the weaving; to separate entangled threads, and hence, to clarify a mystery. To "ravel" means exactly the same thing, though it carries the meaning of "tangle" as well. Thus a "half unravel'd web" is a woven construction undecidably in the process of deconstruction and/or reconstruction. This easily naturalizes to the example of the spider's web, but a more convenient paradigm for such a web is Penelope's weaving and unweaving, which makes a similar engagement with the paternal. She weaves a funeral shroud for Laertes, father of Odysseus; in addition, by completing the weaving she admits the death of Odysseus, and must replace him with one of the suitors. Paradoxically enough, the deferral of completion resurrects Odysseus, giving him time to return. The web of Keats stands in similar relation to tradition, deconstructing its precursors, and at the same time recurring to them insistently within its pattern. For Keats, however (as opposed to Crane), there is no ultimate (or no identifiable) telos to this pattern that cannot be completed. The unraveling web remains *in process,* either forward or back but uncertain which. Crane's *Bridge* carefully inscribes origin and telos, whether or not they are emphasized; Hyperion's actual fall, on the other hand, is never completed, any more than a particular point of origin arises within the multiple frames of dream and vision. The self, and the web that is its textual image, is multiply anchored and ever subject to change, to revision, in light of "emergent understandings," emergent epistemes.

In *Don Juan,* on the other hand, there is a consistent *denial* of understanding that acts as a powerful mode or, better, construction of action. Don Juan, like Dreiser's Sister Carrie, remains "a waif amid forces"; the legend that he becomes is exposed as one based in an odd concatenation of circumstance, and one produced through remarkably little agency of his own. The interaction of self and tradition becomes no more and no less meaningful than any other encounter, except insofar as tradition provides the textual tokens whereby heroic legends are depicted:

> My poem's epic, and is meant to be
> Divided in twelve books; each book containing,
> With love, and war, a heavy gale at sea,
> A list of ships, and captains, and kings reigning,
> New characters; the episodes are three:
> A panoramic view of hell's in training
> After the style of Virgil and of Homer,
> So that my name of Epic's no misnomer.
>
>   (1.200)

The organization is laid out deliberately by Byron as a textual experience mocked by reality's very different forms of experience. (It is also mocked by the reader's textual experience of *Don Juan*.) Traditionally epic forms of experience, in other words, are invoked precisely to show their lack of fit with actual human life.[17] In Byron's poem it is precisely the lack of agency that closes the doors on "emergent understandings"; the insistent skepticism demystifies even the "magnetic north" of the self, a fiction so fully explored in the classic Byronic hero of *Childe Harold's Pilgrimage*—"the wandering outlaw of his own dark mind." Such an appealing fiction understandably became a popular pose or trope for young men—this egotistical sublime that fashions the world after its own longings (" 'Tis to create, and in creating live / A being more intense, that we endow / With form our fancy, gaining as we give / The life we image, even as I do now."). In *Don Juan*, the gates of the self are sealed by the realization of the determinative forces that form the hero, and that waft him from place to place, encounter to encounter.

However, even among poets who eschew traditional myths of origin and telos, few attempts at epic are so fully demystifying as Byron's. Most "decouplings" of the fragment from traditional transcendent wholes result only in new mystiques—those of the Symbol, the Image, the "deep image," the organizing principles of the unconscious, or the creative mind, or the political unconscious (in audience, in poet, or in both).

> Preliminaries consist of such eternity,
> rewriting in an unstable text.
> —Lyn Hejinian[18]

The tactics of the fragmented epic has parallels in Lacan's theory of the mirror stage, which comprehends the human organism as a fragmented body—like a fragmented poem—whose coherence can only be imagined.[19] That is, through adopting the "expedient error" of imagining the self as an autonomous whole, we assert a coherence of self that our actual fragmented experience never lives up to; hence this infinite quadrature as we attempt throughout our lives to make up for the fact that we are not who we imagine ourselves to be. We follow forever in pursuit of that narcissistic fulfillment, that illusionary wholeness of self.[20] As in Lacan's example of the mathematical line (the asymptote), the human life is that which "does not fall together with" its whole and fixed "mirage" of itself.

The *imago* or "mirage" of self established in the mirror stage works two ways in this chapter. First, it echoes the work of the oral epic hero in his or her function as ego-ideal. Second, and germane to this chapter, is the notion of self as process, our perpetual "coming-into-being."[21]

The experientially fragmented human is "caught up in the lure" of the mirage of itself as whole, as totality. At first this mirage is "orthopaedic" and protective, but as an "alienating identity" (of unachievable totality) it soon becomes an armor which, like that of Milton's angels, harms rather than helps. While all epics are involved with compensating for the lack inherent in the self, fragmented epics highlight this drama of quadrature by their recursive *méconnaissances*. Their fragmentation is grounded in insufficiency, and is "completed" or "squared"—if at all—only within the minds of the audience, and then only provisionally, in accordance with audience desire (most frequently demonstrated in institutional desires for textual fixity).

In order to follow the various tactics of *méconnaissance*, Lacan's own use of metaphor is suggestive; generated by similar cultural matrices, these metaphors inform the fragmented epic to a surprising degree. Lacan suggests the "orthopaedic" usefulness behind the illusion of total form,[22] and extends this into the potential problem of hypostatizing the self in "the assumption of an armour of an alienating identity." The same essay glances at architectural symbolism, where "the formation of the I" is symbolized by "a fortress, or stadium . . . divid[ed] into two opposed fields of contest where the subject flounders in quest of the lofty, remote inner castle."[23] These metaphors correspond easily with the traditional concentration in epic—perhaps especially in fragmented epic—on protective armor, fortresses, even metamorphosis. The idealized form of the self in Spenser's House of Alma may be the most familiar in a long line of architectural forms—from Aeneas' numerous architectural attempts and abandonments to Crane's installation of all desire within the Brooklyn Bridge.[24] The opening proem of *The Bridge* presents "opposed fields of contest," displaying even their encroachment upon the "lofty, remote inner castle":

> . . . across the harbor, silver-paced
> As though the sun took step of thee, yet left
> Some motion ever unspent in thy stride,—
> Implicitly thy freedom staying thee!
>
> Out of some subway scuttle, cell or loft
> A bedlamite speeds to thy parapets,
> Tilting there momently, shrill shirt ballooning,
> A jest falls from the speechless caravan.
>
> Down Wall, from girder into street noon leaks,
> A rip-tooth of the sky's acetylene;
> All afternoon the cloud-flown derricks turn . . .
> Thy cables breathe the North Atlantic still.

(45)

The archaic invocational rhythm and forms of address reflect a diction redolent of chivalric romance—bedlamite, parapets, caravans, the "tilting" of the tournament.[25] The movement upward and downward (executed by bedlamite, "jest," and the noon sunlight that "leaks" down Wall Street as a jagged crenellation of the sky) displays two opposed fields, that of the "subway scuttle" later to be more fully realized in "The Tunnel," and that of the sun, the purity of the "sky's acetylene." The Brooklyn Bridge is presented not only as the jointure of these two, but also as a reification of constancy in a world of flux, a structure both lofty and remote, "across the harbor, silver-paced," whose "cables breathe the North Atlantic still." Like Keats's "still unravish'd bride," the bridge is fundamentally paradoxical, and it is important that we examine at least two of the potential ambiguities of "still." The clearest reading is that the cables continue to "breathe the North Atlantic," to be inspired by the changeable flux of the surrounding elements. But the bridge should also be seen in the act of inspiring that flux, of breathing it into stillness. This gift of the bridge to inform its environment (in Lacan, the mark of the significatory copula) runs throughout the poem. Like language itself, the bridge is always (at least) bivalent, its freedom providing it with both hindrance and support ("staying thee"). Clearly enough this rewrites Milton's "heroic patience," the virtue of being free to fall yet remaining sufficient to stand. What is somewhat puzzling—and especially enlightening—is the lack of internal and external dimensions to this version of the heroic self; the fortress image of Lacan has been replaced by a vision of the self as the channel, the connection *between* opposed fields. Moreover, the bridge must to a great extent be understood as inherently *divided* between those fields, not only in its (at least heuristic) need for anchoring points, but in its recursive pattern of ambiguity, its constant construction of a thoroughly divided self, as seen in "stay" and "still" above. An exaggerated form of this division may be understood in the division of the human figure of the "bedlamite." While this is primarily a reference to the insane suicide, Giles reminds us that the best known of bedlamites, of course, is Christ (1986, 151).

Lacan stresses that the recurrent images of armor and architecture in the epic "hall of mirrors" are opposed by "imagos of the fragmented body" (1977, 11). All of these are violently diasparactive: "images of castration, mutilation, dismemberment, dislocation, evisceration, devouring, bursting open of the body" (11). The opening of *The Bridge* highlights a few of these fairly clear images—commonplaces of twentieth-century poetry.[26] Dislocation appears as the primary mode of fragmentation in these three stanzas, but it is a dislocation more thorough than the simple movement of the suicide from dungeon, to parapet, to destruction. The dislocation, first of all, is (in Allen Tate's phrase) "original and fundamental": the suicide arises from "subway scuttle, cell *or* loft," a deliberately ambiguous and multiple source, one that contains within it irreconcilable contradictions of height and depth. While part of the effect is to emphasize the general application (any insane person, not a particular one), that effect is part and parcel of the dispersal of identity implicit in such dislocation. More important than the physical dislocation, however, are the figural dislocations imposed by shifts of scene: the bridge "across the harbor," the bridge of the suicide, and then "Down Wall [Street]"; and by shifts of identity: the physical suicide "Tilting there momently" *becomes* the "jest fall[ing] from the speechless caravan," and then, less forcefully, becomes "noon" and the "rip-tooth" of the heavens that "leaks" "from girder into street."

The violence of "rip-tooth," as a coinage by Crane, is particularly intriguing. Giles, in his useful appendix, glosses the term in three ways: (a) as describing the sky between skyscrapers as "like [the] gap where [a] tooth has been ripped out of a man's mouth," (b) rip as a "worthless person, scamp" and (c) as rough water where opposite currents meet ("poem pulling opposite ways") (230). While all of these allow plausible readings, helpful as well would be the psychological significance attached to the loss of teeth in dreams ("as a rule" symptomatic of the fear of castration [Freud 1900, 422–27]). With the addition of the speechlessness of the spectators, and the deflative slang term for urination applied to the "rip-tooth" of light, *imagos* of the fragmented body appear to proliferate.[27] "Rip-tooth" might also be read productively as formed upon the model of "ripsaw"—the coarse-toothed saw used for cutting along the grain.

We might do any number of things with these divergent readings of fragmentation, but I am less concerned with a particular meaning than with the very multiplicity of readings that suggest themselves, a multiplicity that is itself a marker of the fragmented body. These images, in company with the isolate bridge itself, draw the reader in a movement from the potential ecstatic telos of the bridge to the headlong plunge, and then return that reader to equanimity, as "All afternoon the cloud-flown derricks turn." The movement to a place (again) between the opposed fields of contest, and the unelaborated pun (derrick = Crane) return the reader to a phallic identity, but that identity has been undermined to an extent by the action within or upon it, and begins to appear more fragile.

How does this awareness of the errancy involved in forming the self connect with the epic masterplot of violence and sex? Within the terms of the theory, the fragmented epic should, of course, remain sexually unfulfilled; that is, the breakage of one's own text, though it suffices as an aggressive breaking of tradition, remains an image of the fragmented body. As the sexual/maternal goal of the Oedipal script cannot be achieved when the self is perceived as broken or castrated, so the epic goal cannot be achieved; indeed, most frequently we find that, for the fragmented epic, not even the happy substitute—the social and legal referent—can be achieved. We expect to encounter images of violence, threat, and danger, often framed as castration anxiety; such images will predominate, but desire will remain unfulfilled, possibly denigrated to the extent of becoming insufficient as substitute.

This is linked precisely to identity, that is, to the presentation of self (or hero) in the fragment. The hero is essentially hollow, a fiction of agency: Romantic, quixotic, deluded. This fictional, textual self supposedly could attain its projected wholeness, but the fiction is subverted by an awareness of self as fragmented, and/or by the recognition that the goal of fulfillment is unattainable. The quixotic self is one that is precariously maintained against a cruel and chilly world; the half-ironic, cognizantly futile gesture of the narcissistic mind—willfully ignoring the obvious threat. The world is thus "subjected" in two senses, as it is made subject to the desiring self, and as it is thus also correlative to the "perceiving" subject itself. That is, the environment is necessarily enchanted by the romantic, mythopoeic mind, enchanted so as to provide a locus for self, for agency.

Thus, fragmented epic shows not merely the impossibility of the union with maternal wholeness, but the denigration, deconstruction, or deferral of such potentially happy substitutes as the text creates. As with the more conventional "completed" epics, there is a range within the fragment from narcissistic focus (suggested as characteristic of earlier oral and traditional epic) to Oedipal emplotment (typical of chirographic belatedness). In print epics, we have observed the inversion, not only of traditional heroism, but also of the attitude toward tradition; rather than maintaining a precise Oedipal model, modern epic poets frequently follow a model that could be characterized as Oresteian, involving the murder or elision of the maternal in favor of a metonymic connection with the paternal. More precisely, in the Oedipal plot, metonymic fulfillment is deployed within a script we receive as highly sexualized. In an Oresteian plot, the metonymic fulfillment of union with the paternal is deployed through the (often violent) destruction of women, as in Macpherson's slain females, or in Milton's excision of the strictly female from creation. The Oedipal (and predominantly heterosexual) plot remains in cultural ascendancy, and attains such a cultural mastery that poets falling within the modern era's definition of the "homosexual" must, in epics that establish other bases of narcissistic fulfillment, to some extent *write in* the female goal.[28]

As we examine particular fragmented epics more closely, these dynamics

of sex and violence become clearer. Since much fragmented epic directly concerns the "making" (*poiesis*) of a fictionally whole self—a mirage—that works
to heal the fragmented poetic psyche, it is worth exploring this typical formation of the genre, what earlier criticism might have called an "epic hero."

> To fight in another man's armour is something more
> than to be influenced by his style of fighting.
> —C. S. Lewis[29]

It is hardly surprising to find that the heroic figures of the fragmented epic
are themselves fragmented. Lacan's "armour of an alienating identity" recurs
significantly in fragmented epic through its use of traditional military trappings as a kind of second skin for its characters.[30] The way the arms of Achilles
shift between heroes of the *Iliad*, for example, demonstrates the jeopardy into
which an "alienating identity" can place the narcissistically concerned self. The
identity of Achilles is lent along with the armor to Patroklos, and this relin-
quishing of the image of self opens the way for Achilles' narcissistic humilia-
tion and rage;[31] similarly, the mockery of self in the appearance of the armored
Hektor directly undermines the centrality of the hero with the spectral implication of his utter replaceability. Achilles' ultimate victory over Hektor suggests that the shifting of the signifier—the explicitly textual arms—has relatively little to do with a substratum of Achillean identity. This reading is
underscored, as well, by the (almost) invulnerable "real" skin of Achilles (the
product of the Stygian bath).

In later epic, and in fragmented forms in particular, the warrior's arms,
even when they remain in the hero's possession, and even though they continue
to function as signifiers of the heroic identity, become increasingly alienated
from the "inner self" of the hero. Virgil's Aeneas, driven by the strictly textual
imperative of fate (*fatum*, "that which has been spoken") rather than by the older
heroic dictum of glory (of *famam extendere factis*, i.e., *kleos* or *lof*), displays a dramatically insubstantial self. Actually mistaken for a ghost in the third book,
Aeneas is, as one critic has commented, "the ghost of Troy until he becomes the
father of Rome."[32] Since in the epic he never does become "the father of Rome,"
his own relation with his armorial signifier is particularly unsettling.

The shield of Aeneas depicts the future history of Rome, centering on the
climax of internecine struggle in the Battle of Actium. The shield is full of
meaning for those who know how to read it, especially for those who know

something of Roman history; Aeneas himself, however, remains *rerum ignarus,* ignorant of the things displayed (8.725ff.):

> Miratur talia dona parentis per clypeum Vulcani:
> que gaudet imagini rerum ignarus,
> que attollens famam et fata nepotum humero.[33]

At best, he can "admire" this gift (from his mother)[34] as one that is clearly significant, if incomprehensible, and head off to battle carrying on his shoulder the glory and destiny of his descendants (*famam et fata nepotum*). As Lacan points out, "Only a subject can understand a meaning; conversely, every phenomenon of meaning implies a subject" (1977, 9). The dramatic irony in this scene, of Aeneas ignorantly and speechlessly "admiring" the signifier that represents his own fictional telos or point of wholeness, brings a surprisingly tragic outcome to the Lacanian drama of the "mirror stage." The infant arrives at the mirror but refuses to recognize (or misrecognize) the imaged wholeness as representative of its own fragmented body. Because the subject or self is *formed* through that investiture of meaning, the inability to articulate the relation of one's fragmented body to the imagined whole implies a continued "subjectlessness." Aeneas remains a textual ghost, vacillating between the reiterated demands of *fatum* that impel him into the future and the "admiring" but "unspeakable" (*infandum*) attachments to the preverbal world of fulfillment.[35] The hero's departure from the underworld through the gates of ivory rather than of horn is a less puzzling crux: Aeneas himself is a false dream, a textual fiction.

In the world of the *Aeneid,* full of "mysterious prophecies, half-truths, and thwarted attempts,"[36] such an outcome is not terribly surprising. Steele Commager draws attention to this "constant and unhappy gap" between the determinative textual forces and the characters, in phrases that point up the fragmented, subjectless quality of this "heroic self": "how rarely Aeneas is even graced with an active verb. He becomes the creator of Rome, but only [by] becoming a creature of destiny."[37] The distances that radiate from his current, split existence as "scattered remnant" to the potential and past imagined unities are distances literally inscribed by the hero's attempt to merge with those unreachable texts: at Buthrotum, for example, his pathetic attempt to merge with the barren, imitative signifier of the Trojan past (3.347–50); similarly, in the (for him) meaningless establishment of the Greek arms of Abas in memorial of Augustus' future victory at Actium (3.288).[38] In both of these we see Aeneas as signifier, literally and figuratively bridging the gap from the Homeric past, reaching into the Roman future. But it is with these as with the shield: the hollowness, or the instability, which is at the core of this textual fiction, Aeneas, is highlighted by the dissonance between the textual self and the self-referential text of his alienating shield. (The shield inscribes the self of Aeneas and his destiny for the reader; for Aeneas, the shield is "self-referential" in the different sense of its autotelic structure—as far as he knows, it is meaningless apart from its beauty and martial utility.)[39]

There is a dramatic irony here in which the reader plays a significant role, observing the dissonance between infant self and the coherent but alien self of the heroic arms. This kind of dramatic irony is heightened in a work like Spenser's *Faerie Queene*, where the heroic trappings of medieval chivalry play an even larger part in the *méconnaissances* of the work as a whole.[40] Though this is most easily seen in the decomposition of the heroic self into six (and potentially twelve) fragmentary heroes, a slippage similar to that of Aeneas occurs between the various knights and their accoutrements. Sir Guyon, knight of the "pedestrian virtue" of temperance, loses not only his steed, but also, if temporarily, his shield and sword (as well as his guide, the Palmer) (2.2, 2.8). Between the Redcrosse Knight and the shield from which he takes that name lies a broad chasm; apart from the naming, that chasm is bridged only tenuously, ephemerally.[41] A somewhat different attitude to this chasm between the self and its fictional image can be seen in the pentacle—Solomon's "endelesse knot"—as a signifier of perfection in *Sir Gawain and the Green Knight*. But the *Gawain*-poet presents the five fives that lead to such perfection as necessarily ridden by error in the human world. Sir Gawain may be "as a perle amoung quyte pese" but it is his personal tragedy that he cannot live up to his own image of himself, to the projected (i.e., fictional) whole. In *Sir Gawain and the Green Knight*, the poet's irony directly emphasizes the specific *méconnaissance* between the images created by self and society (the ultimate telos of perfect fulfillment portrayed upon the shield) and the fragmented experience of life, of its happy or unhappy substitutions. The knot of the self's infinite quadrature is "endless" in more ways than one, of course; it is this multiplicity and its inherent fragmentation that redeem Spenser's (and the *Gawain*-poet's) vision: Though perfection and equally full selfhood cannot be attained within the world, something approaching such a state can be grasped, if only momentarily.

Clearer in structural terms is the case of Spenser's Calidore: His capture of the Blatant Beast causes much rejoicing, but it is closely followed by the beast's escape. The poet like the knight follows "an endelesse trace, withouten guyde" and the recursive establishment and disruption of harmonious wholes in book 6 come to seem the pattern of the entire poem. As Jonathan Goldberg puts it, the *Faerie Queene* "offers continuous disequilibrium, frequent disruptions in narration, and characters who exist to disappear."[42] Dixon phrases a similar concern more pungently: "Nor is the form of the poem more bracing than the content, in grammar and spelling lawless, in language and rime licentious in every articulation of its limbs."[43] The metaphor explains the poem as itself a fragmented body, one with specifically "licentious" overtones. And this makes some sense within the traditional framework of sex and violence, where the poem (like the hero) is unable to reach a point of fulfillment: Like Arthur borne down beneath his shield, *The Faerie Queene* is only by an act of grace—through the reader's coercive imagination—conceived as a whole.

"This Arab phantom, which I thus beheld": Fragmented Hero as Specter and Spectator

This armorial recursiveness to fragmented epic implies a textualized conception of reality, even an awareness of the heroic self as a fiction of agency. Both hero and arms are texts, things "written" or "read." Later fragmented epic highlights this textuality by common reference to Cervantes' (textually created and impelled) Don Quixote. The quixotic works as an ironic figure of the poet's own self-delusions (that is, as a carefully distanced figure of narcissistic wish-fulfillment). In Wordsworth's spectral "Arab phantom," the "semi-Quixote" of *The Prelude* (5.71–140), this figure is especially well developed.[44] Though Wordsworth, contemplating the apocalypse (the ultimate diasparactive force), believes that the "living Presence" (5.34) of the eternal psyche will remain, still he fears deeply the loss of earthly identity, the social and human works within the earth's fragmented body (whose "the whole frame" will be "wrenched" "by inward throes" [5.30–31]):

Yea, all the adamantine holds of truth
By reason built, or passion . . .
The consecrated works of Bard and Sage,
Sensuous or intellectual, wrought by men,
Twin labourers and heirs of the same hopes;
Where would they be? Oh! why hath not the Mind
Some element to stamp her image on
In nature somewhat nearer to her own?

   (5.39–47)

The mind's desire to see itself ideally reflected as a complete, eternal whole again parallels Lacan's mirroring fiction of wholeness (opposed to the fragmented sensations of actual experience). In the dream that follows these anxieties, the "kindred hauntings" (56) of diasparactive force give way to the fictional (and textual) agent, the "errant knight" of narcissistic success.

   Between the dreamer (not "exempt" from injury, "seized" by sleep, distress

and fear "creeping over me") and the single-minded, exotic rider of the drome-
dary who emerges "at my side, / Close at my side" there is an ironic distance
parallel but inverse to the slippage between hero and arms. Both dreamer and
dream are textual, but the dream presents a free agent with an absolute goal.
The poet's attitude toward the "semi-Quixote" is ambivalent, recognizing the
madness of the "uncouth shape," and yet wishing "To cleave unto this man"
(5.116):

> Full often, taking from the world of sleep
> This Arab phantom, which I thus beheld,
> This semi-Quixote, I to him have given
> A substance, fancied him a living man,
> A gentle dweller in the desert, crazed
> By love and feeling, and internal thought
> Protracted among endless solitudes;
> Have shaped him wandering upon this quest!
> Nor have I pitied him; but rather felt
> Reverence was due to a being thus employed;
> And thought that, in the blind and awful lair
> Of such a madness, reason did lie couched.
>
>   (5.141–52)

The suppressed violence of the Arab rider and his fool's errand are specifically
opposed to the conventional compromises or substitutes for the Oedipal script
of narcissistic success: there are more than enough men willing to devote themselves to "Their wives, their children, and their virgin loves, / Or whatever else
the heart holds dear" (5.154–55). The poet desires instead "To cleave unto" this
mirroring image of fulfillment, to "share / That maniac's fond anxiety," and go
"Upon like errand" (160–61). In the simultaneous disparagement and elevation
of the quixotic figure, Wordsworth realizes and condemns the illusory quality—
the fool's errand—of narcissistic fulfillment, but at the same time adopts it as a
goal preferable to that of compromise.

What violence is here? The semi-quixote is engaged in the nobly conceived
quest of rescuing the "twofold treasure" of human fictions from the diasparactive realities implicit in the advancing seas: the stone of Euclid's *Elements*, and
the resplendent shell of Poetry.[45] The goal of the quixotic quest as it becomes
known (or misknown) to the dreamer is somewhat puzzling: the Arab explains
the stone and shell, and commands the questioner to hold the latter to his ear:

>   I did so,
> And heard that instant in an unknown tongue,
> Which yet I understood, articulate sounds,

A loud prophetic blast of harmony;
An Ode, in passion uttered, which foretold
Destruction to the children of the earth
By deluge, now at hand. No sooner ceased
The song, than the Arab with calm look declared
That all would come to pass of which the voice
Had given forewarning, and that he himself
Was going then to bury those two books:
The one that held acquaintance with the stars,
And wedded soul to soul in purest bond
Of reason, undisturbed by space or time;
The other that was a god, yea many gods,
Had voices more than all the winds, with power
To exhilarate the spirit, and to soothe,
Through every clime, the heart of human kind.

> (5.92–109)

The attempt at preservation attributed to the Arab rider is oddly in contrast with his decision "to bury those two books," particularly when one of them is precisely that which gives "forewarning" of the deluge. What remains dramatically unclear is how these actions will "preserve" anything, once the books are buried in the midst of "the illimitable waste" and covered by "the fleet waters of the drowning world" (5.136–37).

Moreover, "the Ode"—later equated with the "poor earthly casket of immortal verse, Shakespeare, or Milton" (5.164–65) and destined equally for burial—is multiple and strangely threatening, despite the soothing disclaimers of the last lines above (5.108–9). The "calm" of the rider at this point reminds us of Achilles' narcissistic fantasy of extinction, but more important, the shell conveys the oral text of the threatening parental figure. As a solid emissary of the approaching deluge—in terms both of its appearance and its message—the shell conveys the threat of punishment in the diasparactive image of the devouring flood and the fragmentation of its own voices, "more than all the winds." As a shell from the beach, of course, its synecdochal relation with the apocalypse is hard to ignore, and the familiar voice of the ocean that we hear in seashells becomes the "prophetic blast" of the castrating, fragmenting threat.[46] The precise gender-coding of this threat is uncertain; though readers have argued that Wordsworth locates the absent father in Nature (at least in her "severer interventions") here at least that precision of specification is lacking.

What appears to be happening, then, is an attempt both to rescue and destroy the parental figure or figures, in an act of burial (repression) that is both an affirmation of self and simultaneously a destruction of that self. This last may not yet be clear, so it is important that the "semi-quixote" gains his identity only through the quest undertaken; indeed, by his possession of the shell and its voice, he appears to call up the very deluge he precedes. The precise form of the self-mutilation to be undergone as punishment is most readily visible, perhaps, if we contrast the ever deferred goal of the quest (the abandonment and burial of shell and stone) with the earlier picture of this fictional agent in his uncompromising quest for narcissistic fulfillment:

> Close at my side, an uncouth shape appeared
> Upon a dromedary, mounted high.
> He seemed an Arab of the Bedouin tribes:
> A lance he bore, and underneath one arm
> A stone, and in the opposite hand, a shell.
>
> (5.75–79)

Viewed in the context of this argument, the "uncouth shape" of the erect penis is almost unmistakable; the lance he bears, the draped and flowing clothing associated with the Bedouins, and the "twofold charge" or "treasure" become immediately explicable. The self-castration implicit in the discharge of the quest (significantly remaining incomplete) is ultimately a narcissistic victory, for such a breakage of the self is also a destruction and burial of the representatives of the parental images, the stone and the shell. Moreover, it is a victory that aggrandizes the self in its maintenance of identity.

Though his anxieties soon surface again, it is not surprising that the figure of the spectatorial dreamer or poet is initially pleased with this phallic manifestation:

> At the sight
> Much I rejoiced, not doubting but a guide
> Was present, one who with unerring skill
> Would through the desert lead me . . .
> I looked and looked, self-questioned what this freight
> Which the new-comer carried through the waste,
> Could mean. . . .
>
> (5.80–86)

In Chapter 3, I emphasized the importance of the gaze as an expression of phallic dominance in the voyeuristic aspect of the scopophilic tendency. Here a similar mechanism is at work, the phallic exhibitionism of the Arab rider fully matched by the dreamer who "looked and looked" trying to keep the semi-quixote "full in view" (5.135) both as phallus and as empowered (or not yet compromised) image of self. In fragmented epic in general, this position as passive yet interested, "questioning" spectator is of vital importance.[47] In Wordsworth and Crane, we see it balanced most clearly by the quixotic principle. In poets such as Whitman and Keats the questioner comes to be of even greater import, as such a figure *seems*, at least, to be integrally less fragmented.

In Crane's epic we see again the textual figure of quixotic delusion and narcissistic fulfillment involved in a visual and textual sacrifice for the benefit of the interested spectator(s):

> Out of some subway scuttle, cell or loft
> A bedlamite speeds to thy parapets,
> Tilting there momently, shrill shirt ballooning,
> A jest falls from the speechless caravan.
>
> (45)

The ambivalent interpretations of the suicide are finely realized in the single word "jest," which functions ambiguously: as an appositive, renaming the suicide; as a paradoxically unspeakable textual jeer or taunt from the spectators in the "speechless caravan"; and as heroic jest or exploit. (Though "jest" in this sense is obsolete, it is familiar within the tradition from the *chansons de geste*.) This last in particular suits the act of suicide as *eine Tat*, the Nietzschean and existential act of self-assertion, the *gesture* that asserts a free space and defines its own morality. These readings appear antithetical, but of course the point is that the antitheses are a complex choreography of the divided self. Like Wordsworth's "semi-Quixote," the "jest" is both foolishly deluded and romantically, narcissistically noble. The fiction of agency is reduced in power to a single act, one that literally depends upon the bridge.

This quixotic retrieval of agency is one that Crane alludes to in his letters at a point of crisis similar to Wordsworth's in its concern with precursor-texts. He writes to Waldo Frank, pointing precisely to the necessary error, the evasive *méconnaissance* of "faith" required to construct *The Bridge*, for *The Bridge*

> is an act of faith besides being a communication. The symbols of reality necessary to articulate the span—may not exist where you expected them, however. By which I mean that however great their subjective significance to me is concerned—these forms, materials, dynamics are simply non-existent in the world. I may amuse and delight and flatter myself as much as I please,—but I am only evading a recognition and playing Don Quixote in an immorally conscious way.
>
> The form of my poem rises out of a past that so overwhelms the present with its worth and vision that I'm at a loss to explain my delusion that there exist any real links between that past and a future destiny worthy of it. The "destiny" is long since completed. (231–32)

Crane goes on to remark further on his belatedness with regard to other poets. Accurately enough, he isolates the two poles of the diasparactive tension we have outlined: the voyeuristic observer caught in and fragmented by deterministic forces, represented in the letter by "Laforgue, Eliot, and others of that kidney [who] have whimpered fastidiously"; and the deluded agency of a poet like Whitman, with his "increasingly lonely and ineffectual . . . confidence" (232). The same tension is figured as the gap between the "intellectual" judgment of the bridge's absurdity and the "emotional" commitment of belief (231). The consistently spectatorial role of "the protagonist" of the poem (and through that protagonist allocated to the reader) is countered throughout by the ironized view of the narcissistic and deluded figure, most notably in Rip Van Winkle, as Crane points out in a letter to Otto Kahn: "The walk to the subway arouses reminiscences of childhood, also the 'childhood' of the continental conquest, viz., the conquistadores, Priscilla, Capt. John Smith, etc. These parallelisms unite in the figure of Rip Van Winkle who finally becomes identified with the protagonist, as you will notice, and who really boards the subway with the reader. He becomes the 'guardian angel' of the journey into the past" (250). Rip Van Winkle is a quixotic figure akin to Wordsworth's Arab rider, though the American version emphasizes his childlike faith. As "guardian angel," he too constructs (and is part of) the bridge through time, the "hero" under construction in Crane's epic. The fragmentation of his life's narrative is the most significant thing about him, perhaps, and it is the fiction of a continuing identity that allows him, in Irving's story, to resume his life with little change. These dreams of continuity, however, are questioned by diasparactive forces: the breaking of his life, of course, but also the breaking with tradition implicit in his name—not just a chip off the old block, but a rip off the old "winkle." (Partridge's *Dictionary* includes "winkle" as contemporary slang for the penis.)[48] Numerous other fragmentary figures merge with and separate from this combination of the quixotic Rip Van Winkle and the spectatorial protagonist/reader as we move through Crane's *Bridge*. Keats offers a somewhat different way of imaging the hero of the fragmented epic.

The Chameleon Poet

Keats in *The Fall of Hyperion* manages to recombine the spectral and spectatorial aspects of heroism through the strategy of the "camelion Poet," as he explains it in a well-known letter on his own "poetical Character" (as distinct "from the wordsworthian or egotistical sublime"):

[I]t is not itself—it has no self—it is every thing and nothing—It has no character—it enjoys light and shade; it lives in gusto, be it foul or fair, high or low, rich or poor, mean or elevated—It has as much delight in conceiving an Iago as an Imogen. What shocks the virtuous philosop[h]er, delights the camelion Poet. It does no harm from its relish of the dark side of things any more than from its taste for the bright one; because they both end in speculation. A Poet is the most unpoetical of any thing in existence; because he has no Identity—he is continually in for—and filling some other Body—The Sun, the Moon, the Sea and Men and Women who are creatures of impulse are poetical and have about them an unchangeable attribute—the poet has none; no identity—he is surely the most unpoetical of all God's creatures. (1959, 279)

For Keats, the revolutionary narcissist (Iago) and the heroically patient "heavenly angel" (Imogen) both "end in speculation," the visualization of consequences. This process of heroism is close kin to the spectatorial and passive aspect of the fragmented hero (the Wordsworthian dreamer). Through a metonymic process of sympathy ("in for . . . filling some other body") the poet creates a self. This process of selfless sympathy (as Keats recognizes) requires the *loss* of any prior identity, and therefore results in a self that is neither identity nor nonentity, but rather one whose temporary definitions rely on other entities, on "creatures of impulse" with "an unchangeable attribute." The "camelion Poet" develops a self that is always only its parts: inherently fragmentary, "it is every thing and no thing," a fundamental dehiscence that is only maintained through its repeated metamorphoses and its consistently speculative, questioning attitude. A thing primarily perceptual, it "enjoys" and "delights" with both taste and relish.

The connection of this form of heroism to the typical hero and the armorial trappings of fragmented epic eluded me for some time, until I realized the answer was hidden in plain sight: Like the "alienating identity" of armor, the "camelion Poet's" sympathetic imagination is psychologically a form of protective coloration. Rather than the assimilative "egotistical sublime" of Wordsworth or Whitman (with its consequent repressions), the Keatsian strategy is that of recursive accommodation to the tradition and his precursors. That is, while both strategies are metonymic in their embedded desires to repeat the past, a poet such as Wordsworth aims to repeat the past as a repetition of the self: "the Child is father of the Man" (or Whitman: "I am the Acme of all that has been accomplished, / And the Encloser of all that is to come"). Keats, on the other hand, creates through sympathetic identification a self that only *exists* insofar as it is a recursion to the past, figured much like Rupert Brooke's "pulse in the Eternal Mind." The Keatsian strategy of the chameleon parallels to some extent the disguised "gift" of self in the *Odyssey*, but shows less of Odysseus' deliberately aggressive maintenance of the interior self. For Keats, the effort is precisely to become (as fully as possible) the other, thus to construct and reconstruct the self or selves that we eternally lack.

Rather than an interior self armored with patriarchal (or parental) signifiers (as with Aeneas, Wordsworth's semi-Quixote, or Rip Van Winkle), the individual self, such as it is, is instead lost, camouflaged, within a landscape that is *itself* the signature of the father. (What matters here is emphasis, not mutually exclusive recursions to the paternal.) Twentieth-century epic develops its sleeping giants in response to a still increasing sense of the world as always already text, always already the father's (as in Macpherson's myths of the Highlands). This fully worded world leaves the perceiving subject a highly circumscribed role. Operating primarily as perceiver, his or her contribution is limited to the collection of fragments, fragmented images of a body once (in imagination) whole.[49] The "shavings and shale of lost cultures" encountered in the landscape are "tokens" of the precursor, tokens that are questioned and found meaningful—or not.[50]

Look on my works, ye mighty, and despair!

The fragmentary *Fall of Hyperion* develops a processual and provisional theory of self—a chameleon poet—decoupled from absolute forms of transcendence.[51] In the earlier, heavily Miltonic *Hyperion: A Fragment,* Keats rewrites the opening books of *Paradise Lost* through the older myths of the classical poetic world. In his next rewriting the poet develops the same story of the changing world around a central first-person narrator and places that speaker within multiple layers of dream and vision. Both texts depict a poetic rite of passage—the transformation of an idle dreamer by progressive experience into a poet with a full understanding of the tragic nature of life; but in the earlier *Hyperion*, the god Apollo undergoes the transformation, rather than the poet himself as in the *Fall of Hyperion*. This adoption of the leading role shows the poet quite clearly repeating for himself a precursor's development. It is not just a usurpation of poetic godhood, but rather an identification with Apollo so complete as to displace him entirely. This recursive process of usurpation through identification, literally or metaphorically displayed, plays a significant role in the developing poet.

Understanding this watchful hero, recurrently (and recursively) "questioning," helps us understand fragmented epic (and especially Keats's epics). Such a hero is most easily explicated through exploring the "ruin-poem" and its essential paradox, a paradox that Martin Aske (1985) limits to the function of "epitaph." But Aske underestimates the ambivalence involved in contemplating ruin, and the agency of spectator and audience. These texts deliberately parade human frailty and the inevitability of change. The heavily ironic inscription on the pedestal of Shelley's Ozymandias, King of Kings, is a famous example. About the broken statue of Ozymandias lies a wasteland, and the poet carefully portrays the futility of the mightiest efforts by the mightiest of humankind. A less ironic parallel in *The Fall of Hyperion* (and in *Hyperion*) is the vision of precursors "Like sculpture builded-up upon the grave / Of their own power" (*Fall of Hyperion* 1.383–84):

> Along the margin sand large footmarks went,
> No farther than to where old Saturn's feet
> Had rested, and there slept, how long a sleep!
> Degraded, cold, upon the sodden ground
> His old right hand lay nerveless, listless, dead,
> Unsceptred; and his realmless eyes were closed;
> While his bow'd head seem'd listening to the Earth,
> His antient mother, for some comfort yet.
>
> (*Fall of Hyperion* 1.319–26)

Keats extends the frailty of humans to the gods. All is broken and (as Aske points out) "voiceless" (1985, 11) in this vision, where even "the Naiad 'mid her reeds / Press'd her cold finger closer to her lips" (*Hyperion* 13–14; *Fall of Hyperion* 1.315–18). This deliberate silencing of the living poet is just as clearly displayed in the textual imprints of the powerful precursor, those "large footmarks" beyond which one can go "no farther." In spite of these, however, as in Shelley's sonnet there is an ironic satisfaction for the modern poet in the fallen impotence of the precursor, the projected satisfaction of Apollo in *Hyperion* as the ancient figures give way before the young "by course of Nature's law" (2.181). But simultaneously, fragmented poems also subscribe to the tradition, continuity, and the permanence of effort as they display the beauty of ruin and fragmentation *for the spectator*.[52] In the sonnet, both the pedestal with its "vast and trunkless legs of stone," and the fallen head of the statue remain. The pedestal, basis of Ozymandias' work, bearing the recorded word, is also (one supposes) the last work commanded. A small testament, no doubt, but at least this trace of effort remains: The audience of Shelley's poem, like the poet, like the "traveller from an antique land," like the original "sculptor," is enabled, in the dominant role of living spectator, to understand "well those passions . . . / Which yet survive, stamped on these lifeless things" (6–7). Within and because of the poem, the giant in the earth undergoes a resurrection and dissemination of still greater magnitude. Thus the fame and "passions" of Ozymandias wind into a spiralling tradition of continuity, beyond the ruin of a kingdom's kingdoms to our own classrooms. Ozymandias, unlikely though it seems, becomes a figure of the dying god, an Anfortas for "Parsifal" Shelley to resurrect (by watching and by asking the appropriate questions). By encapsulating an antique, fragmented effort within a compact, inexpensive, and widely dispersable form—the sonnet—the poet militates against mutability, change, and death.

However, the sonnet (especially) *glorifies* the diasparactive process by enforcing an ironic view of the stark beauty (perceived and related) of the tyrant's last works. The ruin-poem and the fragment make the *pretense* of diminishing human effort, but in its effect on the living, perceiving reader, the opposite is accomplished; the poem becomes an affirmation of effort, particularly on the part of the spectator.

The essential paradox of the ruin-poem, which is also the paradoxical strategy of the fragmented poem, forms a commentary on both *Hyperion* and *The Fall of Hyperion*. The ritual aspects of the poetic initiations in the *Hyperion*-poems have been remarked on with some frequency, and these aspects can be seen as particularly relevant in light of the myth of the grail, as in Shelley's "Ozymandias." By visiting the Chapel Perilous, the grail-quester takes the responsibility of posing questions, usually pertaining to the nature of the grail (and/or the lance). Passing this test, the quester gains the power—often through use of the grail—to restore health to the sick or wounded king (a figure of the Dying God, as Fraser points out, but more pertinent here, a figure of the precursor, the tradition); thereby the quester brings life and fertility back to the wasted lands.

While the *Hyperion*-poems lament the change implicit in the defeated portrayals of the precursors (figured as Saturn, Hyperion, and Apollo), they also militate against change, by their repetition and preservation of the magnificence, and of the falls themselves, of those precursors; yet the poems also glorify that change, those deaths. This becomes particularly clear in *The Fall of Hyperion*, where "with the fine spell of words alone" the poem perceives and relates the beauty of the process of the fall through its performance. "Militate against change" may seem a strong phrase. But as the poet points out in his proem, "words alone can save / Imagination from the sable charm / And dumb enchantment" of death (1.9–11). Keats in this poem is preserving the myth, the old story, and not the outmoded mirage of the self; it is not only a fall, but a shedding or sloughing off of the ideal worlds and selves that the poet wants to portray, while at the same time preserving the imaginative play of myth and history. For without that tradition, that tribal record, human life seems very little indeed.

Aske sees the Titans of *Hyperion* as "grotesque and violent distortions of

[Keats's] monumentalized precursors" (1985, 93), a role continued in *The Fall of Hyperion*. Saturn is Milton, according to Aske, but also "the body of the writer of *Hyperion*, unable to write, bereft of inspiration, his imagination already defeated and deadened through his homage to Milton" (93). "Refusing to banish their names from his lips, the dead writers stifle the voice of the modern poet, and strike him dumb at the very moment when he desires to speak the sublime" (90–91). But the difficulty is that Aske's view does not recognize the ability of the reader to complete the text, and therefore he fails to understand that the difference between, say, Hazlitt's view of the past and Keats's (91–94), is a difference that frees the poet and the reader to a great extent.[53] While Aske does note that Keats "repeats but also questions" Hazlitt's view of "benign anteriority" in his *Hyperion* (93), Aske underestimates the power of that questioning stance. Like Bloom, he insists too heavily on the dangers rather than the joys of identification with, and repetition of, the paternal, focusing instead on Keats's "kaleidoscopic" view of "bewildering forms which interpose" (94). The point is, however, that Keats's view is his own, and through his, the reader's own. The clouding, "bewildering forms" that open the epic function much the same way as shield and armor in the epic, acting primarily to emphasize the power of the assaulting weapon or here, the penetrating vision, and not literally to defend or mask:

> Deep in the shady sadness of a vale
> Far sunken from the healthy breath of morn,
> Far from the fiery noon, and eve's one star,
> Sat gray-hair'd Saturn, quiet as a stone,
> Still as the silence round about his lair;
> Forest on forest hung about his head
> Like cloud on cloud.
>
>   (1–7)

The multiple barriers to vision, rather than actually blocking any vision, instead serve to intensify the poet's and the reader's perception of "gray-hair'd Saturn." Like the corresponding place where "there is no light" in the *Ode to a Nightingale*, the perceiving, questioning abilities of the hero are emphasized in a new intensity of perception. (He, and we as readers, "cannot see" the flowers, but can "guess each sweet" in his carefully detailed catalog.) Thus, in *Hyperion*, the "voiceless" stream is clearly mocked by the continuing voice of the poet. The figure of Saturn, one of the many precursors who "In strength and nature . . . have not been surpassed," is literalized in just such an attitude ("large footmarks went, / No further than to where his feet had stray'd, / And slept there since" [15–17]), but the perceiver (and narrator) of the vision clearly does "surpass" (literally, to go beyond the limit, powers, or extent of; to transcend) the precursor, and it encourages the reader to do the same. The poem thus is much more than mere epitaph; rather, through the chameleon function of repeating (identifying with) the father and of showing that father as fallen, the poet and the reader are allowed the spectatorial and speculative agency of "admiration, expectation, and regret."[54] The difficulty with the poem remains, however, and Aske's sensitivity to the diasparaction foisted upon the reader is not without basis. The poet creates powerful identifications, but no full *identity* can be established independent of the precursor.

The revisions we encounter in *The Fall of Hyperion*, particularly its installation of a specifically human agent, clarify this. The difficulty with the first version, as D. G. James and other critics have pointed out, is that the ghost of Milton is too powerful to identify with safely; for Keats to give "Life to him" in chameleon fashion, as he points out, "would be death to me."[55] Hence, the introduction of a fictional agent, a questioning observer for the reader, is a logical means of developing an identity, a "self," through a process of surrogate maieutics—a surrogate nursing or bringing to birth.[56]

Keats creates, then, in his most significant revision of the earlier *Hyperion*, a fiction of agency—a hero whose heroism appears to consist precisely in his willingness (and his ability) to sympathize with and recreate the joys and aches "proportioned to a giant nerve," which are, paradoxically, described as "Too huge for mortal tongue, or pen of scribe" (2.23, 9). The difficulty for such an agent still lies in his lack of self, even though this is also where his ultimate victory lies. The chameleon poet, with his or her protective (but self-alienating) coloration, always hungers for the emergent understanding of the identity adopted. This new identity, however, must always be taken in a strictly provisional sense, and then absorbed, and questioned. The "understanding" becomes a temporary mode of action—action *as if* the current understanding held a form of truth.

In the *Odes*, personal desires submit to the poet's critical judgment and the realization that dreams are only dreams.[57] In *The Fall of Hyperion*, Keats accomplishes a more ambitious project, applying critical intelligence to the dreams of the race, the oppressive fictions (or tales of the tribes) by which people live. After establishing and identifying with such visions through the naive agency of the dreamer, he then questions, subverts, and otherwise demolishes these forms of the ideal, showing them, too, as limited fantasies, provisional fictions of the immutable and the golden age; further, he emphasizes the importance and beauty of mutability and decay; and paradoxically, he asserts the importance of human forms of durability and even permanence.

Both the evanescence and the durability of human visions are emphasized in the eighteen lines that open the poem, where the poet, as opposed to the naive dreamer, outlines the relation between dreams, the consequent process of repeating/expressing the dream ("weav[ing]," "Guess[ing]"), and Poesy, which "alone" of these "can tell her dreams."

> Fanatics have their dreams, wherewith they weave
> A paradise for a sect; the savage too
> From forth the loftiest fashion of his sleep
> Guesses at Heaven; pity these have not
> Trac'd upon vellum or wild Indian leaf
> The shadows of melodious utterance.
> But bare of laurel they live, dream, and die;
> For Poesy alone can tell her dreams,
> With the fine spell of words alone can save
> Imagination from the sable charm
> And dumb enchantment. Who alive can say,
> "Thou art no Poet—may'st not tell thy dreams?"
> Since every man whose soul is not a clod
> Hath visions, and would speak, if he had loved,
> And been well nurtured in his mother tongue.
> Whether the dream now purpos'd to rehearse
> Be poet's or fanatic's will be known
> When this warm scribe my hand is in the grave.
>
>   (1.1–18)

Dreams, such as the one "now purpos'd to rehearse," are common to all: poet, fanatic, savage—"every man whose soul is not a clod." Not all dreams, however, reach the stage of expression; they must be shaped, woven, into a subjectively construed "paradise." The *méconnaissance* implicit in the "fanatical" bent of such constructions is reinforced by the savage's "guesses" toward heaven. The expression of dreams, more generally, is seen to depend on the relation of love and nurture between the speaker and his "mother tongue." The distinction between oral and written forms of expression, between the "guesses" seen as primitive and the traced "shadows of melodious utterance" is displayed as the difference that creates "Poesy." Oral forms, due to their ephemeral quality, cannot participate in the traditional poetic interchange of the laurel; despite the close connection with the "mother tongue" argued by their "melodious utterance," oral poets, according to Keats, have no way to save their imaginative creations from the silence of death—"the dumb enchantment." Only the white magic of poetry, through the spell of words, can counteract the "sable charm" of time and death.

A psychoanalytic reading of this passage notes the necessary connection with the maternal, but notes as well that the connection is not sufficient for poetry. To maintain the full connection with the maternal is to remain "bare of laurel"—effectively castrated, in the terms of poetry. Though Keats does not mark it so at this point, "Poesy," the act of "tracing upon vellum," *appears* to be an act of paternal identification that enables the poet to gain the laurel. The stress on the singleness of poetry (in the repetitions of "alone") adds weight to a view of identification with the father (and separation from the maternal) as a means of gaining autonomous identity. Since Keats has suggested a somewhat different form of identity for the poet—as chameleon—it should be pointed out that here identity is defined only through question and negation: "Who alive can say, 'Thou art no Poet—may'st not tell thy dreams'?"[58] While the implication is that no one can make this injunction to silence, its formation as question leaves the conclusion in some doubt. Moreover, it suggests rather broadly the possibility that someone who is dead (i.e., a precursor) *can* say "Thou art no Poet." Due to the confusion over punctuation the parental injunction appears to say two very different things: first, a statement of lack of identity, "Thou art no Poet"; second, a question (probably) that appears to contradict the statement, "may'st not tell thy dreams?" (i.e., may you not be a poet?). If we continue to view this as the expression of a parental image, however, the paradox is explicable as a manifestation of the classic double-bind: Be like me, but do not be like me (some things are my prerogative). The very shiftiness of the referential system here is suspect as a form of miscognition; though identity at first appears to be formed through simplistic question and negation, the shifting quality of the language allows a different—chameleon—identity, as though Keats answered the parental double-bind with one of his own. Especially striking is the way the reader is sharply and suddenly included in the discussion by the use of the second person; included, that is, not merely as one who dreams and may tell, but as one subjected to the same threat of nonidentity, and as one included in the ongoing dreaming and weaving of the social fabric.

Another important aspect of the proem lies in the distinctions made between fanatic, savage, and poet. The "savage" must be read (in accord with Schiller and the usual forms of Romantic primitivism) as a naive fashioner of dreams who, because unlettered, lacks poetic identity. Both poet and fanatic, however, are clearly capable of rehearsing the dream that follows, and the uncertainty that attends this realization is simultaneously a realization of the self's fragmented nature. While the same physical body writes the dream, the self that consciously orders this expression remains suspended between the two possibilities. The image of the fragmented body that follows (the burial of "this warm scribe my hand") reiterates the threat of diasparactive force.

The "fanatic" is most easily seen as Keats's mutation of the quixotic hero of the fragmented epic, here more ritualist shaman than chevalier. As Northrop Frye has pointed out, Don Quixote is not merely exemplary of the pursuit of an imaginative vision, but is by definition possessed of fanatical "diseased vision": "It would be easy to see in Quixote a relatively harmless example of a very sinister type, one of the line of paranoiacs culminating in Hitler, who have attempted to destroy the present on the pretext of restoring the past."[59] In Keats's vision of the fanatic creating "a paradise for a sect" there is a more general applicability; it is not necessarily tied, as is Quixote's vision of the golden age, to the sentimental view of the past, but as easily to any ideal state. The "poet" envisioned by Keats, it should be noted, still makes no claims to whole truth.[60]

> Fanatics have their dreams, wherewith they weave
> A paradise for a sect

As is traditional in dream-visions, Keats's dreamer gains a new understanding through the process of dreaming. This is worth noting, since some critics fail to take into account the significant temporal shift of Keats's persona after the proem—the fact that the speaker of the proem is no longer the naive dreamer depicted in the past tense of the dream. The careful imprecision of the proem's poet, who introduces the dream, takes place at a point in the unconcluded process of self-formation that we can only guess at, as the poem ends before the naive dreamer reaches a similar state.

In a dream-vision we may expect moral lessons (as in *Pearl* or *Piers Plowman*), but in Keats the lesson, such as it is, has to do (as W. J. Bate observed) with "the nature and uses of the self." It is vital, however, that the "self" which arises in the dreams is caught up not only within what is clearly a repetition of Keats's own poetic progress, but as well a repetition of the poetic progress known as the epic tradition.

The opening lines of the proem suggest that a "paradise" is being depicted—someone's dreamed "Guesses at Heaven." But the "paradise" Keats weaves is ultimately a dismantled paradise, a humanist rather than an idealist vision. The uncertainty of specification (Is the dream that of poet or fanatic?) reinforces our reading for *méconnaissance*. The reader, too, is snared in uncertainty.

The opening dream places the reader in a locale that is both a version of Milton's Eden and a classical, pastoral elysium, the place of "Proserpine return'd to her own fields" (1.37). But apart from the initial descriptions of the dreamer's sensual perceptions, which, as I have suggested, are simultaneously cloaked and intensified, we find that "nearer seen" (1.30), the paradise is antithetical to the models, appearing rather as a paradise deconstructed into di-asparactive forms, emblems of death and decay. While "Trees of every clime" grow here, some of those named carry strong funereal overtones: palms, myrtle, sycamore. Moreover, the trees "made a screen" (20) that blinds the dreamer to his surroundings. The "drooping roof" of the Edenic arbor is not only the "whisp'ring roof / of leaves" from Keats's *Ode to Psyche* (10–11), as Bloom has suggested, but also is kin to the "droop-headed flowers" of the *Ode to Melancholy* (13). The flowers of *The Fall of Hyperion* droop "in bells, and larger blooms, / Like floral censers" (26–27). Along with the funereal woods, then, there is the apparatus (albeit flowery) of the graveside ceremony. Only a grave is needed to make the image complete, and this is provided in the "mound of moss" (28–29) that stands before the arbor. The "feast of summer fruits" thus takes on the char-acter of a wake, a funerary feast more than anything else, perhaps "For Proser-pine, return'd to her own fields, / Where the white heifers low" (37–38). These lines have been interpreted as a celebration of Proserpine's return to earth and life with spring. But the "banqueting" is that of harvest, autumn—"a feast of *summer* fruits"—and as Proserpine is Queen of Hades, "her own fields" are ar-guably those of the Underworld, not those of the world above. (In the land of the dead, ghostly "white heifers" might not seem out of place.)[61]

The process of sensual dissolution within this environment is also a met-onymic identification with it, carried to the epic and traditional level by the dreamer's identifications with Proserpine and Eve. Like them, he eats the food of the enchanted land, and he drinks the milk of paradise—"the parent of my theme"—a drink immediately compared with fatal drugs, a "domineering po-tion" more deadly than the worst that the tyrannies and conspiracies of human-ity can devise (46–54). The dreamer, like Apollo in Hyperion, "struggled hard," but then sinks into textualized oblivion, dead drunk "Like a Silenus on an an-tique vase" (56). The temporary fantasy of quadrature, of becoming whole through the narcissistic exercise of "appetite More yearning than on earth I ever felt Growing within" (38–40), is threatened by the images of the fragmented body that surround the dreamer; the comparison with the satyr reinforces that diasparactive movement, rendering the dreamer half-bestial, as well as textual, no longer approaching a human identity. As he is imprisoned within the simile of the *corps morcéle,* he is likewise textually imprisoned in an "antique" image of paradise, a beautiful but diasparactive and potentially deadly Eden made up only of "remnants."

Aside from the recurrent images of death in this preliminary dream, there are other, more insistent forms of fragmentation. The "screening" quality of the foliage restricts vision, but other senses are equally limited: hearing is muffled by "soft showering" fountains, and the perfumes of "floral censers" beguile the sense of smell. Paradise, like the Isle of the Lotos Eaters, is a dulling spot indeed. It should be remembered that, for a chameleon self that is able to form itself only on the basis of perceptual observation, such sensual masking may well serve as a type of the fragmented body; parts of that sympathetic agency are metaphorically "cut off" by the limiting environment. In short, through so close an identification with the type of a fanatic's paradise, the dreamer is "rapt un-willing" and selfless into a leftover (and outmoded) vision of wholeness, and so is lost in fragmentation. Like Aeneas, the dreamer becomes one of the *reliquias*, a textual and fragmented part of the recursion itself.

The paradisal feast through which the dreamer enacts this recursion is also fragmentary, only the "refuse of a meal" (30):

> For empty shells were scatter'd on the grass
> And grape-stalks but half bare, and remnants more,
> Sweet-smelling, whose pure kinds I could not know.
> Still was more plenty than the fabled horn
> Thrice emptied could pour forth. . . .
>
>   (32–36)

The diasparactive quality of this passage is clear, its implications for the para-dise envisioned perhaps less so. The dreamer is in a "leftover" paradise, a fallen Eden, a realistic world. Shells and half-bare grapestalks are strewn about the burial site at random, all sorts of "remnants" that are explicitly not "pure." Even the "fabled horn" of plenty, the cornucopia with its infinitude, has been "Thrice emptied."

This "fabled horn" is a key element in Keats's paradise. The cornucopia is the horn broken from the head of the goat whose milk was fed to Jupiter by Amalthea (Bush 1959, 356). Through fragmentation arises prosperity; through breakage comes fullness (of a kind). Moreover, the poet himself, by partaking of this feast, is thus identified with Jupiter, the revolutionary usurper of Saturn's throne. The comparison with Eve is thus extended in its revolutionary aspects, and the outcome of Proserpine's eating of the pomegranate is remembered in both positive and negative lights. Keats's emphasis on the beauty of diasparac-tion in this passage does recur to the ideal, but recreates it as a paradise of mu-tability more akin to Spenser's Gardens of Adonis (*Faerie Queene* 3.6.29ff.): "Still was more plenty."

The ascendance of mutability and mortality is emphasized again by the dreamer's toast, "pledging all the mortals of the world, / And all the dead whose names are in our lips" (44–45). Aske selects this passage as symptomatic of the names of the dead precursors that stifle the modern poet, but neglects the pertinent fact of agency: It is the dreamer himself—the speaking artist—who

is able to make this salute. Surrounded by things he once thought ideal, touched
by angels or gods, and most important, *through* his sympathetic identification
with Eve and the human appetite, the dreamer moves onward. By means of repeating the questioning nature of Eve, the dreamer comes to affirm mortality
instead, the living and the dead. That the names of the dead, our histories, "are
in our lips," points once again to the poet's role as continuator, sympathetic
scion of tradition. But he also celebrates the living as he reweaves the "paradise"
for just such a sect; in other words, despite the determined position of the human within a world that is (especially for the chameleon) too much with us, the
poet/dreamer reiteratively questions, explores, and finally moves beyond the
limits to vision, the prescribed boundaries of the already written vision, the
myths of paradise.

> These fragments I have shored against my ruin.

The dream within the dream follows, reiterating the fact that the entire
poem takes place within the mind. This doubled acknowledgment of the
dream-state imparts an encompassing agency to the living human figure, and
hence to humanity in general ("May'st not tell thy dreams?"): The supposedly
supreme and originary titans are mere fictions in the human mind. The precursors are dependent upon the perceiving mind. The latest dream is one
in which the recursions are similarly clear, enforcing an awareness of the
paradisal framework.[62] The dreamer "start[s] up / As if with wings" (1.59) into
a new form of reality (repeating Eve's empowering dream), and finds himself
in an "old sanctuary" (1.62).

> So old the place was, I remember'd none
> The like upon the earth: what I had seen
> Of gray cathedrals, buttress'd walls, rent towers,
> The superannuations of sunk realms,
> Or Nature's rocks toil'd hard in waves and winds,
> Seem'd but the faulture of decrepit things
> To that eternal domed monument.
>
>   (1.65–71)

In this frame of understanding, the reader and dreamer are faced with another poetic ideal, that of the permanent edifice, made of perfect marble and
"Builded so high, it seemed that filmed clouds / Might spread beneath, as o'er
the stars of heaven" (1.63–64). This "old sanctuary" from the ravages of time is
a puzzling one. Established as an explicit type of the Christian heaven, it is an
"eternal domed monument," where "the moth could not corrupt" (1.71, 75; see

also Matthew 6.20). As most criticism views this stage in Keats's "successive phantasies," the ancient sanctuary is "a temple of knowledge and art" (Bush 1959, 357n). In part we may agree with such a determination, but the poet's *dismantling* of this ideal vision is especially important.

In light of Lacan's architectural metaphors of the self, Keats's "dismantling" takes on added effect. Through the agency of the dreamer, Keats first develops a metonymic connection with the outmoded structures of the superego—the "understandings" of ancient images of the self; at the same time, his recurrent questioning shows a thinly veiled aggressive stance toward those imagos. The dreamer attempts to "fathom the space every way" (1.82), etymologically, to bring it within his embrace (OE *fæthm*); but he also criticizes the objects of his embrace, as seen first in the strictly limited nature of this heavenly realm. As with the Garden, the perceptual apparatus is denied full play, already raising subversive questions about the latest frame of understanding: The dreamer can *imagine* things beyond the sanctuary, but nothing beyond it can be perceived. In a sense, the heaven depicted is more a prison than an unfading telos. Though spacious, it is circumscribed and domed; there is *room* within for "filmed clouds" to appear, but they do not: Nothing breaks the static enchantment of the ancient telos. The heavy claustrophobia of the dreamer is increased by "The embossed roof, the silent massy range / Of columns north and south, ending in mist / Of nothing" (83–85). Within the realm of these inscribed ancestral halls, there appears to be no potential for life or sound—not even for poetry. Though the dreamer raises his eyes and tries to embrace this space, the "massy range" of columns acts as a solid limit to his investigation, and no "beyond" is available. Further, we find him sympathetically attuning himself with the vision: "[R]epressing haste, as too unholy there" (1.93). The "mist of nothing" suggests a certain insubstantiality to the entire edifice, an insubstantiality underscored throughout the dreamer's visit. Perhaps even worse, no hope of rebirth or fertility presents itself in this static sanctuary; it closes out all new expression: In the east are "black gates," "shut against the sunrise evermore" (85–86). To the west awaits a literalized *imago* of the chastising parental figure, "An Image, huge of feature as a cloud" (88). Sealed off from rebirth, imprisoned with the forbidding precursor, escape seems unlikely for the poet-dreamer. The potential attraction of this mode of understanding one's relation to tradition is conveyed well by the ambivalent language of the passage.

The lines (1.65–71) might seem to support a converse vision of this heavenly "sanctuary," viewing the "eternal domed monument" as a good thing in comparison with "the faulture of decrepit things." Likewise, the collection of beautiful human artifacts (72–80) and the lengthy metaphor of the "Maian incense" (97–104) appear at first to undermine the reading I have suggested. I hope to show that the exact opposite is true, that despite the initial sympathetic identification of the chameleon poet's praise and involvement with the place, Keats's emphasis throughout is on the stultifying and stifling effect of the archaic structure.

In the very first lines of this dream, the age of the "eternal domed monument" is emphasized. "So old the place was," in fact, that the word "old" is used twice in four lines (62, 66). The insistence on the structure's antiquity despite its "eternal" and unchanging quality is rather odd. Permanence, apparently, allows nothing new in the way of architectural fashion; in a sense, this ideal place—the telos of so many—has been outmoded by more recent structures. Then, too, the sheer *number* of things opposed to this "cold pastoral" of marble is important. Religions, states, whole empires ("sunk realms"), have their ebbs and flows, though ruins ("rent towers") remain to mark their passing. What this disproportion implies is that the earth, with its natural and human works, is far more interesting to dreamer, to poet, and to audience. (One might respond that Milton had similar trouble portraying the splendor of heaven, and thus heaven in *Paradise Lost* is rather dull: That is exactly my point.)

In a "temple of knowledge and art" we would expect the natural world, and especially the works of humanity (which the dreamer views with awe), would be cherished. And indeed, tokens of human art and handiwork at their best are here, but they are "All in a mingled heap confus'd" (78). The ideal denizens of an ideally described "paradise" have a diasparative unconcern with the things of earth. This heap of broken images acts as yet another warning for the self in process of formation, that even this frame of understanding threatens with fragmentation.

This dynamic is at work to an even greater degree in the simile describing the flame beside the altar:

> When in mid-May the sickening east wind
> Shifts sudden to the south, the small warm rain
> Melts out the frozen incense from all flowers,
> And fills the air with so much pleasant health
> That even the dying man forgets his shroud;
> Even so that lofty sacrificial fire,
> Sending forth Maian incense, spread around
> Forgetfulness of everything but bliss.
>
> (97–104)

As in the Homeric epic, where the natural and rural similes of peace provide relief from (and a critique of) the ongoing warfare, so again in Keats's simile, the natural world is much more interesting to poet and audience than the useless (even threatening) sacrifice in a sterile heaven. Additionally, the *earth* is here seen as a place of restorative power, bringing the dying man to forgetfulness of death. The Maian incense that brings "Forgetfulness of everything but bliss," seems to bring no such forgetfulness of death to its dramatic receivers. Moreover, "Forgetfulness of everything but bliss" is not at all the same as forgetting one's death. The typical Keatsian warning to such dreamers is easily recalled: "No, no, go not to Lethe. . . . " The dynamics of remembering and forgetting in epic poetry are rather important, and it is worth dwelling for a moment on the Maian aspect of this encounter.

Maia, in the Greek tradition, is one of the Pleiades, the eldest daughter of Atlas, the mother of Hermes; her name comes from the Greek *maia,* meaning mother, midwife, or nurse. This is crucially related to the term and the process of *maieutics,* the "bringing of ideas to birth," in both Socratic and psychoanalytic discourse. In the Roman tradition, she is the goddess of spring, daughter of Faunus, wife of Vulcan, and her name comes from the Indo-European suffixed stem *mag-ya-,* "she who is great" (the same root stem, *meg-,* leads to Modern English magnanimous, majesty, etc.). Both of these traditions come into play in Keats's "Fragment of an Ode to Maia," where she is presented as directly connected with issues of poetic succession, a goddess and powerful mother who has been "hymned on the shores of Baiæ," "woo[ed] in Sicilian" and "sought, in Grecian isles,"

> By bards who died content on pleasant sward,
>   Leaving great verse unto a little clan[.]
> O, give me their old vigour, and unheard
> save of the quiet primrose, and the span
>   Of heaven and few ears,
> Rounded by thee, my song should die away
>   Content as theirs,
> Rich in the simple worship of a day.

The presentation here of an Oedipal fulfillment, the young poet's song "Rounded by"—completed, made full by, but also echoed by, repeated (as in a round)—by the maternal figure. The poet's request for "their old vigour" shows the Oedipal jealousy of the precursors, the desire to be "great" rather than one of the "little clan." More important, it recognizes that this vigor of the old is subject to maternal dispensation, and that the goal is metonymic fulfillment—to die away into the landscape.

Individual identity and begetting great verse for one's descendants are elided in favor of ultimate centrality and metonymic identity with the maternal lover. I bring this up because in *The Fall of Hyperion,* despite the maternal qualities of Moneta, there is a substantial change from this earlier vision; the goal of individual identity becomes increasingly important. Most obviously, this occurs precisely in the evocation of Maia, where the burning incense is directly connected with the dreamer's own fate. He will die "if these gummed leaves be burnt" before he mounts the steps (1.116). In the fragment, Maia brings bliss only, but here that bliss is attended by its opposite and consequent diasparactive force, threatening to return the dreamer to "the common dust" (1.109). "Forgetfulness of everything but bliss" would lead to that return and dissolution in the maternal landscape. Instead, the threat of death leads the dreamer up the steps, toward a form of the self that necessarily recognizes itself as fictional, and toward a remembering rather than a forgetting.

The poetic interlocutor of *The Fall of Hyperion* is no longer that of the *Ode to Maia*, nor that of the first *Hyperion*. In the earlier version of the epic, Mnemosyne (Memory) is more purely a bestower of gifts, a maternal figure of whom Apollo has dreamt. Mnemosyne gives the lyre to the young Apollo, who learns to "weep, so gifted" (3.68), and whose lyre through his informing fingers gives "birth" to "pain and pleasure" for "all the vast / Unwearied ear of the whole universe" (3.61ff.). From his melancholy and his ignorance, he too must "die into life" (which is the same, apparently, as dying into "knowledge enormous," and becoming a god [3.90–130]). The dreamer of *The Fall of Hyperion*, of course, does the same thing, not once, but twice. Part of the reason for this is that Moneta, rather than presenting memory of "names, deeds, grey legends, dire events, rebellions," etc., is quite a different character indeed. As the change in name suggests, she functions far more clearly as an "admonitory" figure, and the "gift" she offers is far more open to question than that of Mnemosyne.

From her first vague but somewhat threatening appearance as "one minist'ring" to the monstrous statue of Saturn (the "Image, huge of feature as a cloud") she is not more precisely limned; instead, her very inscrutability is emphasized: "that shade," "the veiled shadow" (141), "Majestic shadow" (188), the "tall shade, in drooping linens veil'd" (216). Where Mnemosyne's eyes held "eternal calm," Moneta's are "visionless entire" and are reflective only, "beam'd like the mild moon" (257, 269). Moneta functions in part as a demystification of the earlier maternal figure, but also as a mirror wherein the dreamer envisions his fictional wholeness and attempts (yet again) to establish a coherent sense of self. The self is primarily defined against this Other, and, through his ambivalent intercourse with her, against the powerful (but "faceless") statue whose face remains invisible (because of "the broad marble knees" [213–14]).[63] Moneta's "planetary eyes" give back only what light they are given, and hence argue a kind of solipsistic fictional quadrature (a shortened form of the "maieutic" in psychoanalysis) in which the "dreamer" is brought to face his own reality. As in psychoanalysis, the analysand—the dreamer—to an extent creates his own vision. Not surprisingly, this vision is also the Freudian primal scene, that of the "high tragedy / In the dark secret chambers" of the maternal figure's "hollow brain" (277–78, 276). The solipsistic—ultimately narcissistic—reading tends to reduce the mechanism of poetic inspiration by the muse to a purely self-reflexive level, a level which, like Keats's notions of "negative capability" and the "Camellion poet," can be seen as based in a thoroughly metonymic understanding of the development of self. However, it should be clear from the "high tragedy" of paternal debasement that the text offers as well a reading couched in Oedipal rather than solipsistic terms, when Moneta agrees to be "kind" to the dreamer in exchange for his "goodwill."

> "My power, which to me is still a curse,
> Shall be to thee a wonder; for the scenes
> Still swooning vivid through my globed brain,
> With an electral changing misery,
> Thou shalt with those dull mortal eyes behold,
> Free from all pain, if wonder pain thee not."
> As near as an immortal's sphered words
> Could to a mother's soften, were these last:
> But yet I had a terror of her robes,
> And chiefly of the veils, that from her brow
> Hung pale, and curtained her in mysteries
> That made my heart too small to hold its blood.
>
> (1.243–54)

The "high tragedy" the dreamer is about to witness in "the dark secret chambers" is readily legible as the Oedipal drama itself. The dreamer's aim is to establish himself—as poet and as "father" within the epic tradition—by perceiving himself as whole, defined, within the maternal eyes. This gift of wholeness is the gift of power: While the father is not absent, he is effectively "effaced." In an archaic "rebellion," that is, the father has already fallen and lost much of his identity: His "carved features wrinkled as he fell" (225), leaving the power—to be read as phallic power—in the "supreme" charge of Moneta, "Sole priestess of his desolation" (227).

The law of the father exists, but is blinded, is mute, and has lost much of its ancient meaning: "the silent massy range / Of columns . . . ending in mist / Of nothing . . . " (83–85). The commands and instructions of patriarchy—and its power—are given through the agency of the maternal—the mother tongue, one might argue, but initially at least, the maternal eyes. The dreamer must reach these eyes, "visionless entire," by penetrating all the terrifying veils that "curtained her in mysteries" (253), and by restraining his own terror and sense of impotence. In Chapter 2 the "heart"—as the golden hall of Heorot, and also as the hart that quails at the Mere—was discussed as a phallic referent symbolizing the imposition of order, pointing up the impotence of attempts besides Beowulf's to maintain that order. In *The Fall of Hyperion,* the heart of the dreamer is "too small to hold its blood" (254), and functions in similar fashion; the dreamer remains paralyzed before the powerful woman until she herself "Part[s] the veils."[64] Perhaps the most important expression of this impotence is the dreamer's silence upon Moneta's self-disclosure. Like Eliot's speaker with the "hyacinth girl," Keats's dreamer is unable to speak, to respond in any way except for his continued, shifting gaze:

> I had no words to answer, for my tongue,
> useless, could find about its roofed home
> No syllable of a fit majesty. . . .
>   . . . [T]he altar's blaze
> Was fainting for sweet food: I looked thereon,
> And on the paved floor, where nigh were piled
> Faggots of cinnamon, and many heaps
> Of other crisped spice-wood—then again
> I looked upon the altar, and its horns
> Whitened with ashes, and its languorous flame,
> And then upon the offerings again;
> And so by turns. . . .
>
>   (1.228–40)

This is a puzzling and unremarked instance of silence in a poem full of silences and gaps, but it is, I think, analogous to the speaker's silence in Wordsworth, when in the presence of the "unerring guide," "[He] looked and looked, self-questioned what this freight / Which the new-comer carried through the waste, / Could mean" (5.80–86). In the context of *Hyperion'*s repeated acts of silent "self-questioning" observation, it is worth examining the dreamer's reaction to Moneta's speeches.

The early speeches of Moneta have traditionally been seen as conducive to the dreamer's education and initiation as poet, but the exchange between dreamer and maternal figure is also, as I have suggested, freighted with more tragedy than earlier criticism has pointed out. Not without good reason does Keats's dreamer hesitantly focus on the offerings and altar. The Wordsworthian dreamer is fascinated with the dismembered fragments of the precursor (the stone and shell) that are re-membered into the quixotic agent as a phallic image

of the self. Similarly, the offerings, and the speed with which they are burned
at the altar, are closely tied in with the personal survival of Keats's dreamer, as
Moneta states in no uncertain terms:

> "If thou canst not ascend
> These steps, die on that marble where thou art.
> Thy flesh, near cousin to the common dust,
> Will parch for lack of nutriment—thy bones
> Will wither in few years, and vanish so
> That not the quickest eye could find a grain
> Of what thou now art on that pavement cold
>
> . . . .
>
> . . . if these gummed leaves be burnt
> Ere thou canst mount up these immortal steps."
>
> (107–17)

Without undergoing the (phallic) definition of self implicit in the "hard task
proposed," the dreamer will suffer the metonymic dissolution into the landscape.[65] In the offerings, then, the dreamer sees himself: The "Faggots of cinna-
mon, and many heaps / of other crisped spice-wood" are images of his own
fragmented body, seen under the "fierce threat" of Moneta. Keats proposed earlier, in the *Ode to Psyche*, to "build a fane / In some untrodden region of my
mind" (49–50).[66] Here, within that fane, the dreamer is forced to move through
the fane, to "pro-fane" it indeed. The responsibility for such profanation, however, is explained in the dreamer's election by the maternal figure. The threat
incumbent upon his profanation, his breakage of the law of the father, can be
best seen earlier in the poem, in his "Repressing haste, as too unholy there" (94).
The sleeping altar, he notes at this point in the poem, is one that should be approached slowly by the steps, in "patient travail / To count with toil the innumerable degrees" (91–92). But as with Odysseus and Calypso, the gift of agency,
of phallic power, is given by the female interlocutor, and is similarly expressed
in *The Fall of Hyperion* as the only alternative to annihilation. (The disintegration of heroic identity implicit in remaining on Ogygia suggests the potentially
similar consequence for the Homeric hero.)

Oddly enough, this threat of metonymic dissolution in Keats is shown as a
chameleon-like identification *with* the father. Like the frost-rimed trees around
(and Beowulf within) Grendel's Mother's Mere, the dreamer in Keats's poem
experiences a "palsied chill" beginning to paralyze his limbs, and the onset of
the threatening "numbness." The symbolic efficacy is similar, and, as in *Beowulf*,
this impotence brings the hero into identification with the impotent father, be-

fore whose frozen image he has paused. This is underscored by the later presentation of Saturn in the vision, as a paternal figure who has lost power, an image again of the *corps morcéle:*

> Degraded, cold, upon the sodden ground
> His old right hand lay nerveless, listless, dead,
> Unsceptred. . . .
>
>   (1.322–24)

And when Saturn speaks, it is as one who is lost in a textualized landscape: his words are effaced by their very omnipresence as "the moist scent of flowers, and grass, and leaves" (1.404):

> "Moan, brethren, moan, for we are swallowed up
> And buried from all godlike exercise . . .
> Moan . . . for thy pernicious babes
> Have changed a God into a shaking palsy."
>
>   (1.412–26)

The dreamer must at the same time repeat the precursor and differentiate himself from that precursor; in short, he ought not to be "repressing haste," for it will involve him in dissolution; but he ought not be too hasty, for this is profanation. Caught between the chameleon form of identification (and dissolution), and the quixotic fantasy of fulfillment, the dreamer stops, and looks, and looks again, asking,

> What am I that should so be saved from death?
> What am I that another death come not
> To choke my utterance, sacrilegious, here?
>
>   (1.138–40)

The dreamer understands himself primarily as a question inserted between two forms of death, and the answer returned to him is hermetic, but contains an affirmation of a limited power on his part: "that thou hadst power to do so / Is thy own safety" (1.143–44). Moneta explains further that the only people who reach this point are "those to whom the miseries of the world / Are misery," and goes on to draw further and further distinctions. The first is between those just mentioned and those who "may thoughtless sleep away their days" (1.151). The next lies between the dreamer himself and those who know "misery" but "are no vision'ries . . . They are no dreamers weak." This isolates the dreamer as

> a dreaming thing,
> A fever of thyself—think of the Earth;
> What bliss even in hope is there for thee?
> What haven? every creature hath its home;
> Every sole man hath days of joy and pain,
> Whether his labours be sublime or low—
> The pain alone; the joy alone; distinct:
> Only the dreamer venoms all his days,
> Bearing more woe than all his sins deserve.
>
>   (1.168–76)

Noting briefly the referents toward an appropriate place for the self (haven, home), and drawing the conclusion that the dreamer is apparently still caught in the drama of quadrature, still "homeless," it is worth pausing for a moment. D. G. James and Harold Bloom, in their influential readings of this epic, have both seen Moneta in this passage as making important distinctions, and have seen her as a type of Christ, outlining a peace or love that passes understanding. Bloom reads this passage as dramatic self-condemnation of Keats himself, pointing out perceptively that "the poet is a fever of himself, caught in the anguish of his own selfhood"; but Bloom goes on to make a rather puzzling claim: "Moneta strikes at what is most central in Keats, his inability to unperplex joy from pain. Men, humanists or not, except the dreamer, can experience joy and pain unmixed" (1971, 427). Not to be contrary, but I would suggest that *no one* experiences "joy and pain unmixed" and that this is Keats's point. To say it is possible is to promote the same kind of transcendental idealism that Keats opposes in this poem of the death of gods.[67] Rather, this "inability to unperplex" is part of the human condition. Moreover, Keats explicitly states this view of the human condition in the proem, directly opposing the limiting poetic divisions drawn by Moneta (and provisionally adopted by the dreamer). The speaker of the proem, at least, knows that no one may say:

> "Thou art no Poet—may'st not tell thy dreams?"
> Since every man whose soul is not a clod
> Hath visions, and would speak. . . .
>
>   (11–13)

Moneta, on the other hand, remains perfectly willing to make exactly this sort of distinction, and what is at first surprising is that the dreamer appears to agree with her; he does not feel he is a poet, but feels "as vultures feel / They are no birds when eagles are abroad" (1.191–92). The dreamer adopts through this *méconnaissance* a self defined by its refraction through external images. Vultures are birds, whether eagles fly or no. Like the vultures, the dreamer makes a mistake in feeling when he accepts Moneta's purposely limiting definitions. The poet of the proem, on the other hand, is aware of the danger attending such definitions, and would have us question closely those who attempt to say "Thou art no Poet."

Dramatic irony is certainly at work here. Our own experience tells us, as does Keats, that all people have dreams. Does this, then, "venom all [their] days"? To an extent, yes, if to be human means always to be alienated from some (fictional) wholeness. The "venom" is affirmed especially when such dreams become oppressive institutions with their reified distinctions, the ideological freight of worn-out Edens, Heavens, Golden Ages.

Moneta's name-change (from Mnemosyne) has been explored by K. K. Ruthven, who examines her new descriptions as both "monetary" and "admonitory" figure: "the double name of Keats's goddess was intended to designate a Janus-like figure, a *dea bifrons*."[68] While the reflective exchange between dreamer and moonlike goddess as well as the exchange of her kindness for his "good will" have been mentioned, developing the definition of Moneta as "money, mint, or stamp" shows that the framework of trade is in fact set up with the initial questions, continuing in Moneta's reply that the dreamer has "dated on [his] doom" (i.e., decreased his account of years). Though it appears that the dreamer has relatively little time or capital within this framework of exchange, Moneta's admonitory distinctions provide him with a means of identifying with, and of working his way up, as it were, the poetic corporate ladder. The distinctions she makes are class distinctions of a kind, and the more power the dreamer gains within Moneta's system, the more willing he becomes to oppress the class perceived as lower, finally crying (in "Spite of [him]self"):

> Apollo! faded, far-flown Apollo!
> Where is thy misty pestilence to creep
> Into the dwellings, through the door-crannies
> Of all mock-lyrists, large self-worshippers,
> And careless Hectorers in proud bad verse?
> Though I breathe death with them it will be life
> To see them sprawl before me into graves.
>
>   (203–10)

The annihilative joy is analogous to Achilles' extinction fantasy, but the metaphoric opposition to bad poets is identified with the attitude of Moneta, and is curiously at odds with Keats's usual metonymic tropes (even though this form of identification is brought in, seeing himself "breath[ing] death with them"). Along with these class divisions Moneta also inspires greed in the dreamer, at least temporarily. Though as he says, he would "have fled away" from her ghastly Sibylline countenance ("deathwards progressing / To no death was that visage" [260–61]), the dreamer stays, for in Moneta's eyes he finds poetic coin:

> As I had found
> A grain of gold upon a mountain's side,
> And, twing'd with avarice, strain'd out my eyes
> To search its sullen entrails rich with ore. . . .
>
>   (271–74)

Moneta is a poetic gold mine, a "mint" brought out of the golden age. Here Keats demystifies the inspirational gift of the Muse, revealing it not only as Oedipal, but more pertinently, as a self-reflexive and narcissistic rifling of nature, history, and myth.[69]

Thus, Keats's dreamer to the "old sanctuary" comes, where he poses questions of Moneta. As the grail of myth is often depicted as a coin, it becomes increasingly easy to see Moneta as the grail itself. Like Apollo in *Hyperion,* the dreamer invokes or "conjures" (291) the grail: "Let me behold, according as thou saidst, / What in thy brain so ferments to and fro" (289–90). From the liquor "swooning vivid . . . / With an electral changing misery" (245–46) through Moneta's "hollow brain," the dreamer drinks. Inspiration pours in at the eyes, again as with Apollo.[70] The dreamer adopts/usurps Apollo's place in the ritual initiation into poetic inspiration. Moreover, as we have seen, the dreamer actually inspires himself. With the combined grasp of "Knowledge enormous" and his or her own imagination, the poet bypasses the traditional mystical explanations of poetic ability. Through knowledge and experience of the external world and history, and through the play of imagination with these externals, the poet becomes a self-created God.

This assumption of godhead by the poet is laid out in *The Fall of Hyperion,* at the beginning of the vision (within a dream within a dream), after the voice of Moneta whispers

> "So Saturn sat
> When he had lost his realms"—Whereon there grew
> A power within me of enormous ken,
> To see as a God sees . . .
>
> .   .   .   .

> . . . I sat myself
> Upon an Eagle's watch, that I might see,
> And seeing ne'er forget.
>
>   (301–10)

Through the poetic interplay of imagination and world, the poet can "see as a God sees." This "Eagle's watch" is far above the level of the fallen gods, and creates an equation between the chameleon poet and

> one of the whole eagle-brood [who] still keeps
> His sov'reignty, and rule, and majesty;
> Blazing Hyperion . . .
>
>   (2.13–15)

The poet thus raises himself or is raised to the level of a god. The gods themselves are thrown down to human terms, at least. "Apollo! faded, far-flown Apollo" (203) is almost nonexistent, degraded here despite the invocation, but he is also eliminated by the poet taking his place (which leaves us with the poet as both Muse and God of poetry). Saturn and Thea (like the dreamer as Silenus earlier in the poem) barely rise above the level of "sculpture builded up upon the grave" (383). Saturn, with his "faded eyes" (400), has become "a shaking palsy" (426), "some old man of the earth / Bewailing earthly loss" (440–41).

Even Hyperion, though as yet unfallen, is "unsecure" (2.17) and the poem's title shows his end. Even among the gods, it seems, joy and pain cannot be "unmixed" for there are "horrors, proportioned to a giant nerve, / [which] Make great Hyperion ache" (2.23–24). His palace is that of Cassandra's dream, and "Glares a blood-red through all the thousand courts" (2.27). His voice is only that of "earthly fire" (2.59). Hyperion is a figure equivalent to the poet himself, and knows that "the meek ethereal hours" (2.60) are merely biding their time. And here, I think, as we have understood the dreamer as a question of identity suspended between two forms of death, we may leave him. At this point Keats leaves us trapped in a paradox, the solution of which is certainly the temporary "flare" of the self, but also the gaze of the watcher whose "quick eyes ran on" (2.53). The oxymoronic last sentence of the poem returns us to the Anglo-Saxon thane's description of human life as the time of a sparrow in a meadhall: "the bright blink of an eye, and the least space." Hyperion's brief burst of light is brilliant, but not eternal: "On he flared" (2.61).

Thus, the rejuvenation of the Fisher King, the Dying God, takes place not through the resurrection of the gods, but though the assumption of their power on the part of the human poet. The mythic figures are resurrected with each reading, in the sense that their fall is recorded by the poet. But they are mythic, historical; they are not gods. The waste land is no longer waste, humanity no longer in exile, for the horrors of changeless Edens and barren, eternal Heavens have been exposed. On we flare with what little we have, with "the fine spell of words alone" (1.9).

It coheres, all right: the American epic

According to Cid Corman, Hart Crane is "the very instance of American incoherence."[71] I suggested earlier that Crane's *Bridge* enacts a fantasy of identity. Close reading of the epic reveals this, but it also appears in the avowed connection between *The Bridge* and Crane's notion of himself, as poet and as man; in the literature of psychoanalytic theory, as well, the symbol of the bridge is equated with identity, and especially with phallic identity. That is, Jacques Lacan and Hart Crane refer essentially to the same "transcendental signifier" when they speak of the ultimate connectivity of their respective metaphors.[72] The phallus as signifier is that which speaks in and through the human being (1977, 284), and comes to stand for the relation of the human to the signifiable. As the copulative signifier, the phallus connects the human to its environment and thus represents all processes of signification. Likewise, "The bridge came to be anything and everything Crane wished," as Yingling observes (1990, 187). The chameleon quality of the bridge as "significatory copula" is reiterated in Crane's letters ("The real connective experience, the very 'sign manifest' on which rests the assumption of godhead" [224]): "[The bridge] in becoming a ship, a world, a woman, a tremendous harp (as it does finally) seems to really have a career" (232). In a letter to Charlotte Rychtarik in the summer of 1923, he recalls the "room in Cleveland" where he first thought of the epic (echoing Keats's remarks on the Chamber of Maiden-Thought); *The Bridge* is persistently interwoven with issues of personal and poetic identity:

> When I think of that room, it is almost to give way to tears, because I shall never find my way back to it. It is not necessary, of course, that I should, but just the same it was the center and beginning of all that I am and ever will be, the center of such pain as would tear me to pieces to tell you about, and equally the center of great joys! *The Bridge* seems to me so beautiful,— and it was there that I first thought about it, and it was there that I wrote "Faustus and Helen," which Waldo Frank says is so good that I will be remembered by that, whether or not I write more or not. (1952, 140)

Crane goes on in the next sentence to say that "all this is, of course, intimately connected with my Mother, my beautiful mother." The consciously Oedipal revelation is somewhat less important, I think, than the practical identity be-

tween Crane's recognition of the "center and beginning of all that I am and
ever will be" and the "beautiful" *Bridge,* an identity that is vital to an understanding of the dynamics of sex and violence in *The Bridge.* Ambivalent extremes of feeling toward his mother constitute a dominant theme of Crane's
letters, a theme that is thoroughly reflected within the dynamics of the poem,
but that relationship, too, is symptomatic of Crane's establishment of self in his
epic.[73]

Allen Tate, who remained a sensitive reader of Crane despite their quarrel,
noted that whereas Rimbaud had created "disorder" out of a received or "given"
order, by the early twentieth century "the disintegration of our intellectual systems is accomplished. With Crane the disorder is original and fundamental.
That is the special quality of his mind that belongs particularly to our own
time."[74] The conception of "original and fundamental" disorder is one that
Crane shares with Lacan.[75] As we have seen, Lacan's concern with the dehiscence (or fragmentation) at the core of the human organism led him to postulate
in the drama of the mirror stage a movement from early experience of the fragmented body to the adoption of a fictionally whole image of the self, like that
seen in the mirror: This fundamentally expedient error marks the beginning of
the human subject's attempt at the "inexhaustible quadrature of the ego's verifications" (4), as the human subject tries to live up to its imagined wholeness. In
Crane's vision this process of "quadrature," of "squaring the circle," is rather
different: As "The Tunnel" demonstrates, in the traditional descent to the underworld Crane deconstructs both the fictional self projected within "Time's
Square" and the originary American myth of self, "Columbus Circle":

> Performances, assortments, résumés—
> Up Times Square to Columbus Circle lights
> Channel the congresses, nightly sessions,
> Refractions of the thousand theatres, faces—
> Mysterious kitchens. . . . You shall search them all.
>
> . . . .
>
> As usual you will meet the scuttle yawn:
> The subway yawns the quickest promise home.
>
> Be minimum, then, to swim the hiving swarms
> Out of the Square, the Circle burning bright—
> Avoid the glass doors gyring at your right,
> Where boxed alone a second, eyes take fright
> —Quite unprepared rush naked back to light:
> And down beside the turnstile press the coin
> Into the slot.
>
>   (108–9)

By moving out of Times Square (and time's square, the grid of logic) to the ideally originary circle, "you" apparently go in quest of something. The logic of Crane's tunnel, however, permits only decay within the multifaceted, mirroring circle of social art and intercourse—"the garden [is] dead." What is learned is "each famous sight," and what is gained is further alienation, not unity: You "wish yourself in bed, / With tabloid crime-sheets perched in easy sight," and "exclaim . . . subscription praise[s] for what time slays" (108). Crane deliberately evokes the infernal figure of Eliot's "Prufrock," who is lost in a self determined only by his understanding of his social existence; in Crane's rewriting, however, this Prufrockian self, rather than having "known them all" instead "search[es] them all" as if looking for its own reflection; if it finds this correspondence at all, it is not in the "famous sight" of socially acceptable art, but in that other sensationalism of "tabloid crime-sheets." The Eliotic indecisions continue until the subway entrance, where the self must be brought to its "minimum, then, to swim the hiving swarms," but where to be "boxed alone" with the self "unprepared" in a revolving door is even worse.

The division of self here is parallel to that of Cape Hatteras, where the humiliating knowledge of the analytic spectator is alleviated by its contradiction in the beguiling tale of power: "Seeing himself an atom in a shroud— / Man hears himself an engine in a cloud!" (89). But in the dark atmosphere of "The Tunnel," the inflation of the self contingent upon speed and power is not that of "the engine" but of one who has made "penguin flexions of the arms," and the tales told are only "The phonographs of hades in the brain . . . tunnels that rewind themselves" like shrouds (110). With this view of Crane's versions of the self, it is easy to see why Tate would have judged the disorder to be "original and fundamental" where the self arises, fragmented, out of (perhaps) "the muffled slaughter of a day in birth," already prepared to become minimum, ready for the modern machine

> To spoon us out more liquid than the dim
> Locution of the eldest star, and pack
> The conscience navelled in the plunging wind,
> Umbilical to call—and straightway die!
>
> (111)

Though not far different, it is decidedly more pessimistic than Keats's understanding of the self as a temporary "flare" of consciousness. In this naturalistic portrayal of generation, the "conscience" is already (as I read it) "pack[ed]" "to call" "Umbilical," that is, for the maternal, as we will see more clearly in the discussion of "Three Songs."

But Crane is interested in "affirming" the twentieth century, and the grimy "penny" of modern consciousness is returned from the underworld to the surface, where recursion itself no longer "freezes," and the "links" no longer seem so weak (109). Rather, and in part *because* of the radical dislocation of the speaker ("Tossed from the coil of ticking towers" [112]), his recursions to Shakespeare are freeing, not freezing, especially in their incomplete state. By identification with the precursor he identifies with "some Word that will not die" (instead of that art which "time slays"), and is able to recuperate for the self some useful fragment, at least, of the "famous sight[s]." Moreover, his recursions are, in their incompleteness, able to bridge paratactically the past, future, and present, by means of the self formed in just such recursions:

> Tossed from the coil of ticking towers. . . .
>   Tomorrow,
> And to be. . . .
>
>   (112; original ellipses)

Neither the square of the commercial and industrial world nor the circle of social intercourse or art provides the sense of wholeness that Crane appears to desire. The self that is discovered thus far is inherently fragmented and gains a sense of itself primarily through that fragmenting experience of dislocation, a recursion which ensures that, whatever he may be, he is not that—or not that alone. This sense of radical dislocation is most readily related to Crane's experience of marginalization as a homosexual. (Like Wilde, he was "empowered to speak, but unable to say" [Yingling 1990, 26].) It can also be usefully extended to a reading of American epics in general, founded as they are in multiple experiences of dislocation (e.g., exclusion, transplantation, enslavement, genocide, etc.).

Taking a different focus, a close look at "Southern Cross" (first of the "Three Songs" in *The Bridge*) reveals Crane's awareness of the fragmentation inherent in the human condition, even at birth.

> And this long wake of phosphor,
>   iridescent
> Furrow of all our travel—trailed derision!
> Eyes crumble at its kiss. Its long-drawn spell
> Incites a yell. Slid on that backward vision
> The mind is churned to spittle, whispering hell.
>   (98)

While a principal image portrayed here is that of light within the ocean waves—the "long wake of phosphor"—Crane's simultaneous invocation and inversion of the Wordsworthian conception of the infant "trailing clouds of glory" suggests a clearer reading of the "Furrow of all our travel" that recognizes it as birth canal.[76] The strongly negative imagery of the process of birth is, of course, consistent with the vision of female sexuality in this song (and, indeed, throughout the epic). While we shall return to this issue momentarily, the points I would like to focus on are the recognized *méconnaissance* of "trailed derision," and Crane's version of the Virgilian *infandum*.

The specific form taken by *méconnaissance* here, which may not be immediately clear, is the egocentrism that supposes the trail of light to be directed toward itself. The common assumption of the centrality of the self to the phenomena of the natural world, while understandable (as based on the experience mediated by the perceptual apparatus), is a miscognition, a misreading of the universe we might expect from the quixotic figure of narcissistic fulfillment. "Trailed derision" functions as a recursion that not only mocks Wordsworth, but also describes the mockery implicit in all human observations of the universe. Rather than a reassurance of faith in the world's attention to the self, this similar but antithetical perception is of a world that derides, or laughs at, the self. Reading the "iridescent / Furrow" of travel as birth canal clearly requires that the same reading be applied to the self's relation with the maternal. The next line, difficult to apprehend in terms of natural phenomena, becomes more coherent in an Oedipal reading, where the fact that eyes should "crumble" (or become blind) at the "kiss" from the maternal source, is readily comprehensible.

Similarly, the distinction between the (relatively) articulate "yell" evoked by the mother's life-long "spell," and the "backward" movement toward the preverbal chaos of "spittle, whispering hell," centers us again between the *infandum*—the unspeakable—and the fate that is cried out against. As Crane goes on to describe the crisis, conveyed in this poem as both romantic and Oedipal, he recalls images from Aeneas' descriptions of Troy's fall: "It is blood to remember; it is fire / To stammer back . . . It is / God—your namelessness" (98). The parallel between "God" and the lover's namelessness is surprisingly similar to that found in H. D.'s *Helen in Egypt* where Thetis remains (for Achilles) the unnameable. And as "Helena" is Achilles' password to the maternal, so for the speaker in this song, several names are used—ineffectually—as passwords to the "nameless woman of the South" (who is—also like Thetis—a creature of the sea):

Eve! Magdalene!
        or Mary, you?
Whatever call—falls vainly on the wave.
O simian Venus, homeless Eve,

> Unwedded, stumbling gardenless to grieve
> Windswept guitars on lonely decks forever;
> Finally to answer all within one grave!
>
>   (98)

This broken quatrain implies that all the male speaker's calling and grieving will be answered only in his death, apparently in that absolute form that is also the "answer" in *Voyages II* to "The seal's wide spindrift gaze toward paradise" (answered only "in the vortex of our grave") (36).

The "windswept guitars" form a difficulty in a lyric that easily seems, as Edward Brunner remarks, "a nearly incoherent set of fragmented outcries." In part this "incoherence" results from the refusal of readers to recognize fully the impact of Crane's homosexuality on his work. Brunner, for example, generalizes in order to see the lyric as examining "a nostalgic and backward-looking vision" and the consequent "hatred for the present" bred by such a vision.[77] In contrast, earlier critics comment (following John R. Willingham's influential article) on the generally "unflattering" portrait drawn of modern women as archetypes in the "Three Songs." These portraits, in turn, are held to contrast with the ideal feminine figure of Pocahontas.[78] Yingling is much more promising in his analysis of the way "the homoerotic content of the poem [*The Bridge* as a whole] is incrementally displaced . . . in favor of a purely literary one" (214–15). His reading is not fully carried out in terms of this particular lyric, unfortunately, but he does suggest it is the "complaint" of the homosexual over the "enforced and disempowering liminality express[ed] . . . not as desire for a female object of desire, but, curiously enough, as a kind of gender envy" (216). If I read Yingling correctly, he is saying that the speaker in "Southern Cross" envies (in particular) female reproductive power.

My own reading of "Southern Cross" runs across the grain of these to suggest the primacy, first, of a maternal reading of the "nameless woman": Insofar as a name is settled upon, it is Eve, the first mother, or in the more jaded (and Darwinian) reading a "simian Venus." Still more clearly, she is equated with the personified feminine Night, and finally the Medusa, with her stony offspring:

> Water rattled that stinging coil, your
> Rehearsed hair—docile, alas, from many arms.
> Yes, Eve—wraith of my unloved seed!
>
> The Cross, a phantom, buckled—dropped below the dawn.
> Light drowned the lithic trillions of your spawn.
>
>   (99)

The accusation of promiscuity leveled in these and preceding lines ("You crept out simmering, accomplished . . . ") is of a piece with the prevalent virgin/ whore dualism of "Three Songs." The speaker's implicit fear of the woman appears in his perception of the Medusa, and more clearly still in the impotent "buckling" of the phantom constellation ("that seemingly transcendent phallus," as Yingling puts it). But it is woman as the "wraith of my unloved seed" that puzzles. Perhaps this is explicable in Yingling's interpretation as the homosexual's enforced barrenness. But it seems clearer to read it as consonant with the other images discussed above (and with the accusations of sexual competence), as a recognition of the speaker's own lack of centrality to the maternal figure. The mother is that apparition which haunts the "unloved seed" of the self, much as she haunts his "memory" elsewhere in the poem with a smile so expressly not meant for the speaker:

> . . . is it the Sabbatical, unconscious smile
> My mother almost brought me once from church
> And once only, as I recall—?

> It flickered through the snow screen, blindly
> It forsook her at the doorway, it was gone
> Before I had left the window. It
> Did not return with the kiss in the hall.
>
>   (60–61)

The "almosted" equation in "Southern Cross" between "your namelessness" and "God" can be recalled here, and it leads to an interesting figuration of Crane's particular version of Romanticism. The opening of "Southern Cross" attempts to outline the idealist union:

> I wanted you, nameless Woman of the South,
> No wraith, but utterly—as still more alone
> The Southern Cross takes night
> And lifts her girdles from her, one by one—
>
>   (98)

Despite Yingling's claim that there is no "desire for a female object of desire," and despite the misogynist imagery encountered in immediately succeeding lines, it is difficult to argue with "I wanted you," except to note its past tense. The pastness of that past tense may be seen to arise from two different encounters within the lyric—the wraithlike quality of the woman as she is known, and the sexual horror that attends the unveiling in the lines above, as the girdles are lifted

High, cool,
              wide from the slowly smoldering fire
Of lower heavens,—
                        vaporous scars!

    (98)

I have suggested that that wraithlike quality arises from the speaker's acknowledgment of his own lack of centrality, and this is reinforced by the fact that he
desired her "utterly." His rewriting of Keats's sonnet is at this point most relevant, for where Keats emphatically desires to be "*Not* in lone splendour hung
aloft the night," Crane stresses this to its uttermost, striving to be as the stars,
"still more alone." Similarly, if we read (as we might as easily) "No wraith" as
applying to the speaker rather than to the woman, Crane's lyric becomes a consistent refusal of the happy substitutes suggested by Keats's lyric, the Keatsian
desire to be not alone, but

       still steadfast, still unchangeable,
Pillowed upon my fair love's ripening breast,
To feel for ever its soft swell and fall,
Awake for ever in a sweet unrest,
Still, still to hear her tender-taken breath,
And so live ever—or else swoon to death.

The condition proposed by Keats is, in Crane's terms, that of the wraith; that
is, Keats's speaker demonstrates a romanticism that fails to realize its own lack
of centrality, that chooses to endow natural phenomena with sexlessness to
avoid decentering competition: The star becomes "Nature's patient, sleepless
Eremite," watching "The moving waters at their priestlike task / Of pure ablu-
tion." Crane's rewriting, on the other hand, sexualizes and decenters the scene,
depicting not only the Southern Cross as phallus, but the water, too, as antithetical to the celibate, anthropocentric Keatsian vision:

All night the water combed you with black
Insolence. You crept out simmering, accomplished.

    (99)

Rather than remaining "Awake for ever in a sweet unrest," which is seen as
dramatically uncertain, decentered and "wraithlike," Crane seeks other options
that avoid this compromise. First of these, and perhaps ultimately most attractive, is to "swoon to death," to join the maternal in the sea.[79] Second, and most
relevant to the epic under consideration, is that of the "windswept guitar." Like
the Southern Cross, it is isolated ("lonely"); unlike the constellation, it suffers

no impotence in the changeable world: where the Southern Cross "buckles" with daylight, the windswept guitar grieves "forever." More important, it requires no investment of self: Whether or not the guitar is central matters not; like the Eolian Harp, it merely "perceives" after its musical fashion. The ideal type of the spectatorial epic hero, the windswept guitar identifies as needed with the world around it, "As wild and various as the random gales / That swell and flutter on this subject Lute!"[80]

As should be apparent, the "windswept guitar" is analogous to the bridge itself, and hence analogous with the poet's own self-conception, at least with the spectatorial aspect of the hero. Moreover, the bridge, as "harp and altar, of the fury fused" (46), insinuates by the action of "the fury" that harp and altar come together as a result of crimes against kinship (those crimes that bring the Furies to bear on the criminal). In the most familiar form of the story, the *Oresteia* of Aeschylus, Orestes kills his mother Klytaimnestra and her lover Aigisthos for the sake of the dead Agamemnon; he is pursued by the Furies—the Eumenides, or "kindly ones"—until he obtains the intercession of Apollo and finally Athena.

(An Aside)

(This reading of an Oresteian rather than Oedipal plot in no way undermines the deeper narcissistic concerns of recursive epic desire. A plot that [a] slaughters both parental figures and [b] includes the projected sexual infidelity of mother and seducer as the reason for both murder and subsequent guilt makes for little difference. Moreover, in this light some of the dominant and fundamental preoedipal concerns neglected by Freud may be seen to emerge even in the *Oedipus* itself. Love and war become matters of emphasis, not inextricably linked to the mechanisms of gender.)

There is no art of poetry, save by the grace of other poetry.
—William Carlos Williams

Despite Crane's high opinion of Aeschylus (that "there is none in the English language to compare him with"), the significance of his plays for *The Bridge* appears to have gone undeveloped. Aeschylus is "a revelation of my ideal in the dynamics of metaphor—even through the rather prosy translations one gleans the essential density of image, impact of substance, matter so verbally quickened and delivered with such soul-shivering economy" (1952, 235). Transparently enough, Crane's use of the "fury" as an enforcing agent in the construction of the bridge is particularly intriguing to me because of the old story that lies beneath it: For the sake of his dead father (and to remove the family curse of the Atreidae), Orestes murders his mother. This ought to be more fully explored as to its function throughout *The Bridge*, but even with this limited reading, the outline of a particular attitude toward tradition becomes visible.

The point of a "windswept guitar" is to create articulate sound without requiring the presence of a human agent. Action is removed to its source in the unknowable. As outlined in "Three Songs," the ultimate source is the maternal abandonment, and the ultimate unknowable is the maternal answer. The windswept guitar functions as a removal of self-identification with that maternal: that is, by choosing to abandon the maternal centrality to the self, the self is able to assuage—somewhat—the overwhelming fear of its own lack of centrality. Orestes functions as an aggressively invested form of the instrument ("played upon" by Apollo, Pylades, and Elektra), one that retaliates against the mother for the (aggressively understood) abandonment, the primal dislocation.[81] To Crane the epic is "an act of faith besides being a communication," an altar as well as a harp. Moreover, his "faith" is quite clearly built upon patriarchal tradition, which he sees as having suffered a loss of power, as fragmented (like Agamemnon): "Where are my kinsmen and the patriarch race?" he asks in "Quaker Hill." His affirmation of faith in tradition is primarily antagonistic toward T. S. Eliot, and more generally toward the forces of determinism and belatedness. As he wrote in 1923 and repeatedly thereafter, he would consistently oppose Eliot's pessimistic, "whimpering" acceptance of the perfection of death:

> Certainly the man has dug the ground and buried hope as deep and direfully as it can ever be done. . . .
> After this perfection of death—nothing is possible in motion but a resurrection of some kind. Or else, as everyone persists in announcing in the deep and dirgeful *Dial*, the fruits of civilization are entirely harvested. . . .
> All I know through very much suffering and dullness . . . is that it interests me to still affirm certain things. (1952, 115)

To draw out the tenuous classical analogy, Crane's Oresteian drama involves not only the (temporary) defeat of the maternal in favor of a homosocial bond with patriarchal tradition, but as well the defeat of the precursor as usurper—the "whimpering" Eliot as Aigisthos, Klytaimnestra's lover. Through his "affirmation" of patriarchy and antagonistic response to Eliot, Crane's Orestes enacts a loving resurrection of the father. Though promising, the analogy at this point is unable to bear such conjectural weight. Our reading of "Southern Cross" does reinforce such conjecture, however, especially in the identification we have seen there between the phallic constellation "still more alone" and the lonely "wind-swept guitars." The constellation "buckles" in its confrontation with the female object of seduction, but the Eolian harp goes on for ever, in its more constant emulation of the paternal.

Looking at the epigraph to "Three Songs," a phrase misquoted from Marlowe's *Hero and Leander* ("The one Sestos, the other Abydos hight" [97]), we see another evocation of the bridge, built, as it were, on the back of Leander swimming the Hellespont. The point of the epigraph, however, is not only in its rehearsal of a heterosexual love affair "completed" across the channel, but as well with the homoerotic interlude that is central to Leander's experience of the Hellespont. (The miscognition of the "inverted" quotation only adds to this reading.) For in Marlowe, of course, young Leander is the beloved of Neptune as well as of Hero; in the outcome of the original tale, Leander drowns, and Hero throws herself into the sea. Though Marlowe's fragmented poem does not include that outcome, the ending is implicit in the opening admission of the channel's guilt: "On Hellespont, guilty of true-loves' blood, / In view and opposite, two cities stood."

An important parallel exists between Marlowe's poem and the functional significance of the bridge in Crane. Though the putative goal of Leander's voyage is the heterosexual union with Hero, the significance of that which he bridges is homoerotic—the blandishments of Neptune—and is, like Crane's "Atlantis," a submerged realm of sexual (and textual) pleasure.[82] Crane's epic works in much the same way, where the homoerotic functions (in limited regard) as a bridge to something else. I am *not* suggesting by this that the homosexual is at all (actually or transcendentally) a "stage" in some other process. But given the effectiveness to this point of the Oedipal reading of *The Bridge*, it seems worth remarking the prevailing image of a transcendence marked specifically by difference, but a transcendence that is not the entire (or even the principal) point of the poem. As suggested earlier, the maternal origin and telos are inscribed as a means of emphasizing the antitelic dynamic, the recursive and homosocial engagements allowed by the space *between* origin and telos— the "Lie" of Maquokeeta, the dance, the bridge itself. The dazzling display of recursive desire at the epic's close, just short of the submerged Atlantis, is the best evidence of this vital homoerotic jouissance, necessarily framed (in Crane) by the different, specifically maternal poles of birth and death.

Yingling, despite his sensitive reading of much of the poem, is understandably puzzled by "Atlantis." Though he sees it as the scene of Crane's "most ecstatic readerly marriage" (220), homosexual desire "disappears completely from the surface of 'Atlantis' ": "Unable to depict full-bodied unions throughout the poem, either homosexual or heterosexual, the only union imaginable for Crane is a completely figurative one, a music that has no referent, no body to become trapped in, no ideological weight" (221). My reading is perhaps overinformed by the epic recursions within this part of the poem, but I see them working together in an unmistakable manner:

> Sheerly the eyes, like seagulls stung with rime—
> Slit and propelled by glistening fins of light—
> Pick biting way up towering looms that press
> Sidelong with flight of blade on tendon blade
> —Tomorrows into yesteryear—and link
> What cipher-script of time no traveller reads
> But who, through smoking pyres of love and death,
> Searches the timeless laugh of mythic spears.
>
> Like hails, farewells—up planet-sequined heights
> Some trillion whispering hammers glimmer Tyre:
> Serenely, sharply up the long anvil cry
> Of inchling æons silence rivets Troy.
> And you, aloft there—Jason! hesting Shout!
>
> (115)

Between the observing, though weary, eyes, and the "towering looms" of the bridge that "press ... Tomorrows into yesteryear,"[83] is an implicit contract, which allows the eyes to "link," or put together, the "cipher-script of time." The eyes, of course, must be those of one "who, through smoking pyres of love and death, / Searches the timeless laugh of mythic spears." That is, by looking at the bridge in the right way, with the right sort of eyes, one reads the timeless laugh of spears, connected as one, here, in "blade on tendon blade." By the extension of the epic imagery, these are connected as well in the long process of forging the modern epic, the tale of the tribe, through the traditional "hails, farewells," by a process of repeated ("a trillion whispering hammers") invocations and linkages—the "rivets" that hold Troy to the modern poet and the bridge, both because and in spite of the "long anvil cry / Of inchling æons." Crane's poem has been eons in the making, he implies, and is, like the bridge and the communal (but male) laughter of mythic spears, "One Song, one Bridge of Fire":

> So to thine Everpresence, beyond time,
> Like spears ensanguined of one tolling star
> That bleeds infinity—the orphic strings,

Sidereal phalanxes, leap and converge:
One Song, one Bridge of Fire!

(117)

In Yingling's reading of these lines, he avoids the issue of "thine Everpresence,"
to see the "Sidereal phalanxes" of spears as "a vision of homosexuality as a cen-
tered, unifying experience capable of inspiring redemptive verse" (224). Yingling's interpretation is certainly accurate as far as it goes, but why evade the
apparent transcendence? Other recent criticism similarly attempts to efface the
transcendental from *The Bridge:* a noble goal, but one that threatens to undermine the poem's structure (and Crane's repeated expressions of affirmation).
Allen Grossman's excellent work points out Crane's "rhetoric of shadowed
wholeness (the impossible simultaneity of all the implications of desire) that
struggles to include all meanings in the space of one appearance."[84] That "all
meanings" should be implicit in the bridge itself, which we have read as the
Lacanian transcendental signifier, is not surprising. Nor is John Carlos Rowe's
contention that "Word, Myth, Bridge, Atlantis . . . are defined repeatedly as
metaphors." When he goes on to suggest, however, that Crane's "primordial
One is the energy of differences, never a synthesis that would destroy those ten-
sive and productive relations," it seems to me he undervalues—both literally
and biographically—Crane's relation with Grace.[85]

Migrations that must needs void memory
Inventions that cobblestone the heart,—
Unspeakable Thou Bridge to Thee, O Love.
Thy pardon for this history, whitest Flower,
O Answerer of all,—Anemone,—
Now while thy petals spend the suns about us, hold—
(O Thou whose radiance doth inherit me)
Atlantis,—hold thy floating singer late!

(116)

The "Answerer of all" appears earlier (in "Southern Cross"), equated with the
maternal image of death. So it is here through the Anemone, but the clearest
portrayal of the feminine principle appears in the debased "burlesque" version
from "National Winter Garden," where the female dancer—like Pocahontas—is
both the source of the male and the ground of male acrobatics, she whose
"spasm" engenders horror in the male spectators and apparently causes bonding between men (100):

Yet, to the empty trapeze of your flesh,
O Magdalene, each comes back to die alone.

Then you, the burlesque of our lust—and faith,
Lug us back lifeward, bone by infant bone.

(101)

While this does not suggest transcendence *per se,* it certainly, through the vagaries of its "burlesque" of lust and faith, supports the reading I have outlined for the feminine in *The Bridge.* Especially interesting is the unknowability of the burlesque dancer's smile, like that of the speaker's mother in "Van Winkle." "Virginia," the last of the "Three Songs," has been substantially slighted by critics for its "almost overtly trivial" quality (Yingling 1990, 218). As Crane notes in a letter, it depicts a virgin (Mary) in the process of "being built." Like "National Winter Garden," the lyric emphasizes the speaker's own position as spectator and his discursive elaboration of the female, either as whore or as virgin.

In the more idealistically pitched octave from "Atlantis" quoted above, however, that unknowability of the maternal is translated as "Unspeakable," and the "empty trapeze" to which men return is inscribed as "Love," or "Thou whose radiance doth inherit me." And as the Anemone or "windflower" is the transcendent goal of the bridge, she is also the source of chaos—and we have here a hint again of that fear of lost centrality (notable in the pun on "suns" and the sexual meaning of "spend"): "while thy petals spend the suns about us, hold— . . . hold thy floating singer late!" One cannot be sure, but Yingling's (and Bloom's) reading of this as the dismembered Orphic head seems to miss the point, which is precisely to be *late* in arriving, last of the "suns" to be spent, so that there will be time for "the orphic strings, / Sidereal phalanxes" to converge in "One Song, one Bridge of Fire!"

> I cannot make it cohere.
> —Ezra Pound

Through fragmented epics, poets deconstruct their precursors, and consequently have difficulty reconstructing a valid argument. As the tradition is progressively fragmented, it is harder and harder to conceive a valid basis for action—within the world or within the discursive domain of epic. Demystifying the bases of old values is a traditional strategy, but fragmentation (including in its work the values implicit in narrative) also implies a radical critique of any *new* basis of value: That too will have to be demystified and deconstructed. Speaking broadly, fragmented epic is narratively less dependent upon recursion (but perhaps more dependent in its recursive details) than inverted epic, since fragmentation tends to deny even the initial, temporary validity of epos (in direct proportion to the denial of its own validity). Inverted epic, by contrast, creates the fiction of a new dispensation that (not accidentally) is an inverse of the old, and the recursion seems a negative exposure of the originary text.

Despite Tillyard's claim that "No pronounced homosexual . . . could be an epic poet, not because he is one, but because of what his being one excludes him from" (1954, 8), much of the modern epic—from Milton, perhaps from Chaucer onward—is produced from a stance toward tradition that is in part passive and metonymically engaged, from what I have characterized as an Oresteian rather than strictly Oedipal position. This is fairly clear in the epics of Whitman and Crane. The (lately defined) sexual orientation of poets is of less interest than the fact that this metonymic (stereotypically "feminine") response to tradition produces new epics and that this gradual return toward a metonymic response to tradition coincides with the development of women's epic. Only after the advent of print do epics by women—Elektran epics—circulate widely. The epics of women, moreover, like more recent epics by men, return to formal traditions of coherence, and even to narrative.

6

Sleeping with the Enemy

Women and Epic

WOMEN'S INVOLVEMENT with epic is fraught with peril. As the exemplary genre of patriarchy, epic appears to perpetuate the exclusion of women from cultural power.[1] In consequence, figures of women as scripted *within* epic have received a fair amount of attention. But women's own epic expressions have been ignored, perhaps due to the threatening brevity of the topic; women's exclusion from producing epic in earlier centuries has been so thorough as barely to discover a footnote. Isolated and occluded by the tradition as it is currently framed, these earlier epic poets are precursors who do not precur, "female Homers" without Homeridae.[2] Elizabeth Barrett Browning and H.D., however, provide a clearly polarized set of strategies for coping with patriarchal epic tradition, and—happily enough—also suggest the workings of influence between women as poets and precursors.

The impulse toward epic, then, based, as I have argued, in narcissism and in the narcissistic drive toward fulfillment, is one that (within Western culture) is repeatedly scripted as a search for the mother. The search for the mother in epics produced by women raises two possible objections. The difficulty I would like to explore first is that exposed by a psychoanalytic approach, and the question is a very old one: What do women want? The second is more specific, and is the subject of the chapter as a whole: What are the dynamics of a woman's desire when, as a poet, she chooses to repeat the epic tradition by writing her own epic?

> I grante thee lyf, if thou kanst tellen me
> What thyng is it that wommen moost desiren.
> —Guenevere[3]

A number of excellent studies demonstrate that the plot of female development need not follow the traditional male path of individuation.[4] The question of female desire, too, has been a focus of attention in the last twenty years; much feminist scholarship specifically revalues the important connections established by children in the preoedipal stage, connections that are maintained by females throughout their lives. As Elizabeth Abel remarks, the identity of women is "shaped primarily by the fluctuations of symbiosis and separation from the mother. Rather than being superseded by the Oedipal relation to the father, this process of identification and differentiation endures throughout adult life" (1983, 10). To extend this, female identity is formed and maintained without significant regard for male identity in general and particularly for the heterosexual "Oedipal relation to the father."[5]

Women's desire, then (apart from the inscribed heterosexual code), is demonstrated most clearly in these "fluctuations of symbiosis and separation from the mother." This desire might be most easily (because familiarly) explained in the traditional terms of male desire, as having a "source" and "goal."[6] Women, however, insofar as they already fluctuate between symbiosis and separation from the mother, cannot have such a "goal." These are inappropriate terms, because women are (sometimes more and sometimes less) already in a symbiotic relation with the mother. The "goal" is always already achieved. Luce Irigaray, in a display of anatomy as destiny similar to Lacan's, outlines the fluctuations of female desire in opposition to the necessarily instrumental quality of male desire: "But a woman touches herself by and within herself directly, without mediation, and before any distinction between activity and passivity is possible. A woman 'touches herself' constantly without anyone being able to forbid her to do so, for her sex is composed of two lips which embrace continually. Thus, within herself she is already two—but not divisible into ones—who stimulate each other" (1981, 100). This nonteleological autoeroticism can appear alien to male desire, but more particularly to the patriarchal investment in heteroeroticism and the primacy of the phallus (witnessed, as Irigaray suggests, by "the almost exclusive, and ever so anxious, attention accorded to the erection in Occidental sexuality" [1981, 100]). Male desire, and the logic that is joined to the transcendental signifier, implies "the prevalence of the gaze, discrimination of form, and individualization of form," all of which, according to Irigaray, are "particularly foreign to female eroticism," which in all likelihood "does not speak the same language as man's desire" (1981, 101).

An inscription of female desire like Irigaray's, which insists on the plurality of female "selves" and sexualities, would as insistently lead to chaos, to a state of selflessness or nonbeing. This should not be seen as problematic, since this state of nonbeing is equally the goal of the male desire for maternal union. Moreover, Irigaray asserts that this simultaneous desire for "nothing and everything" (1981, 103), suspended as it is in *jouissance*, in sexual pleasure, does not in fact lead (quite) to chaos: "It is a sort of universe in expansion for which no limits could be fixed and which, for all that, would not be incoherency. Nor would it be the polymorphic perversion of the infant during which its eroge-nous zones await their consolidation under the primacy of the phallus" (1981, 104).[7] Women's autocatalytic desires, however, cannot be the whole story, par-ticularly not when we come to speak of epic tradition. While it is attractive to suggest with Irigaray that women and their desires are sufficient unto them-selves, such an understanding at this point seems hazardous in two different ways. On the one hand, the anatomical and essentialist thesis falls too easily into stereotypical codes of the feminine, displacing agency and necessarily revolutionary goals as somehow "unwomanly." Second, and if possible, more dangerous, is the kind of eloquent worship of women—gynolatry, if you will—suggested in the following passage from Jean Baudrillard: "We have dreamt of every woman there is, and dreamt too of the miracle that would bring us the pleasure of being a woman, for women have all the qualities—courage, passion, the capacity to love, cunning—whereas all our imagination can do is naively pile up the illusion of courage."[8] Disturbing here is not the gallant admission of male anxiety (with its naive "illusion of courage"), but rather the indelible fa-miliarity of this elevation of womanhood. This is most obvious in Baudrillard's insistence on "our" (continued) inscription of women. The phallic "imagina-tion" is only able to accomplish so much with regard to "us" and our illusions, but the phallic imagination is also that which actually *forms* women as idolized objects (once again) through its "dreams."

Fortunately, these theories of desire can easily strike the reader as ulti-mately an inadequate explanation for actual human desire, which does seem, due to the loss or alienation contingent upon consciousness (at all) of self, ac-tually unfulfillable. Closer examination reveals that the absolutist and essen-tialist psychoanalytic paradigms—whether valorizing phallic autonomy or the female sex which is not one, but always plural—are (even if useful) simplistic.

As with the alternate (and similarly exclusive) psychoanalytic polarizations of "male self" and the "female selflessness," this distinction of desire is only useful insofar as we regard it as a heuristic fiction, an "expedient error" that facilitates our interactions with our environments. As soon as it becomes a reified construction—what men or women "are"—it becomes dangerous. What is needed, then, is an ameliorated explanation of desire. If to be human is, in the largest sense, to be desirous for the maternal (in this psychological frame), then insofar as women fluctuate between symbiosis and separation from the mother, they become plural selves (as Irigaray has demonstrated); but this plu-rality does not *negate* the integrity of those selves, or more accurately, we can only imagine such integrity being negated by a condition of utter fulfillment—the return to the mother. Instead, the individual integrity of such selves becomes provisional, useful within a certain context of relations between or among the plurality.[9]

A fundamentally similar dynamic inheres in men's fluctuations of symbiosis and separation from the mother (for these are necessarily fluctuations, analogous in type if not in duration). As seen in the discussion of Keats in Chapter 5, the provisional selves created form temporarily expedient means of functioning within the perceived environment. These provisional selves do their work primarily through metonymic connection—through the chameleon poet Keats's sympathetic involvement or "negative capability." Whereas in Odysseus such duplicity worked to preserve a frequently hostile inner self—a core of narcissism—the plural selves of the fragmented epics imply plural sexualities as well as selves. While the "prevalence of the gaze" that Irigaray notes as prominent in male desire does indeed figure strongly in my (simplified) model of observer and actor, the attenuation of this model in Keats's *Fall of Hyperion* is rather remarkable.[10]

Male desire, moreover, is not always focused only on the phallus, regardless of the reductivist claims of traditional psychoanalytic theory. While it may be true that "woman has sex organs just about everywhere" (Irigaray 1981, 103), it remains unclear why the same should not be understood of men, insofar as men also have erotic responses "just about everywhere." Even according to Freud, the erotogenic capacity of epidermal, aural, and ocular sensation, of oral and anal as well as genital sexuality is extraordinary; this is (in Irigaray's phrase) "the polymorphic perversion of the infant," but it is particularly clear in Freud that these capacities are not elided by genital sexuality.[11] Rather, the "primacy of the phallus" in psychoanalytic theory, I would propose, is almost as debilitating to our understanding of male desire as it is to our understanding of female desire.[12]

> Phallocentrism is the enemy.
> —Hélène Cixous

> But the margin is not "purer."
> —Lyn Hejinian[13]

Unfortunately, neither female nor male autoeroticism is sufficient to explain adequately the necessarily different eroticism implied in women's performance of epic. Within a dominant tradition perceived as thoroughly masculine, the fulfillment of women's desire cannot be understood as autocatalytic: If, as I have argued, the impulse to repeat the tradition is a defining characteristic of the genre, then the establishment of recursion on the part of a female poet is, as Sharon Doubiago suggests in her epic, *Hard Country*, a process of "sleeping with the enemy." That is, writing epic poetry involves women in patriarchy, and involves them, moreover, in a recursion such that they appear to participate in their own continued subversion. However, as Irigaray suggests, women's unnecessary but traditionally "compulsory" engagement with phallocentric culture *can* provide a "vicarious" pleasure for woman, if only through the "masochistic prostitution of her body to a desire that is not her own" (1981, 100).[14] Given the way women are directed toward such vicarious desire by phallocentric culture—and the ways in which other forms of female desire are steadily feared, condemned, and ignored—it is not surprising that identity, for women, is in such a culture bound up with being passive, yet central to male desire. But that culture also presents a substantially different model of identity, bound up with power, agency, and maleness, one that has been typically (but not always) discouraged in females.[15] When this second model of identity is adopted and is encouraged, a child may find herself fulfilling some requirements of both models.

It is hardly surprising that the strategy of imitating the father can result in a simultaneous adequacy to both forms of identity: Imitating the father results in focused parental attention, and the father's encouragement (as representative of male desire) is especially important in suggesting such behavior as appropriate for the child. The act of identifying with and imitating the father teaches as well the efficacy of power and active ("masculine") agency. When this act of imitating the father manifests itself as writing, as the expression of discursive rather than physical power, the imitation is less actively discouraged, and may indeed be encouraged.[16] Thus, within a patriarchal system that begins to encourage its daughters as active agents, the fluctuations of symbiosis and separation from the mother become heavily weighted in favor of separation and the development of "identity" in the traditional sense.[17] This is not without its costs; the development of identity on the basis of the paternal model involves "radical surgery" in the daughter's effort to elide the close connection with the maternal.[18] The movement toward the father and toward active agency enforces a surrender of maternal connection, a denial of the "feminine" in favor of the "masculine." If to be the passive heterosexual woman required by patriarchal culture allows one only "vicarious" pleasure, through the "masochistic prostitution of her body to a desire that is not her own," then to become an active agent within that culture enforces participation in that process. For the *particular* self thus formed through separation from or rejection of the feminine, pleasure is no longer vicarious, but is now instrumentally focused upon the feminine (the maternal goal), in fulfillment of a desire that is adopted as her own.[19] To restate this ambivalent position in Irigaray's terminology, the woman subjects herself to her own (phallic) desires, gaining vicarious pleasure through her masochistic prostitution to her desires, and gaining fulfillment of those desires through the sadistic conquest or purchase of herself.

This rather grim-looking scenario, despite its exaggerated simplicity, does provide an explanatory paradigm to account for the persistent and troubling centrality of violence against women that takes place in some significant epics by women. The act of rape, in particular, is central to both *Helen in Egypt* and *Aurora Leigh*.[20] The problem of the "father's daughter" who abandons the maternal and the feminine connection to ally herself with patriarchal forms of identity is here inseparably linked to the problem of epic recursion, of her complicity with a "masterplot" that is read as predicated on another's conquest and slavery. Since recursion in epic is also closely tied up with identity, particularly with the aggrandizement of the self in poetic fame or glory, it is easy to see that women's production of epic (within the tradition as it has been perceived) *could* be socially destructive of women, however much it might do for the individual poet.[21] Or if we choose to see such violence as an expression against the self, performance of epic could be seen as an act akin to that of Dido, as a self-immolation, insofar as it appears to require the sacrifice of the maternal, the alternate self, in favor of fidelity to the masculine ideal of epos. Epics such as these, then, would clearly feed back into the strategies of patriarchy.

Fortunately, though such textual productions are possible, they are not the *necessary* corollary to women's performance of epic, and seem at least unusual among women who choose to write epics. The grim paradigm of explanation still applies, as rape is still a central focus of these epics, but the consequences are contingent upon other circumstances, as well as the epic script that cannot be escaped, the complex masterplot required of women who would be their fathers' daughters.

> This virilization of woman makes of her, ideally,
> a typical militant who can, in fact, become a
> veritable striking force in the social revolution.
> —Kristeva

Kristeva, remarking on women's writing "associated with the privileged father-daughter relationship," carefully elides the important issue just discussed, of women's sacrifice of women, through her use of "ideally" in the passage above. "[I]deally" suggests viable alternatives to the behavior of powerful women that remain unstated; the possibility of women extensively invested in patriarchy taking a militant stance *against* "the social revolution" is, as we know, entirely conceivable. The alternative extreme to the adoption of phallic

power is seen by Kristeva as women's "denial," "the valorization of a silent un-
derwater body . . . abdicating any entry into history."[22] The trade-off of the epic
poet *appears* to be one of women for power, and power can be (and is) used by
epic poets as a catalyst for change. Thus, one of the particular difficulties facing
feminist scholars focusing on epic is the fact that "it gets hard core."[23] However,
if instead of avoiding the acts of sexual violence that organize these epics we
attend closely to their potential and significance, we may not only recuperate
an ameliorative view of women's production of epic, but also (following the poets) find ways beyond the dichotomy of power and denial.

There are, with the addition of Kristeva's point concerning the potential
for militant feminism, three major ameliorative points to consider in the rather
depressing process of self-subversion I have outlined. First, it is true that both
Barrett Browning and H.D. provide powerfully feminist epics. "The Woman
Question" is central to *Aurora Leigh,* and Barrett Browning's championship of
women's causes—her willingness to write about the unspeakables—was the
subject of both extreme praise and blame.[24] Where *Aurora Leigh* has an unmis-
takably contemporary setting and ideological focus, *Helen in Egypt* does not.
However, H.D.'s striking feminist revision of Homer, "the fount itself" of epic
and of Western tradition as a whole,[25] necessarily focuses the reader's attention
on the relations between the sexes in what is, as we shall see, a conflict between
scripts. Epic poetry produced by women thus serves as a powerful tool for rewriting—"re-visioning," as Friedman terms it—women's position with regard
to patriarchy. But we should hesitate and expand this, for the other poets dealt
with in this study use that power in similar ways, rewriting their own positions
with regard to patriarchal scripts, sometimes establishing themselves as new
patriarchs. As with the other epic poets examined, Barrett Browning and H.D.
are engaged as discursively powerful agents in constructing and validating
themselves. Like other epics, these are quite deliberately opposed to epics that
have gone before. The key difference in these epics by women, however, is that
this opposition is explicitly phrased in terms of gender, usually against male
inscriptions of the female self, and by implication or statement, against such
inscriptions of women in general. Is this shift in gender merely a concealment
and reinscription of the same old elitist poetics, or does it move beyond?

Aurora Leigh and *Helen in Egypt* are beautifully paradigmatic epics to consider: Their prime concerns, respectively, are the cursor and the cursed, active
and passive forms of experience. *Helen in Egypt* parades the ultimate fate of
much-inscribed Helen, textual dream of poets: "She herself is the writing" (22,
91). *Aurora Leigh,* by contrast, is the story of a writer, narrating the growth of a
poet's mind (like Wordsworth's *Prelude*) and constructed, in part, as an answer
to Byron's *Don Juan.*

Both of these epic heroes have "sisters" who work in diametrically opposite ways. Clytaemnestra, in avenging Iphigenia's sacrifice at Aulis, essentially writes her name and agency in the blood of Agamemnon ("Clytaemnestra struck with her mind, / with the Will-to-Power" [97]). Marian Erle, raped and impregnated in a Paris brothel, is "written" as a typically Victorian "fallen woman" by patriarchal force. "Man's violence, / Not man's seduction" (6.1226–27)—carefully portrayed as *any* man's violence—curses her, inscribing her fate by a single act.

Following up on this, Dorothy Mermin makes the suggestion that for women in *Aurora Leigh*, "writing is a kind of sexual submission" to a male muse: "while Marian's narrative of her early life has to be retold by Aurora, after she has been raped she speaks eloquently for herself" (1989, 211). This disturbing reading would satisfy the grim paradigm sketched earlier, but we should note that Aurora (not submitting) writes both Marian's earlier and later life. Mermin also portrays Marian as apparently "inspired" by rape; Marian, however, specifically invokes her "male muse" not as rapist but as the child of that rape. She "bears the word" in a profound making of meaning, inscribing her son with purpose for herself and for her universe and thereby "draw[ing] the threads" of her text (and her life) out fully:

> "All the rest
> Is here," she said, and signed upon the child.
> "I found a mistress-sempstress who was kind
> And let me sew in peace among her girls.
> And what was better than to draw the threads
> All day and half the night for him and him?
> And so I lived for him, and so he lives,
> And so I know, by this time, God lives too."
>
>   (7.106–13)

Perhaps more disturbing than Mermin's reading of inspiration is Aurora's complicity in inscribing Marian as "damned" (6.366) and in her sudden recursion to the plot of masculine rescue/rape. Indeed, in the next few lines, she echoes Romney's first proposal of marriage as she invites Marian to live with her, an angel in the house:[26]

> "Come with me, sweetest sister," I returned,
> "And sit within my house and do me good
> From henceforth, thou and thine! ye are my own
> From henceforth."
>
>   (7.117–20)

Questions surround this ambivalent relationship. Though Aurora connects closely with this maternal and sororal figure, her coercive agency here and her complicity in conventional condemnation raise doubts, as does her demonizing attitude toward Lady Waldemar.

Similarly, Helen's closeness to the maternal goddess (Isis/Thetis) contrasts sharply with a considerable fracture in relations with other women. This abandonment of other women depends primarily on her transcendent relationship with Achilles. Though she must "tell and retell the story" (84) of Clytaemnestra and Iphigenia, this re-telling arises not out of concern for sister and niece but "because Achilles was involved somehow" (80).[27]

Helen's encounter with Theseus contains an extended discussion of Achilles' earlier loves (or sacrifices). Theseus recalls for her the women sacrificed to War: Chryseis, Briseis, Deidamia, Polyxena. But he recalls them in a way "unrelated to our Achilles" and inaccurate besides (172–73), confusing Pyrrhus with Helen's nephew Orestes. And Helen finally interrupts, rejecting the cold Athenian rationality of Theseus' "snow-palace" (174), recalling instead "the burning ember" of Achilles.

> does the ember glow
> in the heart of the snow?
> yes—I drifted here,
> blown (you asked) by what winter-sorrow
> but it is not sorrow;
>
> .   .   .   .
>
> there is a voice within me,
> listen—let it speak for me
>
>   (174–75)

Here, Helen replaces the scripts of Theseus with an inner voice (which itself contains a plurality of voices). Like the "thousand-petalled lily," and the "white crystal," Helen cannot deny that she is constituted by what she has been. The voice is heroic, also lyric; but neither facet of that voice denies the "Star in the night," the love of Helen and Achilles.

> what of that other—
> and that other, you speak of,
> the loves of Achilles?
>
> do I care? I am past caring
>
>   (176)

In the "lyric" she repeats the advice of Thetis: "seek not another Star (she said), O Helen, loved of War" (178). Though critics persist in attempting to rescue Helen from herself, she repeatedly implicates herself in war, and to an extent rejects connection with other women; war is part of what she is. Such a "masculine" concern is something that Paris and Theseus (like critics) would deny Helen. But it should be remembered that the initial conflict of Helen and Achilles is over exactly whose war it was:

> this was his anger,
> they were mine, not his,
> the unnumbered host
>
> mine, all the ships,
> mine, all the thousand petals of the rose,
>
> . . . .
>
> the thousand sails,
> the thousand feathered darts
> that sped them home
>
>   (25)

Theseus tries again to restrict her, lest she "flame out, incandescent" (187). His return to the standard Athenian dualities returns as well to the paternalistic nursery-rhyme:

> Thus, thus, thus,
> as day, night,
> as wrong, right
>
>   (190)

But on the next page, Helen eludes both father-figure and commentator: "Helen understands, though we do not know exactly what it is that she understands." For the reader, however, the imagery of Achilles' ember is very clear:

> yes—it breaks, the fire,
> it shatters the white marble
>
> . . . .
>
> day, night, wrong, right?
> no need to untangle the riddle
> it is very simple
>
>   (191–92)

Helen "refutes the Labyrinth" of the riddle, the tangle of scripts, by means of the unsayable, the intuitive "simple path." This is a characteristic strategy. Whether reading the hieroglyphs on the temple wall, or the "pictures" of the zodiac, or the speech of another character, H.D.'s Helen always "breaks off, as it were, from the recorded drama to remind us of the unrecorded . . . her first meeting with Achilles, 'on the ledge of a desolate beach' " (234). The strong implication of these intuitive leaps is that Helen, though not "instructed," already knows the answer. As in feminist theory, she is always already there, present to the maternal, and hence *needs* only to "re-tell the story" to establish her contiguity with other women. The possibility alerts us to a dangerously simplistic reading of women's epic texts. If men traditionally establish a concluding telos of the mother, what do women do? Apparently access to the maternal, ambivalently inscribed, is likely to be condensed, intermittent, occasional rather than terminal. Even in *Aurora Leigh*, the more traditional narrative, Aurora's relation with Marian (as with other women) fluctuates drastically from "damn[ing]" her (6.366) to canonizing her as a "saint" (7.127). This is a second (and significant) structural difference from male epics, in that women's differentiation from and contiguity with the maternal describes a series of arcs (possibly of little or no differentiation, or possibly exaggerated) rather than describing one more or less continuous arc.

A third ameliorative point to be made concerning writers of epic as father's daughters is that women's approach to fame and epic status may be different. Rather than deliberately attempting to outdo all earlier epics as, say, Milton or Whitman might, they set themselves up within a tradition, reading and responding to earlier epic. While both H.D. and Barrett Browning clearly desire to establish a significant poetic self in relation to tradition, they also see themselves as fundamentally connected to or allied with that tradition, rather than separate from it. The clearest example of this is H.D., whose epic not only critiques and reverses the *Iliad* and Achilles, but also reveres them and (bluntly enough) sleeps with that precursor text and hero. Recognizing and exposing the destructive elements of Homeric epic, the "iron-ring" of the warrior caste and death-cult, H.D.'s epic nonetheless depends upon the *Iliad* and the "wrath of Achilles" in order to attain its epic impact. *Helen in Egypt* presents Helen as neither the tradition's chief exponent nor its chief opponent. Rather, she is a connected part—an essential token—of the living network of exchange between men (and between texts); but H.D. (finally) gives that mere token a voice. The doubled identification of women with both mother and father—their double consciousness—may be seen as encouraging the emphatically dialectical and dialogic structure of women's epic.

Fame, indeed, 'twas said,
Means simply love. It was a man said that. . . .
Aurora Leigh 5.477–78.

Susan Stanford Friedman's excellent essay considers H.D. and Barrett Browning as epic poets, but conceives of them primarily as developing an intersection of genres (lyric, novel, and epic) due to anxiety concerning the patriarchal allegiances of epic. She thus traces the poets' strategic adaptation of the "female forms" of novel and the lyric to epic poetry, a traditionally masculine discursive realm.[28] My own approach to these epics, which takes Friedman's more general reading as a starting point, focuses on the recursive epic dynamic of desire and violence in Barrett Browning and H.D., and the way that dynamic reflects but modifies a set of preoedipal as well as Oedipal concerns with patriarchal tradition. Structural parallels within these epics have been pointed out by Friedman, including the adoption of subject position for the female hero, and the focus on private rather than public. In addition, she outlines the "abandonment of masculine privilege" by the male characters (who do not remain at the margins of these epics but "epitomize both patriarchy and desire") and the development of the heroes through the context of their relationships with other women (216-21).

A cursory glance at these four major structural parallels suggests that little has changed from traditional epic, apart from the dramatically increased emphasis on the female subject position. Given the parallels above, the heroes stay home in the private sector and form heroic identities through relationships with other women, while the male characters go out, get broken, and return. The *Odyssey,* apart from the important shift of subject position, has a similar structure: Penelope stays at home, Odysseus goes out, has his Iliadic heroism broken, forms a new heroic identity—primarily through relationships with women—for himself, but also for Penelope—and returns.[29] I do not intend by this to criticize Friedman's reading of these particular epics, but rather to highlight the vital recursive quality of the genre by directing attention to the way that heroic identity of any kind seems to be formed through relations with women; through, that is, "fluctuations of symbiosis and separation from the mother." The fluctuations of Odysseus in this regard seem to be wilder than most, but similarly directed and far simpler fluctuations occur in the *Aeneid* and, as we have seen, in Chaucer's *Troilus and Criseyde.*

Regarding the structural parallels in *Aurora Leigh* and *Helen in Egypt* there are two important observations to make. First and simplest is that both epics appear to achieve—in the terms of Chapter 3—the happy substitute for union with the maternal. This is not at all striking in the framework of a nineteenth-century novel, but in an epic it seems highly unusual, particularly, it seems, in such a belated age.[30] As I shall suggest, both poets, like the earlier poets, "write beyond" the temporary stability of the happy substitute, but in Aurora's and Romney's vision of the celestial city at the close of the epic, as in "the ultimate mystery" of Helen and Achilles "on the ledge of a desolate beach" (205, 234), we are meant to feel that the writing beyond is temporarily held off, that there is "a pause in the infinite rhythm / of the heart and of heaven" (*Helen* 304). The difficulty with these happy substitutes, however—the absolute conveyed in the unions of hero and heterosexual lover—is that Romney and Achilles are only uneasily seen as maternal. They have functioned, in fact, as exemplary of patriarchal inscription. The "abandonment of masculine privilege" that forms part of both poems is, as Friedman notes, a gradual process.

In *Helen in Egypt,* Achilles ("Greece-incarnate, the hero-god") is ship-wrecked on the coast of Egypt, the land of ghosts, where Helen meets him; he does not recognize her, and as the commentator notes, "though wounded, he carries with him the threat of autocracy" (15). Wounded in the heel and afraid, he is "the new Mortal" (10), but bears still his "shield, helmet, greaves" (18). As the epic continues, we come to realize that Achilles is not as sensitive nor as intuitive a reader as Helen. Where she consistently chooses "the simple path," and can read the zodiac as a single hieroglyph, Achilles must read the zodiac "picture by picture, / the outline of hero and beast" (205), in order to complete his own quest for himself. This quest for the self is as well the Oedipal quest for Thetis, his mother, as the feminine principle within himself, repressed in the interests of patriarchy's "High Command."

"Achilles in Egypt" is no longer Achilles in Troy, but at the moment he is terribly unsure of what he is, as his questions and his fear suggest (13, 15–16). However, we should not simply dismiss him as "the warlord and misogynist of *Helen in Egypt.*"[31] Though much of his diction is "distinctly fascist," indeed, "ty-rannical, elitist, and death-centered" (Friedman 1977, 173), we should carefully remember that Achilles' use of such diction is firmly set in the past tense. "We *were* an iron-ring / whom Death made stronger" (55; emphasis mine). Even in his past "reading" of Helen (or, clearly, of Thetis *through* Helen) on the plains of Troy, Achilles had already begun to change. Helen was "a fountain of water" (48) and her eyes were "as light on the changeable sea" (54). This scene of recog-nition, especially as a scene of unacknowledged maternal recognition and self-recognition (expressed in terms of the sea-imagery that unites all three in a "sea-enchantment") is understood as "weakness" when expressed in the lan-guage of the male "Command," and leads to his death. He had already begun to question Command: "Did the Command read backward?" (54). However, it is this empowerment of his femininity—his liquid "wavering"—that allows his re-creation as "the New Mortal" (10).

> I only remember
>
> how I had questioned Command;
> for this weakness, this wavering,
> I was shot like an underling . . .
>
>   (60)

Achilles, in his violent attempt to rewrite Helen by means of rape, raises serious questions about his reconstructed status as the "New Mortal." His quest for the mother seems off to an unfortunate start, but it is worth noting that the confused Achilles does not (quite) begin with rape. Rather, the gradual quest for his femininity begins (as it should, perhaps) with questions, not impositions:

> what sort of enchantment is this?
> what art will you wield with a fagot?
> are you Hecate? are you a witch?
>
> a vulture, a hieroglyph,
> the sign or the name of a goddess?
> what sort of goddess is this?
>
> where are we? who are you?
> where is this desolate coast?
> who am I? am I a ghost?
>
> (16)

If the quest for the mother is gradual, it is also, however, very sudden—the intuitive leap to the "Star in the Night." Helen shows Achilles this simple path, labeling him ("O child of Thetis"); this invocation of his mother is sudden (too sudden and simple for him), and he does attack her.[32] But still his inscription of her is uncertain; he calls her unreadable, "a hieroglyph" (17). His violent attempt to limit Helen as text (and voice) by throttling her, is, in one sense, the sign of a frustrated reader; he is trying to cut off this particular "writing's" continued evasion or supplementing of his interpretation.

> "O curséd, O envious Isis,
> you—you—a vulture, a hieroglyph";
> . . . .
> *O Thetis, O sea-mother,*
> I prayed, as he clutched my throat
>
> with his fingers remorseless steel,
> *let me go out, let me forget,*
> *let me be lost. . . . . . .*
>
> *O Thetis, O sea-mother,* I prayed under his cloak,
> *let me remember, let me remember,*
> *forever, this Star in the night.*
>
> (17)

Achilles' quest for the mother is solved, in a sense, by this moment of rage and love, though he does not yet understand. But what of Helen and her mother? "It is all very simple." Helen is, as feminist theory would suggest, always already present to the maternal; she *becomes* the goddess, "Isis, forever with that Child, /

the Hawk Horus" (23) in the instant of his anger and that anger's instantaneous change to love. Even more simply, her invocation of Thetis carries enough ambiguity to imply the same thing: *"let me love him, as Thetis, his mother . . . "* (14). Let me love him the way Thetis loves him? Let me love him by *being* Thetis? Or more satisfactorily: Let me love him the way I love Thetis, or love him being Thetis. Most satisfying of all, I think, is to say yes: all of the above. Helen invokes her oneness with the maternal (Thetis) and also accepts Achilles' inscription of her as one with the maternal (Isis). In part, she also loves Achilles because he is an aspect of the mother—as we see from the "sea-enchantment" of his eyes. In this working out of the happy substitute as primarily maternal for both characters, we can see that for Helen the mother is not really a "goal," but a *form of self* achieved intermittently and intuitively by means of the "simple path." However, the mother is *also* really a goal for Helen, insofar as Helen is separable from the maternal, and consequently (as a "self") has an active agency of desire. This active agency is only to be expected, for few are more clearly their fathers' daughters than Helen, daughter of Leda and Zeus-Amen.[33] And the focus of her desiring agency in this scene is Achilles, who is not only the "epitome of patriarchy," a figure of the father, but also feminine and maternal (in that Thetis exists within him). Thus, rather than mere "vicarious" pleasure, she can both imitate the paternal desire and be the object of that desire. The quest for the mother that is primary in both characters, then, is powerfully reinforced by the complementary working out of Helen's agentic or "masculine" desire (as it also fulfills the wish of Achilles to be the object of desire). This balances the equation nicely, though it may leave us rather uncomfortable with assigning an agentic function to her role in the attack. Given the emphasis upon her invocation of Thetis throughout the poem, it may be that in her inscription of Achilles (which is interpreted by him as an assault) we observe this metaphoric movement from subject to object of desire.

I have analyzed this rape as an act of violence based on misreading, frustration. If Achilles sees even the patriarchal Command as "read[ing] backward," it is not surprising that the confused Achilles, desperate to maintain some identity, should attempt to silence, erase this "hieroglyph." This act of attempting, at least, to treat Helen as textual object makes some sense to us; as we know, "She herself is the writing" (22, 91).

> We think back through our mothers if we are women.
> —Virginia Woolf

The theory informing this chapter supposes that women will have powerful and ambivalent recursions to the maternal as well as to the paternal precursor. But even I was surprised, "reading backward" from *Helen in Egypt* to *Aurora Leigh,* to discover the sheer depth of recursion between H.D. and Barrett Browning. The line that first drew my attention to this set of correspondences was Romney's address to Aurora as a "sweet Chaldean":

> you read
> My meaning backward like your eastern books,
> While I am from the west, dear.
>
> (2.818–20)

Like Achilles, Aurora reads "backward," in opposition to patriarchal desire/ command (the "dear" must have been especially infuriating). Aurora's letter responds, however, with Helen's additional intuitive power of "discerning": "We Chaldeans discern / Still farther than we read. I know your heart, / And shut it like the holy book it is" (2.835–38). A small point, this detail of "re-versing" the precursor's "reversal," but it led to other correspondences. Indeed, though the *Iliad* remains the overt principal model for *Helen in Egypt,* the epic recurs thoroughly (in covert fashion, but with more exactitude) to *Aurora Leigh.*[34]

When Romney, patriarch of the Leighs and Aurora's cousin, first approaches Aurora on the subject of marriage, he encounters her placing an ivy laurel on her brow, "arms up, like the caryatid, sole Of some abolished temple" (2.60). They clasp hands, "as shipwrecked men will clasp a hand, indifferent to the sort of palm," and the marginal locale of the beach is invoked, where Aurora thinks of herself as "writing down [Her] foolish name too near the sea" (2.67– 70). (Helen, sole occupant of the temple near the beach, greets the shipwrecked Achilles.) Romney greets Aurora with the following phrases, more than coincidentally related to *Helen in Egypt*:

> "Here's a book I found!
> No name writ on it—poems, by the form;
> Some Greek upon the margins,—lady's Greek
> Without the accents. Read it? Not a word.
> I saw at once the thing had witchcraft in't,
> Whereof the reading calls up dangerous spirits:
> I rather bring it to the witch."
>
> (2.74–80)

This evocation of "witchcraft" and the unread text (obvious in Helen's encounter with Achilles) is followed by H.D.'s source for her famous lyric "Oread." Barrett Browning's image of the Oread "has a Naiad's heart / And pines for waters" (2.83–84); "pines" only makes sense in Barrett Browning as a verb—but H.D.'s reading of the pun ("Whirl up, sea— / whirl up your pointed pines") is not untypical.[35] The fact that Romney has "found" Aurora's book, where

Achilles finds an old flint ("I thought I had lost that" [12]), may stretch this reading too far. However, the discussion of work—that of women and that of men—is pertinent. Aurora provides central images for both Helen and Achilles: The image of the lighthouse is hers, not Romney's (2.365–66), but her aim is like Helen's intuitive knowledge of the ineffable, to "keep up open roads / Betwixt the seen and unseen" (2.469). Romney, though he models different aspects of H.D.'s Achilles, later in this passage becomes one of the sacrifices, as Aurora deplores their fathers' early plans to have the two young cousins marry:

> Ah, self-tied
> By a contract, male Iphigenia bound
> At a fatal Aulis for the winds to change
> (But loose him, they'll not change) . . .
>
> (2.778–81)

A fuller reading of these microstructural correspondences would be beneficial, but it is easiest to see their operation in the image of the Chaldean heart, which returns in reversed form at the end of the epic, where Aurora remarks to the changed Romney, "You have read / My book, but not my heart; for recollect, / 'Tis writ in Sanscrit, which you bungle at" (8.475–77). In the earlier exchange, Romney imagines himself as a text he has written, which Aurora is flagrantly misreading. She claims that an alternate praxis of reading is not necessarily misreading, but can instead provide a more thorough sifting or "discernment" of Romney's "meaning." At the close, however, the (now-blind) Romney has learned to "read backward," or more accurately, has learned a deeper means of "discernment," and becomes the recipient of desire through his acceptance of Aurora's latest book:

> You have written poems, sweet,
> Which moved me in secret, as the sap is moved
>
> . . . .
>
> But this last book o'ercame me like soft rain
>
> . . . .
>
> In all your other books, I saw but *you:*
> A man may see the moon so, in a pond,
> And not be nearer therefore to the moon,
> Nor use the sight . . . except to drown himself:
> And so I forced my heart back from the sight
>
> . . . .
>
>   But, in this last book,
> You showed me something separate from yourself,
> Beyond you, and I bore to take it in

And let it draw me. You have shown me truths . . .
. . . .
                   not yours, indeed,
But set within my reach by means of you,
Presented by your voice and verse the way
To take them clearest.

    (8.592–613)

Romney is textually penetrated by Aurora's book. As I read the imagery here, the intercourse of the book as phallus with Romney's "inner eye" (which is explicitly not the eye of the male gaze, but a "Chaldean" and vaginal deeper discernment), allows Romney access to the maternal "truths" by means of Aurora as the happy substitute.

Aurora, even at this point in the poem, deliberately misleads him, reinscribing her Chaldean heart beyond his ken, because she thinks him married to Lady Waldemar, and does not yet know he is blind. And certainly Aurora miswrites (and misreads) her own heart throughout the epic; but we shall soon return to her heart's "sweet scripture."

In *Helen in Egypt* the implications of the happy substitute ("this Star in the night") can be summarized by noting that Achilles' violent attempt at "close reading" leads directly to his apotheosis, his full knowledge of Helen and himself. For Helen, such full knowledge is less violently, more immediately attained. With Helen's invocation of Thetis, Achilles recognizes *himself* embedded in the alterity of Helen. To put this more clearly, Helen evokes in him (as she always has) the repressed feminine principle, the "sea-enchantment" of his eyes, inherited from his mother Thetis. Brought together, they create a transcendent fusion, "this Star in the night" (17). This becomes clearer as both Helen and Achilles engage in the task of "reconstruction." As Achilles says, "I, too, must question and wonder" (63). In the "Eidolon" section of the epic, his heroic re-integration is followed more closely; through Helen, Achilles has found "the simple path" to his mother, the feminine within himself. "Eidolon" recounts his boyhood, relating the story "picture by picture" and shows the accumulated repression of that femininity, the repression that fitted Achilles for the "iron-ring / Whom death made stronger." But even in the midst of war, to reach merely the image of Thetis on the prow of his ship, he had had to answer the sentries

with the simple pass-word
of Achilles' Myrmidons,
Helena . . .
    (248)

Thetis, as the goal (in a sense) of Achilles' quest, plays a major role in bringing the two lovers together; as Helen is Achilles' "pass-word" to Thetis, so "Thetis," the "secret, / unpronounceable name" (279) is Helen's password to Achilles.[36]

> . . . the name
>
> and the flame and the fire
> would weld him to her
> who spoke it, who thought it . . .
>
>   (278)

The paradigm set up here for achieving the happy substitute applies with equal force to *Aurora Leigh*. In Barrett Browning's epic, though, the paradigm (the union of father's daughter and mother's son) is diffused throughout the text, some elements exaggerated and others—the conclusion for example— muted, so as to present the union of two somewhat alienated humans, each balancing the roles of scriptor and scripted. In H.D., while the characters are more radically alienated (not even knowing whether they are ghosts), they are also semidivine. The act of "reading backward" brought forth in both epics is, we might suggest, essential to H.D.'s strategy of epic recursion. She reads both the *Iliad* and *Aurora Leigh* "backward" to produce *Helen in Egypt*. That is, while she repeats Homer, she reverses the primary subject-position, reading from Helen's position. She thus revises and re-energizes the story "We all know" (1) of Homer's *Iliad*. The Homeric story is that of "the Greek Eve," of woman as seductress and *casus belli* (Friedman 1977, 232). H.D. does not deny the historically and literarily valorized text of the *Iliad*, but by recurring to it so heavily she is able to adjust our readings of that poem as well. In fact, it is by coming so close to the Homeric script that *Helen in Egypt* achieves its considerable impact as an epic; other epic poets have taken characters out of Homer and developed their exploits, or more recently have used Homer as the source of powerful similes, verbal play. No one else (apart from Virgil) so actively engages her poem to the "fount itself" of Western tradition, and H.D. uses a relatively simple strategy of reversal to do so; she does not invalidate Homer—indeed, she depends on him. But by responding to his poem thus, her epic elicits a response from his (in readers and in her text if nowhere else), setting off a string of dialogic echoes at the bedrock of tradition.[37] Though H.D. at several points nudges the traditional view of the Trojan War, for the most part, as Rachel Blau DuPlessis notes, "that tale is taken for granted as the plot that precedes this new alignment of characters and actions" (1985, 191), forming as it were a Bakhtinian orchestral background to the *dramma per musica* presented in the text.

H.D. makes a typical recursion to the Homeric script on the first page of her epic: "Helen was never in Troy. She had been transposed or translated from Greece into Egypt. Helen of Troy was a phantom, substituted for the real Helen, by jealous deities. The Greeks and the Trojans alike fought for an illusion" (1). This "translation" of Helen can be seen as her first evasion of the scripts laid out for her. But still, this comment on the futility of war, and the illusory nature of its causal narrative, is one that has been made before. Both the fragmentary "Pallinode" of Stesichorus and Euripides' late play *Helen in Egypt* revise the Homeric script to this extent, though they establish a more passive Helen than H.D.'s. But by this re-visioning of Homer, and by her obvious concern with "the glory that was Greece, the grandeur that was Rome," H.D. both incorporates and opens to question the voice of the patriarchal literary tradition. We can see this enacted to a great extent in the angry attack itself, which is portrayed largely as the outrage of a jealous and previously dominant script. In Homer, after all, it is "the wrath of Achilles" that is announced in the first lines, not "the beauty of Helen." Their conflict arises in part out of their differing claims—or the differing claims of their poets—to the Trojan War, as Achilles suggests:

> you stole the chosen, the flower
> of all-time, of all-history,
> my children, my legions;
>
> for you were the ships burnt . . .
>
>   (17)

Similarly, by following Helen to Egypt and reconstructing there a mystical, maternal land, H.D. is able to construct a reversal of the Athenian rationality of Theseus and of his contemporary model, Sigmund Freud. H.D. revalorizes the preoedipal attachments of human experience, addressing precisely this "Minoan-Mycenaean civilization" behind the Greek Oedipus complex, a discovery that Freud backed away from in the experience of females.[38]

By her invocation of this magical phase of development in company with her use of the "motherlands" of Egypt and Crete, H.D. also (and again) reveres and reverses Barrett Browning's epic. Aurora Leigh leaves England, her father's land, for Italy, her mother country. With Aurora repeatedly figured as the biblical Miriam (Romney playing a combined Moses and Pharaoh), the action parallels Exodus: escape from the "Babylonian captivity" of England to the maternal land of milk and honey, Italy. The epic's closing vision, building the City of God, Jerusalem, completes the action (and Romney, like Moses, cannot see it).[39] H.D. imitates Barrett Browning in establishing a mothering country, but goes further (in the aftermath of two world wars), to envision the "Western world" itself as a form of captivity; more surely than Barrett Browning, she avoids the simplest trap of just another version of patriarchy.

Narratologically and formally, H.D.'s epic seriously challenges (even as it rewrites) the patriarchal plot. Though *Helen in Egypt* is still written "straight as the Greek," it imitates the shape and plotting of a Sapphic lyric, not Homer's or Milton's (or Barrett Browning's) heroic meters and narrative progression.[40] Instead of organizing her epic toward a telos of battle or marriage, H.D. presents the Absolute early in the epic, and then examines it, questions it. She arranges the balance of the text—the universe, narrative and time itself around this "eternal moment" (the love of Helen and Achilles), this "pause in the infinite rhythm."[41] To illustrate this briefly, what H.D. does with Barrett Browning's linear narrative (which might be represented by a straight line: ———) is not only "reverse" the writing. Rather, she takes the beginning and ending of the story and solders them together across the middle—the rape ("L'Amour/La Mort") of Helen/Marian—thus forming a Moebius strip of narrative, a symbol of infinity: ∞.

The centrality of sexual violence brings us back more forcefully to the question of the rape of Marian who is (like Helen), in the words of Aurora, "not dead, But only . . . damned" (6.365). That is, Marian is written, not the writer, cursed and not curser/cursor. Like Helen, "She herself is the writing" (22, 91). We have seen how, instead of with agency, Helen is carefully associated with that Other inscribed by men, "the Greek Eve." Throughout the poem she is subjected to men's readings, not only those historical scripts of Homer, Stesichorus, and Euripides, of course, but those of the characters, the textual scripts, as well. In Chapter 3, the similar multiplicity and careful juxtaposition of precursor scripts for Chaucer's Criseyde were used to develop the possibility of agency. The "agency" developed by Helen is equally uncertain, because in a sense, for Helen, everything is always already accomplished.

That the diametrically opposed sisters developed in these epics function in part as halves of the projected completion of the heroic self is rather obvious. In condensed versions of the familiar Spenserian and Byronic formulations of love and war Helen is "loved of War," while Clytaemnestra is the principal actor in "a legend of murder and lust" (88). With the maternal, passive Marian and the active Aurora, however, we are placed in a slightly different world: Critics have responded to the infernal atmospheres of the Paris where Aurora rescues Marian, and to a lesser extent that of London (in Aurora's first visit to Marian, 4.758ff., she likens St. Margaret's Court not only to hell, but to a veritable witch's brew that she "charms" with gold). In Paris particularly the images are extended to develop the inverted myth of Demeter and Persephone (or Kore), where in "a room / Scarce larger than a grave" (6.551–52) Marian is interred with her child. The metaphor applied is apropos: Marian

> Approached the bed, and drew a shawl away:
> You could not peel a fruit you fear to bruise
> More calmly and more carefully than so,—
> Nor would you find within, a rosier flushed
> Pomegranate—
>
> (6.562–66)

Aurora is akin to Demeter here, searching Paris for Marian. The city is ruled as if by the wealthy dead (Napoleon's bones " 'neath the golden dome / That caps all Paris like a bubble" (6.130–31), and the "heroic dreams" of the revolution "build instead a brothel or a prison," not a cathedral. But Aurora is thus compared as well to any number of heroes: Pollux, who redeemed his brother, Orpheus the poet, and also, and I think most important, Aeneas. The emphasis of the Sibyl on "cross[ing] the Stygian water / Twice" duplicates the experience of Aurora and Marian, as they traverse their path, twice, "as by a narrow plank / Across devouring waters" (6.482–83, 501–2). Particularly significant are the recursive images of Marian's face or eyes, as "When something floats up suddenly, out there, / Turns over . . . a dead face, known once alive" (6.238–39), or better, the face Aurora "used to liken . . . to a point of moonlit water down a well" (6.314–15). Though when Aeneas meets Dido in the Underworld she really is dead, he sees her "dim form" refracted through a similar image, "as one who sees, / Early in the month, or thinks to have seen, the moon / Rising through cloud, all dim" (*Aeneid* 6.609–13). And the landscapes of the waste land where Marian lives are particularly appropriate to the Fields of Mourning. More important are the overarching concerns of the narrative as a whole, which lead Aurora, like Aeneas, to Italy, there to build a new city. In contrast, the half-developed suburb of Paris, where Marian dwells in "a meagre, unripe house," amid "the half-built habitations and half-dug / Foundations" (6.511–13) evokes the half-built Carthage of Dido.

This deliberate Virgilian underpinning, however, seems a little strange, for as Mermin observes, Barrett Browning "regarded Latin literature as a chilly masculine domain, and Virgil's refusal to let Dido speak in Book VI of the *Aeneid* particularly annoyed her" (1989, 23).[42] Perhaps more accurately, this is not strange at all, as Barrett Browning carefully allows *her* Dido to speak in her own defense against the "chilly masculine domain" that has arranged her fate. This is an interesting use of tradition, much like H.D.'s use of Helen, in part as a response to the tradition itself. It can best be understood, however, in light of larger narrative structures.

An insistently doubled narrative—two quests in one—is maintained throughout *Aurora Leigh* and *Helen in Egypt.* Though we have seen similar doubleness in Chaucer and Milton, in these poems the reader's sympathies remain engaged, I think, with both male and female characters. In *Aurora Leigh,* the larger narrative of the hero's movement from England to Italy is, as Sandra Gilbert has outlined it, a movement "from *Patria* to *Matria,*" from her father's homeland of "the letter" (1.628), where it seems that "Shakespeare and his mates absorb the light" (1.266–67), to her mother's land of Italy (Gilbert 1984, 194–209). Angela Leighton has explained the plot, however, as a quest for the dead father in both England and Italy, noting with Gilbert but placing far different constructions upon the fact that Aurora visits her father's grave but not her mother's.[43] Italy is "only an outer shell of something that has fled: her father's presence" (Leighton 1986, 133). Thus, the feminine hills of Italy invoked at the very end of book 5 (1266–78) are subjected to widely divergent readings: "Are you 'ware of me, my hills, / How I burn toward you . . . As sleeping mothers feel the sucking babe / And smile?" (1267–71). The simile is a key to Gilbert's construction of Italy as "matria," serving as one of the epigraphs to her essay (1986, 194). Leighton, however, records the "negative" answer Aurora provides to the question, quoting lines 1273–74: "Still ye go / Your own determined, calm, indifferent way." This suggests to her that Aurora's "retrogressive desire for a mother" is denied (1986, 132). To read the whole passage, I think, is to come to a rather different conclusion:

> Are you 'ware of me, my hills,
> How I burn toward you? do you feel tonight
> The urgency and yearning of my soul,
> As sleeping mothers feel the sucking babe
> And smile?—Nay, not so much as when in heat
> Vain lightnings catch at your inviolate tops
> And tremble while ye are steadfast. Still ye go
> Your own determined, calm, indifferent way
> Toward sunrise, shade by shade, and light by light,
> Of all the grand progression nought left out,
> As if God verily made you for yourselves
> And would not interrupt your life with ours.
>
> (5.1267–78)

Italy is here figured as maternal; Aurora "burn[s]" with "urgency and yearning" in what seems a very traditionally phallic way, but also, apparently, as a suckling infant.[44] In another phallic attempt on the hills—the impotent and fearful one of the "Vain lightnings"—Aurora is equated with an impotent Jove attempting to ravish the landscape. But the hills go on "inviolate" in a grand, self-sufficient progression—a life *made* by God but as if "for [them]selves," a life not to be "interrupt[ed]" by either Aurora's phallic invasion, or, more clearly in the last line, Aurora's "life," effectively, her birth. This makes some sense. Aurora functions as a phallic agent actively in search of a receptive or "feminine" figure and as an infant seeking preoedipal satisfaction in a maternal figure; her desire is both genital and oral. But she feels impotent, not because she "lacks" lightning, but because she fears her lightnings to be futile, "trembl[ing]."[45] There also seems to be a greater "God" who forbids her access to the maternal, one who has made the hills for themselves, not for Aurora's ravishment or nurture.

This reading has left out the vital point that the "way" of these hills is "Toward sunrise"—toward the sunrise at the end of the epic, that is, and toward Aurora herself. Not to belabor this point (it is at the close of the middle book, however—right in the midst of things), but clearly we may also picture these hills, under direction of God, as moving toward the heroic identity of Aurora, in the same way as Aurora herself is moving toward that self. More precisely, in her steadfastly maintained "inviolate" and "indifferen[t]" attitude to Romney's relations with other women, she is moving toward Italy, the maternal, and herself, refusing to interrupt her own life with Romney's.[46] Even in this detail, then, the paradigmatic self-integration through recursion emerges, like that in *Helen in Egypt;* in the poem's conclusion, naturally, it reaches its fullest explanation.

Thus, Aurora's removal to Italy appears to move toward fulfillment of self through "masculine" intercourse with the maternal *and* toward a metonymic form of union with a maternal Italy in the Italian hills, all of it subtended to the hand of God.[47] What strikes one immediately as a recursive element of the epic is the evocation of Aeneas in this quest for self (and the mother) in Italy, leaving the jaded world of Troynovant.[48] She is also going to Dante's Florence, and her epic ends, not unlike theirs, by evoking the foundation of the imperial city. Aurora cannot bear her father himself on her shoulder, as Aeneas did, for her father is long dead. But the marked absence of her father, as Angela Leighton suggests, is quite important to her; like Aeneas, Aurora moves into a land of maternal immanence, but also the realm of paternal "latency," Latium.[49] Aurora, however, must choose between her "household gods." In order to pay for the trip, that is, she must sell some of her father's books.[50]

> I wrote my name in blue ink on the
> first page of every one of his books.
> —Lyn Hejinian[51]

Aurora Leigh's choice of books (only two are mentioned by name) is pertinent to the dynamics of the father-daughter relation. Her father's hand maintains its presence through his marginalia, and as in her earlier description of his teaching (1.187–98), her father questions traditional structures of knowl-edge.[52] His Greek editions are "overwritten by his hand / In faded notes as thick and fine and brown / As cobwebs on a tawny monument" (5.1220–21). Her father, in a sense, deconstructs or defaces the ancients, and has taught Aurora to do likewise, not through violence, but through a contiguous affection, a like-ness of neglect.

She keeps the text of Proclus because of its link with paternal punish-ment—a rare form of attention in Aurora's life, one would suppose. The "blame of love" connects directly with her gender; the imagery, as usual, is ambivalently sexual:

> Ah, I stained this middle leaf
> With pressing in't my Florence iris-bell,
> Long stalk and all: my father chided me
> For that stain of blue blood,—I recollect
> The peevish turn his voice took,—"Silly girls,
> Who plant their flowers in our philosophy
> To make it fine, and only spoil the book!"
>
> .   .   .   .
>
> Ah, blame of love, that's sweeter than all praise
> Of those who love not! 'tis so lost to me,
> I cannot, in such beggared life, afford
> To lose my Proclus,—not for Florence even.
>
> (5.1234–45)[53]

Instead, Aurora chooses to sell an edition of Homer. The particular edition is important, for it shows Aurora—and Barrett Browning, I think—simultaneously erasing and reestablishing the precursor narratives, always more grandly than before. The rejected edition is that of Friedrich Augustus Wolf, foremost of the early Homeric Analysts; the ironic contrast between the magnificence of his book and his deconstructive, "atheist" attitude toward the author elicits a strong reaction:[54]

> The kissing Judas, Wolff, shall go instead,
> Who builds us such a royal book as this
> To honour a chief-poet, folio-built,
> And writes above "The House of Nobody!"
> Who floats in cream, as rich as any sucked
> From Juno's breasts, the broad Homeric lines,
> And, while with their spondaic prodigious mouths
> They lap the lucent margins as babe-gods,
> Proclaims them bastards. Wolff's an atheist:

And if the Iliad fell out, as he says,
By mere fortuitous concourse of old songs,
Conclude as much too for the universe.

    (5.1246–57)

Pope had said that to copy Homer was to copy Nature; here we find that to deconstruct Homer is to deconstruct the universe.[55] Aurora sells not Homer, but
Wolf, "that kissing Judas" as he in turn "sold" Jesus, or here, Homer's *Iliad*. By
her metaphoric distancing from Wolf, she increases her metonymic connection
with the "real" Homer—that is, with a Homer she is free to reconstruct as desired. But she also gets rid of Homer, who in effect finances her epic status, her
agency, and her move to Italy. (She continues to see herself, too, as a kind of
"Judas"—selling off this Homer, "those Platos.") The Homer she reconstructs
(in rather too-gorgeous lines) is intriguingly androgynous, combining the
mythic maternity of the creamy page with recertified paternity—the lines and
the name of Homer. Aurora's equation of *Iliad* and universe suggests a similar
reading of Homer and God; both are susceptible to atheistic deconstruction, as
well as passionate reconstruction. By assuming meaning for the universe and
the ordering principle of Homer, she is able to muster meaning for herself as
creative poet; the correspondence between herself and the divine author vali-
dates her own acts of self-creation.

    The difficulty, of course, is that there is no check on the correspondence be-
tween the divine ideal and the phenomenal world, and in the same sense, no
mechanism within the self for ensuring any form of correspondence. Wolf, similarly, divides the divine artist from the universal text: He asserts that no necessary correspondence exists between the *Iliad* and a single controlling mind, but
rather, it was a "fortuitous concourse of old songs." Thus, in Barrett Browning's
view, it is necessary to have faith, to take the next step:

               Never flinch,
But still, unscrupulously epic, catch
Upon the burning lava of a song
The full-veined, heaving, double-breasted Age:
That, when the next shall come, the men of that
May touch the impress with reverent hand, and say
"Behold,—the paps we all have sucked!
This bosom seems to beat still, or at least
it sets ours beating . . .

    (5.213–21)

This passage emphasizes even more clearly the maternal quality of the epic poet
as the source of song, "the paps we all have sucked." The correspondence estab-

lished between true art and its audience is phrased in terms of the beating
heart, as between mother and child, and as between Homer and the present
poet, to a degree. The phrase "unscrupulously epic" picks up on the necessary
duplicity, I think, as well as the need for fidelity, both to the Age and to eventual
correspondence between work and audience (and ultimately God), despite
either the artist's own scruples—like those of Proclus—or what the age demands. The discrepancy between "backward" and "forward" scriptures of the
heart (Aurora's Chaldean heresy) begins to make more sense now.[56] I have
called Barrett Browning's strategy one of erasure and reestablishment. The
"rule for Proclus" and his "fantastically crumpled" Neoplatonism is similar,
though it appears to be what one does to one's own text, not to one's precursor:
"[R]ound twice / For one step forward, then . . . back / Because you're somewhat giddy" (5.1230–34). As I read it, one works around a thought or question
twice, takes a step, and hesitantly withdraws. This makes epic sound more like
a dance-step than anything else, and Barrett Browning's specific injunctions
suggest this may be a plausible alternative:

> Nay, if there's room for poets in this world
> A little overgrown (I think there is),
> Their sole work is to represent the age,
> Their age, not Charlemagne's,—this live, throbbing age,
> That brawls, cheats, maddens, calculates, aspires,
> And spends more passion, more heroic heat,
> Betwixt the mirrors of its drawing-rooms,
> Than Roland with his knights at Roncesvalles.
>
>   (5.200–208)

Perhaps a dance-step for epic is not so far off; the "passion" and "heroic heat"
arise, still in primarily public situations, between mirrors.[57] This suggests quite
nicely the epic hall of mirrors, but more appropriate for Barrett Browning is the
image of the lighthouse lamp, followed up on later in the book: The artist "never
felt the less because he sings":

>   Does a torch less burn
> For burning next reflectors of blue steel,
> That *he* should be the colder for his place
> 'Twixt two incessant fires,—his personal life's
> And that intense refraction which burns back
> Perpetually against him from the round
> Of crystal conscience he was born into
> If artist-born? O sorrowful great gift

Conferred on poets, of a twofold life,
When one life has been fond enough for pain!

   (5.372–82)

The lighthouse recurs occasionally throughout *Aurora Leigh*; it forms a continuing thread in *Helen in Egypt* as well. The "twofold life" refers to earlier lines
where Art "Sets action on the top of suffering: / The artist's part is both to
be and do" (5.366–67). We can also see it leading back farther, to the exhorta-
tion that

           poets should
Exert a double vision; should have eyes
To see near things as comprehensively
As if afar they took their point of sight,
And distant things as intimately deep
As if they touched them.

   (5.183–84)

The importance of the "double life"—of action "on the top of" suffering—is
clearly relevant to the work at hand, where Aurora *acts* on the basis of Marian's
suffering. Why else make her a saint save to allow agency? The implication,
perhaps, is like that of the so-called confessionalist poets of this century, that
someone, usually the artist, must suffer to produce art; must, by "transfixing"
suffering experience, and then "turning outward . . . the thing" (5.368–73), transform it into public Art. In *Aurora Leigh* that consciousness is split into different
persons, a fact that could easily lend power to the self-consciousness inherent
in these overcrowded, doubly mirrored drawing-rooms, where one must both
"be and do." The relationship toward past epics, again, seems rooted in the
"double vision" of near things and distant as though they were exchanged—a
rather extreme form of identification with the precursor, and one that, perhaps,
enforces the same "double vision" upon the precursor?

   The doubleness of Aurora's identity, as well as of her vision, is especially
well presented in Vincent Carrington's two sketches of Danaë, the "Two states
of the recipient artist-soul":

A tiptoe Danaë, overbold and hot,
Both arms a-flame to meet her wishing Jove
Halfway, and burn him faster down; the face
And breasts upturned and straining, the loose locks
All glowing with the anticipated gold.
Or here's another on the selfsame theme.
She lies here—flat upon her prison-floor,

The long hair swathed about her to the heel
Like wet seaweed. You dimly see her through
The glittering haze of that prodigious rain,
Half blotted out of nature by a love
As heavy as fate.

    (3.122–33)

Even more fully polarized by the male point of view, the passive figure of Danaë shows "more passion" to Aurora because "Self is put away. . . . She is Jove, / And no more Danaë—greater thus" (3.135–37). This dichotomy is reiterated in Barrett Browning's work, but it is important to recognize the careful exclusion of love between women which such a heterosexual dichotomy appears to entail.[58] Carrington's alternate sketches are of a single personage; in the stereoscopic play between them, however, the dual nature of the woman is evoked in striking terms. As Irigaray has suggested of woman, "within herself she is already two—but not divisible into ones—who stimulate each other" (1981, 100). While it is clear that the divergent heterosexual views of Danaë are presented in the characters of Aurora Leigh and Marian Erle, the narrative fact is that the Danaës are resolved into a single model—Kate Ward, who adores Aurora's poetry. Moreover, this double Danaë is resolved into singleness through her connection with Aurora. Vincent Carrington changes his style of painting and "leave[s] mythologies" to paint

The whole sweet face; it looks upon my soul
Like a face on water, to beget itself.
A half-length portrait, in a hanging cloak
Like one you wore once; 'tis a little frayed,—
I pressed too for the nude harmonious arm;
But she, she'd have her way, and have her cloak—

    (7.591–99)

The bond between women can serve as a source of strength for empowerment, but it is not empowerment directed only toward power of the patriarchal sort; rather, the dichotomy is resolved into one face (or rather, due to the ambiguity, two faces): the first is an image that directs its looks upon the soul of Carrington, as though re-creating him in its image; the second is the illumination of Lacan's mirror stage, and Carrington's "upon my soul" is read as exclamatory. The painting looks like a "face on water, to beget itself," in a kind of perpetual sexual pleasure, a duplicitous and self-sufficient feminist narcissism. Such self-sufficiency is reinforced by the bond with Aurora, which provides a "cloak" from the male gaze in which to establish an integrity of self. What seems a difficulty is the continued existence of the male gaze as a mirror to that self-sufficiency; and indeed, Kate Ward and Vincent Carrington are married within two months.

A similar difficulty attends the usual image noted of sororal bonds in *Aurora Leigh*:

> The magic circle, with the mutual touch
> Electric, panting from their full deep hearts
> Beneath the influent heavens, and waiting for
> Communion and commission.
>
>   (1.623–26)

Like Gilbert, Mermin reads this passage describing the Italian mountains as paralleling "the sororal bond with Marian [which] is deeper than the differences of class and education that circumscribe friendship, and as a poet [Aurora] too effects something like a 'magic circle' of female connection" (1989, 207–8). Again, there seems to be a significant problem, not only in the quite different images of Italy that precede this passage,[59] but also insofar as the "magic circle" is always "waiting for Communion and commission" most arguably from the "influent heavens."

The importance of the images of Danaë as models for the recipient artist has been remarked on before, of course; Mermin in particular stresses that "[t]he gender of the poet, and also the fact that the plot is impelled by sexual passion and has at its center an actual rape, foreground the literal meaning of these metaphors in a very disturbing way" (1989, 211). Further, Mermin points to the way the passive figure of Danaë foreshadows the initial sale of Marian by her mother (Marian's hair "like a sudden waterfall," leaving her "drenched and passive" [3.1046–47]) as well as her later rape in the Parisian brothel (1989, 210–11). Another resonant image of inspiration is Lord Howe's—"the god comes down as fierce / As twenty bloodhounds" (5.943–44)—which is closely tied in with the persistent description of Marian in the circumstances of maternal betrayal as a small hunted animal.

Such images (somewhat muted) haunt Aurora herself later on. Her partner Romney is less elemental, less brutal, than the "Thunderer" whom Barrett Browning associated with her father, and who is arguably the uncaring force behind the brutal rape of Marian at the point "[w]hen mothers fail us" (1229). The sun shines radiantly on both occasions of Marian's betrayal.[60] Aurora's own self-betrayal is engineered carefully. She makes a long speech to the effect that "Art is much, but Love is more!" (9.656), in which she not only compares herself

to the fly that "[r]efused to warm itself in any sun" (6.666), but abases herself—
in sentiments that cannot but remind us of Marian's degradation (in a sense,
the *felix culpa* that allows her redemption):

> . . . indeed
> If now you'd stoop so low to take my love
> And use it roughly, without stint or spare,
> As men use common things with more behind
> (And in this, ever would be more behind)
> To any mean and ordinary end,—
> The joy would set me like a star, in heaven,
> So high up, I should shine because of height
> And not of virtue.
>
> (9.673–81)

The invitation (and the phallic descent of the male implied) is clarified further
in Aurora's desire for the now blind Romney to "see [her] bare to the soul"
(9.704). This rather disturbing speech is followed by the embrace and kiss:
Where the less "passionate" Danaë had been "overbold and hot" (3.122),[61] the
newly impassioned Aurora combines both figures to a remarkable extent, sustained by the ambiguity of the text:

> Did I drop against his breast,
> Or did his arms constrain me? were my cheeks
> Hot, overflooded, with my tears—or his?
> . . . There were words
> That broke in utterance . . . melted, in the fire,—
> Embrace, that was convulsion, . . . then a kiss
> As long and silent as the ecstatic night.
>
> . . . .
> I have written day by day
> With somewhat even writing. Did I think
> That such a passionate rain would intercept
> And dash this last page?
>
> (9.715–28; first and fourth ellipses mine)

This synthesis of the two Danaës may be weighted on the side of the passive
image. The "passionate rain" that appears to silence her as an agent is the familiar "prodigious rain" that leaves Danaë "Half blotted out of nature by a
love / As heavy as fate" (3.131–33). The silence is extended in the lines immediately following, which also underscore Romney's place as a diminished—indeed, a substitute—Jove:

> What he said,
> I fain would write. But if an angel spoke
> In thunder, should we haply know much more
> Than that it thundered?
>
>   (9.737–40)

From the very opening of the epic, the power of the writer is reinforced; moreover, the task of the epic poet—which I have said to be the construction of a coherent self—is outlined:

> Of writing many books there is no end;
> And I who have written much in prose and verse
> For others' uses, will write now for mine,—
> Will write my story for my better self,
> As when you paint your portrait for a friend,
> Who keeps it in a drawer and looks at it
> Long after he has ceased to love you, just
> To hold together what he was and is.
>
>   (1.1–8)

The poem is that which can "hold together what [one] was and is," and in the case of Aurora, the poem holds together a "better self" (akin to the fictional wholeness encountered in Lacan's mirror stage). Two things here demand comment, however. First of all, while the first line of the poem says quite literally that there is no end to the production of books, it can easily be read as saying that for many books, no end is produced. This hint at writing beyond the ending connects not only with the provisional conclusion of Barrett Browning's epic, but also with the similarly endless task of self-formation. More important here is the conception of the "better self" as a male friend who has "ceased to love," but who remains in possession of, and indeed, observes for his own benefit, an earlier version (or draft) of that self. This self-conception, then, appears strongly divided by gender, time, and emotional distance; the division is bridged by art. But this bridge is itself rather uncertain; we remain unsure of the friend's "use" of the portrait, except as a means of self-confirmation, more mirror than bridge to another.

Such a divided self-conception is not surprising in this hero, who continues to open the poem with descriptions of her English father, her Florentine mother, and her childhood in Italy and England. Most important, however, remains the present tense—"I write" (1.29).[62] *Aurora Leigh* is full not only of "mother-want" (1.40), as critics have noted, but of the continuing desire for paternal approval.[63]

The past tense of "I felt a mother-want about the world" contrasts sharply with Aurora's present tense invocation of the father:

> O my father's hand,
> Stroke heavily, heavily the poor hair down,
> Draw, press the child's head closer to thy knee!
> I'm still too young, too young, to sit alone.
> I write.
>
>   (1.25–29)

Aurora writes of herself, and for herself, and continues to write, from Leigh Hall to London's Grub Street, from London to Italy, until the poem's close in the striking last scene where she both writes and reads herself for the male protagonist, the now-blinded Romney Leigh. The scene shows the hero building the City of God;[64] this city, of course, is built in Aurora's own image, for she describes the sunrise:

> "Jasper first," I said;
> "And second, sapphire; third, chalcedony;
> The rest in order:—last, an amethyst."
>
>   (9.962–64)

As with the "many books" that open the epic, there is no real end to the writing of this one; the reader is left to read "beyond the ending" of the text, although ultimate closure is not eliminated. The self both read and written in the dawn is left deliberately unspecified—the first three jewels are named, to correspond with Aurora's three decades of life, and the last—the amethyst—as radiant telos.[65] While the end and the orderly progression thereto are assured, eight of the twelve jewels of the holy city's foundation are silent, for the revelations of Aurora are as yet incomplete.

To read this scene as an act of "writing" in the heterosexual fulfillment of the plot, however, is not exactly fair, insofar as it is also so clearly a recursion to the already written. The last act of writing described as such within the poem is the one interrupted by her union with Romney (9.719–43): repeatedly she writes "I fain would write it down,"

> But what he said . . . I have written day by day,
> With somewhat even writing. Did I think
> That such a passionate rain would intercept
> And dash this last page? What he said, indeed,
> I fain would write it down here like the rest,
> To keep it in my eyes, as in my ears,
> the heart's sweet scripture, to be read at night

When weary, or at morning when afraid

. . . .
                              What he said,
I fain would write. But if an angel spoke
In thunder, should we haply know much more
Than that it thundered?

    (9.725-40)[66]

The passage shows a (somewhat unwilling) disavowal of agency in favor, first, of recording another's words: The active present tense "I write" with its unlimited possibilities has been intercepted by "what he said" as the appropriate text; active authorial power has been displaced by mere desire for power, and for limited scribal power at that. And "what he said," insofar as it is recorded at all, becomes "the heart's sweet scripture," the inscription of Aurora by the mystery of heavenly thunder, the "passionate rain." The alignment of Romney with the patriarchal Jovian script, which figures centrally as a script of rape, is disturbing. What Rachel Blau DuPlessis might call a script for romantic thralldom (1985) is, according to Barrett Browning, "the heart's sweet scripture." At this point Aurora may almost become H.D.'s Helen: "She herself is the writing" (22, 91). This is a difficult moment for a reading such as Angela Leighton's, which emphasizes the quest for the paternal in *Aurora Leigh* as a "laying to rest of ghosts," and reads "the poet's last quest" as the perfectly self-sufficient sororal quest for Marian. But it seems clear that if the ghosts were once laid to rest, they have now returned. Much of Leighton's excellent work on Barrett Browning is concerned with the agency of the self-conscious Aurora: "I write." But the fact of Aurora's sudden inability to write is troublesome.

Perhaps these isolated examples of Aurora writing and not writing are insufficient. In the midst of the epic, in Paris, Aurora encounters Marian and her child, and loses them in the chase that follows (6.226-80). She vacillates between writing and not writing to Romney. Her reasons are several—on the one hand, she wants to resurrect Marian (thought lost or dead) for Romney: "I ought to write to Romney, 'Marian's here; / Be comforted for Marian' " (6.333-34). But on the other hand, Aurora "cannot write to Romney" for she must then condemn Marian, cannot, as she imagines the letter, cannot "choose, being kind, to write" and say to Romney: " '[S]he's not dead, / But only . . . damned' " (6.364-66).

The mere act of writing in *Aurora Leigh* appears to be deeply associated with the condemnation of women, an association demonstrated again once the truth of Lady Waldemar's plotting is known. Again Aurora considers a letter to Romney, but finds herself again condemning a woman, the "Lamia-woman." She is also considering (again) the effect on Romney, not at all on the woman involved, to "write" that which "stops his marriage, and destroys his peace" (7.152–53). And again she resists the act of writing:

> No, Lamia!
> . . . . . .
> I will not let thy hideous secret out
> To agonize the man I love—I mean
> The friend I love . . . as friends love.
>
>   (7.170–74)

For Aurora Leigh, then, writing provides the power to inscribe women; the inscriptions she imposes on women are predominantly condemning, violations of an *unheimlich* secrecy, that of the Lamia, or that of Marian. Aurora's proposed hunt for Marian contains the same images of quarry and pursuit that were applied to both the rape and Marian's earlier betrayal:

>   The police
> shall track her, hound her, ferret their own soil;
> We'll dig this Paris to its catacombs
> But certainly we'll find her, have her out,
> And save her, if she will or not.
>
>   (6.384–88)

Like the proposition that villages must be burned in order to save them, the arrogance of "rescue" is closely tied to the arrogance of rape. Aurora's role as cursor implicates her in a master narrative predicated on the quite violent imposition of power upon women, one that reinforces her epic bond with men, and one that agrees quite easily with the Oedipal paradigm initially sketched. There are, however, additional points to be considered in Aurora's role as writer.

First, despite my comments above, the poem as a whole suggests that Aurora does indeed keep writing, despite the deviations connected with Romney. *Aurora Leigh*, too, is a book that inscribes a woman, a portrait of the artist designed to render the artist's self coherent, to "save" or "keep" for confirmation (as described in the opening lines). Second, and more clearly, it is through her writing, her earlier book, that she is able to "conquer" the proud Romney (8.469) who had earlier "built up follies like a wall / To intercept the sunshine and [Aurora's] face" (8.381–82). Her book, like the voice of Miriam, rescues him from his own "male ferocious impudence" (8.324–37). Third, her status as a *non*-inscriber of women is critiqued (to some extent) by the narrative; through her repeated acts of *not* writing to Romney, the entire plot is drawn out for several extra years, when swiftly subjecting either Marian or Lady Waldemar to inscription in the passages quoted above would have brought the poem to a swift close. Denying her power as cursor results only in her deeper entanglement in the plot. On a different level, even her phallic rage to "rescue" Marian from herself is brought, not exactly to nothing, but rather, is circumvented by the "simple chance" of her sleepless evening in Paris, and her recognition, not of the father's English nor the mother's Italian, but of "stranger's French" (6.419–42).[67]

"Lie still there, mother!"
Aurora Leigh 2.769

In conclusion, I should reiterate the importance of the simultaneous allegiance to and rejection of the maternal. Developed most fully in H.D.'s recursions to *Aurora Leigh,* these recursions repeat yet transform the female precursor—perhaps more deeply and completely than the male precursor. Barrett Browning, writing without "poetic grandmothers,"[68] not only recurs to the women's novelistic tradition, but also rewrites the patriarchal tradition as maternal, inscribing her own plural identity, her own "double vision," as if on a nurturing source as well as on an alien law. Her "heart's sweet scripture" thus *corresponds* to God the Father's universal law. As suggested earlier, for a woman who chooses to write epic, the tradition already stands as a powerfully defining force, and the rejections of the poet are likely to be cast as immediately recursive: As the heterosexual partners appear designed to complement the epic heroes, so these two women's epics are designed in part to respond quite specifically to eminently male precursors. The reactions of the poets to female precursors, on the other hand, are more problematic. As is not infrequent in male productions, women (apart from the epic hero) are effectively silenced in favor of the poet/hero. To paraphrase Judith Fetterley, "Die then, women must, so that [male or female] poets may sing."[69] In epics by women, however, this separative fluctuation is not without its positive side, the movement back toward the maternal. Less immediately obvious than the sometimes bitter dismemberings, rejections, and erasures of women are the rememberings of women, of the mother, conveyed primarily through (provisional) self-integration. The tactics of self-integration are polarized about the metonymic and metaphoric sororal bonds (as in Marian and Lady Waldemar), but are finally resolved (in these two epics) by the invocation of the maternal or feminine within a male object of desire. To explain this more clearly, I hope, the presence of a male *object* of desire functions as a legitimation of female agentic desire. It is not that desire is "unnatural" to women, but rather that women are trained in cultures that support the notion that any female desire can only be, at best, stolen. The object of heroic desire—

the reconstructed patriarch Osiris whom the poet as Isis must re-member, even as she re-members herself (and hence the maternal), functions as a validation of female heroism, even as he functions simultaneously as desiring agent himself. As this "new mortal" is also an emblem of the desiring father, the polarized selves of the hero are provisionally, temporarily, brought together into a vision of the absolute, the Holy City, this Star in the Night.

7

In This Late Century

Radical Pluralism and the Future of Epos

> What is the end of fame? 'tis but to fill
> A certain portion of uncertain paper.
> —Byron[1]

BYRON, ONE OF many poets regrettably excluded from this book, remarks that there is "Nothing so difficult, as a beginning, in poesy, unless perhaps the end." Beginning to conclude would seem a doubly difficult task. When I first thought to write on recursive desire in epic, I did not imagine nearly so long an exile, so many unravelings. In conclusion, I would like to suggest the key threads of this labyrinth, all discussed at greater length in preceding pages. A little metacritical comment is in order, not because it is fashionable, but because it is important; a theory is a powerful tool, and I would prefer that this one be seen as empowering its audience, and apprehended in more complex ways than simple labeling might suggest. In addition, I will sketch the shape of epic as practiced today under the aegis of electronic word processing—not a death mask or a still life, but as charcoal might trace shifting lines, or as magnets pluck roses from steel-dust.

> I leave the thing a problem, like all things.
> —Byron

I have focused on epic poets and their powerful desire to repeat rather than evade their precursors. Epic recursion demonstrates remarkable tenacity and equanimity through drastic shifts of medium and worldview. Despite the significant impact such changes—from oral, to literate, to print, to electronic technologies—have on humans, and on their construction and perception of epic texts, epic poetry conveys a high degree of commonality, a family resemblance in detail and in plot that is striking considering the temporal, spatial, and linguistic gulfs to be bridged. Thus a work by a postcolonial poet, marginalized by European imperialism and its aftermath in the Caribbean, both recurs to and recoils from a poetic precursor whose varied inscriptions are both empowering and constrictive. Derek Walcott's *Omeros* first appeared as I completed the draft of this book, and works as an excellent argument for the thesis of recursive desire and violence. This is clearest in the poem's attitudes toward a doubled myth of tradition, conveyed in the distinction between "Omeros" and the traditional English "Homer."

> I said, "Omeros,"
>
> and *O* was the conch-shell's invocation, *mer* was
> both mother and sea in our Antillean patois,
> *os*, a grey bone, and the white surf as it crashes
>
> and spreads its sibilant collar on a lace shore.
> Omeros was the crunch of dry leaves, and the washes
> that echoed from a cave-mouth when the tide has ebbed.
>
> The name stayed in my mouth.[2]

In this passage the association of the Greek—the native—pronunciation (Oμηρον or Ómeros) with the Oedipal focus of desire for the maternal (here also associated with a Greek woman in exile in the United States) is particularly clear. The desire focuses as well upon death, which with the maternal is strongly linked with the sea, the "common ground" of Homer and Walcott as native islanders. In substantial contrast to this deconstructed but still fluid presentation (*O-mér-os*) is that of the Anglicized, Americanized, stationary and static "tradition" of "Homer and Virg[il]." These also are broken, but broken in their alienation from the sea and their embeddedness in commerce (especially the poetic marketplace of Pegasus), capitalism, and the associated concern with defense:

"Homer and Virg are New England farmers, and the winged horse guards their gas-station."[3] Walcott's epic needs more exploration than I can afford here and now. In these passages, however, he uses a loose hexameter line (following Omeros rather than Pope); the speaker becomes the locus for the recursive "echo" of Homeric seas ("The name stayed in my mouth" just as Omeros is still "echoed from a cave-mouth when the tide has ebbed"); and he recurs, as well, to the celebrated Homeric simile that likens human lives to the generation of the leaves.[4]

Walcott's *Omeros* not only exemplifies epic recursion, but highlights another point, that those who feel themselves to be deeply conditioned by loss—through cultural stratification based on race, sex, sexual orientation, class, age, or re-gion—have much at stake in recuperating epic traditions. This helps explain the increasing production of epic poetry by people otherwise marginalized. Epic, far from being merely a masculine attempt to compensate for the deficien-cies of gender, is more radically an attempt made by men, or women, or other marginalized groups to compensate for the perceived deficiencies of the self. In its largest sense, epic tries to make up for the perceived condition of loss that constitutes the human condition.

This reading of epic proposes that we displace the monolithic, monoglot views in favor of comprehending the tradition as an open and shifting array (and disarray) of textual forces. Though many people like to think that the only good epic is a dead epic, this definition, this strategy of reading, asserts that epic, old and new, is surprisingly vital. Thus, though Walcott's Achille and Hec-tor still struggle over Helen in the isles of the West—in "the New / World, made exactly like the Old"—still everything changes and changes. As Walcott ob-serves of the sea (and the Homeric connection of "the noise of the surf lines wandering") at the close of the epic: "The sea was still going on."[5]

The same two paradoxes are fundamental to this vision of epic: first, that everything is in constant change; second, that nothing ever changes. Thus, no epic is ever the same epic twice: Vastly different media and contexts of produc-tion, transmission, and reception disallow any epic "essence"; at the same time all epic is always the same, to judge at least from our experience of reading and rereading. Wittgenstein's theory of "family resemblance" between members of a set and Bloom's application of the Oedipal scenario to his idiosyncratic poetic tradition prepare the way for a powerful explanation of epic tradition as psy-choanalytic family romance, emphasizing the deeply recursive nature of desire. Recursive desire explains more fully and accurately why poets continue to com-pose epics in spite of their belatedness. Moreover, the genealogical metaphors frequently used of (and within) epic tradition make this a logical—indeed, com-monsensical—shift in our paradigms of understanding epic.

Since the traditional matter of epic poetry concerns love and war, the step to the Oedipal plot described by Freud is simple: The son desires the mother and wishes to slay the father. Recent revaluations of preoedipal concerns with separation and contiguity provide corrections to twentieth-century overestima-tions of the Oedipal plot. While this "master plot" works fairly well for the *Od-yssey* and after, this plot is certainly only the gender-linked coding of the more basic narcissistic plot (or processes) of union and separation. While we may *read* the death and glory complex of narcissistic epic as analogous to the Oedipal, this is only our sexualized reading of the more fundamental narcissistic script. The Freudian "master plot" is already a sublimation—a search for the happy

substitute. Thus it is only within a culture hierarchized by gender and characterized by literacy that the Oedipal plot becomes preeminent. Moreover, the continuing shift from print literacy to electronic coding, and the imaginable de-
regulation of gender and family suggested by theorists such as Judith Butler and
Donna Haraway, open the way for substantial changes in the human masterplot
as it becomes more clearly preoedipal and polymorphous, even (in Haraway's
view) "non-Oedipal," a narrative "with a different logic of repression."[6] This
emphasis on preoedipal configurations not only improves our comprehension
of oral and literate epic, but usefully clarifies women's relationship to epic tradition. Recognizing that both female and male infants are required to adjust
their relations (of separation and connection) with the mother and with other
powerful forces in their environment and considering these adjustments as formative of later strategies of interaction with the world allow us a view of epic
as not *necessarily* Oedipal, and of tradition as not necessarily patriarchal. I think
this adoption of the preoedipal may also reduce confusion with regard to gay
and lesbian epic, where the maternal may be figured as the absolute, but the
process of epic—its aiming if not its aim—is homosocial. The point is not the
goal, but the working through of our desires and the life lived; not the ending,
but the story in its telling.

This critique of gendered and sexualized narratives arises from the premise
that oral epic is analogous to literary epic. Such a premise also suggests that we
question more thoroughly the absolute foci of desire. While later centuries, epics, and psychoanalysis have considered both self and mother as absolutes (in
both positive and negative senses), what we need, perhaps, is a little more of
Heisenberg's uncertainty with these atomic structures of the psyche. Reading
Beowulf or *Helen in Egypt*, where absolute identity and otherness disappear in
favor of matrices of exchange, charged fields of relative and contextual value,
may suggest additional fields of exploration.

In the historical contexts of performance in Western culture, epic has been
used primarily to allow men a form of substitute contiguity to make up for the
fact of lost connection with the maternal. This account of epic generalizes usefully to incorporate the increasing value placed on the individual, on self-fash-
ioning in Western culture, and more recently the increasing value of epic (and
agency) to marginalized groups. Thus, we compose epics to make up for the
human condition, the sense that we are not even (not always, not ever) quite
ourselves. And the coherence gained by epic recursion becomes especially useful to those who feel themselves most deeply struck by loss.

Throughout this book I have focused on the way poets recur to and reconstruct tradition as a means of gaining power for their own epic expression. This

concern is deeply connected to other, more recent attempts at salvaging distinct traditions; while I am thinking particularly of the feminist recovery of women's texts, a similar strategy operates in pluralist invocations of other marginalized traditions. These "rememberings" will be especially difficult as long as Western epic is only read as dead, monolithic, and instrumental in the very marginalization or destruction of other traditions. It is problematic. Insofar as the performance of epic is subject to the dynamics of recursive desire, then these acts of recovery appear to be denied epic status from their very inception: If a poet does not repeat the tradition, a poet does not create an epic.[7] And if a poet *does* repeat the patriarchal, imperial, or exploitative script, there is considerable danger of merely reinscribing that narrative. Alternately, if a poet recurs only to the newly recovered tradition, then an epic is composed within *a* tradition, but that tradition itself may appear alien to the Western tradition, and hence the epic not "really" an epic within Western tradition. So the attempt at epic power and status appears to be subverted, continuing the perceived pattern of the voiceless margins within Western epic tradition. This problem, however, arises from our limited perceptions of tradition and our undervaluing the processes of change. Looking backward, we can see that *Beowulf* still stands in a starkly tangential relation to the classically informed "mainstream" of Western tradition, only associated more firmly with epic in this century. Milton's *Paradise Lost*, now the prime example of the English epic, was not accepted as "traditionally" epic until the middle of the eighteenth century. Only quite recently is the appellation of epic applied to works of the nineteenth and twentieth centuries, and this in itself is counter to the usual received wisdom concerning the demise of epic. Just so, the latest marginalized traditions and epics require the continued broadening of "tradition" before they can be usefully explained as epic. Reading an epic like Judy Grahn's *Queen of Swords* requires not only that we understand the different complexities of women's epic, but that we decenter the Homeric focus of Western epic studies to include other vital precursors. The Sumerian *Descent of Inanna to the Underworld*, for example, is the primary focus of Grahn's recursions to the maternal text, repeating that ancient story of death and rebirth as a modernized poetic drama.[8] Grahn avoids indulging in simplistic mythic answers, but turns—as the title implies—to reclamation of women's swordwork, "female blood powers" that were lost and/or stolen within patriarchy. She does not bypass patriarchy entirely, as the names of the characters imply. Helen/Inanna's deconstruction and rebuilding take place in an underworld lesbian bar, and the Amazon Penthesilea is a key figure leading to the main character's rebirth, Helen's remembering of herself as "queen of Heaven and Earth" (not mere goddess of love and beauty). "Pen," as the Amazon warrior is called, rightly represents the lost (but reclaimable) tooth, dagger, and voice for a woman who has become—through patriarchy's dominion—"so fragile / and unimaginative . . . [with] no expectations except to shine."[9]

It is troubling that the tradition does not broaden itself faster; that Walcott's epic is taught in undergraduate courses while others, less or differently traditional, are avoided. The question *can* become one of what possible value inheres in a tradition that so carefully excludes nontraditional forms of expression, labeling them alternately as "idiosyncratic" or "alien." This, I think, is the wrong approach. More productively, the epic tradition can be seen as one of inclusive strategies, one that moves in an ameliorative direction, though it moves rather slowly. In this light, what we see in the history of epic thus far is a gradual inclusion of different voices and differential forms of tradition—the Roman, the Anglo-Saxon, the biblical, the personal, the feminist, the American, the Caribbean. This shattering of a tradition *perceived* as monolithic is made most explicit in the deconstructive strategies of fragmented and feminist epic; this opening outward of tradition continues in the compositional and reading strategies of contemporary theorists, as well as in their poetic precursors. Opening up a tradition perceived as "central" and monolithic allows the traditions of the marginalized to be expressed, discovered, invented (in their root senses). The ethical choice of pluralism, thus, is not so much a negation of tradition as it is continuation, the continuation of an inclusive practice of reading.

> If I suddenly notice that a poet's poems have become a lot
> longer, I make a mental note to ask the poet if he or she is now
> working on a word processor. The answer is invariably yes.
> —William Matthews[10]

This kind of inclusive reading is supported by—perhaps made inevitable by—emergent technologies that enable or force us to deal differently with texts. In the latter years of "this late century," as Doubiago phrases her belatedness, most poets compose their epics on word processors.[11] The epigraph from William Matthews suggests the important connection between this new medium of production and what has been called "a widespread but mostly unheralded revival of the book-length poem in America during the last decade or so."[12] A full exploration of the potential for new strategies available to our latest epic poets must be deferred, but brief comments might sketch this expanding field.

As many remark, these changes in technology change literature itself (both as constructed and as comprehended): "No longer is a text fixed on the printed page." A new form of reading, interactive, reader-controlled, takes shape, "chang[ing] the balance of power. We can now draw mustaches on the Mona Lisa."[13] Epic tradition, like the Mona Lisa, thus begins to show its discursive power as not unlike our own, constructed and provisional. Precursors who are, like ourselves, ephemeral, tentative and revisable, have a substantially different impact on would-be epic poets. The example of the Mona Lisa stresses the destructive, satiric edge this new power can attain: The danger may lie in the human cursor's metaphoric distancing of self from screen, analogous to the (aggressive, or violently indifferent) distancing that can occur in watching television and video-games. But perhaps this change in the balance of discursive power—this interactivity—allows more than an increased destructive power; one hopes it also offers possibilities of increased sympathy with other people wandering the labyrinthine *selva oscura* of a world become text, the collocation of bits of information. If poststructuralism is in part a signal of "our own repressed desire for the whole world to become a literary text,"[14] the question remains: Is this a desire to recreate the world as Other, or instead, a desire to establish equity between that textual world and a textual self?[15]

The potential movement outlined above involves a radical democratization of epic, akin to but possibly more thoroughgoing than that imposed by print technologies. Mass-market works argue for a coming age of globally aware, discursively and technologically empowered individuals within varying systems of community and connectivity.[16] Among other developments, they emphasize such buzzwords as "interactivity," "mobility," and the global concerns of the late twentieth century. A quick survey of contemporary long poems suggests a surprising relevance. The idea of an "interactive" epic is not far from the reader-oriented aspect of a fragmented epic like the *Aeneid*, but this interactivity is heightened by the potential for reader revision and use. Lyn Hejinian expects a surprising degree of such interaction in a work like *My Life*. ("Are your fingers in the margins?" she asks.) Collaborative epics (like the fantasy sequence of Sylvia Kantaris and Philip Gross, *The Air Mines of Mistila*) demonstrate another aspect of interactivity.[17]

"Mobility" is vital to contemporary epic (especially in its North American forms), recurring to the ancient epic journey. Generally, recent epics stress the process of dislocation, mobility itself, rather than origin or telos. Dewey stated that "All art is local," but the concept of "local" itself has changed. Robert Pinsky suggests this in his *Explanation of America*, noting that "motion from place to place itself / May come to be the place we have in common."[18] And according to Doubiago, that "motion from place to place" is indeed a common heritage:

The particular direction of travel in an epic like *Hard Country* is less important than the *fact* of travel, of remembering the many subnarratives of travel that underlie her own, latest migration: the Oregon Trail, the Trail of Tears, the poet's own ancestors in their quests for jobs in California. As with the idiosyncratic potential in interactive epics like Hejinian's, there is a danger of insularity in this mobility, the deadly Lawrencian isolation and stoicism of mobile citizens who "begin with loss," well evoked by Doubiago:

> We don't love our land
> because we're the ones
> who always left our land
> for some notion of it[19]

The global concerns of contemporary epic are worth remarking, though the same potential for loss and aggression presents itself. The political skeptic is not set at ease by the prospect of glossy-pictured coffeetable "green epics" such as Heathcote Williams's *Whale Nation*,[20] nor by Doubiago's proposition that there is a true law, "cosmo logic, astro logic, geo logic."[21] Archly, one might suppose that the struggle with one version of logocentrism had been enough.

I do not wish to appear negative about these possibilities, but wish to maintain an awareness of the potential hazards as well as benefits of the poetics implicit in technological change. The energizing potential of the word processor as an interactive device for dealing with twentieth-century versions of belatedness is particularly well laid out by Umberto Eco. The passage that follows weaves together quite helpfully a number of the textual strands in this work, including those just discussed. This key passage from *Foucault's Pendulum* shows a more immediate case of the human reconstructing its being, its identity, through the convergence of epic tradition and the word processor. The character Belbo shifts from mere "intelligent spectator" to "protagonist" through interacting with his computer-file, Abu: Because he realizes it is "not writing but only the testing of an electronic skill. A gymnastic exercise," Belbo finds in the machine "a kind of LSD," and loses his old identity, "forgetting the usual ghosts that haunted him," to form a new identity "without fear of being judged": "His natural pessimism, his reluctant acceptance of his own past were somehow dissolved in this dialog with a memory that was inorganic, objective, obedient, nonmoral, transistorized, and so humanly inhuman that it enabled him to forget his chronic nervousness about life." And what is it that Belbo writes?

> O what a beautiful morning at the end of November, in the beginning was the word, sing to me, goddess, the son of Peleus, Achilles, now in the winter of our discontent. Period, new paragraph. Testing testing parakalo,

parakalo, with the right program you can even make anagrams, if you've written a novel with a Confederate hero named Rhett Butler and a fickle girl named Scarlett and then change your mind, all you have to do is punch a key and Abu will global replace the Rhett Butlers to Prince Andreis, the Scarletts to Natashas, Atlanta to Moscow, and lo! you've written war and peace.[22]

The mind-altering, reality-altering potential of the computer as an interactive device for dealing with inevitable twentieth-century insecurities is well demonstrated in Eco's pastiche of epic texts, if only in a form akin to drawing mustaches on the Mona Lisa. The democratizing implications of the word processor are rather staggering, if it makes all would-be writers into Homers or Tolstoys. But there is a difficulty encountered in the capability to inscribe (and endlessly revise) the self as both epic hero and poet. As in Byron's proposed poetics, each poet is suddenly his or her own Aristotle, his or her own Virgil: A predominantly elite discursive structure such as epic loses power and definition (and hence perhaps its attractiveness to new poets) when everyone may be an epic poet. The incentive to fame may appear small, if that fame is universally attainable. (But maybe one *can* readily imagine a world of epic poets, creating hermetic, idiosyncratic empires of the mind, but remaining unread.)

In a world still so stratified, still stubbornly entrenched in old wars, cold wars, and faithless loves, the proposition that epic can thus democratize so far as to disappear seems highly implausible. This should be regarded as neither a bad nor a good thing, I think, but rather more usefully as one aspect of that *jouissance* which continues the tale of the tribe, life itself, which C. S. Lewis once described as "the mere endless up and down, the constant aimless alternations of glory and misery, which make up the terrible phenomenon called a Heroic Age" (1942, 28). The question of recursive desire, violence, and epic tradition must be left, therefore, as all things must be left, an ongoing problem.

AOI

. . . .
Co dit la Geste e cil ki el camp fut,
Li ber Gilie, por qui Deus fait vertuz,
En fist la chartre el muster de Loüm.
Ki tant ne set ne l'ad prod entendut.

   —*La Chanson de Roland* 155

The geste says this and the man who was on the field . . . and who wrote the book . . . the man who does not know this has not understood anything.

   —David Jones, *In Parenthesis* 187

It was an epic where every line was erased

yet freshly written in sheets of exploding surf
in that blind violence with which one crest replaced
another with a trench and that heart-heaving sough

begun in Guinea to fountain exhaustion here,
however one read it, not as our defeat or
our victory . . .

    —Derek Walcott, *Omeros* 296

Notes

Chapter 1. Fierce Warres and Faithfull Loves

1. See, for example, M. A. M. Ngal, "Literary Creations in Oral Civilization," *New Literary History* 8.3 (Spring 1977): 335–43.

2. The "name" approved in *oral* contexts would differ still more from the later, literately imposed label: "The homecoming of Odysseus, raider of cities," for example. I use the term *text* to denote both oral and literate productions (despite objections to its affinities with *textus* and the weaving of cloth and hence to book manufacture), because it is the common term most relevant to oral productions (as compared with the oxymoronic "oral literature"). See as well A. N. Doane's discussion in *Influence and Intertextuality* (Madison: University of Wisconsin Press, 1992).

3. As Adena Rosmarin puts it, "A genre is a kind of schema, a way of discussing a literary text in terms that link it with other texts and finally, phrase it in terms of those texts." See Rosmarin, *The Power of Genre* (Minneapolis: University of Minnesota Press, 1985), 21.

4. Richard Rorty, *Philosophy and the Mirror of Nature* (Princeton: Princeton UP, 1979), 31. Kenneth Burke draws similar conclusions: "there are terms that put things together, and terms that take things apart." See Burke, *Language as Symbolic Action* (Berkeley: University of California Press, 1966), 49.

5. Ernst Von Glasersfeld, in *The Invented Reality*, ed. Paul Watzlawick (New York: Norton, 1978). This is typical epistemology for the radical constructivist philosophers.

6. As Freud remarks: "In biological functions the two basic instincts operate against each other or combine with each other. Thus, the act of eating is a destruction of one object with the final aim of incorporating it, and the sexual act is an act of aggression with the purpose of the most intimate union" (1940, 6).

7. At first glance obvious counterexamples appear, but appearances are deceptive: The first step to enslaving anyone is telling her how free she is. The Amazon in epic is almost invariably subjected to male desire, often becoming a convenient (if noble) sacrifice; indeed, much of her nobility seems enabled by the fact of her death. Figures like Klytaimnestra and Medea emphasize the horror of women's violence; midway between the nonhuman (Medusa, Sphinx) and the human (Eve, Penelope), they partake of both worlds, becoming subhuman through their assertions of violent power against male culture and hierarchy. Like Lady Macbeth, they are "unsex'd"; and if they are neither woman nor man, they are (by virtue of received cultural categories) transformed to the monstrous, the nightmare. Women have often, however, chosen to reject cultural categorization as "human" or "feminine" in order to gain for themselves a positive form of agency. Categorization protects the power structure and Lady Macbeth "unsex'd" is enabled to attack that power structure. The sacrifice of gender will free her from traditional roles and let her assert her own desires. Women who assert power over their own sexuality, or who assert desire at all, are similarly denied status as fully "human" within male-dominated cultures. The assertive woman is typically portrayed as temptress and seductress, but the labels tend to shift, either toward the alienated figure of the prostitute (e.g., with Helen and Criseyde) or toward that of the sorceress (e.g., Kirke and Duessa). Similarly, portrayals of women within these realms of action often deny agency to the woman in favor of a male agent: The woman is instrumental to another's desire, rather than agent on her own behalf, and her ability to exercise power is borrowed or given rather than being stolen or owned. Behind Eve

is the Serpent, behind Klytaimnestra is Aigisthos, behind Britomart is the impulse of Merlin and the borrowed magical lance. Behind every notable woman, the story goes, is another man.

8. To be a bit more precise, what I mean by "Self" is (as in the earlier example of Socrates) that constellation of conceptual and perceptual experiences that has traditionally been described or labelled as an "I" or a "Self." Self and Other are capitalized here for the purpose of clarity.

9. This sense of separation between Self and Other has been called by many names, but perhaps we can try to avoid the violent imagery of the Heideggerian "breakage," which leads to consciousness, the "fall from grace," and the *descensus ad inferos.*

10. Traditionally described "male" and "female" mindsets may well have somewhat different interactions with the Other, the fulfilling wholeness. The main thing here, common to both, is the fact of consciousness, the realization of some constellated Self as opposed to some Other.

11. This may argue against some current formulations of the fashionable critical concept of desire. For a coherent and insightful summary, see Jay Clayton, "Narrative and Theories of Desire" (*Critical Inquiry* 16 [1989]: 33–53), and his *Pleasures of Babel* (New York: Oxford UP, 1993).

12. The paradigm of difference I'm suggesting is parallel to Vaihinger's "degrees of truth," where some forms of action are seen as more expedient than others in certain contexts. As there are times when the sacrifice of all else to the fulfillment of the self appears (at least to that self) to be necessary and most expedient, so there are times when the absolute sacrifice of the self to a "greater cause" is perceived as the most expedient course of action.

13. See my "Or(e)ality: The Nature of Truth in Oral Settings," *Oral Tradition in the Middle Ages,* ed. W. F. H. Nicolaisen (Binghamton: Medieval and Renaissance Texts and Studies, 1995).

14. Both metaphor and metonymy have a long critical history. In this century they have particular resonance from the work of Roman Jakobson and Jacques Lacan, where they are recognized as the essential tropes of linguistic existence, corresponding with human experiences of similarity and contiguity. Similarly, Kenneth Burke presents the tactic of metaphor as "a device for seeing something *in terms of* something else." It is rooted in the sense of the "self," a construct that allows us to see any thing Other "*in terms of*" the Self. Metonymy attempts to present an "incorporeal or intangible state in terms of the corporeal or tangible," a project only accomplished through the tangible because of the problematic, self-extinguishing goal of metonymic desire. Burke's philosophy of action develops along lines similar to those suggested by Hans Vaihinger, Mikhail Bakhtin, and Paul Watzlawick, outlining the way that inherently social meanings are exchanged within symbolic systems. This understanding of reality is parallel to my own analysis of discursive structures (epics) as performative acts within given matrices of culture and power. Moreover, Burke shows sensitivity to the way that such "orders of power" are not necessarily but merely contingently opposed, the way, as he puts it, that people "make themselves over in the image of their imagery." See Burke, *A Grammar of Motives* (Berkeley: University of California Press, 1969), 117–24, 503–17. Kaja Silverman provides a useful discussion in her *Subject of Semiotics,* where she distinguishes her view of the tropes from the Freudian and Saussurean "versions" of them. "Whereas condensation and displacement treat similarity and contiguity as the basis for absolute identification, and paradigm and syntagm establish an irreducible difference among similar and contiguous elements, metaphor and metonymy respond to similarity and contiguity as the basis for the temporary replacement of one signifying element by another. In other words, metaphor and metonymy mediate between the extremes represented by the other two sets; they assert neither the complete identity nor the irreducible difference of similar and contiguous terms, but rather what Proust would call their 'multiform unity.' Within metaphor and metonymy the primary and secondary processes find a kind of equilibrium, one which permits profound affinities and adjacencies to be discovered without differences being lost." See *The Subject of Semiotics* (New York: Oxford UP, 1983), 109. This suggests the general placement of the tropes as I see them; I tend to allow them

more leeway than does Silverman, in accord with their comparable expressions in epic, where love and war can illustrate wild extremes of identification and/or difference. (It is no surprise that the tropes of metonymy and metaphor echo the familiar dualities of stereotypical feminine and masculine relationships to the Other. Similarly, though not an essential point for this study, the status of the tropes as mediators between the primary and secondary processes renders them particularly applicable to the study of texts.)

15. See Teresa L. Ebert, "Ludic Feminism, the Body, Performance, and Labor: Bringing *Materialism* Back into Feminist Cultural Studies," *Cultural Critique* (Winter 1992–93): 5–50, and Judith Butler's *Gender Trouble* (New York: Routledge, 1990), as well as her amplification of the argument in *Bodies That Matter* (New York: Routledge, 1993).

16. This relates directly to Bloom's desire for a transcendent subject, an ego that can rise above historical forces. His imposition of violence on differences more readily explainable by other phenomena is potentially Bloom's most dangerous habit, readily seen in students like Camille Paglia as well as among politicians.

17. Underlining the expedient function of these constructions is the fact that the character of Oliver, projecting a newer set of values, is a relatively late addition to the *Roland* tradition.

18. For a deeper biographical discussion of Freud's "essential conservatism," see, e.g., Daniel Gillis, *Eros and Death in the Aeneid* (Rome: "L'Erma" de Bretschneider, 1983), 18–25.

19. MacDonald argues that this *is* a form of "revisionist" subterfuge, but seems himself somewhat unconvinced (1987, 189–92).

20. See Hume's *Enquiries Concerning Human Understanding and Concerning the Principles of Morals* (1777. Oxford: Clarendon, 1975), 26.

21. The developing scientific branches of complexity theory remind us as well that our old notions of cause and its proportional effect are highly selective, based on ignoring the way most things in the universe operate in favor of discrete and heuristically simplified (i.e., fictionalized) systems.

22. This highlights the point that Herakleitos' statement of the sixth century BCE is self-contradictory. By its very existence (perhaps especially in translation) here at the end of the twentieth century CE, the phrase belies its content. All is flux, and nothing solid, except for the impressive fact that the words continue to bear meaning and form within the (admittedly quite limited) context of twenty-odd centuries of Western civilization, even expanding from that initial statement to its use in classrooms, doctoral dissertations, and the community at large. Thus language is both a thing ephemeral and a thing that—by reason of its changing—resists change. This paradox of language, its constant flickering between diasparactive and cohesive force, is well brought out by Mikhail Bakhtin, where the object of discourse is always already "overlain with qualification, open to dispute, charged with value, already enveloped in an obscuring mist. . . . It is entangled, shot through with shared thoughts, points of view, alien value judgments and accents" (1981, 276). Consequently, any word seeking this "entangled" object of desire follows an obvious plot, implies a narrative, a quest: that of Oedipus, that of Odysseus, that of Parsifal. The desire of the Oedipally plotted word, directed toward its maternal object, enters not a simplex *agon,* but "a dialogically agitated and tension-filled environment of alien words" where it attempts to replace the precursor words, and thus come to the (unattainable but ever desired) union with its putative mother, the *Ding an sich.* By its very existence, the word admits its fundamental condition of loss; however, in its attempt to fulfill desire despite the resistance of both the object and the earlier word, the word works against loss—it exists. In the religious framework of the grail-quests, the perfect word, like the perfect knight, can reach the transcendent Word, the presence of Christ. In a more realistic (but still romantic) world, like that of Odysseus, the word comes home, but not to the transcendent goal; the Odyssean word moves through its quest, asks its questions of the dead (as in the grail-myth) and comes to rest with its conventional and legal referents, its Penelope, its Ithaka. In other words, and in good Saussurean style, it finds itself at home *in other words.* Perhaps the most important aspect

of all of these verbal quests, especially so of the Odyssean type, is the recognition that the quest itself, the playing out of desire against resistances, is the real story (as it is the real life). The *Odyssey* is not the story of the return of Odysseus to Penelope and Ithaka, but the story of his *returning* (and as often as not, the story of the *story* of his returning). Similarly, the *Oedipus* is not a play about a man sleeping with his mother, but the story of that man unwittingly struggling to discover that he sleeps with his mother. So once again we come to the importance of play, the *jouissance* between unattainable absolutes, implicit in the single word.

23. Brooks's claims for the Freudian "masterplot" are not perhaps as far-reaching as my own, since he limits his analysis to the canonical novel as if to the epitome of narrative. Thomas Maresca in *Three English Epics* (1979) applies a variant of this psychological script, focusing on the *descensus ad inferos* as the single marker of the genre in English, a topos of plot that he regularizes to the psychological and philosophical descent; the descent to hell becomes both a descent into consciousness and a descent into time, history, and matter.

24. We must be cautious in our use of Bakhtin, especially when speaking of poetry, for around this "unitary" language, which he sees as "authoritarian, dogmatic and conservative" (287), Bakhtin constructs a kind of poetic death-cult, where "Everything that enters the work must immerse itself in Lethe, and forget its previous life in any other contexts" (297). Though fundamentally untenable, such a statement is understandable as a critique of decontextualizing formalist methods of criticism, and still more as a clearing of territory for his valorization of the novel.

A second cautionary stance must be taken toward Bakhtin's conception of the musical nature of poetry. Rhythm and rhyme, according to Bakhtin, "destroy in embryo those social worlds of speech and of person that are potentially embedded in the word" (298). That is, the poet, yet again seen as bringer of death, uses musical devices to "police" the monological borders of that "unity and hermetic quality of the surface of poetic style" (298). This perception is accurate, to a certain extent; coherence is indeed induced by a repeated pattern of sounds, as is found, for example, in the musical coherence of a Mozart concerto. But sound can also be used to destroy coherence, to create and manipulate dissonance and discontinuity within a given work. Rhythm, like language, constitutes socially constructed codes of signification. Hence, the use of a culturally dominant rhythmic code, such as iambic pentameter, bears a significance similar to the invocation of tradition implicit in a Ciceronian periodic sentence. And, though rhythm is intrinsic to language, present in every spoken word, prosaic discourse—and criticism in particular—largely ignores it. The conscious manipulation or orchestration of this pervasive linguistic musicality remains almost exclusively the domain of poetry.

25. While Wilkie's emphasis on tradition is very useful, his understanding of what "genre" is, if not something defined by tradition (i.e., by repetition), comes to seem rather incomplete.

26. As Louis MacNeice remarks, "Nothing could be more vicious than the popular legend that the poet is a species distinct from the ordinary man and that poetry can flourish only in certain places or people." See "The Traditional Aspect of Modern English Poetry," in *Selected Literary Criticism of Louis MacNeice*, ed. Alan Heuser (Oxford: Clarendon, 1987). Many other criticisms of Bloom exist, notably for this study Annette Kolodny's often-anthologized "The Influence of Anxiety: Prolegomena to a Study of the Production of Poetry by Women" (1987).

27. "I sing of warfare and a man at war. From the sea-coast of Troy in early days He came to Italy by destiny, To our Lavinian western shore" (lines 1–3). Citations in Latin are from *The Aeneid of Virgil* (Ed. R. D. Williams. 2 vols. 1972, 1973. Rpt. London: Macmillan, 1988). English citations are (unless otherwise noted) from Robert Fitzgerald's translation of the *Aeneid* (New York: Vintage-Random House, 1984).

28. See Jack Goody and Ian Watt, "The Consequences of Literacy," in *Literacy in Traditional Societies*, ed. Jack Goody (Cambridge: Cambridge UP, 1968: 27–68), 31–32.

29. Though the act of "re-visioning" is developed by Adrienne Rich as a specifically femi-

nist response to patriarchal culture, I here broaden that application. For a more strictly feminist approach to this terminology, see Susan Stanford Friedman (1977).

30. See *Poetry as Discourse* (London: Methuen, 1983), 9. Easthope's remarks clearly suggest that such repetition characterizes all discourse, especially poetic discourse. The difference of the epic tradition from, say, the lyric, lies in the extreme emphasis that epic places upon such repetitions over the course of an extended work.

31. See Joanne Feit Diehl, " 'Come Slowly—Eden': An Exploration of Women Poets and Their Muse," *Signs* 3.3 (Spring 1978): 572–87; Ellen Moers, *Literary Women* (New York: Anchor, 1977); Sandra Gilbert and Susan Gubar, *The Madwoman in the Attic: The Woman Writer and the Nineteenth-Century Literary Imagination* (New Haven: Yale UP, 1979); Elizabeth Abel, "(E)merging Identities: The Dynamics of Female Friendship in Contemporary Fiction by Women," *Signs* 6, no. 3 (Spring 1981): 413–35; Kolodny (1987). Unrevised Freudian or Lacanian models would largely replicate Bloom's exclusion of feminine experience.

32. Friedman's important article "Gender and Genre Anxiety" (1986) provides significant discussion of the familiar but usually unstated dichotomy between the "masculine" epic and the "feminine" forms of lyric and novel.

33. My broader use of "self" should be distinguished from a strict Althusserian notion of a modern unified subject produced within Western capitalist ideology. Clearly, different cultural ideologies produce different forms of subjectivity, diffuse as well as unified. By using a more general and inclusive term I intend to include these multiple possibilities. Among numerous scholars working to shift "modernity" earlier and earlier is Valeria Finucci, who demonstrates the applicability of subjectivity to the study of Renaissance epic in *The Lady Vanishes: Subjectivity and Representation in Castiglione and Ariosto* (Stanford: Stanford UP, 1992). More to the point is Elizabeth Bellamy's psychoanalytically based *Translations of Power* (1992), which broadens "epic 'subjecthood' " as she calls it to extend throughout dynastic epic from Virgil to Spenser. Part of my aim is to push the varieties of "subjecthood" farther still.

34. See Tillyard 1954; Maresca 1974; Newman 1986; MacDonald 1987. They follow numerous studies of epic, some cited in the next note but one. Good selected bibliographies are available in Merchant 1971 and Yu 1973.

35. See Lukács, *The Theory of the Novel*, trans. Anna Bostock (1920. Cambridge: MIT Press, 1971).

36. While earlier critics often agree with the "death of epic" theory, the embedded awareness of epic's elite status among earlier scholars lets them escape the epic to novel theory. Such an awareness, or at least the high valuation of elite status, is eradicated in later novelizing critics. Among the earlier critics, see, e.g., John Clark, *A History of Epic Poetry* (London, 1900); Lascelles Abercrombie, *The Epic* (London, 1914); A. C. Bradley, "The Long Poem in the Age of Wordsworth," in *Oxford Lectures on Poetry* (1908. London: Macmillan, 1962: 177–205); William MacNeile Dixon, *English Epic and Heroic Poetry* (London, 1912).

37. Shelley's use of "unacknowledged" does point to a crisis in the production of epic: an increasing separation of the discursive elite from the ruling elite on one hand, and on the other the growth of a middle sector—a bourgeois or prosaic sector—which increases in discursive as well as economic power. The split between discursive and ruling elites, though detectable in the earliest epics, becomes a recurrent strain in elite forms of discourse as they encounter improved technologies of composition, until a theorist such as Umberto Eco, rather than hearing the echoes of a dominant cultural code, can hear the rhythmical (ins)urgencies of poetry as "semiotic guerrilla warfare." In connection with elitism see also Timothy Steele's *Missing Measures* (Fayetteville: University of Arkansas Press, 1990): 71–85: "Prior to the nineteenth century, most imaginative literature of prestige is metrical" (71). Note, however, that this hierarchical difference is culturally specific to English and a few other traditions.

38. The phrase is William Hayley's, from *An Essay on Epic Poetry* (1782. Gainesville, FL: Scholars' Facsimiles and Reprints, 1968).

39. They also turn the Oedipal scenario from explanatory paradigm into oppressive metanarrative, something I am struggling to avoid because it imposes awkwardly and reductively on both our earliest and our latest epics.

40. Women poets, for example, in general show less affliction by this particular influence of tradition. Bloom shows little concern for them.

Chapter 2. *Worda ond Worca*

1. William W. Lawrence, *Beowulf and Epic Tradition* (New York: Hafner, 1963), 128. He refers specifically to the Finnsburh episode and fragment.

2. This will be the subject of further discussion below; for the moment, the relation between the initial (and therefore striking) alliterative consonant and its more "fragile" shadows may be considered pertinent.

3. That is, it makes up for the fact that they are unable to reconcile their fragmented, unsatisfying experience of life with their projected images of themselves as whole, as in the Lacanian mirror stage.

4. See Robert P. Creed, "The Making of an Anglo-Saxon Poem," in Fry 1968, 141.

5. Alford draws primarily on Heinz Kohut and Otto Kernberg. See Kernberg, *Borderline Conditions and Pathological Narcissism* (New York: Jason Aronson, 1975); Kohut, *The Restoration of the Self* (New York: International Universities Press, 1977); or, especially, Kernberg's "Contrasting Viewpoints Regarding the Nature and Treatment of Narcissistic Personality Disorders," *Journal of the American Psychoanalytic Association* 22 (1974): 255–67.

6. As Peter Hägin notes, this was a dominant tendency in neoclassical theories of the grand epic cause, which "overemphasiz[ed] the importance of apparent 'causes', i.e. the defeat of Troy (which is never completed within the twenty-four books of the *Iliad*), or the destruction of Penelope's suitors in the *Odyssey*, whereby the latter cause, being only of a domestic kind, embarrassed the critics considerably and caused them to slight the whole poem as quite inferior to the *Iliad*" (1964, 35).

7. G. E. Lessing, *Laocoön*, ed. and trans. William A. Steel (1930. Rpt. London: J. M. Dent, 1970). The "blindness" of Achilles that Lessing suggests is interesting for its connections with Oedipus.

8. *The Iliad of Homer*, trans. Alexander Pope (London, 1715–20). Other citations of the *Iliad* will be to Richmond Lattimore's well-known translation. Citations of the *Odyssey* are to Robert Fitzgerald's translation. Greek citations (rare) are to T. W. Allen's Oxford Classical Text (*Homeri Opera*, 2d ed., Oxford, 1917, 1919). For the sake of familiarity and continuity I have chosen to adopt the traditional Anglicized versions of the Homeric names most frequently encountered: Helen, Achilles, Jason, Medea, Troy. Those appearing less often I have left to their native usage.

9. Pope's translation allows momentary confusion over the antecedent of "Which" ("me" or "this sacred sceptre"), nicely underscoring both the future of Achilles and the relative impotence of the Greek army without him.

10. It will be remembered that Thetis was destined to give birth to a child more powerful than the father. This is the reason Peleus was aided in his rape of the goddess (according to Ovid, at least), and the reason Zeus was able to restrain himself (for once) in his desire.

11. And, according to most psychoanalysts, the prerequisites of homosexuality. Alford, in his discussion of cultural narcissism, follows Chasseguet-Smirgel in a distasteful analogy, but one that comments aptly on Achilles' fixations: "The 'pervert's mother' . . . plays temptress when she leads the child to believe that he has no need either to grow up or to identify with his father in order to be her perfect partner. This allows the child's ego ideal to become fixated at a level at which archaic ideals of fusion and oedipal victory predominate" (1988, 63). See Janine Chasseguet-Smirgel, *The Ego Ideal: A Psychoanalytic Essay on the Malady of the Ideal*, trans. Paul Burrows (New York: Norton, 1984), 33. Alford removes the quotation marks from "per-

vert" on the next page of his work: "one might define cultural narcissism as simply the cultural analog of the pervert's mother" (64).

12. *Gilgamesh*, typically, has it both ways, focusing on the narcissistic in the first half of the epic and shifting to a more clearly Oedipal quest and compromise in the second half.

13. Though I have modernized the Anglo-Saxon thorns and edhs throughout, all references to *Beowulf* are based on the standard third edition of Fr. Klaeber, *Beowulf and the Fight at Finnsburg* (Lexington, MA: D. C. Heath, 1950). All translations, except where noted, are my own.

14. Many of the analogues, as well, suggest a reading that emphasizes the place and power of the wicked mother or stepmother, e.g., the figure of Hvít in *Hrolfs saga kraka* and in *Bjarkarímur*. See *Beowulf and its Analogues*, trans. G. N. Garmonsway and Jacqueline Simpson (New York: Dutton, 1968), 95–112.

15. Christine Fell, *Women in Anglo-Saxon England* (London: British Museum Publications, 1984). The name's meaning "must have been instantly understood by any Anglo-Saxon audience." Though the rise in her fortunes is obviously "not a commonplace of Anglo-Saxon society . . . it was a readily imagined possibility." Fell also cites the example of the female slave Balthild, who married King Clovis of the Franks, and went on later to become a saint (66).

16. My colleague Karen Grossweiner, following R. M. Lumiansky's argument in "The Dramatic Audience in *Beowulf*" (Fry 1968, 76–82), reminds me to be cautious in proposing what may appear a literalizing of details, which are (a) subject to drastic change in oral settings, and (b) designed only for the immediate context of performance, not for comparison with other details. However, as my concern must be with the extant record of the poet's performance, such details—"Freudian slips" or not—have clear significance as traces of a context-dependent and provisional composition. I do not suggest that there are no other textual forces behind such details; however, psychoanalytic theory provides at least a coherent explanation of this and similar phenomena. Oral-formulaic composition does not, any more than written composition, negate the impact of the composing mind—in fact, oral texts may demonstrate that impact more freely than written texts.

17. As Pound wrote: "The *Nekuia* shouts aloud that it is *older* than the rest, all that island, Cretan, etc., hinter-time, that is not Praxiteles, not Athens of Pericles, but Odysseus." See *The Letters of Ezra Pound: 1907–1941*, ed. D. D. Paige (New York: Harcourt, Brace, 1950), 274. The alliterative four-stress lines, imitative of Anglo-Saxon verse, need no comment.

18. "As for race, we are liegemen of the Geatish people, and belong to the fellowship that sits at Hygelac's own hearth. My father was famous among many nations, a high-born war-leader whose name was Ecgtheow. He lived to see many winters, until in old age he passed away from his courts; every wise man in all parts of the world remembers him well. It is with friendly hearts that we have come to visit your lord, the son of Healfdene, the protector of your people; show goodwill to us by your advice! We have weighty business with the renowned lord of the Danes, and I intend that none of it should remain hidden once we are there.

"You know—if what we have heard tell as the truth is so—that in the land of the Scyldings there is some sort of scourge, some mysterious foe whose deeds give proof of hatred, and who in the darkness of night, by the terror he brings, reveals unbelievable spite through humiliations and carnage. In this matter I can give Hrothgar good counsel from a generous heart, teaching him how he, so noble and ripe in wisdom, may overpower his foe, so that his restless cares may be quieted—if indeed his tormenting troubles are ever fated to change, and if relief is to be found. If not, he will evermore endure a time of hardship and inescapable distress, so long as that finest of halls still stands as his royal seat" (258–85; Garmonsway's translation).

19. Emphasis mine, throughout the paragraph.

20. Note that the *landweard* appears to see through this fairly easily, suggesting in his response that Beowulf goes to face "the onslaught of battle" (299). A warrior like Beowulf (248–51) does not offer counsels only.

21. Not to underestimate the coastguard, it should be noted that his position, having both to challenge and to maintain the social contract, is one of some difficulty.

22. Klaeber outlines classical and Germanic analogues (1950, 149); Ward Parks develops these in a full-length study, *Verbal Dueling in Heroic Narrative: The Homeric and Old English Traditions* (Princeton: Princeton UP, 1990). A wider cultural range is found in Vansina (1985, 102ff.).

23. The question is a sly put-down as well, with its implication that the present Beowulf cannot easily be equated with the more famous one who strove with Breca. The use of the question, however, exposes Unferth's lack of certain knowledge.

24. The name's etymological significance has been remarked on before. For discussion and summary, see Eugene Greene, "Power, Commitment, and the Right to a Name in *Beowulf,*" *The CUNY English Forum* (New York: AMS, 1985), 133–40.

25. Klaeber, pointing to "the admirable use of variation, the abundance of sea terms (ll. 508ff.), the strong description of the scene," claims that these speeches "show the style of the poem at its best" (1950, 150).

26. David K. Crowne, "The Hero on the Beach: An Example of Composition by Theme in Anglo-Saxon Poetry," *Neophilologische Mitteilungen* 61 (1960): 362–72, 368.

27. Ibid., 370.

28. This is reduced from MacCary's explanations (1982, 90ff.). The conception of the partial object is drawn from Kohut's analyses of narcissism, which distinguishes between the metonymic sense of fusion in the archaic, narcissistic self-object (the secondary narcissistic state of Freud) and the metaphoric "true objects" of instinctual investment, i.e., what we usually consider the mature, post-oedipal objects of desire and aggression. See also Heinz Kohut, *The Analysis of the Self* (New York: International Universities Press, 1971), 50–51.

29. For example, Achilles to Patroklos, *Iliad* 16.97–100: "If only not one of all the Trojans could escape destruction, not one of the Argives, but you and I could emerge from the slaughter, so that we two alone could break Troy's hallowed coronal" (trans. MacCary 1982, 219).

30. There are also numerous examples of narcissistic pairing in *Beowulf* and in Germanic texts in general, the most important being the hero and sister's son (e.g., Beowulf and Wiglaf [2602ff.], Sigemund and Fitela [879ff.]). It is worth noting that, despite the mention of Fitela in this context, a main point of the passage is that in the conquest of the dragon, *ne wæs him Fitela mid* (889).

31. See Stanley B. Greenfield, "The Formulaic Expression of the Theme of the 'Exile' in Anglo-Saxon Poetry," *Speculum* 30 (1955): 200–206.

32. Greene 1985, 138.

33. J. R. R. Tolkien, "*Beowulf*: The Monsters and the Critics," in Fry 1968, 8–56.

34. For example, 893, 1269, 1512, 2592. I have quoted Wyatt and Chambers's alternative translations of the term in *Beowulf with the Finnsburg Fragment*, ed. A. J. Wyatt, revised with notes by R. W. Chambers (Cambridge: Cambridge UP, 1920).

35. For example, Heorogar, older brother of Hrothgar, and both of Hygelac's elder brothers. It is worth noting that Herebeald, the eldest of the latter, is killed by the middle brother Hæthcyn under somewhat questionable circumstances.

36. This agonistic and binary framework of violence can be best exemplified, perhaps, by the *Battle of Maldon*, a poem E. V. Gordon has characterized as "the greatest battle-poem in the English language," one that even more consistently than *Beowulf* displays "the clearest and fullest expression known in literature of the ancient Germanic heroic code." The quintessential statement of this code has long been regarded as lying in the famous speech of Byrhtwold:

> Hige sceal the heardra,   heorte the cenre,
> mod sceal the mare,   the ure mægen lytlath.

[Thought shall be harder, heart the keener, / spirit shall be greater, as our strength dwindles.] The Other (unexpressed in this passage) is the Viking host, the soon-to-be victorious *wicinga* on the shores of the Panta river. The metonymic linking of same with same is enforced by the adverse conditions—*because* the Anglo-Saxon warriors are surrounded, outnumbered, and their leader lies dead on the riverbank, the bonds between the members of the comitatus become even more powerful. See E. V. Gordon, ed., *The Battle of Maldon* (New York: Methuen, 1937), 29, 26.

37. Joan Blomfeld, "The Style and Structure of *Beowulf*," in Fry 1968, 57–58.

38. Joseph Russo and Bennett Simon, "Homeric Psychology and the Oral Epic Tradition," *Journal of the History of Ideas* 29 (1968): 483–98, conveniently reprinted in *Essays on the Iliad*, ed. John Wright (Bloomington: Indiana UP, 1978). The phrase is from Fränkel's *Dichtung und Philosophiedes frühen Griechentums* (Munich, 1962): "Das ich ist nicht abgekapselt, sondern ein offenes Kraftfeld" (89). As Russo and Simon elaborate, "The Homeric self or ego is simply not clearly conceived of or defined, either with regard to its component parts or to those forces that impinge upon it from without. Any one of the parts can be equivalent to the whole person. *Pars pro toto* is here no mere figure of speech, but a reflection of a poorly differentiated concept of self" (43).

39. Dorothy Whitelock, *The Audience of Beowulf* (Oxford: Clarendon, 1951), 67.

40. Edward B. Irving, Jr., *A Reading of Beowulf* (New Haven: Yale UP, 1968), 198.

41. Ibid., 155–56.

42. Calder (1972, 23–24n) provides a useful summary of the interpretations up to 1972, and his own article has been especially useful in the discussion that follows. Richard Butts, in "The Analogical Mere: Landscape and Terror in *Beowulf*," *English Studies* (1987) 2:113–21, though correct in his emphasis of the psychological grounding of the landscape, does not go very far with that emphasis, hindered perhaps by his idea that "the poet's prime concern" is "the collective terror of men in the face of the unknown" (113). Closer to my reading of action is Jane Chance, in "The Structural Unity of *Beowulf*," in Helen Damico and Alexandra Hennessey Olson's *New Readings on Women in Old English Literature* (Bloomington: Indiana UP, 1990), 248–61; Jeffrey Haverman provides a Jungian analysis in "*Beowulf*: The Archetype Enters History," *ELH* 35 (1968).

43. Whitelock 1951, 67.

44. See, e.g., Chance 1990, 248; Butts 1987, 114.

45. Chance 1990, 253ff., arrives at a reading of action in some ways similar to my own, but her reading and hence her argument as a whole are weakened by her insistence on female "passivity" in Anglo-Saxon culture. As Christine Fell suggests, in this insistence we project patriarchy and underestimate Anglo-Saxon culture.

46. As noted above, signification itself is the phallic "copula," the linkage or copulation with the world. As the eminent jointure of the masculine exertion of power over the Anglo-Saxon worldview, *earm ond eaxl* cannot easily be read as other than phallic. The euphemistic form of displacement, to thigh rather than joint, is found in Mediterranean as well as Celtic myths of the Dying God.

47. The prone position for giving birth—without the aid of gravity—was uncommon prior to the Renaissance.

48. See Page duBois, "On Horse/Men, Amazons, and Endogamy," *Arethusa* 12 (1979): 34–57, and her amplification of these and related ideas in *Sowing the Body: Psychoanalysis and Ancient Representations of Women* (Chicago: University of Chicago Press, 1988).

49. Daniel N. Stern, *The Interpersonal World of the Infant: A View from Psychoanalysis and Developmental Psychology* (New York: Basic Books, 1985).

50. Earl also cites the *Rig Veda* and Hesiod's *Theogony*. On the *Voluspá*, see the comments of G. Turville-Petre, *Origins of the Icelandic Eddas* (1953. Rev. reprt. Oxford: Clarendon, 1967), 57.

51. Tolkien, in Fry 1968, 45–46.

52. *Bede's Ecclesiastical History of the English People*, ed. and trans. by B. Colgrave and R. A. B. Mynors (Oxford: Clarendon, 1969), 182–85.

53. Charles R. Dahlberg, "Beowulf and the Land of Unlikeness," *The CUNY English Forum* (New York: AMS, 1985: 105–27), 114.

54. Fell (1984) provides a helpful supplement in this regard. One of her illustrations reproduces a scene from an Anglo-Saxon manuscript (MS. Harley 603, f. 67v). Fell's caption notes: "*As a child that is weaned of his mother:* she appears to be giving him a ring" (77). Considering the later role of the Anglo-Saxon lord as *beaggifa* or "ring-giver," there are important observations to be made. The Anglo-Saxon mother is powerful but not all-encompassing as in the Greek drama, and here is seen as introducing the child to the vitally important system of exchange. She is herself a figure of the later power exerted by the king in his hall, where the comitatus and kinship in a sense make up for the warriors' lost sense of connection with the mother. This maternal mastery of exchange is also shown by Wealhtheow, who like her husband is a giver of treasure; and Hygd, Hygelac's queen, who has the power to award Beowulf the throne after her husband's death.

55. I emphasize the literal "delightfulness" of this specifically social *locus amoenus* rather than the natural setting of more conventional association.

56. For convenience I am referring to the N. K. Sandars translation of *The Epic of Gilgamesh* (Middlesex: Penguin, 1972). Though unmarked blending and homogenizing take place in this version, it is probably the most familiar and readily available text. The fragment that serves as an epigraph to this book is from Maureen Gallery Kovacs's translation of *The Epic of Gilgamesh* (Stanford: Stanford UP, 1989), 92–93.

57. The people of Uruk lament that Gilgamesh leaves no son to his father, and "his lust leaves no virgin to her lover," yet he should be "the shepherd of the city, wise, comely, and resolute" (62).

58. As Joan Blomfeld points out with regard to the poem, "As far as his medium, a sequence of words, will allow, the poet has detached his theme from the processes of time and space and disregarded the appearances which for practical purposes constitute reality" (in Fry 1968, 64).

59. For a more thorough exploration, see John Miles Foley, "*Beowulf* and Traditional Narrative Song: The Potential and Limits of Comparison," *Old English Literature in Context: Ten Essays,* ed. John D. Niles (Woodbridge, Suffolk: D. S. Brewer, 1980), 117–36.

60. See, e.g., James F. Doubleday, "Two-Part Structure in Old English Poetry," *Notre Dame English Journal* 8.2 (Spring 1973): 71–79; Fred C. Robinson, *Beowulf and the Appositive Style* (Knoxville: University of Tennessee Press, 1985); and John Leyerle, "The Interlace Structure of *Beowulf,*" *University of Toronto Quarterly* 37 (1967): 1–17.

61. John Miles Foley 1980, 120.

62. One might add that the phenomenon of nearly identical beginnings of Anglo-Saxon epics (e.g., the opening lines of *Andreas* and *Beowulf*) reflects that tradition's principal recursive device; thus the Beowulfian tradition can be seen to alliterate with itself, insofar as it continues.

63. James W. Earl, "The Role of the Men's Hall in the Development of the Anglo-Saxon Superego," *Psychiatry* 46 (1983): 139–60.

64. Again, there are clearly differences between various traditions with regard to the separation caused by the margin of silence. The Anglo-Saxon poet appears to occupy a position midway between the professional bard of the Homeric epics and the far more informal milieu of, say, the *Orkneyinga Saga* or the Icelandic *Eddas,* where the extemporaneous making of verses is far more commonplace. The examples of Cædmon and Aldhelm in Anglo-Saxon show a higher degree of separation in their performances.

Chapter 3. Twice Faithless Troy

1. "Oedipus" is equivalent to "clubfoot," and the injury is conventionally related to the castration complex. On the recurrent identification of Odysseus and Hephaistos, see Rick M. Newton, "Odysseus and Hephaistos in the *Odyssey,*" *Classical Journal* 83.1 (October–November 1987): 12–20. Unless otherwise noted, I cite from Robert Fitzgerald's translation of *The Odyssey* (Garden City, NY: Anchor-Doubleday, 1963).

2. The relative identity of Odysseus and Polyphemos in this episode is more fully laid out below, following Norman Austin's remarkable "Odysseus and Cyclops: Who is Who?" in *Approaches to Homer,* ed. Carl A. Rubino and Cynthia W. Shelmerdine (Austin: University of Texas Press, 1983), 3–37.

3. In Antikleia's speech (11.200) the emphasis is clearly placed on all the ways she did not die; the effect is similar in Eumaios' explicit omission of cause (15.350). The legend is that she hanged herself.

4. Although the *Odyssey,* like the *Iliad,* is oral in character, its later provenance is traditional. I follow the common view that the poet of the *Odyssey* is reacting to an already monumentalized *Iliad.* Thus, the gradual shift in attitude toward "twice faithless Troy" is also a shift from oral attitudes to literate ones despite a continuing orality of poetic performance, even in Chaucer's rewriting of the already written.

5. Some have suggested that the *Odyssey* shows evidence of the skepticism that appears in partially literate cultures, and indeed the thesis outlined here places it in that progressive modern "lettering" of a vocalic world. See, for example, Julian Jaynes, *The Origins of Consciousness in the Breakdown of the Bicameral Mind* (Boston: Houghton Mifflin, 1977).

6. Henry Fielding, *The History of Tom Jones, a Foundling,* ed. Fredson Bowers (Oxford: Clarendon, 1974), 509.

7. Howard W. Clarke, *The Art of the Odyssey* (Englewood Cliffs, NJ: Prentice-Hall, 1967), 5. For an excellent but more general discussion of Odysseus' attentiveness to food, see W. B. Stanford's classic "The Untypical Hero," conveniently reprinted in Steiner and Fagles' *Homer: A Collection of Critical Essays* (Englewood Cliffs, NJ: Prentice-Hall, 1962), 122–38.

8. Among other critics, see Chris Emlyn-Jones, "True and Lying Tales in the *Odyssey,*" *Greece and Rome* 33:1 (April 1986): 1–10; and C. R. Trahman, "Odysseus' Lies (*Odyssey,* Books 13–19)," *Phoenix* 6 (1952): 41ff.

9. The characterization of Odysseus' speeches as "gifts" is indebted in part to Helene P. Foley, " 'Reverse Similes' and Sex Roles in the *Odyssey,*" *Arethusa* 11.1 (1978): 7–26, where she discusses them as part of the "complex exchanges of favor between host and guest" (14).

10. According to Nestor, we might add Odysseus' extra trip, to Tenedos from Troy and back again, due to dissension caused by Zeus and Athena (3.163); but see my discussion of the hero's ambivalence below.

11. George deForest Lord, "The *Odyssey* and the Western World," in *Essays on the Odyssey,* ed. Charles H. Taylor (Bloomington and London: Indiana UP, 1963: 36–53), 44. The fact that the Kikones are almost unattested in other sources renders the incident, as one without apparent cause or consequence, particularly resonant as a recursive psychological manifestation.

12. In the story told to Eumaios, the labor in exile seems somewhat mitigated by the intervention of a fatherly intercessor, the Egyptian king. Similarly, in both "fantasies," the paternal figure of Zeus is explicitly the initiator of the trip that leads to the raid. Since this raid is portrayed as an assault on the father, one could apply E. R. Dodds's theory of projection as a psychological defense to such an incident; in a sense, the paternal figure "was asking for it." See E. R. Dodds, *The Greeks and the Irrational* (Berkeley: University of California Press, 1951). For a more detailed reading of the differences in these tales, which focuses on the contextual differences of audience and performative intent, see Emlyn-Jones 1986.

13. Odysseus' tears, here and earlier (8.70–94, in response to the song of the clash between Odysseus and Achilles), are perceived by Alkinoös despite the hero's attempt to conceal them. This strikes us as odd, since he is able in his meeting with Penelopê to "weep inwardly," his eyes "like horn or iron" (19.212). Two alternative readings suggest themselves: Either he weeps with intent in book 8, hoping to coax questions from the Phaiakians; or he is more deeply moved by the bard's evocation of the Oedipal struggles of Troy than he is by his wife's tears. These are not, however, mutually exclusive readings.

14. See related stories at, e.g., 1.320–40, 3.130–98, 3.254–312, 4.351–586; the two *nekuia,* 10.153–650, 24.1–203; the song of the Sirens, 12.184–91; for the parallel homecoming of

Agamemnon, in particular (e.g., 1.29–35, 1.298–304, 3.194), see Edward F. D'Arms and Karl K. Hulley, "The Oresteia Story in the *Odyssey*," *Transactions of the American Philological Association* 77 (1946): 207–13. Heubeck's characterization of the poem as the story "The Victors' Return from Troy" (1988, 14) can best be understood in an ironic light.

15. Heubeck makes no claims, but does cite Mattes's claim that the choice of song reflects Odysseus' increasing self-confidence.

16. I am aware of the dangers in connecting poet and hero too closely here; nonetheless, given the poet's evident reworking and revaluation of the *Iliad*'s primary ethical values, and at the same time the *Odyssey*'s clear dependence on a knowledge of the Iliadic tradition, it seems worthwhile to explore the connection more thoroughly. Moreover, Odysseus, whose various accounts encompass a substantial portion of the text, seems on that basis alone worth analyzing as a figure of the poet.

17. Eliminating Hektor, "master of horses," has allowed the "sons of the Akhaians" to penetrate the city wall, inside of yet another horse standing "tall on the assembly ground of Troy" (8. 524). Αιπος, "high-lying" or "steep" (8.516), is a common epithet for towns, and especially for Troy (Heubeck 1988, 380). Here, however, the phallic height of the city (and hence also of the Trojan Horse) is emphasized by the presence of the cliffs (πετρης, 8.508) down which the Greek gift might be cast. (These cliffs do not appear in the *Iliad*.) According to prophecy, the city of Troy must fall on the day she harbors the "great horse of timber." Here as in many of the poem's episodes Odysseus initiates and leads the killing/castration of a father figure (Priam and his armies, but also Troy), which is simultaneously the possession of the mother (Troy, but also Helen, Kassandra, and the other women of Troy).

18. This in turn suggests that the precursor tradition is not exclusively figured as patriarchal.

19. The balance of the passage clarifies this: "Mental work is linked to some current impression, some provoking occasion in the present which has been able to arouse one of the subject's major wishes. From there it harks back to a memory of an earlier experience (usually an infantile one) in which this wish was fulfilled; and it now creates a . . . future which represents a fulfillment of the wish" (1908b, 147–48).

20. Changing readings of the Homeric poems over the centuries define our own repressed wishes rather than those of the poet: the medieval love for the Trojans, the continuing Romantic improvement in the fortunes of Helen (often at a cost to Achilles), the twentieth-century preference for the *Odyssey* despite its earlier disparagement. For earlier adaptations of Helen (prior to Landor, Poe, H.D., and others), see Mihoko Suzuki, *Metamorphoses of Helen: Authority, Difference, and the Epic* (Ithaca: Cornell UP, 1989).

21. Another clear example of exhibition is Odysseus' embarrassing encounter with Nausikaa (6.100–215), where he breaks off an olive branch "to shield his nakedness." (The questionable effectiveness of this concealment is not discussed.) The girls' shouts are "most like the cry of nymphs," evoking Odysseus' recent experience with Kalypso. Moreover, the tension of the moment is increased by the dramatic, warlike simile (cf. *Iliad* 12.299–307) of the "lion with burning eyes . . . his hungry belly taking him near stout homesteads for his prey": "Odysseus had this look, in his rough skin / advancing on the girls with pretty braids; / and he was driven on by hunger, too" (6.135–40). The suspense is clear—will Odysseus react as he would to a figure like Kalypso, "the nymph with pretty braids"? In other words, will the rape of Troy be enacted yet again? The sexual tension is quite high in this scene, as seems evident from the readers who wish that Odysseus had stayed with Nausikaa. At this point in the story, too, the audience may know relatively little about Odysseus. How does a conqueror of Troy, especially one who uses poisoned arrows, react to this isolated young maiden? Odysseus' long, complimentary speech, issued with extreme tact, and Nausikaa's dry and somewhat moralistic reply, ease this tension a good bit. (Odysseus' references to marriage, matching so well with Nausikaa's dream, create a new set of expectations and tensions.) But in a sense the conquest of Troy has already occurred, satisfied as wish by the act of exhibition itself. According to Freud, the

relatively "indifferent" spectator involved in exhibition-dreams analogous is "nothing more nor less than the wishful contrary of the single familiar individual" "upon whom our sexual interest was directed in childhood" (1900, 276–79). (Indeed, Freud uses this particular episode to illustrate the exhibition-dream in *The Interpretation of Dreams* [1900, 279–80].) Odysseus reiterates the Fall of Troy in fantasy, seducing his mother in the person of her "wishful contrary" Nausikaa.

22. Lattimore's more literal translation of these "sweet coupled airs" prevents overemphasis on the "wounds" borne: "everything that the Argives and Trojans did and suffered in wide Troy."

23. Freud's terminology of "hallucinatory wishful psychosis" seems a bit extreme to characterize Odysseus' story. Three things should be said here. First of all, Odysseus does not seem to me to reach this extreme state of melancholia, but neither can he be explained as undergoing a simple process of mourning, as his final adjustment to his loss (if, indeed, it occurs) takes such a very long time. Second, his creation of his story, subject as it is to verbal and interpersonal structures, is a far different thing than the highly personal "hallucinations" of the psychotic. Third, Freud's epistemology (i.e., here, his view of the difference between "hallucinatory" and "real" experience) is naive and reductive, as Lionel Trilling points out in "Freud and Literature," *The Liberal Imagination: Essays on Literature and Society* (Garden City, NY: Anchor-Doubleday, 1953).

24. One would think so, at least. But the *nekuiai* in general are controversial, and the presence in Hades of these figures of punishment is often adduced as evidence of "impurity" or interpolation. See Heubeck 1988, 75–77; for older controversies, see J. G. Petzl, *Antike Diskussionen über die beiden Nekyiai* (Meisenheim: Anton Hain, 1969).

25. Leto is known almost exclusively as mother to Apollo and Artemis. These two also recreate the brother-sister pair of Odysseus' youth with Ktimene.

26. As Heubeck notes, the scene "vividly illustrates the tragedy of the hero with his limited outlook" (1988, 130–31). But Heubeck, in calling Odysseus' arming "heroic" (130) despite Kirke's warning of the possible extra tragedy involved, seems to praise rashness.

27. The gifts correspond to the two originally separate folktales that have been fused in this episode. See Denys Page, *Folktales in Homer's Odyssey* (Cambridge: Harvard UP, 1973).

28. Norman Austin remarks on the Cyclops becoming "a stupid and savage trickster, a gigantic parody of our own endearing hero" (1983, 13).

29. The tradition of Homer's blindness hints at ways to interpret this outraged father-figure: The *Iliad*-poet was "Much-Famed" already; the poet of the *Odyssey* perhaps virtually *outis*—"nobody."

30. Samuel Butler, *The Authoress of the Odyssey* (1897. London: Fifield, 1908), 10.

31. Though the "nine days" of his journey to Ogygia is a standard formula for a long voyage, the number is not without relevance to his process of rebirth.

32. M. I. Finley's assertion in *The World of Odysseus* that this reunion is an unmitigated "scene of love and devotion between father and son" is forced ([London: Chatto and Windus, 1956], 95).

33. Any number of other important incidents of empowered—and threatening—female sexuality in the epic ought as well to be studied. There is little space in this chapter, but an example that certainly deserves mention is that of the women of Lemnos, who have killed all their husbands, but (in an elegant fantasy of maternal seduction) adopt the Argonauts for a year. See *The Voyage of Argo,* ed. and trans. E. V. Rieu (London: Penguin, 1971). All citations of the epic are taken from this readily available—though unfortunately prose—translation.

34. Chaucer's carefully maintained distance from the traditional figure of Criseyde renders his work far more complex than the simple equation of separation, betrayal, and sexual promiscuity noted in other versions. See, e.g., Gretchen Mieszkowski, "The Reputation of Criseyde, 1100–1500," *Transactions of the Connecticut Academy of Arts and Sciences* 43 (1971): 71–153, and Janet Adelman, " 'This Is and Is Not Cressid': The Characterization of Cressida," in

The (M)other Tongue: Essays in Feminist Psychoanalytic Interpretation, ed. S. N. Garner, C. Kahane, and M. Sprengnether (Ithaca: Cornell UP, 1985), 119–41. Citations from Chaucer are drawn from F. N. Robinson's second edition of *The Works of Geoffrey Chaucer* (Boston: Houghton Mifflin, 1957).

35. As adapted from Chaucer by Carolyn Dinshaw in *Chaucer's Sexual Poetics* (1989). Dinshaw emphasizes the way that Criseyde's "slydynge of corage" plays directly into patriarchal necessity, a point discussed more fully below. See also her source in Gayle Rubin's "Traffic in Women: Notes on the 'Political Economy' of Sex," in *Toward an Anthropology of Women,* ed. R. R. Reiter (New York: Monthly Review Press, 1975), 157–210. Rubin remarks, apropos my equation of literacy and increasing "traffic in women," that such practices "seem only to become more pronounced and commercialized in more 'civilized' societies" (175).

36. M. Naimuddin Siddiqui, "*Troilus and Cressida:* Treatment of the Theme by Chaucer and Shakespeare," *Osmanian Journal of English Literature* 4 (1964), 110, 109. For other examples of Troilus' "Lack of forthright masculinity," see Howard Rollins Patch, *On Re-reading Chaucer* (Cambridge: Harvard UP, 1939), 89. These readings of Troilus' passivity are not fully satisfying except for the middle portions of the poem. His activity at beginning and end, though primarily ocular, makes a surprising contrast to his bedridden self-exhibition.

37. A comparable incarnation of this increasing sense of being written is the fate that rules Aeneas, an "already spoken" destiny that he is condemned (or chosen) to repeat: His recursive attempts to discover a happy substitute for the ancient motherland are insistently broken off in favor of the script (itself broken off prior to its fulfillment).

38. For the original of arguments in this area, see Walter Clyde Curry's essay on destiny in *Chaucer and the Mediaeval Sciences* (2d ed., rev., New York: Barnes and Noble, 1960). Persuasive and more recent is Jill Mann, "Chance and Destiny in *Troilus and Criseyde* and the *Knight's Tale,*" in Boitani and Mann 1986, 75–92.

39. To illustrate these at length is beyond the scope of this chapter, but they include the women of the Isle of Lemnos, the Clashing Rocks, the loss of Hylas (and hence of Herakles); on the return journey, the voyage up the Danube and the multitude of rivers (real and imagined) that allow the *Argo*'s return to the Mediterranean, the Wandering Rocks, the Isle of Shkeria, the grounding in Syrtis (Libya) and consequent portage, the encounter with Talos, etc.

40. Euripides' *Medea* had been produced in 431 BCE, while Apollonius Rhodius wrote in the third century BCE.

41. Briefly summarized, Medea rejuvenates Jason's father Aison and murders the usurping uncle Pelias. Pelias' son Akastos banishes the couple from Iolkos; in Corinth, Jason abandons Medea for the daughter of Creon. Medea arranges the deaths of king and daughter, then those of her own children as revenge upon Jason. She flees to Athens; Jason dies in Corinth, killed, as one version has it, by a falling piece of woodwork from the maternal *Argo.*

42. The good paternal figures—Aison (42–43) and Phineus (77–87)—deserve some mention, despite their frailty and inconsequentiality.

43. For example, Jason responds thus to her desires concerning Apsyrtos and his forces (157–60), and the entire crew tries to put off her pleas on the Phaiakian isle (174–76).

44. It should be noted that the poet portrays the Fleece as stolen away—along with Medea herself—at Medea's injunctions.

45. See, e.g., Eleanor Shipley Druckett, *Hellenistic Influence on the Aeneid* (Smith College Classical Studies 1. Northampton, MA: Departments of Greek and Latin of Smith College, 1920), 2–3. Pavlock draws a similar equation (1990, 65).

46. "Phrixus sacrificed the ram at its own suggestion to Zeus alone, because he is the god of fugitives; and Aeetes made him welcome in his palace and married him in all good will to his daughter Chalciope without extracting the usual gifts" (104).

47. The fact that the Fleece is also the bedding that "carries" Jason and Medea on their wedding night should be noted: Though the wedding takes place prematurely (on Phaiakia, not at Iolkos) in the opinion of the protagonists, who desire stronger paternal sanction of the

marriage, an early marriage is the only way to maintain—with whatever fragility—the happy substitute.

48. See, e.g., Rieu's introduction (1971, 14–15), where he argues that the ship itself is the centrally unifying device of Apollonius' epic.

49. Epistemophilia, "the instinct for knowledge or research" (Freud 1905b, 112) is described somewhat equivocally by Freud, primarily as it "makes use of the energy of scopophilia," and indeed its instruments, to conduct its researches. Its genesis remains uncertain (it appears between the ages of three and five), but indeed, Freud suggests that "the instinct for knowledge in children is attracted unexpectedly early and intensively to sexual problems and is in fact possibly first aroused by them" (1905b, 112–13). See also Freud's "Notes upon a Case of Obsessional Neurosis" (1909b, 244–47).

50. Freud calls the question of origins "the oldest and most burning question that confronts immature humanity" (1907, 176–77 and the editors' notes), but later suggests that for girls, and for some boys, the questions of sexual difference (i.e., the castration complex and penis envy) are prior and more important. See "Some Psychical Consequences of the Anatomical Distinction between the Sexes" (1925, 336n).

51. Their theoretical failure is caused, according to Freud, by their "undeveloped" state, where they remain ignorant of "the fertilizing role of semen and the existence of the female sexual orifice" (1905b, 115).

52. Freud relates an anecdote of a three-year-old boy who is told that the stork fetches babies from the water: He "disappeared—to the terror of his nurse. He was found at the edge of the big pond adjoining the country house, to which he had hurried in order to see the babies in the water" (1908c, 191).

53. Herakles had abandoned the *Argo,* in mourning for the slain Hylas, in book 1.

54. See Pavlock, who points out that the shift from Homeric focus on the artisan to the Apollonian focus on the object itself is remarkable (1990, 24–39).

55. Another focus could be followed here, placing emphasis on the (relatively numerous) quite conscious medieval rewritings of the Argonautica legend. See, e.g., Frank A. Dominguez, *The Medieval Argonautica* (Potomac: Studia Humanitatis, 1979).

56. That is, while Troilus himself is briefly mentioned in the *Iliad* and the *Aeneid,* the important linkage to Briseida/Criseyde only occurs in the twelfth century. By "cloaked" I mean here the adoption of the Homeric mantle of authority, not whether the written is disguised as an oral text.

57. For example, see, in addition to Benoît, Guido de Columnis's *Historia Destructionis Troiae* (1287), Boccaccio's *Filostrato* (1336), and Beauvau's *Livre de Troilus* (1380s). While the story remains popular throughout the Renaissance, one might suppose that as the medium of print prevails in succeeding centuries, this form of the repeated narrative loses some of its power. Other causes, however, including the decisions of such influential figures as Shakespeare and Dryden to render the story, may well contribute more heavily to the apparently diminishing impact of the tale. On this, however, see Piero Boitani's collection, *The European Tragedy of Troilus* (Oxford: Clarendon, 1989), particularly his own essay, "Eros and Thanatos: Cressida, Troilus, and the Modern Age," 281–304.

58. "De mei n'iert ja fait bon escrit / Ne chantee bone chançon. / Tel aventure ne tel don / Ne vousisse ja jor aveir." The translation is Robert Kay Gordon's, from his *Story of Troilus* (London: 1934), 19. See also Mieszkowski's difference of emphasis here, 1971, 85–86.

59. The pun has thus been useful in establishing the date of the poem. See Robinson's (1957) introduction and notes.

60. "La vostre C.," "Le vostre T.," etc. (5.1421, 1631).

61. Notable in this connection is the not infrequent Middle English use of "Alpha to Tau" rather than "Alpha to Omega"; this would lead us to an extreme (but not inconsiderable) thesis concerning the connections of Troilus/Troy and Criseyde/Christ. See *Brewer's Dictionary of Phrase and Fable,* ed. Ivor H. Evans (1817. Centenary Edition, Revised. New York: Harper and

Row, 1981). These and all biblical citations (except as noted) are from the *The New Oxford Annotated Bible with the Apocrypha*, ed. Herbert G. May and Bruce M. Metzger (New York: Oxford UP, 1977).

62. Donald Howard, *Chaucer: His Life, His Times, His Works* (New York: E. P. Dutton, 1987), 353.

63. Arthur Mizener, "Character and Action in the Case of Criseyde," *Chaucer: Modern Essays in Criticism*, ed. Edward Wagenknecht (Oxford: Oxford UP, 1959: 348–65), 348.

64. Ibid., 349.

65. Mieszkowski 1971, 103–4.

66. Graydon in his "Defense of Criseyde" argues that two months elapse between her departure from Troy and the date of her last letter, and that two years pass before the sexual consummation of her relationship with Diomede. Citing Graydon, Arthur Mizener (1959) notes Chaucer's deliberate confusion of temporal sequence as a means of heightening the tragic contrast by juxtaposing Criseyde's betrayal (at two years) and Troilus' agony (at ten days and following).

67. "Matere" also, of course, derives directly from Latin *materia* ("the mother of something") and hence from *mater*. See also Freud 1925, 156, 159–60; and 1900, 434n, etc.

68. See Howard 1987, 352, and Robinson's (1957) notes.

69. On a simpler Freudian level, of course, one could argue that the reason this question is left undecided is to allow the poet—despite his distance from the hero Troilus—to remain the child of the maternal Criseyde.

70. Amor est passio quaedam innata procedens ex visione et immoderata cogitatione formaealterius sexus, ob quam aliquis super omnia cupit alterius potiri amplexibus et omnia de utriusque voluntate in ipsius amplexu amoris praecepta compleri. Cited in Dodd, "The System of Courtly Love," *Chaucer Criticism II: Troilus and Criseyde and the Minor Poems*, ed. Richard J. Schoeck and Jerome Taylor (Notre Dame: University of Notre Dame Press, 1960:1–15), 4, 14n2.

71. Who cannot keep secrets cannot love.

72. Ibid., 4–6.

73. Ibid., 5.

74. Boccacio's language, somewhat appropriate to his more jaded Troilo, takes on a significantly different point when placed in the mouth of the inexperienced Troilus.

75. See also, for this uncertainty, the "Canticus Troili" (1.400–420).

76. The same dilemma—in a sense, the castrating effect of the fear of castration—reaches submerged expression in the earlier song of Troilus, in the living death experienced by the lover as so very *unheimlich*: "O quike deth, O swete harm so queynte" (1.411).

77. Additional depth could be added by following through to the song of Troilus in book 5, where the star is lost to Troilus, and clearly parallel to the "lanterne" (in which Robertson sees such a "bitter" pun): "O thow lanterne of which queynt is the light" (5.543). See *A Preface to Chaucer* (Princeton: Princeton UP, 1962).

78. The lies are primarily those of Pandarus (e.g., of the "Greek espie," or his pretended interest in "yonder hous" to maneuver Criseyde into the window [2.1112, 2.1185–90]), but there are also the narrator's overarching fiction of Lollius as well as his smaller fabrications (e.g., of "every word right thus" of Troilus' song, where Lollius gives "only the sentence" [1.393–97]). See also Mark Lambert, "Telling the Story in *Troilus and Criseyde*," in Boitani and Mann 1986, 59–73.

79. I have in mind not only the precursor narratives already discussed to some extent, but as well, e.g., the feigned sickness of Troilus as a stratagem that allows access to Criseyde in book 2.

80. Most clear in this regard is the role of Pandarus. The consistent presentation of the researcher's gaze through gaps and intermittencies, however, should not be ignored (e.g., "thorugh a route," noted above, and in the celebrated window scenes [2.649–51, 2.1256]).

81. See Joseph A. Longo, "Apropos the Love Plot in Chaucer's *Troilus and Criseyde* and

Shakespeare's *Troilus and Cressida," Cahiers Elizabéthans* 11 (1977): 1–15. While in part the image is a commonplace by Chaucer's time, it is worth noting the significant symbolic recursion to the earlier epics discussed, especially since in its later manifestations it directly invokes the *Odyssey* (*Troilus and Criseyde* 5.638–44).

82. The fabricated father is investigated further in Chapter 4, in the similarly useful textual figure of James Macpherson's Ossian.

83. Mizener 1959, 349–50.

84. See, e.g., Curry 1960 and Mann, in Boitani and Mann 1986; for related work, especially as it applies to Criseyde, see, for example, David Aers, *Chaucer, Langland, and the Creative Imagination* (London: Routledge and Kegan Paul, 1980), 135–38; Dinshaw 1989, 3–18.

85. "The pattern of the story," obviously, relies on Chaucer's willingness to repeat that story for epic status, to "kis the steppes" of Virgil, Ovid, Homer, Lucan, and Statius (5.1791–92). Essentially I have in mind the same structural claustrophobia that informs Donaldson's (1983) "logic of fact" (as [incongruously enough] opposed to the "logic of love"); Lambert's "poetry of contract" as opposed to the "poetry of grace" (Boitani and Mann 1986, 66); and Jill Mann's metaphor of the tapestry in process of being woven, where all "necessitee" relies on one's perspective (Boitani and Mann 1986, 78–79).

86. Robinson points out that this incident is original with Chaucer's version.

87. Howard 1987, 373.

88. This also takes place in the *form* of the precursors—"Go, litel bok, go, litel myn tragedye."

89. This passage is often interpreted as a joke: Donaldson calls it an "outrageous inversion of morals" and the narrator's "excursion into farce" (1983, 95). In suggesting that the poet is not merely joking, nor simply denying his own responsibility for the tale as he has told it, I hope to arrive at a different reading of *Troilus and Criseyde*. In a poem that has involved such a textual wariness, and such a heightened awareness of the way "other bokes" or language itself form character, as well as interpretations of character or behavior, a reading that denies the worth of textual instructions (on behalf of the matter of the poem) in favor of the "correct" (because assumed) antifeminist moral seems unwise.

90. See also Robertson (1962) and Donaldson (1983), who suggest (with famously different emphases) that the distinction is between the charms of "pagan fable" and the contrasting lure of Christian morality.

91. Carolyn Dinshaw, in her "Quarrels, Rivals and Rape: Gower and Chaucer" delivered at MLA in Chicago, 1990, and in a more elaborate version read at Madison (February 1991), analyzes the textual figure of rape and the critical history of Chaucer's case of *raptus* as acts of "violent indifference" aimed at making coherent the identity of the Self through the erasure of the Other's subjectivity. The close of *Troilus and Criseyde*, not surprisingly, eschews physical assault in favor of the patriarchal rhetoric of abandonment and *contemptus;* the voyeuristic and hostile gaze upon "this wrecched world" thus becomes the mechanism of violence. Though Chaucer's attitude toward such a monolithic indifference is highly ambivalent, the ending of the epic threatens to do away with the dissonant "matere." The deliberate confusion of the ending's "linguistic apocalypse," however, does militate against a simple patriarchal reading.

92. This could be related to the increasing distance between Chaucer and his precursors, who come to him refracted through "sondry ages, / In sondry lands" (2.27–28).

93. The observation that "Toas" might be construed as a childlike mispronunciation of "Troilus" is interesting, but should not be stressed too heavily.

94. Janet Adelman, in Garner, Kahane, and Spregnether 1985, 134n17.

95. Dinshaw 1990, 1991.

96. Glancing ahead to Chapter 6 and H.D.'s *Helen in Egypt,* one might suggest it is in great part *because* of the heroine's earlier scriptedness that the poet is allowed such a strategy. Her destiny Chaucer leaves unstated, perhaps to allow the audience to write (or read) beyond the ending according to their chosen reading of the matter itself. Piero Boitani remarks on the ten-

dency of later writers to "finish" *Troilus and Criseyde* as an index to the unsatisfactory quality of the ending (1989, 299).

Chapter 4. Fierce Loves and Faithless Wars

1. Byron's *Don Juan* 7.8. All citations are from Leslie Marchand's edition (Boston: Houghton Mifflin, 1958).

2. An epic hero like Virgil's Aeneas, on the other hand, is left in his fragmented epic almost where he begins, caught between the conflicting, unfulfilled desires for an originary home on the one hand, and a future home, "this ever-receding Italy," on the other. "Completions" of the *Aeneid* (e.g., the fifteenth-century "Thirteenth Book" by Maffeo Vegio, which Gavin Douglas includes, with hesitation, in his translation) indicate that the poem's ending has long been perceived as unsatisfactory, fragmentary. The story of Virgil's deathbed instructions to burn the *Aeneid* performs a similar explanatory function. (The *Aeneid* could profitably be explained as an inverted epic as well. One writer, indeed, has already suggested that Virgil's epic is an enormous pun.)

3. The phrase is Peter Hägin's (1964), and he provides useful précis of a number of important "neoclassical" attempts at epic. A longer list of eighteenth-century epics may be found in R. D. Haven's *Influence of Milton on English Poetry* (Cambridge: Harvard UP, 1922).

4. Joseph A. Dane points out that the critical conception of parody only arises in the seventeenth and eighteenth centuries (12); the critical "literariness" of the genre as he describes it clearly connects, I think, to increasing literacy. See *Parody: Critical Concepts Versus Literary Practices, Aristophanes to Sterne* (Norman: University of Oklahoma Press, 1988).

5. Personal communication, November 1990. Homer's *centrality* to the conflict and the exaggerated antagonism or devotion to him and to the classical past, not the (certainly increasing) ascendancy of the Moderns, is the primary issue. As Donald Foerster makes clear, the alternating homage to and doubt of Homer is a hallmark of the "modern age." See especially the first chapter of his *Fortunes of Epic Poetry: A Study in English and American Criticism, 1750–1950* (Washington, DC: Catholic UP, 1962).

6. "Frangam Saxonicas Britonum sub Marte phalanges!" (*Mansus*, line 84). This, and all quotations from Milton (except as noted), are taken from *John Milton: Complete Poems and Major Prose*, ed. Merritt Y. Hughes (Indianapolis: Odyssey, 1957).

7. Joseph Spence, *Joseph Spence: Observations, Anecdotes, and Characters of Books and Men, Collected from Conversation*, ed. James M. Osborn (Oxford: Clarendon, 1966), 1:15. Byron's planned epic on Bosworth Field and the satiric results in *Don Juan* make an appropriate later example.

8. *Selected Poetry and Prose of John Dryden*, ed. Earl Miner (New York: Random House, 1969), 112. It is this attitude that Richard Blackmore complains of in his preface to *Alfred*: "I should be glad to know what Gentlemen mean when they affirm that nothing is to be admitted into the Poem we are discoursing of, but Action. Sure they cannot think that we are to be entertained there only with Musters, Camps, Battles, and Sieges. If this were a true maxim, it would exclude the greatest Part of Homer's Ulysses and of Virgil's Aenead." See *Alfred: An Epick Poem in Twelve Books* (London, 1723), 30.

9. *The Task* 1.1, *Selected Poems of William Cowper*, ed. Nick Rhodes (Manchester: Fyfield-Carcanet, 1984).

10. See G. Douglas Watkins, *Quests of Difference: Reading Pope's Poems* (Lexington: University Press of Kentucky, 1986), 138–45; also George M Ridenour, on Byron and Pope shifting from "the 'high' and 'heroic' in favor of the 'low' and 'true' " in "My Poem's Epic," in Yu 1973, 311.

11. See, e.g., Watkins 1986; Ellen Messer-Davidow, " 'For Softness She': Gender Ideology and Aesthetics in Eighteenth-Century England," in *Eighteenth-Century Women and the Arts*, ed. Frederick M. Keener and Susan E. Lorsch (Westport, CT: Greenwood, 1990); Ellen Pollak, *The*

Poetics of Sexual Myth: Gender and Ideology in the Verse of Swift and Pope (Chicago: University of Chicago Press, 1985), 22–76.

12. Macpherson, writing as a Scot and a Highlander, had a significantly higher opinion of martial action than many of the English. Ploughing and sowing grain were (then as now) typical of Lowland (or English) life, and therefore unheroic in the extreme.

13. With regard to the massive social changes taking place in England, Laslett points to (among other things) the effects of "National war, conscription and disbandment," the increased "social mobility" available in industrialized society (1971, 184), as well as the increase in literacy.

14. Even in translation as a form of epic recursion, the concerns of the younger poet can be only too clear. The epigraph, Dryden's translation of the Virgilian *tum virgam capit* ["then he takes the wand"] (*Aeneid* 4.242), shows an overcompensating inflation of the phallic signifier of Mercury that is "comic," as L. Proudfoot comments in his excellent study of *Dryden's Aeneid and its Seventeenth Century Predecessors* (Manchester: The University Press, 1960). It is well to note with Proudfoot that this is "one of his [Dryden's] *most* pompous expansions" (45; my emphasis).

15. This contrast, in Augustan poetry, at least, is graphically evoked by Peter Hughes in a review for *Eighteenth-Century Studies* 22.1 (Fall 1988): 78, where "a bulimic passion for the consuming and voiding of genres and subjects" is balanced by the "ventriloquist mockery of the voice of the bard out of the poet's own mouth."

16. Elizabeth Wright, *Psychoanalytic Criticism: Theory in Practice* (1984. London: Methuen, 1987), 138. By my formulation of this "double-tongued" aspect of literature as analogous to the "double movement" of jokes, I do not mean to imply that Milton's *Paradise Lost,* or any other work of literature, is only a "joke" in the usual sense. I am interested in the Freudian formulation as useful to an explanation of texts.

17. See Freud 1905a, 41–42, for his summary of primarily linguistic contrasts in jokes. Though the example that springs readily to mind is the parodic contrast of God and Satan in Milton's poem, this doubling of discourse is more clearly seen in close parodies of epic: the *Pelerinage de Charlemagne,* or Paul Scarron's *Vergile Travesti;* English examples might be John Philips's parodic Miltonisms in *The Splendid Shilling,* or Henry Reed's parody of Eliot in *Chard Whitlow.*

18. I should not be taken as saying that parody is neither enjoyable, nor worthwhile. Skillfully done, it can be as playfully "loving" as any translation; in its recursion, it is clearly affirmative as well as critical of the precursor.

19. See, e.g., Jonathan Culler, *Structuralist Poetics* (Ithaca: Cornell UP, 1975), 152–53; J. A. Cuddon, *A Dictionary of Literary Terms* (London: Andre Deutsch, 1977), where the "calculated and analytic technique" of parody uses its "subversive mimicry"; and Dane 1988, 5–12.

20. George Steiner, in a review of D. Weissbort's *Translating Poetry: The Double Labyrinth* (Iowa City: University of Iowa Press, 1989), remarks on translation as an act "at once loving and somewhat desperate" (*Times* [London], 3 December 1989). The fuller study of the translator as poetic child of the parental text remains to be written.

21. Joseph Spence 1966, 1:15. Pope's early epic *Alcander* (burned at an early reader's behest) similarly contained "all the beauties of all the great writers of the past."

22. As Cuddon notes, pastiche may be a "serious and loving" attempt to create a new text, or alternately may be "disrespectful and deflationary," highlighting ambiguities implicit in the original. This latter becomes a dominant practice in the documentary style of much twentieth-century epic, though increasingly the originary text is that of history rather than that of the poetic tradition.

23. *Timber, or Discoveries,* in *Seventeenth-Century English Prose,* ed. Mary R. Mahl (New York: J. B. Lippincott, 1968: 114–30), 129.

24. For Bate, see, e.g., "The English Poet and the Burden of the Past, 1660–1820," in *Aspects of the Eighteenth Century,* ed. Earl R. Wassermann (London: Oxford UP, 1965), 245–64.

25. Howard Weinbrot, "William Collins and the Mid-Century Ode: Poetry, Patriotism, and the Influence of Context," in *Context, Influence, and Mid-Eighteenth-Century Poetry,* ed. Howard Weinbrot and Andrew Price (Los Angeles: William Andrews Clark Memorial Library, 1990: 1–39), 4.

26. William Hayley, *An Essay on Epic Poetry,* facsimile reproduction with introduction by Sister M. Celeste Williamson, S.S.J. (1782. Gainesville, FL: Scholars' Facsimiles and Reprints, 1968). Ian Watt's *Rise of the Novel* outlines several continuing influences: increasing power of what he calls the "middle classes," ongoing industrialization and concomitant forms of alienation, the Cartesian splitting of *res cogitans* and *res extensa* (Berkeley: University of California Press, 1957), 9–59. Elizabeth L. Eisenstein, in *The Printing Press as an Agent of Change,* emphasizes the ongoing democratizing influence of the specific technology of movable type, and the proliferation of the printing press, as having a significant impact on poetic creativity (Cambridge: Cambridge UP, 1983).

27. Even so publicly invested a poet as Jonson, of course, realized the differences of status implicit in genre and in the audience he approached: "Make not thyself a page to that strumpet, the stage; But sing high and aloof, Safe from the Wolf's black jaw, and the dull Ass's hoof." See "An Ode: To Himself," in *Ben Jonson,* ed. Ian Donaldson (Oxford: Oxford UP, 1985), 343–44.

28. In English, primarily. Classical education, like epic poetry, remained the preserve of a very small elite, consisting of the "possessing minority" and those close to them in the social structure (Laslett 182). Despite Johnson's opinion that England had become "a nation of readers," the most generous estimates suppose that half a million people, less than 10 percent of the population, were even newspaper literate (Watt 1957, 35–37).

29. Jonson 1968, 116–17.

30. College students today are still somewhat shocked by the "lack of originality" or "plagiarism" in Chaucer's and Shakespeare's use of preexisting stories. The lines quoted are from *Beowulf* (1) and from Pope's *Essay on Criticism* (293). All quotations from Pope, except as noted, are from John Butt's one-volume version of the Twickenham edition, *The Poems of Alexander Pope* (New Haven: Yale UP, 1963).

31. Thomas Greene remarks in his study of Renaissance epic on the inevitable burden of imitating Virgil that devolved onto poets from Petrarch to Milton. See *The Descent from Heaven: A Study in Epic Continuity* (New Haven: Yale UP, 1963).

32. See, e.g., Dryden on the importance of conveying "the spirit of an author" in "Preface to Ovid's Epistles," in *John Dryden: Selected Criticism,* ed. James Kinsley and George Parfitt (Oxford: Clarendon, 1970), 179–88. See also his "Preface to Fables, Ancient and Modern" and the end of his "Discourse on Satire." There are, of course, cases where the translation is thought to exceed the original. These can be rather idiosyncratic, as in Ezra Pound's preference for Douglas's *Eneados* over Virgil's original, because Douglas "had heard the sea." Regardless, the necessary recurrence to an originary text urges us to see the translator as secondary, as belated to that original.

33. This double-bind is certainly not restricted to the seventeenth and eighteenth centuries. See, e.g., Greene, for a similar dynamic throughout the Renaissance (1963, 3–8). However, given the "will to epic" characteristic of some principal seventeenth- and eighteenth-century poets, and the similarity of their actual texts in relation to their epic precursors, these statements can be seen as applying with special force to those centuries.

34. Alexander Pope, "Preface to the Translation of the *Iliad,*" in *Eighteenth-Century Critical Essays,* ed. Scott Elledge (Ithaca: Cornell UP, 1961), 1.266.

35. Charles Gildon, *The Laws of Poetry* (London, 1721). See also Joseph Addison, *The Spectator,* 5 January 1712, 9 February 1712. For readings of Milton's ironic attitude toward tradition, see, among many others, Hägin 1964; T. J. B. Spencer, "Paradise Lost: The Anti-Epic," in *Approaches to Paradise Lost,* ed. C. A. Patrides (London, 1968), 81–98.

36. Coleridge, for example, suggests that "John Milton himself is in every line of *Paradise Lost,*" cited in Tulsi Ram, *The Neo-Classical Epic (1650–1720): An Ethical and Historical Interpreta-*

tion (Delhi: National Publishing, 1971), 83; see also Denis Saurat's similar thesis in his *Milton, Man and Thinker* (1946. London: Archon, 1964). In the same vein is Stephen J. Nimis's section on Milton in *Narrative Semiotics in the Epic Tradition: The Simile* (Bloomington: Indiana UP, 1987): "What propels *Paradise Lost* forward is language's inexhaustible 'interpretability' or 'readability,' its capacity for unlimited displacement and deferral" (175).

37. This trend develops further in the "personal epics" of the nineteenth and twentieth centuries, where the poet, more than a bit like Ossian, becomes the primary protagonist.

38. Pope, "Preface to the Translation of the *Iliad*," 1.263.

39. Charles Gildon, *The Complete Art of Poetry* (London, 1718), 1.269.

40. Though the Scandinavian king Swaran's attempt at usurpation of rule in Ireland is significant, this is underlain, as Macpherson notes, by the earlier love of Fingal and Agandecca (Swaran's sister), and her death at her father Starno's hand, related at the beginning of book 3.

41. William Kerrigan, *The Sacred Complex: On the Psychogenesis of Paradise Lost* (Cambridge: Harvard UP, 1983), 6.

42. E. M. W. Tillyard, *Milton* (1930. Rev. ed., New York: Collier, 1966), 246. As Tulsi Ram reminds us, Tillyard shifts his ground remarkably following World War II.

43. For a brief survey of the principal identifications, see J. B. Broadbent, *Some Graver Subject: An Essay on Paradise Lost* (London: Chatto and Windus, 1960); the section on Satan (70–80) is usefully reprinted in the Norton edition of *Paradise Lost*, ed. Scott Elledge (New York: Norton, 1975), 460–68.

44. According to William Cunningham's *Cosmographical Glasse*, 1559 (in Milton 226n).

45. The primary myth evoked here is that of Alpheus and Arethusa, which in *Lycidas* as well as in this passage is connected with the question of poetic succession and inspiration. For more discussion of this passage and ways in which Satan continues to "muddy the waters of the source" (212), see David Quint's *Origin and Originality in Renaissance Literature* (New Haven: Yale UP, 1983), 207–20. Much of his book pertains to my argument as it focuses on the progressive development of "originality" as a newly enshrined "source of authority" (220).

46. Noteworthy in Satan's "final" repression within the epic is its lack of finality; far from complete eradication, he is instead dissolved into the landscape, becoming the soul, as it were, of the "universal Hiss"; like Milton's God (in Empson's controversial reading of the epic), Satan becomes immanent, implicit in the very dust of earth until the end of Time (when "God shall be All in All" [*PL* 3.341]). See William Empson, *Milton's God* (Norfolk, CT: New Directions, 1961), 132–33. See also Hughes's headnotes (Milton 1957, 194): "[M]an's spiritual root and perfecting character are both said to end in heaven." His quotation from the theologian William Ames is particularly apt to Milton's organicist view of life and art: "all natural things tend to God."

47. Christopher Kendrick, "Milton and Sexuality: A Symptomatic Reading of Comus," in *Re-Membering Milton: Essays on the Texts and Traditions* (New York and London: Methuen, 1987: 43–73), 49.

48. See the discussion of this, Milton's Arminian heresy, in James Holly Hanford and James G. Taaffe, *A Milton Handbook* (1954. 5th ed., New York: Meredith, 1970), 191–94.

49. The old analogy used against this argument—that a person knowing a train will strike an object does not thereby cause the train to strike it—is fallacious. The observer has no power over the situation, and does not *know* the train will strike the object, but *assumes* it will, based upon the customary law of relation between cause and effect. But the viewer's perceptions are radically faulty (unlike God's), and his or her power drastically limited.

50. Edward Young, *Conjectures on Original Composition* (London, 1759).

51. *The Complete Works of William Hazlitt*, ed. P. P. Howe (London: J. M. Dent, 1930), 5:15. By "settled" I have in mind the findings and decisions of the 1805 Committee; many enthusiasts remained convinced the poems were genuine.

52. Boswell continues: "He said Mrs. Sheridan and he had fixed it as the standard of feeling. . . . 'These poems give us great light into the history of mankind. We could not imagine

that such sentiments of delicacy as well as generosity could have existed in the breasts of rude, uncultivated people' " (1950, 182).

53. The parallel with Byron is striking; an additional, and clearly related kinship, as Roderick Watson points out in *The Literature of Scotland* (London: Macmillan, 1984), is that of Ossian (and Macpherson) with the "noble savage" of Rousseau (188).

54. Samuel Weber, *The Legend of Freud* (Minneapolis: University of Minnesota Press, 1982), 80.

55. Despite the apparent preeminence of such jokes in their accession of "nonsense" and "the original sources of verbal pleasure," Freud refuses to admit them to serious discussion of legitimate jokes—in much the same way that he laments the hermetically sealed personal worlds of those with narcissistic psychoses (1914, 75ff.). Freud puts this in stronger terms in the 1917 lecture on "Libido Theory and Narcissism" (1966, 422–25).

56. This solution is one that still finds adequate representation in the numerous hoaxes of our own century, of course, as well as in the tendency toward the hermeticism of "secret narratives" in modernist and contemporary long poems (e.g., the esoterica of Eliot, Pound, and [in his own way] Williams, or the opacity of [still widely divergent] works by John Ashbery, Lyn Hejinian, and Blake Morrison).

57. Anthony Grafton, *Forgers and Critics: Creativity and Duplicity in Western Scholarship* (Princeton: Princeton UP, 1990), 37–40; see also H. R. Trevor-Roper, "Wrong but Romantic," *Spectator* (16 March 1985): 14–15.

58. Recent scholarship (notably Fiona Stafford 1988, who offers the first booklength attempt at a reading of the poems) has begun to refocus our attention on important aspects of Macpherson's work. Like Bailey Saunders's *Life and Letters* (1894), Stafford's work tends toward biography rather than the textual, since she is still engaged in settling the ghosts of the controversy. More recent is Paul J. de Gategno's *James Macpherson* (Boston: Twayne, 1988), which offers brief readings of individual compositions. Unfortunately, his arch Johnsonian bias is not balanced by an awareness of Stafford's work. David Quint's excellent *Epic and Empire* (1993) addresses the Ossian phenomenon briefly in its concluding chapter, in a historical analysis troubled only by the problematic thesis of epics by "winners" and "losers" (343–61). Joseph Bysveen's study of parallels between Homer's *Iliad* and *Fingal* is cogent but limited, and it too finds necessary a rehearsal of the issues of fraudulence (*Epic Tradition and Innovation in James Macpherson's Fingal* [Stockholm: Uppsala, 1982]). See also Ian Haywood, *The Making of History: A Study of the Literary Forgeries of James Macpherson and Thomas Chatterton in Relation to Eighteenth-Century Ideas of History and Fiction* (Cranbury, NJ: Associated University Presses, 1986).

59. A phrase used of him by numerous contemporaries.

60. Henry Mackenzie, ed., *Report of the Committee of the Highland Society of Scotland* (Edinburgh, 1805). Such reconstruction has been particularly facile in its construals of various testimonies, depending on (usually) a view of the character of the witness. As noteworthy as usual among early commentators is Samuel Johnson: "he told [his host, minister of Kilmuir, Dr.] Macqueen flatly that he did not believe his . . . testimony. . . . When Macqueen took no notice of this affront, Johnson supposed himself to have hit the right nail upon the head; 'he wished me,' said he, 'to be deceived for the honour of his country, but would not directly and formally deceive me' " (Saunders 1894, 243). See also Johnson's *Journey to the Western Islands of Scotland*, ed. Mary Lascelles (New Haven: Yale UP, 1971), 118. At the outset, Johnson appears to have believed that there was, in Saunders's phrase, "a national conspiracy of falsehood" among the Scots. There was little, it appears, that could have changed his mind. On the other extreme there is the enduring naiveté of William Blake, who penned in 1826, in his "Annotations to Wordsworth," "I Believe both Macpherson & Chatterton, that what they say is Ancient Is so" (cited in Stafford 1988, 77).

61. Specifically, Macpherson appears to have used some fourteen or fifteen ballads: The principal sources for the plot include *Garbh mac Stairn* and the *Magnus* ballads. Thomson pro-

vides full and clear discussion in *The Gaelic Sources of Macpherson's "Ossian"* (Edinburgh: Oliver and Boyd, 1952).

62. Thomson 1952, 84. The Gaelic "originals" of Ossian so long demanded were finally published in 1807, and were not of a character to assuage any doubt or engage any new converts. See Saunders (1894, 303–17), and Maclean, "On the Gaelic Poetry of known and unknown Bards, Published and Traditional," in William Sharp's (1924) edition of the poems. Watson (1984) describes how oral poets of the Highlands (e.g., John MacCodrum) "did not fit Macpherson's idea of the 'antique sublime,' singing instead about village events, etc." (199).

63. A facsimile is readily available in the series of the Augustan Reprint Society (number 122 [1966]), and it is from this text all quotations will be cited. Macpherson's statement to similar effect in the preface to his *Iliad*, that he has "translated the Greek VERBATIM" (1773, xix) is surprisingly brassy, suggesting the inflation of ego consequent upon his early achievement of fame.

64. Alfred Nutt, in his introduction to *original* Ossianic ballad literature of the Scottish Highlands, has only one pithy (and pertinent) remark to make concerning Macpherson's use of that source: "[H]e worked up many of its themes into his English Ossian, which is, however, almost as much his own composition as 'Paradise Lost' is the composition of Milton." See *Ossian and the Ossianic Literature* (1899. Rpt., New York: AMS, 1972), 2.

65. See Thomson 1952, 3–7, and Watson 1984, 198–99. That Macpherson took strong exception to actual oral style is suggested in his few statements concerning the difficulties of transcribing recitations in the Highlands. In a similar vein, a writer in the *Critical Review* of March 1773 lambasted Macpherson's *Iliad* for its liberties with the original: among other things, for his numerous and various translations of κορυθαιολος ("with glancing helm"), one of Hektor's formulaic epithets (cited in Saunders 1894, 223).

66. See Stafford 1988, 165, and Haywood 1986, 24–26.

67. Cited in Dunn's introduction to the *Fragments* (1760, vi). Laing (1805), on the other hand, points to the use of prose as the principal reason that Macpherson's "plagiarism" was not detected with more certainty and immediacy.

68. The now-conventional supposition that epic poetry gave way to the more "realistic" prose of the eighteenth-century novel is more fantasy than fact. In the most noteworthy proposal that the novel could be an "epic in prose" (in Fielding's *Joseph Andrews*) the statement is largely ironic; like parodic epic forms such as Harington's *Ajax* or Jonson's *Famous Voyage*, it makes no claim to real stature within the elite tradition of epos. (As Fielding explains, the low social standing of the characters leads to the choice of comic action and of prose as a medium.) Fielding's focus on the grand ancestry of the comic novel in the *Margites*, the lost comic epic that Aristotle attributes to Homer, suggests his awareness of the invisibility, the practical nonexistence, of his own work as acceptably epic; as a strategic evasion as well as adoption of the precursor, it is a whimsical "mis-reading" akin to Macpherson's. Rather than "ghost-writing" for, or reinscribing the blind bard himself, Fielding recurs to a ghostly text. See also P. J. H. Titlestad, "The English Epic," in Geoffrey Cronjé, ed., *Die Epos* (Pretoria: J. L. van Schaik, 1970), 75.

69. See Wallace Cable Brown, *The Triumph of Form* (1948. Westport, CT: Greenwood, 1973); William Bowman Piper, *The Heroic Couplet* (London: Case Western Reserve UP, 1969).

70. That Ossian's diction was to become, as Dunn points out, "the staple diction of the greater Romantic lyric" (1760, viii) is not surprising. "Democratic" is perhaps the wrong word for a poem about monarchs, but "populist" might be more accurate, with the usual suspicions accorded to such politics. Pertinent anecdotal evidence exists in the report that Napoleon carried his Ossian with him on campaigns.

71. Though Macpherson was born in Scotland, he is *writing* in London, for an English audience.

72. The ill success of Lord Bute (Macpherson's patron, but also Tory, Jacobite, and Scot),

whose Ministry followed that of the famous Pitt, helped matters little. The reactions of the Irish (from whom Macpherson had "stolen" national heroes) were as vociferous as those of the English. But typically enough, the outcries from that country were ignored.

73. "The Influence of Ossian," *English* 7 (1948): 96. It is, naturally, difficult to be precise about such a matter. Meyerstein is clearly speaking of twentieth-century poetic form.

74. Possibly many more, but no fewer than five such "re-translations" of the six books of *Fingal* alone were published in the late eighteenth and early nineteenth centuries.

75. See Donald S. Taylor, *Thomas Chatterton's Art: Experiments in Imagined History* (Princeton: Princeton UP, 1978); see also Haywood 1986, 121.

76. Laing points out the testimonial letter of George Laurie, minister of London (18 January 1782): "One great argument he used against the printing them [the *Fragments*] was, That his Highland pride was alarmed at appearing to the world only as a translator" (1805, xv). Moreover, it seems that as he became more deeply involved with the establishment himself, Macpherson "sold out" (to some degree) to establishment attitudes. See, for example, the conclusion to his *Rights of Great Britain Asserted Against the Claims of America* (London, 1776 [2d ed.]): "The law of God and Nature is on the side of an indulgent Parent, against an undutiful Child; and should necessary correction render him incapable of future offence, he has only his own obstinacy and folly to blame" (80).

77. This from a man who translates θεα γλαυκωπις Αθηνη (*Iliad* 1.206)—the bright-eyed goddess Athena—as "the blue-eyed maid." Rightly enough, Macpherson's *Iliad* was scathingly reviewed. As Donald M. Foerster notes, "almost every literary man rose in indignation." See *Homer in English Criticism: The Historical Approach in the Eighteenth Century* (1947. Hamden CT: Archon, 1969), 67–68.

78. Stafford provides a good case for Macpherson's idealization of both the Highland culture of his childhood and the remote "primitive" past under the aegis of his education at Aberdeen. Moreover, Macpherson had seen enough evidence of the futility of words and action for these notions to make a great deal of sense to him: At nine years old he observed the consequences to his own clan of the 1745 rebellion and its bloody aftermath in the Highlands, and at Aberdeen he learned of the continuing dissection of classical epic and heroism; hence his desire for fame in the person of Ossian is equivocal, ambivalent.

79. The tale is that of Grudar and Cairbar, who "strove for the spotted bull." Grudar's sister, who secretly loved Cairbar, dies of grief after she discovers his death (1924, 47–48).

80. Dryden, "Discourse on Satire," *Selected Criticism*, 278.

81. An alternate strategy is used in Spenser's *Faerie Queene*, where the *katabasis* is fragmented (like the ideal virtuous character and the epic itself).

82. That the ghosts of the ancestors maintained an existence on earth is familiar from Celtic mythology. But they have additional and significant roles in *Fingal*, both as manifestations of the "epic underworld" as outlined above and as an echo of (and typical reaction against) the "machinery" of epic. Divine intervention in particular was seen as detracting from the virtue of the hero it aided.

83. That the "dark red stream of fire" should be seen as a meteor is apparent from Macpherson's note (1924, 49) on the long-held "opinions of the ancient Scots."

84. Lattimore translates the passage from the *Iliad* where Patroklos appears "all in his likeness for stature, and the lovely eyes, and voice, [wearing] such clothing as Patroklos had worn" (23.66–67).

85. The phallic metaphor could be followed further, of course, examining the "curling head" of the spirit here more closely.

86. Noted there, following Alford, were the narcissist's "grandiosity and fragile self-esteem," the recursive withdrawal from interaction, the lack of a rigid superego, frequent feelings of emptiness and isolation, of not being real, of being an observer of one's own life. Though the narcissist functions socially at a relatively high level, the cost of such functioning is a rigid self-structure, highly resistant to change.

87. Among the *Fragments,* however, some are dialogues related by the two lovers, and more often, by the female lover of the slain youth before she too expires.

88. The *Iliad* provides a good contrast. The deeds of youthful Achilles are sung, as occasionally in *Fingal,* but they are in no way overshadowed by the warlike deeds of the old. Moreover, the youthful figures in Homer most frequently have their own voices, where in *Fingal* the young are consistently inscribed by the aged bards.

89. See, e.g., *Paradise Regain'd* 3.43–108, 4.285–364.

90. As before, my use of a word such as "duplicitous" is not designed to invoke a moral judgment of any kind. Duplicity—the double state of being "like, and not like"—is the human condition.

Chapter 5. With Half Unravel'd Web

1. When these labels denote modes rather than periods they can be useful in application, if not in terminology. As chronological divisions, they obscure more than they illuminate.

2. As Valéry points out, a poem is never finished, merely abandoned.

3. Most epics at least gesture toward a Golden Age: Hrothgar's Heorot before the coming of Grendel, Troy before the Fall, Eden, etc.

4. Epics based in teleologies might more properly be considered "unfinished," in the sense developed by Balachandra Rajan's *Form of the Unfinished* (1985). "Fragment," a more general term, may connote for too many readers an unexpressed whole, but "unfinished" seems even more clearly based on an eventual "finished" quality. (Rajan's observation that "finished" is not a desirable state for contemporary public figures seems beside the point [1985, 7].) The term becomes especially puzzling when he applies it to a poem such as *Paradise Lost* (among "the most militantly organized [poems] in the language" [126]). As he points out, Milton's epic "achieves closure only by placing a completed structure of understanding around a deeply uncertain outcome" (3). This "completed structure of understanding" is in fact the only determinant of closure, the reader's, and while it is one which Rajan nods to briefly, he fails to privilege the reader sufficiently. A vital aspect of the fragment is its engagement with the reader, an aspect made particularly clear in the following passage from Rajan: "Incomplete poems are poems which ought to be completed. Unfinished poems are poems which ask not to be finished, which carry within themselves the reasons for arresting or effacing themselves as they do. If an unfinished poem were to be finished it would ideally erase its own significance" (1985, 14). The language of "ought to be" and "asking" alerts you to a central problem of fragment-criticism: It tends to ignore or avoid the issue of the audience's power to make or unmake the fragment. But the "fragmented" quality of any epic is most evident in its relation to its audiences; I have tried to remain aware of this in my selections and discussions of texts.

5. Even this simple construction allows a useful division of epic, placing the greater part of British epic of the nineteenth and twentieth centuries in the former, and the mass of American epic (or colonial epic in general) of those centuries within the latter, utopian vision. Such a framework quickly becomes problematic, however. While Barlow's *Columbiad* and Crane's *Bridge* aim toward a utopian vision of history, we could not so easily adduce Pound's *Cantos* or Williams's *Paterson.* These, though they have their utopian moments, maintain (arguably) a steadier emphasis on past forms of union—the age of Confucius or magical Ecbatan in the *Cantos,* or the originary, undivided "marriage" of city and land in *Paterson.*

6. Anne F. Janowitz, "Parts and Wholes: Romantic and Modernist Fragment Poems," unpublished Ph.D. dissertation (Stanford University, 1983).

7. All citations from Hart Crane's works will be from Brom Weber's convenient edition of *The Complete Poems and Selected Letters and Prose of Hart Crane* (Garden City, NY: Anchor-Doubleday, 1966), unless otherwise noted. This is not simply Romantic extremism, as Crane's use of "hypothetical" demonstrates. Though Crane speaks elsewhere of *The Bridge* as "an act of faith" (231), he sees this faith as a conscious delusion: "The form of my poem rises out of a past

that so overwhelms the present with its worth and vision that I'm at a loss to explain my delusion that there exist any real links between that past and a future destiny worthy of it. The 'destiny' is long since completed" (231–32).

8. "The Dance" is read so even by a critic as perceptive as Thomas E. Yingling. He paraphrases Crane's diction of Pocahontas's flesh as mythic smoky soil: "[H]ere we are on the pure, mythical, and smoky soil of heterosexual union and fertility seen as the natural anthropological origin of human community. The poem rehearses a sky-god/earth-goddess fertility rite, the dance of the title, and is a primal scene in both a Freudian and anthropological sense" (1990, 219).

9. Pocahontas repeatedly figures in *The Bridge* as "the mythological nature-symbol chosen to represent the physical body of the continent, or the soil" (Crane, 248).

10. The critical supposition that no white people appear in this section is surprising, to say the least. See, e.g., Edward Brunner, *Splendid Failure* (Urbana: University of Illinois Press, 1985), 160, and Yingling 1990, 252.

11. In an early letter to his father (5 January 1917), Crane comments on his central fascination with two powerful forces, striving together. See *Letters of Hart Crane and His Family*, ed. Thomas S. Lewis (New York: Columbia UP, 1974), 21–22. Virgil's simile of serpent and eagle (book 11) springs to mind (where Camilla's gendered heroics spur the enigmatic encounter of Tarchon and Venulus), especially because of Crane's reuse of the same image in *The Bridge*.

12. There are critics who imagine that "redemption" is prophesied in Eliot's poem. I find such arguments unconvincing, though indeed delusive hints of such unity cast a long shadow in the poem. This may, as Rajan suggests, show Eliot "establish[ing] the reality of that wholeness through the ineradicable notations of its absence" (17), but in 1922, at least, Eliot seems not to condone such paralogical argument.

13. Janowitz 1983. The quotation is from her abstract.

14. Rajan's understanding of the "classic" or "major unfinished" is based in the traditionally and transcendentally justified "privileging whole" of teleological poets such as Spenser and Milton (1990, 15).

15. The poem is closely related, as many scholars have suggested, to Keats's focus on the evolving self as developed in his letters on the "Vale of Soul-Making" and the "Mansion of Many Apartments." These and other important letters are conveniently found in Douglas Bush's edition of the *Selected Poems and Letters of John Keats* (Boston: Houghton Mifflin, 1959), 274, 287–90. These two letters, in particular, have been a consistent recourse as glosses on the fragmentary epics.

16. Unless otherwise noted, I have used Elizabeth Cook's edition of *John Keats* (Oxford: Oxford UP, 1990).

17. In his letters, the traditionally "epic" appears in contrast to the "human" (e.g., 4 June 1819).

18. Lyn Hejinian, *My Life* (Los Angeles: Sun and Moon, 1987), 113.

19. Body and poem differ less than we might think: Both are (adaptively) postulated as "unities" by the perceiving mind as it "reads" its specular image in mirror or text.

20. I defined the "self" earlier in this study as a conceptual label for a constelled set of conceptions and perceptions. In his exploration of the mirror stage as "formative of the function of the I," Lacan extends this commonsensical but radically fragmentary notion of the human subject into infancy, outlining a masterplot: It is a "drama" that "situates the agency of the ego, before its social determination, in a fictional direction" (1977, 2). Lacan's fullest discussion of this development of the fictional self is found in his essay on "the mirror-stage," but his key term for this necessary errancy (*méconnaissance*) is elaborated upon in "Aggressivity in Psychoanalysis" (1977).

21. The phrase "Coming-into-being" is from *le devenir*. The process is a "drama which manufactures for the subject, caught up in the lure of spatial identification, the succession of

phantasies that extends from a fragmented body-image to a form of its totality that I shall call orthopaedic—and, lastly, to the assumption of an armour of an alienating identity, which will mark with its rigid structure the subject's entire mental development. Thus, to break out of the circle of the Innenwelt into the Umwelt generates the inexhaustible quadrature of the ego's verifications" (Lacan 1977, 4).

22. While "orthopaedic" in its root sense means "right-educating" or "rightly formative," Lacan's periphrastic use of the term and his general ambivalence toward such "rightnesses" remind us that these formative images are "right" only insofar as they are adequate to a particular cultural matrix.

23. In waking thought these symbols are realized in "the structure of fortified works, the metaphor of which arises spontaneously, as if issuing from the symptoms themselves" (Lacan 1977, 5). See also "Aggressivity in Psychoanalysis" (1977, 13).

24. The innumerable forms this construction takes (in Spenser alone) have been the object of substantial discussion. The continuing transformations in the *topos* are especially intriguing, including not only the bridges of Crane and Stewart Brown (*Lugard's Bridge*), but the protective shell (the "home") of animals presented as emblems of poetic identity such as the shellfish in H.D.'s *Trilogy*, or the snail in Peter Jenkins's more recent *Greenheart*.

25. These are from chivalric romance, but primarily such materials are refracted through Crane's reading of Marlowe and Shakespeare (e.g., in "bedlamite"). Paul Giles's (1986) work with puns in the poem pays attention to the medievalizing diction. Harvey Gross, among others, points out Crane's affiliation with the Elizabethan dramatists in *Sound and Form in Modern Poetry* (Ann Arbor: University of Michigan Press, 1964), 219.

26. Lacan makes a compelling case for the exacerbation of these images under the aegis of the subject's desperate maintenance of the self, particularly in the case of paranoia.

27. The castration implicit in "speechless" would appear to apply only to the crowd; as Freud points out, however, the fulfillment of scopophilic desire implicit in the "spectacle" is not either seeing or being seen, but both at once.

28. "Homosexual," as we define it today, must be understood as an invention of the late nineteenth century (the *OED* lists 1892 as a date for the first usage of the term). The chief poets I have in mind here are Whitman and Crane, though certainly earlier epic poets were homoerotically engaged. Homosocial desire "between men," as Eve Kosofsky Sedgwick shows (1985), affects literature quite thoroughly. In part, this book demonstrates the broader recursive forms of that desire, while trying to avoid the naive idea that such recursive desire is entirely benign.

29. So C. S. Lewis speaks of Spenser in the "armour" of the Italian romancers (1936, 304). Appropriate not only to the current discussion, but to the entire essay, it indicates both blessing and bane in the poet's inheritance of a heavily armored genre.

30. Elizabeth J. Bellamy provides a more thorough examination of both Lacan and the armorial signifiers of epic (in Virgil and Ariosto) in the excellent third chapter of her *Translations of Power* (1992, 82–130), pointing to the increasing elaboration of weaponry in connection with identity—"the weapon as fetish object for the individual ego" (83).

31. This transfer opens toward a new construction of identity as well—the new arms and the uncomfortable restoration of Achilles to the Greek forces.

32. C. M. Bowra, *From Vergil to Milton* (Oxford: Clarendon, 1949), 65.

33. In Fitzgerald's translation: "All these images on Vulcan's shield, / His mother's gift, were wonders to Aeneas. / Knowing nothing of the events themselves, / He felt joy in the pictures, taking up / Upon his shoulder all the destined acts / And fame of his descendants."

34. Though I draw brief attention to it here and elsewhere, the recurrent role of the maternal figure as the apparent agent of patriarchal law—the teacher of the "mother tongue"—deserves fuller explication throughout the epic tradition.

35. "Unspeakable" is the recurrent epithet given to the sufferings of Aeneas (the fall of

Troy, the wanderings, the civil wars); in this analysis, it seems they are "unspeakable" because of their relative untranslatability into the patriarchal language of destiny, that fate which has already been textually ordained.

36. Steele Commager, ed., *Virgil: A Collection of Critical Essays* (Englewood Cliffs, NJ: Prentice-Hall, 1966), 6.

37. Ibid., 11.

38. See also Adam Parry 1989, 86–87.

39. Moreover, the fiction itself covers an unstable history, the different point of origin current in Rome before Virgil, and one that remains related to our understanding of the City, as opposed to the Empire: the strife between brothers, Romulus and Remus. This strife echoes the civil wars familiar to Virgil from childhood, and it is one of the unstable sources of the poem which the fiction of Aeneas attempts to heal. Virgil represses this story largely by placing the action of his poem four hundred years earlier. But this repressed version of the story recurs in the continued metonymic violence of civil war (including the killing—twice—of figures named Remulus).

40. The extreme case of such a slippage—a slippage that becomes inversion—occurs in *Paradise Lost,* where armor functions almost exclusively as an intensifier of damage, an entrapment of the combatants in their broken shells: "Thir armor help'd thir harm, crush't in and bruis'd / Into thir substance pent, which wrought them pain / Implacable" (4.656–58). The best defense (according to Milton) is no defense: Arms are the "argument / Of human weakness rather than of strength" (*Paradise Regain'd* 4.401–2). The same inversive strategy displays armor as a troubling emblem of identity in the simile of Satan's shield.

41. A similar dissonance exists between the incomplete Prince Arthur and his shield (another textual version of the law of the father). Arthur is "incomplete" because only human, only prince, only the fragmented topic of an unfinished epic, and his quest is more ephemeral than most (see 1.9.4ff.). The shield is emblematic of the truth which blinds, the absolute Word (1.7.33). Nor does it stop with (Oedipal) blinding; it has additional disintegrative powers associated with images of the fragmented body: "Men into stones therewith he could transmew, And stones to dust, and dust to nought at all; And when him list the prouder lookes subdew, He would them gazing blind, or turn to other hew" (1.7.35). The power of this weapon is not surprising, given the all-powerful scripting of its omniscient, often threatening source. But Arthur, who perfects and contains all virtues (as the Letter to Ralegh remarks), is himself unable to face the shield, and must keep it "all closely cover'd." Indeed, the only way the shield serves him is "by chaunce" (1.8.19) and not at all "when him list." A radical insufficiency informs the difference between the ideally "perfected" agent and the teleological fiction. The *méconnaissance* of the ironic distance or cloaking between the "perfected" knight and his escutcheon, his textually fraught but figurally inexpressible symbol of an ideal self, plays itself out against images of the fragmented body. Perhaps more clearly, Arthur, by gaining control of the Lacanian mirror—the signifying shield of an ideal unity of self—should be able to defend that self against encroaching diasparactive forces. But the poem pointedly shows him as unable to control the shield. For the shield, glossed allegorically as Grace—the manifestation of Logos—is simultaneously the power of God, the Law of the Father. The precisely textual aspect of the shield can be seen more clearly in the description of the giant Orgoglio's reaction, where he has "read his end" in the meaning of the shield, and Prince Arthur, following through, literally inscribes the fragmentation of the body. The right leg follows the left arm, the head follows both, and then "That huge great body" deflates entirely: "of that monstrous mass Was nothing left, but like an empty bladder was" (1.8.24).

42. Jonathan Goldberg, *Endlesse Worke* (Baltimore: Johns Hopkins UP, 1981), xi.

43. W. MacNeile Dixon, *English Epic and Heroic Poetry* (London: J. M. Dent, 1912), 149.

44. All citations of Wordsworth, unless otherwise indicated, are taken from the 1850 version of *The Prelude* in the Norton critical edition, ed. Jonathan Wordsworth, M. H. Abrams, and Stephen Gill (New York: Norton, 1979). The most significant change from the 1805 version of

these passages is the poet's adoption of the dream for himself. In the 1805 version, it is the "friend" who recalls the dream, and in this very change I think we can see the operative *méconnaissance* of self-quadrature.

45. As Laurence Goldstein has observed in *Ruins and Empire,* the Arab rider is responsible for "the preservation of virtue and vision" (Pittsburgh: University of Pittsburgh Press, 1977), 158.

46. The fact that this voice, if followed out more fully still, becomes a "self-questioning" generated by the pulsing blood of the listener himself, is intriguing; an apparently more conscious use of this self-reflection occurs in Keats's fragmented epic.

47. This relation of active specter and (relatively) passive spectator is a reduced form of the double-tongued demonic and Christic opposition from *Paradise Lost.*

48. Winkle also has close connections with the maternal *unheimlich:* a fragmented "rip" from (perhaps) a "wrinkle," but more clearly from the Dutch *Winkel,* as "hiding place." *Cassell's Dutch-English Dictionary.* Also "shop, store," etc. See also, e.g., the German *Winkel* (a corner or angle); and *Wink* (a nod, a sign, hence a hint or suggestion). "Rip" can be related to Dutch *rijp* (ripe) or the idiomatic *rep* (as in English "rip-roarer"); and possibly to German *Rüpel* (bounder or lout) or to *Rippe,* the feminine noun denoting the anatomical rib (and hence another image of the fragmented body) (*Cassell's*).

49. *Paterson, Finnegans Wake,* Geoffrey Hill's *Mercian Hymns* (Deutsch 1971), Jeremy Hooker's *Soliloquy of a Chalk Giant* (Enitharmon 1974), etc. While the giant in the earth is (so to speak) as old as the hills, the increased concentration on this trope in twentieth-century epic deserves more exploration.

50. Philip Pacey, *David Jones and Other Wonder Voyagers: Essays* (Bridgend, Mid Glamorgan: Poetry Wales, 1982), 119.

51. Keats's letters on the "Vale of Soul-Making" and the "Mansion of Many Apartments," among others, develop such a heroism largely independent of the poetry. Keats entertains the idea that "there really is a grand march of intellect," and sees himself, in a surprisingly hopeful interaction with tradition, marching along with various poets within that tradition.

52. One thinks of the nineteenth-century vandalizer of Kenilworth Castle, knocking out window frames to make it look "more like a ruin."

53. Glancing at the list of epic precursors, Hazlitt observes that "These giant-sons of genius stand indeed upon the earth, but they tower above their fellows; and the long line of their successors, in different ages, does not interpose any object to obstruct their view, or lessen their brightness. In strength and nature they have not been surpassed." See *The Complete Works of William Hazlitt,* ed. P. P. Howe (London: J. M. Dent, 1930), 5:45.

54. The phrase is Byron's: "*Hyperion* is the greatest of poetical Torsos. . . . It is perhaps better that it remains a fragment. Had only the two first Books of *Paradise Lost* come down to us, we question if they had not impressed us with a higher opinion of the author's powers than the completed work. Such magnificent mutilations are regarded with a complex emotion, composed of admiration, expectation, and regret." See *Keats: The Critical Heritage,* ed. G. M. Matthews (London: Routledge and Kegan Paul, 1971), 303–4.

55. D. G. James, "The Two *Hyperions,*" in *Keats: A Collection of Critical Essays,* ed. W. J. Bate (Englewood Cliffs, NJ: Prentice-Hall, 1964), 161–69.

56. The term *maieutics* is used in Socratic discourse and in psychoanalysis for the analytic process of bringing ideas to birth; Keats's reiterated use of *Maia*—the maternal—as a generatrix of ideas and of the poetic self will be the subject of further discussion.

57. See, e.g., David Perkins, ed., *English Romantic Writers* (New York: Harcourt Brace, 1967), 1117–18.

58. The quotation marks are puzzling here, conflicting in the MS readings and various editions. Here, as throughout, unless otherwise noted, I follow Elizabeth Cook's Oxford University Press edition, 1990. Even the difficulties, however, are productive in the reading that follows.

59. Northrop Frye, *Fables of Identity: Studies in Poetic Mythology* (New York: Harcourt, Brace and World, 1963), 165. A book could (and should) be written on the overindulged Hitlerian trope in literary criticism, where it plays to a sensationalism far too familiar in more conventionally political realms.

60. This despite the continuing critical tradition of viewing this as the "true poet." Barnard (in *John Keats: Selected Poems*), for example, proposes that "Only '*Poesy*' can give permanent life to the truth perceived by unlettered savages. This poem could itself be either fanatic's dream or truth. The reader must decide whether the narrator is a poet or a dreamer" (Keats 1988, 229–30n). I have already pointed out that the "savage" who "guesses at Heaven," even in "the *loftiest* fashion of his sleep" is hardly more likely to perceive truth than anyone else (my emphasis). Poetry is seen in this poem as maintaining not truth, but "Imagination." Barnard's assertion that the poem could be "fanatic's dream or truth" flouts a text that explicitly calls itself a "dream" of either poet or fanatic, and in which neither figure is given credit for access to the truth. To give Keats his due, he seems to suggest that poetry is necessarily abandoned to human history, through his images of time and death—"the sable charm and dumb enchantment"—and thus, history and the ultimate awards of the laurel are decided upon by the winners. (I read the "sable charm" and "dumb enchantment" as emblematic of the diasparactive force of death, but others [e.g., Bloom 1971, 422] have read differently, seeing these images as reflective of fanatical and savage expression. This reading, while tempting, seems to be immediately contradicted by the lines following.) In short, between the sectarian idiolect of the fanatic, and the universal sociolect that famed precursors appear to control, the difference is principally one of historical accident. Keats's shift in allegiance, from the Puritan Milton in the first *Hyperion*, to the Catholic Dante in *The Fall of Hyperion*, may be in part the basis for his focus here on sectarian partisanship.

61. The development in this poem of the threat of death is embedded more consistently throughout, but enjoins a contrast similar to that invoked in "Ode on a Grecian Urn" by the sudden appearance of the sacrificial procession.

62. Bloom proposes that in this part of the dream no less than "five religious traditions— Christian, Jewish, Egyptian, Olympian, Druidic—" are represented (1971, 423).

63. Though one would not wish to overemphasize Keats's use of the Homeric metaphor of the knees as a phallic referent, it is worth remarking that the metaphor appears to carry such weight here as well as in Homer (see Slater 1968 as well as Bradley 1970).

64. The phallic significance of "heart," discussed in Chapter 2 (and by Slater), is also of relevance to our discussion of Crane's *Bridge*. "Hart," of course, was not Crane's given name.

65. The symbolism of the stairs is traditionally (and rather too simply) linked with phallic expression in the work of Freud. See especially his chapter on dream symbolism in *The Interpretation of Dreams* (1900).

66. Both W. J. Bate and Harold Bloom throughout their work on Keats have addressed the issue of Romantic internalization as a strategy for dealing with the "belatedness" so clearly expressed in the "Ode to Psyche." See also Keats's letter to Reynolds (3 May 1818).

67. See as well K. K. Ruthven, who points out that the Lamia's power to "unperplex bliss from its neighbour pain" (1.192) is precisely that which distinguishes her from Lycius and other mortals. "Keats and *Dea Moneta*," *Studies in Romanticism* 15 (Summer 1975: 445–59): 456.

68. Ruthven (1975) provides an illuminating discussion of the divergent sources even within Keats's copy of the *Auctorites Mythographi Latini*, and connects (with less certainty) Moneta to Keats's own financial difficulties. D. G. James (1964) is but one of the scholars who suppose Keats to have had little real intent in a such a half-hearted re-naming.

69. The parallel—and distinctly Oedipal—description of the freshly fallen angels ransacking the bottom of Hell for gold (*Paradise Lost* 1.678–88) is the source of another of this poem's repetitions.

70. In *Hyperion* it is made explicit that this inspiration consists of certain kinds of knowl-

edge (history, legend, the "sovran voices"), and it is this jumbled synthesis of knowledges that deifies the protagonist:

> Knowledge enormous makes a God of me.
> Names, deeds, gray legends, dire events, rebellions,
> Majesties, sovran voices, agonies,
> Creations and destroyings, all at once
> Pour into the wide hollow of my brain,
> And deify me, as if some blithe wine
> Or bright elixir peerless I had drunk.
>
> (*Hyperion* 3.113–19)

71. Cid Corman, *At Their Word: Essays on the Arts of Language,* vol. 2 (Santa Barbara: Black Sparrow Press, 1978), 67.

72. "The phallus is the privileged signifier of that mark in which the role of the logos is joined with the advent of desire. It can be said that this signifier is chosen because it is the most tangible element in the real of sexual copulation, and also the most symbolic in the literal (typographical) sense of the term, since it is equivalent there to the (logical) copula. It might also be said that, by virtue of its turgidity, it is the image of the vital flow as it is transmitted in generation" (Lacan 1977, 287). See also Freud (1900, 391), where the dream symbolism of the bridge is linked specifically with the phallus.

73. Weber draws attention to their "profound mutual misunderstanding" in his introduction to *The Letters,* emphasizing Crane's alienation from his father rather than the later, agonizingly ambivalent relation with his mother (vi, x–xii).

74. "Hart Crane," *Critical Essays on Hart Crane,* ed. David R. Clark (Boston: Hall, 1982: 115–23), 115. See also his discussion of Crane's narcissism, 121.

75. Giles, following W. R. Bion, notes that such a fundamentally fragmented understanding of self and world is (in its extreme forms) a primary characteristic of schizophrenia (1986, 221).

76. While the most obvious reading of the particular light source is the phosphorescence within the Caribbean seaweed, its contrasting "iridescence" and the sunset's "smouldering fire [and] vaporous scars" in the preceding lines make this specification less exact, possibly pointing to the furrow of the sun's light as it sinks. It makes little difference, I think, to this reading of *méconnaissance.*

77. Brunner 1985, 142.

78. John R. Willingham, " 'Three Songs' of Hart Crane's *The Bridge:* A Reconsideration," *American Literature* 27 (March 1955): 66.

79. Crane committed suicide in 1932, jumping off the S.S. *Orizaba* while returning from the Caribbean.

80. Coleridge, "The Eolian Harp" (42–43). Perhaps more telling still is the poet's earlier description of how the harp, "by the desultory breeze caress'd, / Like some coy maid half yielding to her lover, / pours such sweet upbraiding" (13–14).

81. Klytaimnestra sent Orestes to live in exile long before the murder of Agamemnon.

82. Marlowe's development of this submerged realm is clearest in the following passage:

> [Neptune], the sapphire-visaged god grew proud
> And made his capering Triton sound aloud;
> Imagining that Ganimed, displeased,
> Had left the heavens, therefore on him seized.
> Leander strived; the waves about him wound
> And pulled him to the bottom where the ground
> Was strewed with pearl, and in low coral groves

Sweet singing mermaids sported with their loves
On heaps of heavy gold and took great pleasure
To spurn in careless sort the shipwrack treasure;
For here the stately azure palace stood
Where kingly Neptune and his train abode.
The lusty god embraced him, called him love.

(649–51)

83. In the much-remarked letter of 20 June 1926, Crane comments (despairingly) that "the bridge as a symbol today has no significance beyond an economical approach to shorter hours, quicker lunches, behaviorism and toothpicks" (232).

84. Allen Grossman, "Hart Crane and Poetry: A Consideration of Crane's Intense Poetics with Reference to 'The Return,' " in David Clark, ed., *Critical Essays on Hart Crane* (Boston: G. K. Hall, 1982), 221–54, 229.

85. His mother, as well as the theological machine. Giles (1986) and Yingling (1990) offer similar deconstructions of the received "transcendentalism" of Crane.

Chapter 6. Sleeping with the Enemy

1. For a traditional feminist reading of traditional epic, see Susan Stanford Friedman's incisive reification of the "traditionally masculine domain of epic" in her "Gender and Genre Anxiety" (1986).

2. For example, Krjukova, Balagurina, Anyte, Faltonia Proba, Hrotsvitha of Gandersheim, Mary Tighe, and a few others. I hope that a further study may bring these disparate voices together in a space of their own, and thus revise further the tradition of epic. For now, only Jerold Frakes's *Brides and Doom: Gender, Property, and Power in Medieval German Women's Epic* (Philadelphia: University of Pennsylvania Press, 1994) and Lynne Keller's forthcoming *Forms of Expansion: Recent Women's Long Poems* have begun to remedy this long neglect.

3. In Geoffrey Chaucer, *The Wife of Bath's Tale,* 904–5.

4. See, e.g., Jean Baker Miller, *Toward a New Psychology of Women* (Boston: Beacon, 1976); Carol Gilligan, *In a Different Voice: Psychological Theory and Women's Development* (Cambridge: Harvard UP, 1982); Nancy Chodorow, *The Reproduction of Mothering: Psychoanalysis and the Sociology of Gender* (Berkeley: University of California Press, 1978), and Jessica Benjamin (1988).

5. One is tempted to say that female identity is later maintained "in spite of" the imposed Oedipal relation; what Adrienne Rich has called "compulsory heterosexuality" appears causally related to the fact that women in Western culture are forced to "remain culturally marginal, passive, dependent, and infantile" (Abel, *The Voyage In,* 1983, 10).

6. Lacan in a famous passage notes: "The phallus is the privileged signifier of that mark in which the role of the logos is joined with the advent of desire" (1977, 287). The phallus, "metaphorically" or not, is in this inscription the instrumental focus of male desire; that desire is aimed at the maternal goal (perceived by the male self as distinct, separate).

7. It is a trifle unclear (to me) exactly why this last sentence should be true, except in order for Irigaray to avoid the "infantilization" so familiar from earlier inscriptions of female desire, and above all a misunderstanding of female desire as one which "await[s] . . . the phallus." And this in itself, even if a rhetorical maneuver, is certainly laudable.

8. Jean Baudrillard, quoted in *The European* 1.1 (11–13 May 1990): 9.

9. Clearly enough, some of these selves achieve a relative stability within the individual (e.g., the "private" and "public" selves) insofar as they seem more useful than others in mediating the demands of necessity.

10. Given the visual focus of contemporary media and the changing nature of desire, the association of the gaze strictly with male sexuality seems of limited accuracy; even in historical terms, its consistency of applicability seems highly questionable.

11. I hardly mean to defend Freud; he does inscribe genital sexuality, and particularly that of the male phallus as a telos toward which human development is aimed; moreover, his consistent characterization of other forms of sexuality as "abnormal" or perverse is not pleasant. However, Freud repeatedly stresses the thinness of the line between "normal" and "abnormal"; the placement of such a line, as with any line, depends upon limited social definitions of normality.

12. To illuminate this difficulty, both the "the sex which is not one" and the "primacy of the phallus" function as elegant biological metaphors which have increasingly limited usefulness as descriptions of male or female psyches or behaviors.

13. Lyn Hejinian, *My Life,* 40.

14. As Donaldson points out of Criseyde: "[S]he will behave in such a way as to please the onlooker, and desire what most desires her" (1983, 57).

15. This, clearly enough, provides a simple contextual rather than anatomical source for women's selves seeming not one, but two. It also recurs to a duplicitous background for male development, whose common establishment of (often overlapping) "public" and "private" selves is not accounted for by Irigaray's essentialist theory.

16. That is, within certain classes or ranks of society, primarily within the last two or three centuries. Much of this depends heavily on quite specific circumstances of imitation and centrality to parental attention, including (among other things) birth order, the number and gender of siblings, the number and gender of those in parenting roles, etc., all of which are susceptible to varied social and cultural emphasis.

17. Marjorie Lozoff's study of women who achieve success within the career system suggests that women developed a powerful ego—a sense of active agency—"when the fathers treated the daughters as if they were interesting people, worthy and deserving of respect and encouragement." Cited in Maureen Murdock, *The Heroine's Journey* (Boston: Shambhala, 1990), 30.

18. As Adrienne Rich remarks: "The mother stands for the victim in ourselves, the unfree woman, the martyr. Our personalities seem dangerously to blur and overlap with our mothers, and, in a desperate attempt to know where mother ends and daughter begins, we perform radical surgery." *Of Woman Born: Motherhood as Experience and Institution* (New York: Norton, 1977).

19. Jessica Benjamin notes: "As long as the mother is not articulated as a sexual agent, identification with the father's agency and desire must appear illegitimate and stolen; furthermore, it conflicts with the cultural image of woman-as-sexual-object and with the girl's maternal identification" (1986, 69). As I read these epics, a woman poet can be seen as constructing a "desire of her own" in terms analogous to those of Benjamin's excellent analysis, but the poet does so through a text that is predominantly Oedipal.

20. Specifically, (a) the rape of Helen by Achilles (15–17, 39); see also Helen's dismissals of "the loves of [or sacrifices to] Achilles": Polyxena, Chryseis, Deidamia, Briseis (172–73, 176ff.); and (b) the rape of Marian Erle, Aurora's alter ego, by an unknown antagonist (6.1231–32); see also the "purchase" of Marian effected by her mother (3.1040). All citations are from *Helen in Egypt* (New York: New Directions, 1974) and from *Aurora Leigh* (London: Women's Press, 1978).

21. This might be rephrased to emphasize the hierarchical difference: A woman of active power, the poet wishes to establish herself as part of a discursive elite—the pantheon of epic poets. Epic, long the pinnacle of poetic identity—that which culminates and fulfills a poetic career—is also seen as exemplary of phallocentric legislation. Insofar as a woman participates in ("buys into") the system, just so far she oppresses (or "sells out") women.

22. The epigraph and the quotations from Kristeva in this paragraph are from the interview "Oscillation between Power and Denial," in *New French Feminisms,* ed. Elaine Marks and Isabelle Courtivron (New York: Schocken, 1981: 165–67), 166.

23. See Sharon Doubiago's *Hard Country* (Minneapolis: West End, 1982), 40. The "virilization" of epic poets is vividly evoked by the gendered sexual associations of the terms "hard"

and "country" of Doubiago's title. Poets, too, recognize the peril of exploitation. Fear of sensationalism and complicity haunts much of Doubiago's epic, well expressed by the image of a woman gazing on the romantic prototype of the knight in shining armor: "She looks into his armor and sees herself" (123).

24. See, e.g., Virginia L. Radley, who records the damning critics particularly well, if not the effusive, in her *Elizabeth Barrett Browning* (Boston: Twayne, 1972), 120–25. In sum, she writes, *Aurora Leigh* was received as a " 'noble error.' . . . There is no question, however, that the total work is unwieldy, shapeless, amorphous, and philosophically untenable" (125).

25. The traditional phrase is invoked by Ora Pate Stewart, "Epic: A Comet among Stars," in *The Study and Writing of Poetry: American Women Poets Discuss Their Craft*, ed. Wauneta Hackleman (Troy, NY: Whitston, 1983), 51–64: "All other epic writers since Homer pale into faded copyists. No other epic has ever been created to stand beside his. But from his generous genius, the thirsty imitators may drink. He is the fount itself" (53).

26. For the proposal, see 2.402–3 and especially 2.418, "you want . . . a sister of charity."

27. According to the commentator, at least. The use of multiple voices—of commentator, the male heroes, and the many facets of Helen herself—ensures that the epic shifts in Protean fashion as we read; I offer one explanatory paradigm.

28. These are vital contemporary influences, but Friedman's suggestion that these hybrid forms are the domain of a "distinct women's epic" is puzzling (1986, 222). The adaptation of other genres for epic purposes is not new with H.D. and Barrett Browning. While there are critics who see the *Odyssey* as a "novelizing" form of the epic, the adaptations I have in mind are Spenser, following the Italian poets in adapting romance; Milton's use of tragedy; the immersion in satire of Byron's *Don Juan;* the nearly universal dependence upon lyric and meditative "personal" modes seen in epics of the nineteenth and twentieth centuries. Similarly, when Friedman suggests that the shift of action to the private domain from "the public domain of conventional epic" (1986, 217) is based primarily in the shift of heroism—to female from male— she must be understood as excluding at least the epics of Whitman and Wordsworth, if not even Milton and Chaucer. Concerning the shift of the speaking subject (i.e., the gender of heroic emphasis), she is surely correct, though to reduce figures such as Criseyde, Penelope, Medea, Eve, even Spenser's Una (all of whom are developed in part as heroes) to "the symbolic peripheries as static rewards or temptations" (205), seems a trifle unfair. These heroic attributes can of course be read as critical of the characters. Friedman's is the most useful discussion of the importance of lyric forms to H.D. and Barrett Browning, though Sappho plays a very different role in mythos of each poet. On the novel, see Gardner B. Taplin, *The Life of Elizabeth Barrett Browning* (New Haven: Yale UP, 1957), 313–27; and Cora Kaplan's introduction to *Aurora Leigh* (London: Women's Press, 1978), 14–36. On the novel as dominated by women, see Rosalind Miles's *The Female Form* (New York: Routledge and Kegan Paul, 1987).

29. As the topic of a number of conversations in the epic, and as a reiterated contrast in Odysseus' meetings with women, Penelope's character is developed throughout the epic—to as great an extent, even, as that of Achilles during his famous absence.

30. Mermin, among others, points out the contrast between male and female poets in this regard; for Barrett Browning, "No shadow of past greatness darkened her path, and the scope for aspiration seemed limitless" (1989, 11). Friedman draws the contrast between the epics of these poets and those of their male contemporaries, focusing on Tennyson's "Epic," which projects his plan for *Idylls of the King*, and on Pound's *Cantos*. Barrett Browning and H.D. simultaneously admired and rejected these contemporaries and their epics, with roughly equal force (1986, 209–13). By extending the comparison to a broader tradition I aim to clarify the achievements of H.D. and Barrett Browning.

31. Alicia Suskin Ostriker, "What Do Women Poets Want?: H.D. and Marianne Moore as Poetic Ancestresses," *Contemporary Literature* 27 (1986): 475–92, 486.

32. Note the similar invocation by Romney of the "mother's face" in his attempt to quell Aurora (2.390–93).

33. Exceptions, of course, are Helen's sister Clytaemnestra and the goddess Athena, Elizabeth Barrett Browning's empowering identification in her juvenile epic, *The Battle of Marathon*. When the image is attributed to Aurora (by Lord Howe, near the end of book 5), it seems to function more as a critique of Aurora's loveless autonomy than as an affirmation.

34. Not only are there extensive (if covert) rewritings of Aurora Leigh in H.D.'s *Helen in Egypt*, but (as Friedman notes) H.D. attempted to model her life with Richard Aldington on that of the Brownings (1986, 211–13). Friedman concludes, however, that "Changes in poetic discourse and distortions in literary history . . . prevented Barrett Browning from serving as a sustaining example for H.D. Barrett Browning's effusive poetic style was a distinct negative to modernists in general" (212). Changes in Barrett Browning's critical status may indeed have changed H.D.'s *public* attitude, but evidence in *Helen in Egypt* suggests that the epic was heavily—if silently—influenced by the earlier poet.

35. H.D., *Collected Poems, 1912–1944*, ed. Louis L. Martz (New York: New Directions, 1983), 55. Friedman provides a brief discussion (1986, 212, 226n30).

36. The fact that H.D. puns on the lisping, childlike comparison of Isis/Thetis (279) reinforces this interpretation: The "simple path" of Helen's intuition becomes the "simple password" or "path-word" of Achilles.

37. Derek Walcott attempts a similarly strategic cultivation of Homer in his *Omeros*, with only slightly less success.

38. "Our insight into this early, pre-Oedipus phase in the little girl's development comes to us as a surprise, comparable in another field with the discovery of the Minoan-Mycenaean civilization behind that of Greece" (Freud 1931b, 372).

39. See Exodus 15.20 for Miriam the prophetess, sister of Moses. Her name is from the Hebrew *miryam*, rebellion. Note that the "sea-king" imagery applied to Romney is a form of rebirth in this context, killing the Pharaoh but freeing the visionary leader. I use the typological reading of Egypt as prefiguring the Babylonian captivity to point again to Aurora's "Chaldean" heart: It too must be freed.

40. The quotation is from Ezra Pound. See *The Letters of Ezra Pound: 1907–1941*, ed. D. D. Paige (New York: Harcourt, Brace, 1950), 11. Friedman (1986) has outlined H.D.'s debt to Sappho and the Greek lyricists.

41. This also challenges Bakhtin's praise of the novel for depicting "the present in all its openendedness" (1981, 11). Despite the fact that *Helen in Egypt* is firmly rooted in "the absolute epic past" of Troy (Bakhtin 1981, 14), H.D. depicts that very epic *past* in all of its own "openendedness."

42. Why Barrett Browning did not excuse Virgil with the fact that he was recurring to her beloved Homer (and the silence of Aias) is unclear. Dido's refusal to speak, like that of Aias, may be in many ways a more significant condemnation of Aeneas than speech.

43. The pragmatic explanation that her mother had died nine years and her father only immediately before she left Italy may not be to the point.

44. The consistent references to orality, eating, etc., in *Aurora Leigh* require a fuller explication of the poem in relation to the *Odyssey*. Note as well the prevalence of dogs and canine images—most of them not at all like the Brownings' Flush.

45. A futility reflected in her current poverty and impotence as a poet; her fortunes change after she reaches Italy.

46. She rushes off to Italy so that she needn't attend the supposed wedding—futile as well as a mark of male vanity in her eyes—between Romney and Lady Waldemar (5.1060ff.), and Aurora's "indifference" is not what it seems. We could note also that Romney Leigh is the son— the "leightning"?—of *Vane* Leigh.

47. And, by orchestrating this simile, Barrett Browning is equated with God herself.

48. A closer reading of the party at Lord Howe's in this light might be revealing.

49. So Virgil derives the name from Saturn's time spent in Italy.

50. Gilbert takes brief note of this, but avoids mentioning the books Aurora keeps.

51. Lyn Hejinian, *My Life,* 40.

52. "He taught me all the ignorance of men, / And how God laughs . . . " (1.190–91). For Aurora, books act as "counselling souls confederate" (1.188).

53. Proclus' "rule" clearly correlates with Aurora's own progress: "[R]ound twice / For one step forward, then . . . back / Because you're somewhat giddy" (5.1231–33). Proclus (c. 411–85 CE) was the last major figure of the Neoplatonist school.

54. Friedrich Augustus Wolf, *Prolegomena to Homer* [*Prolegomena ad Homerum*], trans. Anthony Grafton, Glenn W. Most, and James E. G. Zetzel (1795. Princeton: Princeton UP, 1985).

55. Radley speaks of the young Elizabeth Barrett's views, and notes that she always thought of Homer as "more than human" (1972, 15). Though Barrett praises more recent poets too, "she always saves the greatest laurels for Homer, Virgil, and the 'ancients.' Their direct descendant is Alexander Pope" (1972, 28–29).

56. The double narrative movements from London to Florence provide a larger, structural example. We have already glanced at Aurora's return to Italy. The second movement becomes clearer on Romney's arrival from his own Fall of Troy, the destroyed patriarchal mansion that Aeneas/Romney must leave behind. And in his offer to take up the marriage with Marian yet again, Romney, like Aeneas in the Underworld, is only slowly coming to terms with a new life, outside of Troy and its patriarchal forms of responsibility. Romney arrives, like H.D.'s Achilles, a "sea-king," a shipwrecked Aeneas or Odysseus, buffeted by storm and fate (8.60, 9.700, etc.). He too is "bringing his goddis into Latium," in the portrait of the ancestral mother who resembles Aurora. As many critics have noted, he is also equated with the beloved brother Edward ("Bro"), who died at sea in 1840. The intertextual parallels are too many to list, but include the likening of Marian's father (who blinded Romney) to the boar who scarred Odysseus (9.550ff.), the traditional recounting of the fall of Troy/Leigh Hall, the presence of the child. Aurora's role, at first, is less certain. (Indeed, the two characters shift roles with remarkable ease.) Though she is herself Odyssean (8.507), Romney's relationships with other women remain uncertain to her. Their testing of each other's memories is a deliberate reminder of Odysseus' homecoming to Penelope.

57. The game of "fox and goose," mentioned a number of times in the epic, adds weight to this social view of epic. See especially Lady Waldemar's accusations that Aurora thinks she can "rub out" the patriarchal Romney, in a move parallel to that of Proclus (9.153ff.).

58. Though here less violently portrayed, the position is that imagined by the submissive Venus in Barrett Browning's early *Battle of Marathon,* imprisoned ("Transfix[ed]," again) in the lake of fire, subject to the phallic power of Jove. The other figure, "forward, personal, wanting reverence, / Because aspiring only" (3.140–41), is parallel to the early epic's Athena, but is perhaps less attractive in the emphasis of her "anticipat[ion]" of male penetration.

59. For example, "my chestnut woods / Of Vallombrosa, cleaving by the spurs / To the precipices" (1.615–17).

60. See 3.1040, 6.1231–32. The repetition in this last of the imprisonment and ravishment that bring forth utterance is particularly clear.

61. See also her early self-characterization as "overbold / For what might be" (1.1109–10).

62. Angela Leighton (1986, 117–22) emphasizes the active verb here and its import for the poem, discussing the "richly revealing confusion" of the images of parents—necessarily absented so that the poet may write (120).

63. One way of reading this version of the self as a friend who has "ceased to love" is by the biographical analogue in Barrett Browning's father, who not only "ceased to love" upon the occasion of the poet's marriage, but continued to reject her overtures until his death. Indeed, biographically, the second seems the more powerful motive; but see Leighton (1986, 116ff.), and Virginia Steinmetz, "Images of 'Mother-Want' in Elizabeth Barrett Browning's *Aurora Leigh," Victorian Poetry* 21 (1983): 351–67, and Gilbert (1984).

64. Revelations 21:18–20.

65. The traditional significance of the amethyst as a ward against both intoxication (Gr.

a-methusko) and male infidelity may be pertinent, as a warning against Aurora's intemperate indulgence in herself, and against Romney's rather frequent and misguided offers of marriage. As ultimate word of the poem and as ultimate Word (as in Revelations), it elicits a closer reading.

66. Ellipses without clear grammatical correlation are those of the poet.

67. Worth remarking for further exploration and discussion is the fact that Barrett Browning learned French primarily from her own mother. See Peter Dally, *Elizabeth Barrett Browning: A Psychological Portrait* (London: Macmillan, 1989), 15.

68. "England has had many learned women . . . and yet where are the poetesses? . . . I look everywhere for grandmothers, and see none." See *The Letters of Elizabeth Barrett Browning,* ed. Frederick G. Kenyon (New York: Macmillan, 1899), 1.230–32.

69. Judith Fetterley, "Reading about Reading: 'A Jury of Her Peers,' 'The Murders in the Rue Morgue,' and 'The Yellow Wallpaper,' " in *Gender and Reading,* ed. Elizabeth Flynn and Patrocinio Schweickart (Baltimore: Johns Hopkins UP, 1986), 147–64.

Chapter 7. In This Late Century

1. *Don Juan* 1.218.1–2. The subsequent Byron citations are also from *Don Juan* (4.1.1ff., 17.13.1).

2. Derek Walcott, *Omeros* (New York: Farrar, Straus, Giroux, 1990), 14.

3. Ibid.

4. This reading and the consequences of poststructuralist interactivity and hypertextuality are developed to a slightly greater degree in my "High-Tech Epic and the Poetics of Change," *Inner Space/Outer Space: Humanities, Technology, and the Postmodern World,* ed. Daniel Schenker, Craig Hanks, and Susan Kray (Huntsville: Southern Humanities Press, 1993), 87–97.

5. Walcott 1990, 319, 325. As C. S. Lewis notes of *Beowulf:* "Like every other Primary Epic it leaves matters much as it found them: the Heroic Age is still going on at the end" (1942, 31).

6. See Judith Butler, *Gender Trouble* (New York: Routledge, 1990); Donna Haraway, "A Manifesto for Cyborgs," in *Coming to Terms: Feminism, Theory, Politics,* ed. Elizabeth Weed (New York: Routledge, 1989: 173–204), 175.

7. In another phraseology, this classic double-bind would be the "Catch-22" of epic tradition. The sentence that follows rewrites another aphorism: Damned if you do and damned if you don't.

8. Judy Grahn, *The Queen of Swords* (Boston: Beacon Press, 1987). Grahn also provides Betty De Shong Meador's English rendering of *The Descent of Inanna to the Underworld* (149–62).

9. Ibid., 67, 15.

10. Quoted in Robert Kendall, "Writing in the Computer Age," *Poets & Writers* 19.2 (March/April 1991: 40–45): 45.

11. It matters little whether a poet actually uses the word processor: It is enough that the technology is imaginable, but marked when that technology is available. In spite of the old saying, you needn't hold the hammer yourself for everything about you to transform itself into a nail. We needn't look through telescopes ourselves to feel the impact of new planets swimming in our ken.

12. Christopher Clausen, *The Moral Imagination* (Iowa City: University of Iowa Press, 1986), 157.

13. These statements are drawn from Richard Lanham of the UCLA Writing Program, as quoted in the *Chronicle of Higher Education* (15 April 1987): 16–17.

14. As Robert Scholes suggests, *Chronicle of Higher Education* (15 April 1987): 16.

15. That is, between a self and world which are understood as always already textualized. Donna Haraway's excellent "Manifesto for Cyborgs" outlines the implications more fully.

16. For example, Alvin Toffler's *Powershift* (New York: Bantam, 1990); John Naisbitt and

Patricia Aburdene's *Megatrends 2000* (London: Sidgwick and Jackson, 1990). A critique of this optimism can be found in Neil Postman's *Technopoly* (New York: Knopf, 1992).

17. Hejinian, *My Life,* 10. Kantaris and Gross, *Air Mines of Mistila* (Newcastle upon Tyne: Bloodaxe, 1988). More extensive forms of interaction wait on the horizon in hypertext and other interactive software, but I know of no epics yet composed in this medium. For an excellent analysis of the issues raised, see George P. Landow's *Hypertext* (Baltimore: Johns Hopkins UP, 1992).

18. Robert Pinsky, *An Explanation of America* (Princeton: Princeton UP, 1979), 18.

19. Doubiago 1982, 42.

20. John Powell Ward remarks that "the book's clear aim is to match the coffee-table glossies the larger public is more likely to buy," wondering (as do I) "whether these coffee-table monsters are not themselves products of the technology Williams pervadingly castigates." See *Poetry Review* 80.1 (Spring 1990): 29.

21. Doubiago 1982, 146.

22. Umberto Eco, *Foucault's Pendulum,* trans. William Weaver (1988. New York: Ballantine, 1990), 21–22.

Selected Bibliography

Abel, Elizabeth, ed. *Writing and Sexual Difference.* Chicago: University of Chicago Press, 1982.

———, and Emily K. Abel, eds. *The Signs Reader: Women, Gender and Scholarship.* Chicago: University of Chicago Press, 1983.

———, Marianne Hirsch, and Elizabeth Langland, eds. *The Voyage In: Fictions of Female Development.* Hanover: University Press of New England (for Dartmouth College), 1983.

Alford, C. Fred. *Narcissism: Socrates, the Frankfurt School, and Psychoanalytic Theory.* London: Yale UP, 1988.

Apollonius of Rhodes. *The Voyage of Argo.* Ed. and trans. E. V. Rieu. London: Penguin, 1971.

Arthur, Marilyn B. "Early Greece: The Origins of the Western Attitude Towards Women." *Arethusa* 6.1 (1973): 7–58.

Aske, Martin. *Keats and Hellenism: An Essay.* Cambridge: Cambridge UP, 1985.

Bakhtin, M. M. *The Dialogic Imagination: Four Essays.* Ed. Michael Holquist. Trans. Caryl Emerson and Michael Holquist. Austin: University of Texas Press, 1981.

Bate, Walter Jackson. "The English Poet and the Burden of the Past, 1660–1820." *Aspects of the Eighteenth Century.* Ed. Earl R. Wassermann. London: Oxford UP, 1965, 245–64.

Bellamy, Elizabeth J. *Translations of Power: Narcissism and the Unconscious in Epic History.* Ithaca: Cornell UP, 1992.

Benjamin, Jessica. *The Bonds of Love: Psychoanalysis, Feminism, and the Problem of Domination.* New York: Pantheon, 1988.

———. "A Desire of One's Own: Psychoanalytic Feminism and Intersubjective Space." *Feminist Studies: Critical Studies.* Ed. Teresa de Lauretis. Bloomington: Indiana UP, 1986:78–101.

Beowulf and the Fight at Finnsburg. Ed. Fr. Klaeber. 3d ed. Lexington, MA: D. C. Heath, 1950.

Bernstein, Michael. *The Tale of the Tribe: Ezra Pound and the Modern Verse Epic.* Princeton: Princeton UP, 1980.

The Bible. *The New Oxford Annotated Bible with the Apocrypha.* Ed. Herbert G. May and Bruce M. Metzger. New York: Oxford UP, 1977.

Blomfeld, Joan. "The Style and Structure of *Beowulf.*" Fry, *The Beowulf Poet,* 57–65.

Bloom, Harold. *The Visionary Company: A Reading of English Romantic Poetry.* Rev. and enlarged ed. Ithaca: Cornell UP, 1971.

———. *The Anxiety of Influence: A Theory of Poetry.* New York: Oxford UP, 1973.

———. *A Map of Misreading.* New York: Oxford UP, 1975.

———. *Agon: Toward a Theory of Revisionism.* New York: Oxford UP, 1982.

———. *Poetics of Influence: New and Selected Criticism.* Ed. John Hollander. New Haven: Henry R. Schwab, 1988.

———. *The Western Canon.* New York: Harcourt Brace, 1994.

———, ed. *English Romantic Poets.* New York: Chelsea House, 1986.

———, ed. *Modern Critical Interpretations: The Odes of Keats.* New York: Chelsea House, 1987.

Boitani, Piero, and Jill Mann, eds. *The Cambridge Chaucer Companion.* Cambridge: Cambridge UP, 1986.

Boswell, James. *Boswell's London Journal 1762–1763.* Ed. Frederick A. Pottle. Toronto: McGraw-Hill, 1950.

Bradley, N. "The Knees as Fantasied Genitals." *Psychoanalytic Review* 57 (1970): 65–94.

Brooks, Peter. *Reading for the Plot: Design and Intention in Narrative.* New York: Vintage, 1984.

Browning, Elizabeth Barrett. *Aurora Leigh and Other Poems.* London: Women's Press, 1978.

Brunner, Edward. *Splendid Failure: Hart Crane and the Making of "The Bridge."* Urbana: University of Illinois Press, 1985.

Burrow, Colin. *Epic Romance: Homer to Milton.* New York: Oxford UP, 1993.

Bush, Douglas, ed. *John Keats: Selected Poems and Selected Letters.* Boston: Houghton Mifflin, 1959.

Byron, George Gordon, Lord. *Don Juan.* Ed. Leslie Marchand. Boston: Houghton Mifflin, 1958.

Calder, Daniel G. "Setting and Ethos: The Pattern of Measure and Limit in *Beowulf.*" *Studies in Philology* 69 (1972): 21–37.

La Chanson de Roland. Oxford text and translation. Ed. and trans. Gerard J. Brault. University Park: Pennsylvania State UP, 1984.

Chaucer, Geoffrey. *The Works of Geoffrey Chaucer.* Ed. F. N. Robinson. 2d ed. Boston: Houghton Mifflin, 1957.

Crane, Hart. *The Complete Poems and Selected Letters and Prose of Hart Crane.* Ed. Brom Weber. Garden City, NY: Anchor-Doubleday, 1966.

———. *The Letters of Hart Crane: 1916–1932.* Ed. Brom Weber. New York: Hermitage House, 1952.

Dimock, George. "The Name of Odysseus." Steiner and Fagles, *Homer,* 106–21.

———. *The Unity of the Odyssey.* Amherst: University of Massachusetts Press, 1989.

Dinshaw, Carolyn. *Chaucer's Sexual Poetics.* Madison: University of Wisconsin Press, 1989.

Donaldson, E. Talbot. *Speaking of Chaucer.* Durham, NC: Labyrinth, 1983.

Doody, Margaret Anne. *The Daring Muse: Augustan Poetry Reconsidered.* Cambridge: Cambridge UP, 1985.

H.D. [Hilda Doolittle]. *Helen in Egypt.* 1961. New York: New Directions, 1974.

duBois, Page. *History, Rhetorical Description and the Epic: From Homer to Spenser.* Cambridge: D. S. Brewer, 1982.

DuPlessis, Rachel Blau. "Romantic Thralldom and 'Subtle Genealogies' in H.D." *Writing Beyond the Ending: Narrative Strategies of Twentieth-Century Women Writers.* Bloomington: University of Indiana Press, 1985.

Earl, James W. "Apocalypticism and Mourning in *Beowulf.*" *Thought* 57. 226 (September 1982): 362–70.

The Epic of Gilgamesh. Trans. N. K. Sandars. Middlesex: Penguin, 1972.

Foerster, Donald M. *The Fortunes of Epic Poetry: A Study in English and American Criticism, 1750–1950*. Washington, DC: Catholic UP, 1962.

————. *Homer in English Criticism: The Historical Approach in the Eighteenth Century*. Hamden, CT: Archon, 1969.

Freud, Sigmund. *The Interpretation of Dreams*. 1900. Ed. and trans. James Strachey. New York: Avon, 1965.

————. *Jokes and Their Relation to the Unconscious*. 1905a. *Standard Edition*, vol. 8.

————. *Three Essays on the Theory of Sexuality*. 1905b. *On Sexuality*, Pelican Freud Library 7:33–169.

————. "The Sexual Enlightenment of Children." 1907. *On Sexuality*, Pelican Freud Library 7:176–77.

————. "Character and Anal Erotism." 1908a. *On Sexuality*, Pelican Freud Library 7:205–15.

————. "Creative Writers and Day-Dreaming." 1908b. *Standard Edition* 9:143–53.

————. "On the Sexual Theories of Children." 1908c. *On Sexuality*, Pelican Freud Library 7:191–92.

————. "Family Romances." 1909a. *On Sexuality*, Pelican Freud Library 7:217–25.

————. "Notes upon a Case of Obsessional Neurosis." 1909b. *Standard Edition* 10:244–47.

————. *Totem and Taboo*. 1913a. *Standard Edition* 13:1–162.

————. "Two Lies Told by Children." 1913b. *On Sexuality*, Pelican Freud Library 7:285–91.

————. "On Narcissism: An Introduction." 1914a. *On Metapsychology*, Pelican Freud Library 11:59–97.

————. "Remembering, Repeating, and Working Through." 1914b. *Standard Edition* 12:145–67.

————. "Instincts and their Vicissitudes." 1915a. *On Metapsychology*, Pelican Freud Library 11:105–38.

————. "Thoughts for the Times on War and Death." 1915b. *Standard Edition* 14: 275–80.

————. "Mourning and Melancholia." 1917. *On Metapsychology*, Pelican Freud Library 11:245–68.

————. "Beyond the Pleasure Principle." 1920. *On Metapsychology*, Pelican Freud Library 11:269–338.

————. "The Ego and the Id." 1923a. *On Metapsychology*, Pelican Freud Library 11:339–407.

————. "The Infantile Genital Organization." 1923b. *On Sexuality*, Pelican Freud Library 7:303–12.

————. "The Dissolution of the Oedipus Complex." 1924. *On Sexuality*, Pelican Freud Library 7:313–22.

————. "Some Psychical Consequences of the Anatomical Distinction between the Sexes." 1925. *On Sexuality*, Pelican Freud Library 7:323–43.

————. "Libidinal Types." 1931a. *On Sexuality*, Pelican Freud Library 7:359–65.

————. "Female Sexuality." 1931b. *On Sexuality*, Pelican Freud Library 7:367–92.

————. "A Disturbance of Memory on the Acropolis." 1936. *On Metapsychology*, Pelican Freud Library 11:443–56.

———. *The Standard Edition of the Complete Psychological Works of Sigmund Freud*. Ed. and trans. James Strachey. London: Hogarth, 1960.

———. *Introductory Lectures on Psychoanalysis*. In *The Standard Edition*. Ed. and trans. James Strachey. 1966. Pbk. New York: Liveright-Norton, 1977.

———. *New Introductory Lectures on Psychoanalysis*. 1933. Ed. and trans. James Strachey. Rev. ed. New York: Norton, 1966.

———. *On Metapsychology: The Theory of Psychoanalysis*. Pelican Freud Library vol. 11. Ed. Angela Richards. Trans. James Strachey. London: Penguin, 1984.

———. *On Sexuality*. Pelican Freud Library vol. 7. Ed. Angela Richards. Trans. James Strachey. London: Penguin, 1977.

———. *The Origins of Religion*. Pelican Freud Library vol. 13. Ed. Albert Dickson. Trans. James Strachey. Harmondsworth, Middlesex: Penguin, 1985.

———. *An Outline of Psychoanalysis*. 1940. Ed. and trans. James Strachey. New York: Norton, 1969.

Friedman, Susan Stanford. "Creating a Women's Mythology: H.D.'s *Helen in Egypt*." *Women's Studies* 5 (1977): 163–97.

———. "Gender and Genre Anxiety: Elizabeth Barrett Browning and H.D. as Epic Poets." *Tulsa Studies in Women's Literature* 5.2 (Fall 1986): 203–28.

Fry, Donald K. *The Beowulf Poet: A Collection of Critical Essays*. Englewood Cliffs, NJ: Prentice-Hall, 1968.

Frye, Northrop. *Anatomy of Criticism: Four Essays*. 1957. 3d pbk. printing. Princeton: Princeton UP, 1973.

Garmonsway, G. N., and Jacqueline Simpson, trans. *Beowulf and Its Analogues*. New York: E. P. Dutton, 1968.

Gilbert, Sandra. "From *Patria* to *Matria*: Elizabeth Barrett Browning's Risorgimento." *PMLA* 99.2 (March 1984): 194–209.

Giles, Paul. *Hart Crane: The Contexts of "The Bridge."* Cambridge: Cambridge UP, 1986.

Gilligan, Carol. *In a Different Voice: Psychological Theory and Women's Development*. Cambridge: Harvard UP, 1982.

Goody, Jack. *The Domestication of the Savage Mind*. Cambridge: Cambridge UP, 1977.

Grahn, Judy. *The Queen of Swords*. Boston: Beacon, 1987.

Greene, Thomas. *The Descent from Heaven: A Study in Epic Continuity*. New Haven and London: Yale UP, 1963.

Hägin, Peter. *The Epic Hero and the Decline of Heroic Poetry*. Berne: Francke Verlag, 1964.

Harris, John R. *Accidental Grandeur: A Defense of Narrative Vagueness in Ancient Epic*. New York: Peter Lang, 1989.

Havelock, Eric A. *The Muse Learns to Write: Reflections on Orality and Literacy from Antiquity to the Present*. New Haven: Yale UP, 1986.

Heubeck, Alfred, Stephanie West, and J. B. Hainsworth. *A Commentary on Homer's Odyssey*. Volumes I–II. Oxford: Clarendon, 1988.

Homer. *Homeri Opera*. Oxford Classical Text. 4 vols. Ed. T. W. Allen. 2d ed. Oxford: 1917, 1919.

———. *The Iliad of Homer*. Trans. Richmond Lattimore. Chicago: University of Chicago Press, 1951.

———. *The Odyssey*. Trans. Robert Fitzgerald. Garden City, NY: Anchor-Doubleday, 1963.

———. *The Iliad of Homer.* Trans. Alexander Pope. London: 1715–20.

Howard, Donald R. *Chaucer: His Life, His Works, His World.* New York: E. P. Dutton, 1987.

Hume, David. *Enquiries Concerning Human Understanding and Concerning the Principles of Morals.* 1777. Rpt. ed. L. A. Selby-Bigge; 3d ed. rev., P. H. Nidditch. Oxford: Clarendon, 1975.

Irigaray, Luce. "This Sex Which Is Not One." *New French Feminisms: An Anthology.* Ed. Elaine Marks and Isabelle Courtivron. New York: Schocken, 1981: 99–106.

Janowitz, Anne F. "Parts and Wholes: Romantic and Modernist Fragment Poems." Unpublished Ph.D. dissertation, Stanford University, 1983.

Jonson, Ben. *Timber, or Discoveries.* Ed. Mary R. Mahl. *Seventeenth-Century English Prose.* New York: J. B. Lippincott, 1968: 114–30.

Kaplan, Cora. Introduction to Elizabeth Barrett Browning, *Aurora Leigh.* London: Women's Press, 1978.

Keats, John. *John Keats.* Ed. Elizabeth Cook. New York: Oxford UP, 1990.

———. *Selected Poems.* Ed. John Barnard. New York: Penguin, 1988.

———. *John Keats: Selected Poems and Selected Letters.* Ed. Douglas Bush. Boston: Houghton Mifflin, 1959.

Kendrick, Christopher. "Milton and Sexuality: A Symptomatic Reading of Comus." *Re-Membering Milton: Essays on the Texts and Traditions.* Ed. Mary Nyquist and Margaret W. Ferguson. London: Methuen, 1987: 43–73.

Ker, W. P. *Epic and Romance: Essays on Medieval Literature.* London: 1896. Rpt. New York: Dover Editions, 1957.

Klaeber, Fr., ed. *Beowulf and the Fight at Finnsburg.* 3d ed. Lexington, MA: D. C. Heath, 1950.

Kolodny, Annette. "The Influence of Anxiety: Prolegomena to a Study of the Production of Poetry by Women." Ed. Marie Harris and Kathleen Aguero. *A Gift of Tongues: Critical Challenges in Contemporary Poetry.* Athens: University of Georgia Press, 1987: 112–41.

Kristeva, Julia. *Desire in Language: A Semiotic Approach to Literature and Art.* Ed. Leon S. Roudiez. Trans. Thomas Gora, Alice Jardine, and Leon S. Roudiez. New York: Columbia UP, 1980.

Lacan, Jacques. *Ecrits: A Selection.* Trans. Alan Sheridan. New York: Norton, 1977.

———. *Feminine Sexuality: Jacques Lacan and the école freudienne.* Ed. Juliet Mitchell and Jacqueline Rose. Trans. Jacqueline Rose. New York: Norton, 1985.

Laing, Malcolm, ed. *The Poems of Ossian, by James Macpherson.* 2 vols. Edinburgh: Ballantyne, 1805.

Laslett, Peter. *The World We Have Lost: England before the Industrial Age.* 1965. 2d ed., London: Scribner, 1971.

Leighton, Angela. *Elizabeth Barrett Browning.* Bloomington: Indiana UP, 1986.

Lewis, C. S. *The Allegory of Love: A Study in Medieval Tradition.* 1936. New York: Galaxy-Oxford, 1958.

———. *The Discarded Image: An Introduction to Medieval and Renaissance Literature.* 1964. Pbk. rpt., Cambridge: Cambridge UP, 1976.

———. *A Preface to Paradise Lost.* New York: Oxford UP, 1942.

Lord, Albert B. *The Singer of Tales.* Cambridge: Harvard UP, 1960.

MacCary, W. Thomas. *Childlike Achilles: Ontogeny and Phylogeny in the Iliad.* New York: Columbia UP, 1982.

MacDonald, Ronald R. *The Burial-Places of Poetic Memory: Epic Underworlds in Vergil, Dante, and Milton.* Amherst: University of Massachusetts Press, 1987.

Macpherson, James. *Fingal.* London: Becket and Dehondt, 1762a.

———. *Fingal.* Dublin: 1762b.

———. *Fragments of Antient Poetry.* Edinburgh, 1760a.

———. *Fragments of Ancient Poetry.* 1760b. Introd. John J. Dunn. Facsimile, Augustan Reprint Society number 122 (1966).

———. *The Iliad of Homer, Translated by James Macpherson.* London: 1773.

———. *The Poems of Ossian, by James Macpherson.* 2 vols. Ed. Malcolm Laing. Edinburgh: Ballantyne, 1805.

———. *The Poems of Ossian, by James Macpherson.* Ed. William Sharp. Edinburgh, 1924.

———. *Rights of Great Britain Asserted Against the Claims of America.* 2d ed. London, 1776.

McWilliams, John P., Jr. *The American Epic: Transforming a Genre, 1770–1860.* New York: Cambridge UP, 1989.

Maresca, Thomas E. *Epic to Novel.* Columbus: Ohio State UP, 1974.

———. *Three English Epics: Studies of Troilus and Criseyde, The Faerie Queene, and Paradise Lost.* Lincoln: University of Nebraska Press, 1979.

Merchant, Paul. *The Epic.* The Critical Idiom 17. London: Methuen, 1971.

Mermin, Dorothy. *Elizabeth Barrett Browning: The Origins of a New Poetry.* Chicago: University of Chicago Press, 1989.

Miller, James E. *The American Quest for a Supreme Fiction: Whitman's Legacy in the Personal Epic.* Chicago: University of Chicago Press, 1979.

Milton, John. *John Milton: Complete Poems and Major Prose.* Ed. Merritt Y. Hughes. Indianapolis: Odyssey, 1957.

———. *Paradise Lost.* Ed. Scott Elledge. New York: Norton, 1975.

Murrin, Michael. *The Veil of Allegory: Some Notes toward a Theory of Allegorical Rhetoric in the English Renaissance.* Chicago: University of Chicago Press, 1969.

Newman, John Kevin. *The Classical Epic Tradition.* Madison: University of Wisconsin Press, 1986.

Niles, John D. *Beowulf: The Poem and Its Tradition.* London: Harvard UP, 1983.

Nimis, Stephen A. *Narrative Semiotics in the Epic Tradition: The Simile.* Bloomington: Indiana UP, 1987.

Ong, Walter J., S.J. *Orality and Literacy: The Technologizing of the Word.* London and New York: Methuen, 1982.

Parry, Adam. *The Language of Achilles and Other Papers.* Oxford: Clarendon, 1989.

Parry, Milman. *The Making of Homeric Verse.* Ed. Adam Parry. Oxford: Clarendon, 1971.

Pavlock, Barbara. *Eros, Imitation, and the Epic Tradition.* Ithaca: Cornell UP, 1990.

Pope, Alexander. *The Poems of Alexander Pope.* Ed. John Butt. New Haven: Yale UP, 1963.

———, trans. *The Iliad of Homer.* London, 1715–20.

Pound, Ezra. *The Cantos of Ezra Pound.* New York: New Directions, 1986.

Proudfoot, L. *Dryden's Aeneid and Its Seventeenth Century Predecessors.* Manchester: Manchester UP, 1960.

Quint, David. *Epic and Empire: Politics and Generic Form from Virgil to Milton.* Princeton: Princeton UP, 1993.

Radley, Virginia L. *Elizabeth Barrett Browning.* Boston: Twayne Publishers, 1972.

Rajan, Balachandra. *The Form of the Unfinished: English Poetics from Spenser to Pound.* Princeton: Princeton UP, 1985.

Ram, Tulsi. *The Neo-Classical Epic (1650–1720): An Ethical and Historical Interpretation.* Delhi: National Publishing Co., 1971.

Rexroth, Kenneth. "Classics Revisited—IV: *Beowulf.*" Fry, *The Beowulf Poet,* 167–69.

Rieu, E. V., ed. and trans. *The Voyage of Argo.* Apollonius of Rhodes. London: Penguin, 1971.

Robinson, F. N., ed. *The Works of Geoffrey Chaucer.* 2d ed. Boston: Houghton Mifflin, 1957.

Saunders, Bailey. *The Life and Letters of James Macpherson.* 1894. New York: Haskell House, 1968.

Sedgwick, Eve Kosofsky. *Between Men: English Literature and Male Homosocial Desire.* New York: Columbia UP, 1985.

Sharp, William, ed. *The Poems of Ossian, by James Macpherson.* Edinburgh, 1924.

Shawcross, John T., ed. *Milton: The Critical Heritage.* London: Routledge and Kegan Paul, 1970.

Silverman, Kaja. *The Subject of Semiotics.* New York: Oxford UP, 1983.

Slater, Philip E. *The Glory of Hera: Greek Mythology and the Greek Family.* Boston: Beacon, 1968.

———. "The Greek Family in History and Myth." *Arethusa* 7.1 (1974): 9–44.

Spenser, Edmund. *The Faerie Queene.* Ed. Thomas P. Roche, Jr. New Haven: Yale UP, 1981.

Stafford, Fiona J. *The Sublime Savage: A Study of James Macpherson and The Poems of Ossian.* Edinburgh: Edinburgh UP, 1988.

Steiner, George, and Robert Fagles, eds. *Homer: A Collection of Critical Essays.* Englewood Cliffs, NJ: Prentice-Hall, 1962.

Tillyard, E. M. W. *Milton.* 1930. Rev. ed. New York: Collier, 1966.

———. *The English Epic and Its Background.* 1954. New York: Barnes and Noble, 1966.

Vaihinger, Hans. *The Philosophy of 'As if': A System of the Theoretical, Practical and Religious Fictions of Mankind.* Trans. C. K. Ogden. New York: Harcourt, Brace, 1925.

Van Nortwick, Thomas. *Somewhere I Have Never Travelled: The Second Self and the Hero's Journey in Ancient Epic.* New York: Oxford UP, 1992.

Vansina, Jan. *Oral Tradition as History.* Madison: University of Wisconsin Press, 1985.

Virgil [Publius Maro Vergilius]. *The Aeneid of Virgil.* Ed. R. D. Williams. 2 vols. 1972, 1973. Rpt. London: Macmillan, 1988.

Virgil. *The Aeneid.* Trans. Robert Fitzgerald. New York: Vintage-Random House, 1984.

Weber, Brom, ed. *The Complete Poems and Selected Letters and Prose of Hart Crane.* Garden City, NY: Anchor-Doubleday, 1966.

———. *The Letters of Hart Crane: 1916–1932.* New York: Hermitage House, 1952.

Wilkie, Brian. *Romantic Poets and Epic Tradition.* Madison: University of Wisconsin Press, 1965.

Wofford, Susanne L. *The Choice of Achilles: The Ideology of Figure in the Epic.* Stanford: Stanford UP, 1992.

Yingling, Thomas E. *Hart Crane and the Homosexual Text: New Thresholds, New Anatomies.* Chicago: University of Chicago Press, 1990.

Yu, Anthony C., ed. *Parnassus Revisited: Modern Critical Essays on the Epic Tradition.* Chicago: American Library Association, 1973.

Zumthor, Paul. *Oral Poetry: An Introduction.* Trans. Kathryn Murphy-Judy. Minneapolis: University of Minnesota Press, 1990.

Index